Generative AI for Cybersecurity and Privacy

Generative AI for Cybersecurity and Privacy offers a groundbreaking exploration of how generative artificial intelligence is reshaping the landscape of cybersecurity and privacy protection in an era of rapid digital transformation. As cyber threats grow in sophistication and scale, this book provides a timely and authoritative guide to harnessing generative AI to safeguard digital ecosystems, secure sensitive data, and address emerging challenges across diverse domains.

Spanning a series of expertly curated chapters, this volume delves into cutting-edge advancements and practical applications of generative AI in cybersecurity. It covers critical areas such as AI-driven threat detection and response, privacy-preserving AI models, secure IoT and cloud computing frameworks, and robust defenses for cyber-physical systems, including Smart Cities and wireless networks. The book balances rigorous theoretical foundations with real-world case studies, making it an essential resource for researchers, security professionals, policymakers, and organizational leaders.

The book offers comprehensive coverage of key topics, including:

- Leveraging generative AI for proactive threat detection, risk analysis, and automated incident response
- Innovative approaches to data privacy, compliance, and governance in AI-driven systems
- Advanced methodologies for securing IoT, mobile applications, and cloud infrastructures
- Practical frameworks for integrating generative AI into cybersecurity strategies for critical infrastructures
- Emerging applications of generative AI in personalized, secure digital experiences, such as e-commerce and smart systems

Authored by a global team of leading researchers and practitioners, this book stands out by not only addressing current cybersecurity and privacy challenges but also proposing forward-thinking, scalable solutions powered by generative AI. Unlike traditional resources, it emphasizes the transformative potential of AI in revolutionizing risk analysis, threat mitigation, and privacy preservation across multiple domains. Whether you're navigating the complexities of IoT, cloud security, or emerging cyber threats, *Generative AI for Cybersecurity and Privacy* equips you with the knowledge and tools to build intelligent, secure, and future-ready strategies for a dynamic digital world.

Generative AI for Cybersecurity and Privacy

Edited by
Youssef Baddi, Yassine Maleh, Izzat Alsmadi,
and Mohamed Lahby

CRC Press
Taylor & Francis Group
Boca Raton London New York

CRC Press is an imprint of the
Taylor & Francis Group, an **informa** business

Designed cover image: Shutterstock Image ID 1727384935

First edition published 2026
by CRC Press
2385 NW Executive Center Drive, Suite 320, Boca Raton FL 33431

and by CRC Press
4 Park Square, Milton Park, Abingdon, Oxon, OX14 4RN

CRC Press is an imprint of Taylor & Francis Group, LLC

ISBN: 978-1-032-98020-1 (hbk)
ISBN: 978-1-032-98183-3 (pbk)
ISBN: 978-1-003-59747-6 (ebk)

DOI: 10.1201/9781003597476

Typeset in Sabon
by KnowledgeWorks Global Ltd.

Contents

Preface

The rapid pace of digital transformation has ushered in an era of unprecedented connectivity, innovation, and opportunity. Yet, it has also amplified the complexity and scale of cyber threats, challenging organizations, governments, and individuals to safeguard their digital assets and privacy in an increasingly volatile landscape. At the heart of this challenge lies the transformative potential of generative artificial intelligence (AI)—a technology capable of redefining how we detect, defend against, and mitigate cyber risks while preserving the integrity of sensitive data. *Generative AI for Cybersecurity and Privacy* is a comprehensive exploration of this dynamic intersection, offering a rigorous and forward-thinking guide to leveraging generative AI to build resilient, secure, and privacy-conscious digital ecosystems.

This book emerges from a pressing need to address the evolving cybersecurity and privacy challenges posed by sophisticated adversaries, from advanced persistent threats to data breaches in interconnected systems. Generative AI, with its ability to model complex patterns, generate synthetic data, and adapt to emerging threats, represents a paradigm shift in how we approach security. It empowers defenders to anticipate and neutralize attacks proactively, enhances privacy-preserving mechanisms, and enables innovative applications across diverse domains. However, this power comes with dualities: generative AI can also be wielded by adversaries to craft novel attack vectors, underscoring the need for ethical frameworks and responsible deployment. This volume seeks to navigate these complexities, providing both theoretical depth and practical insights to empower a wide range of stakeholders.

Structured in four meticulously curated parts, the book offers a comprehensive journey through the multifaceted role of generative AI in cybersecurity and privacy. Part I: Foundations and Core Concepts establishes the theoretical and conceptual groundwork. Chapter 1 provides a systematic review of machine learning and deep learning applications in information security, tracing the evolution of AI-driven defenses. Chapter 2 delves into the transformative impact of generative AI on cybersecurity and data privacy, setting the stage for the book's exploration of cutting-edge methodologies.

Part II: Applications in Threat Detection and Defense focuses on practical implementations, showcasing generative AI's potential to enhance security operations. Chapter 3 explores the use of generative adversarial networks (GANs) for intrusion and malware detection, highlighting their ability to simulate and counter sophisticated threats. Chapter 4 examines how generative AI strengthens cybersecurity in e-health systems, ensuring the protection of sensitive medical data. Chapter 5 investigates the integration of generative AI with software-defined networking (SDN) to bolster network security, offering scalable solutions for dynamic environments.

Part III: Sector-Specific Use Cases addresses the unique challenges of applying generative AI in critical domains. Chapter 6 aims to systematically classify existing research on AI within the smart city framework. Chapter 7 tackles cybersecurity in agriculture, identifying emerging threats, and proposing resilience strategies for AI-driven farming systems. Chapter 8 introduces blockchain-SDN-based architectures for securing industrial IoT, emphasizing robust and decentralized frameworks. Chapter 9 explores the synergy of generative AI, federated learning, and blockchain in edge-IoT environments, paving the way for next-generation cyber threat intelligence.

Part IV: Ethics, Education, and Future Directions confronts the broader implications and future trajectories of generative AI. Chapter 10 examines its applications, challenges, and ethical considerations in higher education, fostering responsible adoption. Chapter 11 focuses on privacy preservation in IoT ecosystems, proposing generative AI-driven solutions to balance utility and confidentiality. Chapter 12 navigates the dual role of generative AI in cybersecurity, exploring its potential for both defense and attack. Finally, Chapter 13, Generative AI-Driven Penetration Testing: Frameworks, Methodologies, and Ethical Considerations, provides a detailed examination of how AI enhances proactive security testing, with a strong emphasis on ethical and legal accountability.

Acknowledgements

This book is the product of a collaborative effort by an international panel of leading researchers, practitioners, and thought leaders who share a commitment to advancing the field of cybersecurity and privacy. It is designed to serve a diverse audience—security professionals seeking practical frameworks, researchers exploring theoretical advancements, policymakers shaping regulatory landscapes, and organizational leaders navigating digital transformation. By blending rigorous analysis with real-world applications, this volume aims to not only inform but also inspire innovation and collaboration.

We are deeply grateful to the contributors whose expertise and dedication have made this book possible, as well as to the broader academic and industry communities driving progress in this field. As you embark on this exploration of generative AI's transformative potential, we hope this volume equips you with the knowledge, tools, and perspectives needed to build intelligent, secure, and ethical solutions for the digital future.

Editor biographies

Youssef Baddi is a full-time associate professor at Chouaïb Doukkali University UCD EL Jadida, Morocco. He earned a PhD degree in computer science from ENSIAS School, University Mohammed V Souissi of Rabat, Morocco, in 2016. He also holds a Research Master's degree in networking obtained in 2010 from the High National School for Computer Science and Systems Analysis – ENSIAS-Morocco-Rabat. He has been a member of the Laboratory of Information and Communication Sciences and Technologies STIC Lab, since 2017. He is a guest member of Information Security Research Team (ISeRT) and the Innovation on Digital and Enterprise Architectures Team, ENSIAS, Rabat, Morocco. Dr. Baddi was awarded as the best PhD student of the University Mohammed V Souissi of Rabat in 2013. Dr. Baddi has made contributions in the fields of Group Communications and protocols, information security and privacy, Software-defined networks, the Internet of Things, Mobile and Wireless Networks Security, and Mobile IPv6. His research interests include Information Security and Privacy, the Internet of Things, Networks Security, Software-defined Networks, Software-defined Security, IPv6, and Mobile IP. He has served and continues to serve on executive and technical program committees and as a reviewer of numerous international conferences and journals such as *Elsevier Pervasive and Mobile Computing PMC*, *International Journal of Electronics and Communications AEUE*, and *Journal of King Saud University – Computer and Information Sciences*. He was the general chair of the IWENC 2019 Workshop and the secretary member of the ICACIN 2020 Conference.

Yassine Maleh is an associate professor of Cybersecurity and IT Governance at Sultan Moulay Slimane University, Morocco. He is the founding chair of IEEE Consultant Network Morocco and the founding president of the African Research Center of Information Technology & Cybersecurity. He is a senior member of IEEE and a member of the International Association of Engineers (IAENG) and the Machine Intelligence Research Labs. Dr. Maleh has made contributions in the fields of information security and privacy, Internet of Things security, and wireless and constrained network security. His research interests include information security and privacy, Internet of Things, network security, information systems, and IT governance. He has published over 200 papers (book chapters, international journals, and conferences/workshops), 50 edited books, and 10 authored books. He is the editor-in-chief of the *International Journal of Information Security and Privacy* and *the International Journal of Smart Security Technologies* (IJSST). He serves as an associate editor for IEEE Access (2019 Impact Factor 4.098), the *International Journal of Digital Crime and Forensics* (IJDCF), and the *International Journal of Information Security and Privacy* (IJISP). He is a series editor of Advances in Cybersecurity Management, by CRC Press / Taylor & Francis Group.. He was also a guest editor of a special issue on *Recent Advances on Cyber Security and Privacy for Cloud-of-Things of the International Journal of Digital Crime and Forensics* (IJDCF), Volume 10, Issue 3, July–September 2019. He has served and continues to serve on executive and technical program committees and as a reviewer of numerous international conferences and journals such as *Elsevier Ad Hoc Networks, IEEE Network Magazine, IEEE Sensor Journal, ICT Express,* and *Springer Cluster Computing.* He was the publicity chair of BCCA 2019 and the general chair of the MLBDACP 19 symposium and ICI2C'21 Conference. He received Publon Top 1% reviewer award for the years 2018 and 2019.

Izzat Alsmadi is a professor in the Department of Computing and Cyber Security at Texas A&M, San Antonio. He has received his Master's degree and PhD in Software Engineering from North Dakota State University in 2006 and 2008, respectively. He has more than 100 conference and journal publications. His research interests include: Cyber intelligence, Cyber security, Software security, Software testing, Social networks, and Software-defined networking. He is the lead author and editor of several books, including Springer, The NICE Cyber Security Framework Cyber Security Intelligence and Analytics, 2019; Practical Information Security: A Competency-Based Education Course, 2018; and Information Fusion for Cyber-Security Analytics (Studies in Computational Intelligence), 2016.

Mohammed Lahby obtained his PhD in Computer Science from University Malaysia Terengganu in Malaysia. He earned MSc in Computer Information System from Middle East University (MEU), Jordan, in 2011. He is now working as an associate professor in the Department of Computer Networks and Communications at King Faisal University, Saudi Arabia. He has published over 100 research papers in highly reputed journals such as *Engineering and Science Technology, International Journal, Education and Information Technologies*, the *Journal of Educational Computing Research*, and others. Most of his publications were indexed under the ISI Web of Science and Scopus. His current research interests include mobile learning, software quality, network security, and technology acceptance. He is a certified recognized reviewer for IEEE, Elsevier, and Springer.

List of contributors

Abdulaziz Aborujilah
College of Commerce and Business Administration, Dhofar University
Salalah, Oman

Noura Aknin
TIMS Lab, Abdelmalek Essaadi University,
Tetouan, Morocco

A. S. Akshaya
Department of Information Technology, Hindustan Institute of Technology and Science
Bay Range Campus, Chennai, India

Sabaa Ahmed Yahya Al-Galal
Department of Computer Science, Multimedia University (MMU)
Malaysia

Mohammed Al-Sarem
Department of Computer Science, College of Computer Science and Engineering, Taibah University
Medina, Saudi Arabia

Izzat Alsmadi
Department of Computational, Engineering, and Mathematical Sciences, Texas A&M University–San Antonio
San Antonio, Texas, USA

El Hossain Baali
Energy and Agroequipment Department, Institute of Agronomy and Veterinary Hassan II
Rabat, Morocco

C. V. Suresh Babu
Department of Information Technology, Hindustan Institute of Technology and Science
Bay Range Campus, Chennai, India

Youssef Baddi
STIC Lab, Chouaib Doukkali University
El Jadida, Morocco

Rachid Batess
Energy and Agroequipment Department, Institute of Agronomy and Veterinary Hassan II
Rabat, Morocco

Hafssa Benaboud
IPSS Team, Mohammed V University in Rabat
Rabat, Morocco

Akram Bennour
Department of Computer Science, Université de Tebessa
Tebessa, Algeria

Faiçal Bensalah
LARSEM Lab, ENCGJ, Chouaib Doukkali University
El Jadida, Morocco

Khaoula Boukir
SETIME Lab, Ibn Tofail University
Kenitra, Morocco

Akram Chhaybi
Department of Mathematics and Computer Science, National School of Applied Sciences, Abdel Malek Essaadi University
Tangier, Morocco

Garrett Crumrine
Department of Computational, Engineering, and Mathematical Sciences, Texas A&M University–San Antonio
San Antonio, Texas, USA

Hajar Fares
TIMS Lab, Abdelmalek Essaadi University
Tetouan, Morocco

Younes El Fellah
Energy and Agroequipment Department, Institute of Agronomy and Veterinary Hassan II
Rabat, Morocco

Samia El Haddouti
National Higher School for Computer Science and Systems Analysis, Mohammed V University
Rabat, Morocco

A. Jeswin Francis
Department of Information Technology, Hindustan Institute of Technology and Science
Bay Range Campus, Chennai, India

Samir Hammami
College of Commerce and Business Administration, Dhofar University
Salalah, Oman

V. L. Kalyan Kumar
Department of Information Technology, Hindustan Institute of Technology and Science
Bay Range Campus, Chennai, India

Hiba Kandil
IPSS Team, Mohammed V University in Rabat
Rabat, Morocco

Mouna Kaouni
Department of Physics, Faculty of Science, Chouaib Doukkali University
El Jadida, Morocco

Jihad Kilani
STIC Lab, FSJ, Chouaib Doukkali University
El Jadida, Morocco

Fatima Lakrami
Department of Physics, Faculty of Science, Chouaib Doukkali University
El Jadida, Morocco

Ouidad Laouidya
Department of Physics, Faculty of Science, Chouaib Doukkali University
El Jadida, Morocco

Anis Laouiti
Samovar, T´el´ecom SudParis, Institut Polytechnique de Paris
Palaiseau, France

Saiida Lazaar
Department of Mathematics and Computer Science, National School of Applied Sciences, Abdel Malek Essaadi University
Tangier, Morocco

Wissal Lazraq
National School of Applied Sciences, Ibn Tofail University
Kenitra, Morocco

Ralf Leiter
Mobica Cognizant Company
Frankfurt, Germany

Chakir Loqman
LISAC Laboratory, Faculty of Sciences Dhar El Mahraz, Sidi Mohamed Ben Abdellah University
Fez, Morocco

Yassine Maleh
Sultan Moulay Slimane University
Beni-Mellal, Morocco

Ilyasse Mellal
Computer Science Department, Faculty of Sciences, Mohammed V University
Rabat, Morocco

Alaa Eddine El Moussaoui
PRISME laboratory, Higher School of Technology, Hassan 2 University
Casablanca, Morocco

Taoufiq El Moussaoui
LISAC Laboratory, Faculty of Sciences Dhar El Mahraz, Sidi Mohamed Ben Abdellah University
Fez, Morocco

Yuvaraj Munian
Department of Computational, Engineering, and Mathematical Sciences, Texas A&M University–San Antonio
San Antonio, Texas, USA

Michael J. O'Brien
Department of History, Philosophy and Geography and Department of Life and Health Sciences, Texas A&M University–San Antonio
San Antonio, Texas, USA

Anass Sebbar
International University of Rabat, TICLab, College of Engineering and Architecture
Rabat, Morocco

Abderrahim Ait Wakrime
Computer Science Department, Faculty of Sciences, Mohammed V University
Rabat, Morocco

Part I

Foundations and core concepts

Chapter 1

A systematic review of machine learning and deep learning applications in information security governance

Abdulaziz Aborujilah, Sabaa Ahmed Yahya Al-Galal, Samir Hammami, Mohammed Al-Sarem, and Akram Bennour

1.1 INTRODUCTION

Using neural networks with multiple layers, deep learning is a type of artificial intelligence (AI) and machine learning (ML) technique that automatically detects patterns and relationships in vast amounts of data (Hazratifard, Gebali, & Mamun, 2022). Deep learning is used in information security and governance to identify and address a variety of security threats, including fraud, cyberattacks, and data breaches. Deep learning models are an invaluable tool for information security and governance because of their high accuracy in spotting patterns and anomalies and their ability to process and analyse enormous amounts of data in real time (Mughaid et al., 2022). Malware detection, spam filtering, risk management, and data privacy protection are a few examples of applications of deep learning in information security and governance. Deep learning models can also be applied to network traffic analysis or the analysis of massive amounts of log data to find and stop malicious activity (Basit et al., 2021). These are just a few examples of the potential uses for deep learning in the areas of governance and information security. Deep learning is anticipated to play a bigger part in improving the security and privacy of digital systems and data as it continues to develop. Deep learning has the potential to significantly improve information governance and security by delivering more precise and effective means of identifying and addressing security threats.

Information security governance is essential for safeguarding sensitive data and ensuring the security and privacy of data used to train and test ML systems. Businesses have recently been experienced unheard-of financial stress. Additionally, there is a growing need for cyberattacks to be protected from outside threats as they proliferate across the globe. Information security decisions are therefore more important than ever (Bongiovanni, Renaud, Brydon, Blignaut, & Cavallo, 2022). In order to make sure that ML systems are making accurate and impartial decisions, they must be tested and validated. ML systems raise questions about fairness and transparency, especially when they are used to make critical decisions that have

DOI: 10.1201/9781003597476-2

an impact on people or organisations (Alexopoulos et al., 2019). There is ongoing research into how to make sure that ML systems used for information security governance tasks make fair and open decisions. Researchers are working to create ML algorithms that are more precise and efficient at spotting security threats, taking appropriate action, and spotting unusual network activity (Yu, 2021). The following is a list of the sections of this research study. In the second section, which describes the study methodology, including the search terms, web databases, research questions, and methodical mapping procedure that we used, the systematic review methodology and taxonomy analysis are covered. The third section reports the compiled study findings and discussion. Conclusions and suggestions for the future are presented in the final section.

1.2 COMPREHENSIVE REVIEW

A systematic literature review (SLR) is a type of review in which all pertinent studies on a specific research question or topic are identified, critically evaluated, and synthesised. It is a thorough and exact method for putting together all the information on a particular research question. What is already known about the topic, and what gaps in knowledge exist that need to be addressed by future research? A systematic review involves a comprehensive search for relevant studies, which are then screened for eligibility based on predetermined criteria. The quality of each study is assessed, and the findings are synthesised using statistical methods if appropriate. Two major questions will be addressed by this study:

1. What are the main methodologies and frameworks for deep learning and ML in information system security governance?
2. What is the current research trend regarding the use of deep learning and ML in systems security governance?

1.2.1 Systematic review protocol

An SLR typically involves several steps, including defining the research question, conducting a thorough search for relevant studies, choosing studies based on inclusion and exclusion criteria, assessing the studies under scrutiny, and synthesising the findings to reach a conclusion. Typically, a clear protocol is followed consistently and openly to guide this process. The scope of this chapter is to establish by the use of the keywords "information security governance," "deep learning," and "machine learning." The scope of the study was restricted to four digital databases, specifically: (1) Science Direct; (2) ACM; (3) PubMed; and (4) IEEEXplore. The period from 2018 to March 2023 was covered by the search for pertinent literature. It can be difficult to choose pertinent studies, especially given the variety of research fields. Despite the fact that reading papers is important in general, researching a particular topic is especially important.

1.2.2 Taxonomy analysis

A large and complex body of information must be organised and understood, and taxonomy analysis aims to do just that. It is an effective method for synthesising and summarising data and can be used to spot trends, relationships, and other patterns in the data. Deep learning has quickly developed into a powerful tool in the fields of information security and governance. Deep learning is expected to be important in a variety of current and future directions, such as the following: deep learning can be used to automatically identify and protect sensitive information that is present in large datasets, including personal and financial data. Deep learning algorithms can be taught to detect and react to a range of malware and spam threats, including newly emerging ones. Malware and spam detection: deep learning models can be taught to recognise suspicious activity in a range of industries, including financial transactions. Risk management is the process of regularly assessing risks to identify potential threats, weak points, and defences. Deep learning algorithms enable automated decision-making and incident response, enabling quicker and more accurate responses to security incidents. Businesses are able to more quickly recognise and address security threats by using deep learning to analyse how people behave in online and digital environments.

1.2.3 Data protection

Data security and information security are two different but related ideas. Information security is the process of preventing unauthorised access to, use of, disclosure of, modification of, or destruction of all types of information, including data. It includes the procedures, guidelines, and tools applied to safeguard information assets against a range of dangers, such as burglary, theft, and natural disasters [...]. In contrast, data security refers specifically to the safeguarding of data against unauthorised access, use, disclosure, modification, or destruction. Implementing security controls, such as encryption, access controls, backup and recovery procedures, and focusing on the confidentiality, integrity, and availability of data are all parts of this process (Gellert, 2022). Deep learning can be used to automatically find and safeguard sensitive data, including financial and personal information, in sizable datasets. Wylde provides a review of the literature on the connection between blockchain technology, data privacy, and cybersecurity. The authors give a summary of the current state of research on the subject and highlight the main difficulties and opportunities associated with using blockchain to improve cybersecurirty and safeguard personal information. The chapter covers a variety of topics in the area, including the security and privacy concerns associated with blockchain use in various fields and the role of blockchain in resolving these concerns. Additionally, the authors discuss how blockchain technology may be used to enhance cybersecurity and safeguard user privacy, and they emphasise the need for more research in this area (Wylde et al., 2022). In order to more effectively regulate algorithms, Gellert compares how the definitions of data and information are used in ML and data protection law. According to the authors, comprehending the distinctions between the definitions of data and information in these two fields can help create meaningful rules for algorithms (Gellert, 2022). A shallow neural network and homomorphic encryption are used in Hong et al.'s method for secure tumour classification. The authors suggest a system that enables medical imaging data analysis while safeguarding the confidentiality of the patient's private data. Before the medical information is entered into a shallow neural network that has been trained to identify tumours in medical images, the system encrypts the data using homomorphic encryption. The study's findings show that homomorphic encryption and shallow neural networks can be used to securely classify tumours, offering a useful tool for maintaining patient privacy while allowing the analysis of medical imaging data (Hong, Park, Cho, Choe, & Cheon, 2022). Hernandez et al. talked about a technique for continuously and privately authenticating a user's identity using sensor data. The authors suggest a system that continuously verifies a user's identity without jeopardising their privacy by using sensor data from their device, such as touch and gesture patterns. The system uses cryptographic methods to encrypt and securely store the sensor data, making sure that only people with the proper authorisation can access it. Through a series of tests, the authors assess the effectiveness of the suggested system and demonstrate that it can offer strong continuous authentication while upholding the user's privacy (Hernández-álvarez, Fuentes, & González-Manzano, 2021). The article reviews the difficulties and determining elements involved in the creation and application of efficient information security policies. The lack of a clear understanding of the risks and threats, the difficulty of balancing security with business needs, and the lack of employee awareness and compliance are just a few of the difficulties mentioned by the authors. The article also identifies a number of elements, such as organisational culture, legal requirements, and resource accessibility that may affect the creation and application of efficient security policies. The authors come to the conclusion that creating and implementing successful security policies requires a multidisciplinary strategy that considers the technical, organisational, and human factors at play. In order to keep security policies effective and current over time, the article also emphasises the need for ongoing evaluation and monitoring (Alotaibi, Furnell, & Clarke, 2017). A method for measuring compliance with information security governance guidelines is presented by Bongiovanni et al. The authors contend that a more objective and quantitative approach is required because conventional methods for evaluating adherence to these guidelines can be qualitative and subjective. The suggested mechanism makes use of a number of metrics to measure various aspects of compliance with information security governance principles.

Table 1.1 Summary review table for data protection articles

Reference	*Machine learning (ML) method*	*Application*	*Detection*	*Prevention*	*Response*	*Recovery*
Gellert (2022)	Deep learning	Financial data	Y	Y		
Hong et al. (2022)	Neural network	Medical imaging data		Y		
Hernández-álvarez et al. (2021)	Sensor data and cryptographic techniques				Y	
Alotaibi et al. (2017)	N/A					
Bongiovanni et al. (2022)	Metric-based approach				Y	

The authors go over how these metrics can be used to evaluate adherence at various organisational levels, from a single employee to the entire company. A case study illustrating the mechanism's practical use is also included in the article. The authors draw the following conclusions: (1) the proposed mechanism offers a more objective and quantitative approach to assessment and (2) it can help organisations better understand and adhere to information security governance guidelines (Bongiovanni et al., 2022). Table 1.1 shows a summary of data protection papers.

Information security and data security are two distinct but related concepts. The process of guarding against unauthorised access to, use of, disclosure, modification, or destruction of all kinds of information, including data, is known as information security. It includes the protocols, instructions, and instruments used to protect information assets from a variety of threats, including theft, cyberattacks, natural disasters, and unauthorised access, use, disclosure, modification, or destruction. It includes the protocols, rules, and instruments used to protect information assets from a variety of threats, such as theft, robbery, and natural disasters. Data security, on the other hand, specifically refers to the protection of data from unauthorised access, use, disclosure, modification, or destruction. It protects against unauthorised access and data loss by using security controls like encryption, access controls, backup, and recovery procedures, and focusing on the confidentiality, integrity, and availability of data (Gellert, 2022). In large datasets, deep learning can be used to automatically find and protect sensitive data, such as financial and personal information.

Wylde reviews the research on how blockchain technology, data privacy, and cybersecurity are related. The authors provide an overview of the state of the research on the topic and highlight the key challenges and opportunities related to using blockchain to enhance cybersecurity and protect sensitive data. The article covers a wide range of topics in the area, including the role of blockchain in assuaging security and privacy concerns related to its use in various industries. The authors also discuss the potential applications of blockchain technology for improving cybersecurity and protecting user privacy, and they stress the importance of further research in this area (Wylde et al., 2022).

Gellert contrasts how the definitions of data and information are used in ML and data protection law in order to be more effective in regulating algorithms. The authors argue that understanding the differences between the definitions of data and information in these two fields can aid in the development of meaningful algorithms (Gellert, 2022).

The method for secure tumour classification put forth by Hong et al. uses a shallow neural network and homomorphic encryption. The authors propose a system that permits the analysis of medical imaging data while preserving patient privacy and confidentiality. The system encrypts the data using homomorphic encryption prior to feeding it into a shallow neural network that has been trained to recognise tumours in medical images. According to the study's findings, shallow neural networks and homomorphic encryption can be used to securely classify tumours, providing a helpful tool for protecting patient privacy while enabling the analysis of medical imaging data (Hong, Park, Cho, Choe, & Cheon, 2022).

Hernández-álvarez et al. discussed a method for using sensor data to continuously and secretly authenticate a user's identity. The authors propose a system that uses sensor data from the user's device, such as touch and gesture patterns, to continuously verify a user's identity without compromising their privacy. The sensor data is encrypted and securely stored by the system using cryptographic techniques, ensuring that only those with the required authorisation can access it. The authors evaluate the performance of the proposed system through a series of experiments and show that it can provide trustworthy continuous authentication while preserving the user's privacy (Hernández-álvarez, Fuentes, & González-Manzano, 2021).

The article examines the challenges and crucial factors related to the formulation and implementation of effective information security policies. The authors mention a number of challenges, including the lack of a clear understanding of the risks and threats, the challenge of balancing security with business needs, and the lack of employee awareness and compliance. The article also lists a number of factors that may influence the formulation and implementation of effective security policies, including organisational culture, statutory requirements, and resource accessibility. The authors reach the conclusion that developing and implementing effective security policies necessitates a multidisciplinary approach that considers the pertinent organisational, technical, and human factors. The article also highlights how crucial it is to continually assess and monitor security policy in order to ensure that it remains useful and efficient over time (Alotaibi, Furnell, & Clarke, 2017).

Bongiovanni et al. offer a technique for gauging adherence to information security governance guidelines. Because traditional methods for assessing adherence to these guidelines can be qualitative and subjective, the authors claim that a more objective and quantitative approach is necessary. In order to evaluate different aspects of compliance with information security governance principles, the suggested mechanism uses a number of metrics. The authors discuss the use of these metrics to assess adherence at different organisational levels, from one employee to the entire business. The article also includes a case study that shows how the mechanism can be applied in real-world situations. The authors claim that the suggested mechanism can aid organisations in comprehending and following information security governance guidelines. Additionally, it provides a quantitative and impartial evaluation technique (Bongiovanni et al., 2022).

These strategies deal with issues relating to unauthorised data access, use, disclosure, alterations, or destruction. Organisations can effectively reduce risks, ensure compliance with security policies, and improve the protection of their information assets by utilising encryption, access controls, continuous authentication, and quantitative assessment mechanisms. Future studies could concentrate on improving data protection strategies and incorporating them into frameworks for information security governance.

1.2.3.1 Malware and spam detection

A summary of the various AI techniques for phishing attack detection is provided in the research paper. It summarises the various methods for identifying phishing threats, including ML algorithms, deep learning techniques, and others. The paper evaluates the effectiveness of these techniques and provides details on both their benefits and drawbacks. The study's conclusion sheds light on the future course of phishing attack detection research. The paper is probably a review of the literature on phishing attack detection using AI. Cybercriminals use emails, websites, and other tools in phishing attacks to trick victims into disclosing sensitive data like passwords and credit card numbers. The paper might provide an overview of various AI techniques developed and employed for phishing detection, such as ML algorithms, deep learning techniques, and natural language processing (NLP). It might also compare and evaluate the benefits and shortcomings of these approaches. Additionally, the paper may review recent advancements in the field of AI-enabled phishing detection and propose fresh lines of inquiry. This chapter will provide a comprehensive overview of the state of the art in AI-enabled phishing detection techniques in order to better inform researchers and practitioners (Basit et al., 2021). A deep learning-based intelligent system for phishing attack detection is recommended by Mughaid et al. (2022). Using a dataset of trustworthy and phishing websites, the system trains and evaluates deep neural networks, including convolutional neural networks (CNNs) and long short-term memory (LSTM) networks. The proposed system performs better than other traditional ML approaches and achieves high accuracy in phishing attack detection. The results demonstrate how effectively deep learning techniques can be applied to cybersecurity applications (Mughaid et al., 2022). Kula and Choras investigate the application of bidirectional encoder representations from transformers (BERT)-derived disinformation-fighting architectures in their study. The authors focus on using these architectures, which are based on the BERT transformer-based language model, to recognise and classify disinformation in a variety of forms, such as propaganda, fake news, and hate speech. The authors provide a thorough description of these architectures' implementation and evaluate their effectiveness using a variety of datasets pertaining to disinformation. The study's findings show that the architectures derived from BERT are effective at identifying and classifying misinformation and can be useful in addressing the issues that misinformation raises. The authors discuss the study's limitations and possible future directions for this area of research in their conclusion. The application of challenges involving misinformation to architectures derived from BERT is discussed in this chapter. BERT is a state-of-the-art language representation model developed by Google. For the purpose of identifying and correcting false information, the authors of this chapter advise using models derived from BERT. The study shows how well the BERT-derived models perform when it comes to precisely identifying false information in text and discusses how these models can be used in the future to address disinformation challenges. Using architectures derived from BERT is generally considered to be a promising tactic to address the issue of false information in online media (Kula, Kozik, & Choraś, 2022).

Min et al. present an ML-based technique for spotting unusual transactions in horse racing betting using IoT data. To quickly spot unusual betting behaviour, the authors advise using sensor data from a variety of gadgets, such as wearables, cameras, and gaming machines. The authors use ML techniques like clustering and anomaly detection to analyse the collected data and identify transactions that deviate from expected behaviour. The authors evaluate the suggested system through experiments and show how well it can spot unusual betting transactions. The authors conclude that the suggested approach may find use in a variety of other areas and can help improve the overall security and transparency of betting systems (Min, Lee, Park, & Lee, 2021). Lee and Kim present a deepfake detection method based on the rate of change between video frames. The authors advise using computer vision techniques to analyse the rate of change between subsequent video frames and find anomalies that indicate the presence of deepfakes. Using this information, the authors train an ML model that can differentiate between real and fake videos. The authors evaluate the suggested method's performance on a number of benchmark datasets to show how well it performs in identifying deepfakes with high accuracy. The authors claim that the suggested method offers a promising answer for deepfake detection and has potential uses in a variety of fields, including security and entertainment (G. Lee & Kim, 2021). Venters and Mikkilineni discuss the use of knowledge structures and evolutionary algorithms to identify anomalies in financial statements. The authors propose a method where financial statements are modelled as knowledge structures and then genetically evolved to discover potential anomalies. The method is tested using real financial data, and the results suggest that it is effective at identifying potential anomalies. The authors come to the conclusion that the suggested approach offers a potentially useful way to spot fraudulent financial reporting (Venters & Mikkilineni, 2020). Feltus discusses how reinforcement learning (RL) has already proven to be helpful for enhancing network security and will continue to do so. The authors provide a broad overview of RL and the network security tools it can be used with, including anomaly, malware, and intrusion detection. The article also discusses the challenges of using RL for network security, such as the need for large datasets and the potential for adversarial attacks. The authors recommend that future research in RL focus on developing more dependable and scalable models that can quickly recognise and mitigate network threats. They conclude that RL has a lot of potential to improve the efficiency of network security systems and can be a vital tool for safeguarding against fresh cyber threats (Feltus, 2020). The article proposes a conditional Wasserstein Generative Adversarial Network with Gradient Penalty (WGAN-GP) based on data augmentation to detect cross-site scripting (XSS) attacks. The authors claim that data augmentation is used to increase the training set size and generalisability of the model. Additionally, they go into great detail about how extra data samples are created using the WGAN-GP framework and then used to train a classifier to recognise XSS attacks. The authors evaluate the performance of the suggested system on a real-world dataset and compare it to that of other state-of-the-art methods. The results show that the proposed system outperforms competing methods in terms of accuracy and detection rate. The authors conclude that the proposed system can effectively detect XSS attacks and can be a useful tool for web application security (Mokbal, Wang, Wang, & Fu, 2020). The article offers a method for locating adversarial AI samples in Internet of Things (IoTs) settings. The authors explain that these environments are particularly vulnerable to attacks due to their distributed nature and the significant number of devices involved. They recommend a detection method based on a deep learning model that can withstand hostile assaults. The approach combines supervised and unsupervised learning to identify unusual behaviour in the system. The authors evaluate the performance of the suggested method on a real-world dataset and compare it to that of other cutting-edge approaches. The results show that the proposed method outperforms other methods in terms of detection rate and robustness to adversarial attacks. The suggested approach, the authors conclude, can be used to enhance the security of these systems and can successfully detect adversarial samples in IoT environments (Wang & Qiao, 2019). The article examines the application of ML and deep learning algorithms in cybersecurity. The authors stress the importance of cybersecurity in today's society and how ML and deep learning can be used to improve it. A summary of several ML and deep learning techniques, such as malware, intrusion, and anomaly detection, that have been used in cybersecurity is provided in the article. The authors describe each technique's advantages and disadvantages and provide examples of how it has been applied in actual settings. The lack of labelled data and the potential for hostile attacks are just two of the challenges that applying ML and deep learning to cybersecurity presents. In order to address these issues and ensure that ML and deep learning algorithms continue to be effective tools for thwarting cyberattacks, the authors emphasise the significance of ongoing research and development in the field of cybersecurity in their conclusion (Jahwar & Ameen, 2022). The research on ML -based computer network information security is discussed in the paper. The authors stress the importance of information security in the wired society we now inhabit, where sophisticated cyberattacks are occurring more frequently. As part of an enhanced ML strategy for identifying and preventing cyberattacks, the paper proposes a deep learning algorithm for anomaly detection. The advantages of using deep learning for anomaly detection are discussed by the authors, including its ability to handle large amounts of data and its capacity to learn from the past. The paper also includes a case study that shows how the suggested approach can be used in real-world situations. The authors conclude that additional research is necessary to fully realise the potential of the enhanced ML approach, which has the potential to significantly improve computer network information security (Yu, 2021). Zhao et al. discuss the effect of sample duplication on the efficiency of ML-based malware detection for Android apps. Three well-known ML algorithms are used by the authors in experiments that use a variety of datasets with both unique and duplicate samples. They find that sample duplication can significantly improve malware detection models' accuracy, but only to a certain point. In addition, overfitting reduces the models' performance. The authors claim that by using data augmentation techniques, additional samples can be created without the danger of overfitting. The study emphasises the significance of carefully managing datasets when creating ML models for malware detection in general (Zhao et al., 2021). The effectiveness of various automated machine learning (AutoML) techniques for malware detection was evaluated by Kundu, Anatharaman, & Truong-Huu in 2021. The authors use a dataset of both excellent and subpar Android apps to compare the performance of AutoML methods and traditional ML algorithms. They find that some AutoML methods, such as tree-based pipeline optimization tool (TPOT) and H2O, outperform more traditional ML algorithms in terms of accuracy and speed. Additionally, they note that using AutoML techniques can help find brand-new malware samples that haven't been seen before. The authors do mention that using AutoML may require a lot of computational power and that conventional ML algorithms may not always outperform them. The study highlights the need for more research in this area and the potential of AutoML techniques to improve malware detection overall.

H. Wu (2020) compares the performance of different deep learning models, including LSTM networks, recurrent neural networks (RNNs), and CNNs, in detecting malicious Android apps. The authors experiment with different feature extraction techniques and hyperparameters to enhance the performance of the models. The outcomes show that the LSTM network with

TF-IDF feature extraction performs best, with a binary classification accuracy of 99.2% and an F1 score of 0.992. The study demonstrates the value of feature selection, model tuning, and deep learning for Android malware detection in order to achieve the best performance. The study provides a framework for identifying malware that integrates forensic analysis with unsupervised ML techniques. The framework employs static and dynamic analysis to extract features from a given binary file, such as file headers, strings, and API calls. Then, unsupervised ML algorithms like clustering and principal component analysis are applied to these features to identify potential malware samples. The performance of the framework is evaluated by the authors using a dataset of known malware and benign samples. The results show that the framework performs better than current malware detection methods by achieving high accuracy, precision, and recall rates. The study highlights the potential of combining forensic and unsupervised ML methodologies for malware detection and suggests further research to improve the framework's scalability and effectiveness against sophisticated malware attacks (Irfan, Ariffin, Mahrin, & Anuar, 2020). The implementation of ML -based mobile malware detection in a business environment is covered in (Gong et al., 2020). In the process of designing and putting the system into practice, the authors discuss issues with data collection, model selection, feature engineering, and performance optimisation, to name just a few. The system uses a combination of static and dynamic analysis techniques to extract features from mobile apps and then uses a Random Forest algorithm to classify them as either benign or malicious. The authors use a sizable dataset of actual mobile apps to assess the system's performance and show that it achieves high accuracy, precision, and recall rates. The study emphasises how important collaboration between researchers, engineers, and product managers is when creating and delivering effective ML solutions for real-world issues. The authors recommend further research to improve the interpretability, scalability, and resistance of the system to sophisticated malware attacks. The article provides a summary of the state of deep learning research for malware detection (Sahin & Bahtiyar, 2021). The authors discuss deep learning models, including CNNs, RNNs, and Generative Adversarial Networks (GANs), and how they can be applied to identify malware in a variety of settings, such as cloud computing, mobile devices, and the IoT. The survey also covers various feature extraction techniques, such as byte n-grams, opcode sequences, and API calls, as well as the use of ensemble techniques and transfer learning to improve detection performance. The authors discuss the advantages and disadvantages of using deep learning for malware detection as well as a number of research challenges, such as data scarcity, adversarial attacks, and interpretability. The survey provides an in-depth analysis of the current state of deep learning research for malware detection and offers suggestions for new research directions to improve the effectiveness and dependability of deep learning-based solutions in real-world settings (Y. Lee, Lee, & Soh, 2018). The article discusses a development in deep learning for malware detection. The authors provide an overview of the state-of-the-art feature extraction techniques and deep learning models for malware detection research. The study discusses both the advantages and disadvantages of deep learning for malware detection, emphasising both its ability to handle sophisticated and constantly evolving malware threats as well as the challenge of dealing with noisy and unbalanced data. The authors discuss recent advances in deep learning research for malware detection, including explainable AI and adversarial ML, and their potential effects on the efficacy and interpretability of deep learning-based solutions. The study also provides a critical evaluation of the current state of deep learning research for malware detection and offers suggestions for future research directions to address open problems and improve the functionality and effectiveness of deep learning-based solutions in real-world settings. The method for identifying Android malware using deep learning techniques is presented in the paper by Zegzhda, Zegzhda, Pavlenko, and Ignatev (2018). The authors propose a framework to extract features from Android apps, such as manifest files, API calls, and system events, using both static and dynamic analysis. The features are then fed into a deep neural network, specifically a CNN and an LSTM network, to categorise the apps as either benign or malicious. The authors evaluate the framework's performance using a dataset of real Android apps, and they show that the CNN-LSTM network outperforms other ML methods by achieving high accuracy, precision, and recall rates. The study shows the potential of deep learning techniques for Android malware detection and offers ideas for additional research to improve the framework's scalability and effectiveness against cutting-edge and novel malware attacks. The article discusses the application of ML algorithms for Android malware detection (Kakavand, Dabbagh, & Dehghantanha, 2018). The authors provide a general overview of various ML techniques, including naive Bayes, support vector machines (SVMs), decision trees, random forests, and neural networks, and how they can be used to detect Android malware. The study highlights the importance of feature extraction and selection, including static and dynamic analysis and feature engineering techniques like bag-of-words and n-grams. According to the authors' evaluation of the performance of different ML algorithms using a dataset of Android apps, the SVM algorithm with a combination of static and dynamic features achieves high accuracy, precision, and recall rates. The study also discusses the limitations and challenges of using ML for Android malware detection, such as the need for extensive and diverse datasets, the issue of data privacy, and the challenge of identifying novel and undiscovered malware threats. The study has important implications for creating ML-based malware detection systems for secure mobile devices (Sewak, Sahay, & Rathore, 2018). The paper examines a deep learning-based malware detection system. The authors propose a framework that combines static and dynamic analysis techniques to extract features from Android apps, such as API calls, system events, and permissions. A deep neural network, specifically a CNN, would then be fed these features. The study evaluates the framework's performance using a dataset of real Android apps and shows that it outperforms other ML methods by achieving high accuracy, precision, and recall rates. After examining the effects of various hyperparameters, such as the number of layers, filters, and neurons, on detection performance, the authors also give their recommendations for the ideal CNN architecture settings. In order to increase the framework's robustness and scalability in the face of sophisticated malware threats, the study recommends further research into the advantages and disadvantages of using deep learning for malware detection. The research has important implications for creating safe mobile security applications that use deep learning-based malware detection. The article from C. Wu, Shi, Yang, & Li (2018) discusses using RL to enhance a malware detection model based on ML. The authors propose a framework that combines a CNN and an RL algorithm, specifically the Q-learning algorithm, to improve the accuracy of Android malware detection. The features that the framework extracts from Android apps using both static and dynamic analysis and feeds into the CNN include API calls, system events, and permissions. The Q-learning algorithm assists CNN in making better decisions by rewarding accurate classifications and penalising false positives and false negatives. The study evaluates the framework's performance using a dataset of real Android apps and discovers that it performs better than other ML and deep learning techniques by achieving high rates of accuracy, precision, and recall. The best CNN and Q-learning algorithm settings are also suggested by the authors after they examine the effects of different hyperparameters on detection performance. The study presents the feasibility of using RL for ML -based malware detection and proposes future research topics to enhance the robustness and scalability of the framework against sophisticated malware attacks (Sang, Cuong, & Cuong, 2018). The article makes a recommendation for an effective ensemble deep learning framework for malware detection. The framework combines a number of deep learning models, such as CNNs and RNNs, to achieve high accuracy, precision, and recall rates. The authors employ both static and dynamic analysis to extract features from Android apps, including system events, API calls, and permissions. The deep learning models are then fed these features. Using a dataset of real Android apps, the study compares the framework's performance to that of other state-of-the-art ML and deep learning techniques. The authors analyse the effects of various hyperparameters on detection performance and provide suggested settings for the ensemble deep learning framework. The study highlights the value of utilising a collection of deep learning models to improve the generalisation and robustness of malware detection systems and offers recommendations for additional research to increase the framework's scalability and effectiveness against sophisticated malware attacks.

These methods have proven successful in identifying a variety of security risks, such as phishing attacks, false information, fraudulent financial reporting, and adversarial samples. The effective use of these techniques has helped to improve security protocols in a variety of contexts, including smart grid environments, horse racing betting, network security, web application security, and mobile app security. To guarantee the continued efficacy of these strategies, issues like data scarcity, adversarial attacks, and interpretability must be resolved. By overcoming these obstacles, information security governance can be improved even more by implementing cutting-edge malware detection methods and keeping up with new online threats. Table 1.2 shows a summary of malware and spam detection articles.

Table 1.2 Summary review table for malware and spam detection articles

Reference	*Machine learning (ML) method*	*Detection*	*Prevention*	*Response*	*Recovery*
Basit et al. (2021)	Various AI techniques (ML, deep learning, etc.)	Detecting phishing attacks		Y	
Mughaid et al. (2022)	Deep learning techniques (CNNs, LSTM)	Detecting phishing attacks			
Kula et al. (2022)	BERT-derived architectures	Detecting disinformation		Y	
Radoglou-Grammatikis et al. (2021)	Centralised architecture for SIEM system	Monitoring and responding to security threats in smart grid	Y		
Min et al. (2021)	ML (clustering, anomaly detection)	Detecting anomalous transactions in horse racing betting		Y	
G. Lee & Kim (2021)	Computer vision techniques	Detecting deepfakes		Y	
Venters & Mikkilineni (2020)	Evolutionary algorithms	Detecting anomalies in financial statements		Y	
Feltus (2020)	Reinforcement learning	Network security (intrusion detection, malware detection)			
Basit et al. (2021)	Conditional WGAN-GP	Detecting cross-site scripting (XSS) attacks	Y		
Mughaid et al. (2022)	Deep learning	Detecting adversarial samples in IoT environments		Y	
Kula et al. (2022)	ML, deep learning	Various cybersecurity applications (anomaly detection, intrusion detection, malware detection)		Y	

(Continued)

Table 1.2 (Continued)

Reference	*Machine learning (ML) method*	*Detection*	*Prevention*	*Response*	*Recovery*
Radoglou-Grammatikis et al. (2021)	Deep learning (LSTM, TF-IDF)	Detecting and preventing cyber-attacks			
Min et al. (2021)	ML	Malware detection for Android apps			
G. Lee & Kim (2021)	Automated ML (AutoML)	Malware detection			
Venters & Mikkilineni (2020)	Deep learning (CNNs, RNNs, LSTM)	Identifying malicious Android apps		Y	
Feltus (2020)	Forensic analysis and unsupervised ML	Malware detection			Y
Basit et al. (2021)	ML (Random Forest)	Mobile malware detection			
Mughaid et al. (2022)	Deep learning (CNNs, RNNs, GANs)	Malware detection in different contexts		Y	
Kula et al. (2022)	Deep learning	Malware detection	Y		
Radoglou-Grammatikis et al. (2021)	Deep learning	Android malware detection		Y	

1.2.3.2 Risk management

The use of hybrid ML algorithms for ontology learning in disaster risk management is covered in (Contreras, Ballera, & Festijo, 2020). The authors suggest a framework to automatically extract and classify disaster-related concepts from various information sources using a combination of supervised and unsupervised learning techniques. The framework uses SVMs to classify potential concepts into predefined categories after using clustering and NLP algorithms to identify them. The performance of the framework is assessed by the authors using information gathered from social media during a hurricane event. The findings demonstrate that in terms of accuracy and efficiency, the hybrid approach performs better than conventional ML techniques. The study emphasises the potential of applying ML and ontology learning techniques for disaster risk management and recommends additional study to increase the framework's scalability and capacity for various types of disasters. Table 1.3 shows a review of risk managements articles.

The papers that were discussed provided insight into the role that risk assessment techniques have played in information security governance. By concentrating on the U.S. healthcare sector and outlining key themes, Abraham

Table 1.3 Summary review table for risk management articles

Reference	*ML method*	*Security governance related solutions*
Abraham et al. (2019)	Not specified	- Better education and training for employees - More resources for cybersecurity - Greater collaboration and information sharing among organisations
Veale et al. (2018)	Not specified	- Technical measures to prevent model inversion attacks - Legal frameworks to hold data controllers accountable - Education and awareness-raising campaigns for data privacy
Aftab et al. (2021)	Attribute-based encryption	- Secure and dynamic access control mechanism for IoT-based systems - Efficient management of access to IoT devices and associated data - Flexibility in controlling authorisation for different users and groups
Johnson (2020)	Not specified	- Regular security assessments to identify weaknesses and threats - Comprehensive security strategy addressing confidentiality, integrity, availability, accountability, and auditability
Contreras et al. (2020)	Hybrid ML	Not specified

et al. draw attention to the complexity of cybersecurity and the demand for an all-encompassing strategy that strikes a balance between risk management, resource allocation, and patient care. They emphasise how crucial it is to improve cybersecurity in the healthcare industry through education, training, resources, and cooperation. Model inversion attacks are used to violate data protection laws, according to Veale et al. They argue that the problem should be addressed with clear guidelines, technical solutions, legal frameworks, and awareness campaigns. The work of Aftab deals with security and access control in IoT-based traffic systems, and it suggests a safe and flexible access control mechanism based on attribute-based encryption. They provide evidence of the mechanism's potency in delivering secure access control. Johnson also covers the fundamental elements of security and the significance of routine security audits to guarantee a system's safety. Last but not least, Contreras et al. suggest a hybrid ML framework for ontology learning in disaster risk management that performs better than conventional methods in terms of accuracy and efficiency. Collectively, these studies emphasise the significance of risk assessment in information security governance and offer insights into how to deal with issues like data protection violations, access control in IoT systems, overall system security, and disaster risk management.

On the basis of system security and NLP, Shahbazi and Byun present a digital forensic analysis of online social networks. The study's goal is to create a process for looking into and spotting security threats in online social networks using NLP methods. The authors suggest using NLP to analyse text and image content in online social networks in order to identify harmful behaviours like spamming, phishing, and cyberbullying. The results of the study show that system security specialists can efficiently find security threats in online social networks by employing the NLP-based digital forensic analysis method (Shahbazi & Byun, 2022). The creation of an AI bot that can identify fake COVID-19 vaccine certificates is described by Arif et al. The authors outline a system that analyses and verifies the accuracy of vaccination certificates using ML algorithms. The system can be used to spot fake or altered certificates and warn organisations and authorities about possible fraud. The study highlights the potential of the AI bot as a useful tool for preventing vaccine fraud during the COVID-19 pandemic by showing how well it can recognise fake vaccine certificates. The authors also discuss potential drawbacks and future development directions, as well as how to integrate the technology with other technologies and datasets (Arif, Shamsudheen, Ajesh, Wang, & Chen, 2022). A tutorial on the use of ML for dynamic authentication in telehealth is offered by Hazratifard et al. The authors provide a brief overview of the difficulties and prerequisites for authentication in telehealth, including the requirement for easy and secure access to confidential patient data. The subject of dynamic authentication using ML algorithms is then discussed after that. This could offer a more dependable and effective way to confirm the users of telehealth. The tutorial discusses various ML methods, such as SVMs, decision trees, and neural networks, and offers suggestions for picking the best ML strategy for a particular telehealth application. The paper also provides illustrations of how these algorithms can be used in actual telehealth applications. The authors go over the potential advantages and disadvantages of using ML for dynamic authentication in telehealth as well as possible lines of inquiry for additional study in this area (Hazratifard et al., 2022). Shah suggests tackling the problem of mobile number portability using a blockchain-based system. Mobile number portability allows users to change their mobile service provider while keeping their current phone number. The authors argue that the current process for porting mobile numbers is prone to errors and security issues, and they offer a blockchain-based solution to address these problems. Building a decentralised blockchain network to securely store information about mobile numbers and the users connected to them is the suggested solution. The authors demonstrate the viability and effectiveness of the proposed solution through simulations, demonstrating how it can improve the security, dependability, and transparency of the process for mobile number portability (Shah et al., 2021a). Manral and Somani talk about the difficulties in advancing digital forensics capabilities in light of insider threats from superusers. Superuser insiders are people with access to private data and systems who, if they act maliciously, could do a lot of damage. The authors claim that insider superuser threats may be difficult to identify and counter using traditional digital forensics techniques. The authors present a framework for developing forensic expertise to successfully deal with threats posed by superuser insiders. The proposed framework is based on a combination of technical and procedural measures and includes a number of components, including data collection, analysis, and reporting. The authors also go over the shortcomings of the suggested framework and emphasise the need for more research in the field. In light of insider threats from superusers, the paper emphasises the importance of developing forensics capabilities to ensure the security and integrity of digital systems and information (Manral & Somani, 2021). The article summarises how deep learning is used to classify encrypted traffic. According to the authors, conventional techniques for categorising network traffic are losing their usefulness as encryption usage rises. They discuss the classification of encrypted traffic using deep learning techniques like CNNs and RNNs. The authors give a general overview of the various types of encrypted traffic, including SSL/TLS, SSH, and VPN, and they discuss the difficulties in categorising these traffic types. They also go over the different datasets that can be used to train and test deep learning models. According to the authors, deep learning techniques may enhance network security and have the potential to classify encrypted traffic (Rezaei & Liu, 2019). The article discusses how applying ML can enhance the analysis of real-world weaknesses for image-based user authentication based on mouse data. The authors of the article outline a technique for using a dataset of user authentication attempts to train an ML model to distinguish between legitimate and malicious mouse movements. The model is very good at identifying malicious mouse movements, which is helpful for identifying potential security gaps in systems that rely on images for user authentication. The authors come to the conclusion that the use of machine learning can significantly increase the precision and efficacy of vulnerability analysis in this field (K. Lee & Lee, 2020). The paper suggests a mobile number portability (MNP) method based on blockchain. Thanks to MNP, mobile phone users can change service providers while retaining their phone numbers. The suggested method automates and secures the MNP process using private blockchain smart contracts, cutting down on the time and expense of using conventional MNP systems. The functions and data structures of smart contracts are included in the authors' thorough description of the proposed system architecture. They also go over the privacy and security ramifications of the system and make a number of recommendations for potential future advancements. The research highlights how blockchain technology may enhance the overall security and effectiveness of the MNP process (Shah et al., 2021b). Qasaimeh et al. present a new scoring system for assessing the effectiveness of information security governance frameworks (ISGFs) in the banking sector. The authors use deep learning algorithms to analyse various inputs, such as audit reports and security policies, to create a score for each

ISGF component. Using these component scores, they then calculate an overall ISGF score. The proposed system was evaluated using data from a real-world case study involving a bank. The results show that the system is capable of precisely identifying the bank's ISGF's shortcomings and providing helpful recommendations for improvement. Overall, the study demonstrates how deep learning algorithms can benefit information security governance in the banking sector (Qasaimeh, Al-Qassas, & Batayneh, 2021). Barut, Grohotolski, & DiLeo (2020) presented the paper that is a comprehensive evaluated the perfromance of ML-based malware detection on encrypted traffic. The authors evaluate different ML algorithms, feature selection methods, and traffic encryption protocols to find the best approach for detecting malware in encrypted network traffic. The study uses a dataset of authentic encrypted traffic gathered from various sources to simulate different malware attacks. The results show that combining features based on frequency and time improves the accuracy, precision, and recall of the SVM algorithm. The study emphasises the impact of different encryption protocols on detection performance and offers ideas for additional research to address the challenges of detecting sophisticated malware attacks in encrypted traffic. For modern communication networks that heavily rely on encryption, the research has significant implications for developing effective security solutions.

Information security governance has benefited greatly from incident response strategies in a number of ways. Shahbazi and Byun show how NLP techniques can be used to identify security threats in online social networks like phishing and cyberbullying. System security experts can benefit from the insights provided by this NLP-based digital forensic analysis. Similar to this, Arif et al. created an ML -powered AI bot to identify phoney COVID-19 vaccine certificates, helping to stop vaccine fraud during the pandemic. Hazratifard et al. emphasise the use of ML algorithms for dynamic authentication with a focus on telehealth authentication, offering a more effective and secure way to confirm the identities of telehealth users. Shah also suggests a blockchain-based approach to the mobile number portability procedure, addressing security concerns and enhancing the system's dependability and transparency. Manral and Somani talk about the difficulties in detecting and countering superuser insider threats and offer a framework for developing digital forensics capabilities. The security and integrity of digital systems and information are enhanced by this framework. Rezaei and Liu investigate the application of deep learning methods for categorising encrypted traffic and enhancing network security by adjusting to the rising use of encryption. In order to help identify potential security vulnerabilities, K. Lee and Lee present how ML can enhance vulnerability analysis in image-based user authentication systems. The effectiveness of ISGFs in the banking industry is evaluated by Qasaimeh et al. using a scoring system that makes use of deep learning algorithms. They offer insights and suggestions for improvement. Finally, Barut, Grohotolski, and DiLeo assess ML -based malware detection on encrypted traffic, identifying the most effective configurations of algorithms and features for malware detection in contemporary communication networks that heavily rely on encryption. Collectively, these studies show how incident response strategies that make use of deep learning and ML techniques have improved information security governance across a range of domains, as shown in Table 1.4.

Table 1.4 Summary review table for incident response articles

Reference	*Machine learning (ML) method*	*Security governance related solutions*
Shahbazi & Byun (2022)	Natural Language Processing	- NLP-based approach for detecting security threats in online social networks - Valuable tool for system security professionals
Arif et al. (2022)	ML Algorithms	- AI bot for detecting fake COVID-19 vaccine certificates - Combating vaccine fraud during the COVID-19 pandemic
Hazratifard et al. (2022)	ML Algorithms	- ML for dynamic authentication in telehealth - Secure and efficient verification of telehealth users
Shah et al. (2021a)	Blockchain	- Blockchain-based solution for mobile number portability process - Improved security, reliability, and transparency in portability process
Manral & Somani (2021)	Not specified	- Framework for establishing forensics capabilities for superuser threats - Ensuring security and integrity of digital systems and information
Rezaei & Liu (2019)	Deep Learning	- Deep learning for encrypted traffic classification - Enhancing network security through accurate traffic classification
K. Lee & Lee (2020)	ML	- ML for vulnerability analysis in image-based authentication - Improving accuracy and efficiency of vulnerability analysis
Shah et al. (2021b)	Blockchain	- Blockchain-based solution for mobile number portability process - Automation and security in the portability process
Qasaimeh et al. (2021)	Deep Learning	- Scoring system for assessing the effectiveness of information security governance frameworks in the banking sector
Barut, Grohotolski, & DiLeo (2020)	ML	- Evaluating ML -based malware detection on encrypted traffic - Designing effective security solutions for encrypted communication

1.2.4 Result and discussion

When using ML for information security governance, researchers are investigating new strategies for safeguarding private data and safeguarding sensitive data. The ethical ramifications of using ML for information security governance, including concerns about fairness, transparency, and the potential loss of jobs for human analysts, are receiving increasing attention.

Maintaining the confidentiality, integrity, and availability of an organisation's information assets as well as adhering to legal and regulatory requirements depend on effective information security governance. It involves cross-organisational cooperation and necessitates a thorough comprehension of business operations, risks, and compliance requirements.

In order to protect an organisation's information assets from unauthorised access, use, disclosure, disruption, modification, or destruction, a set of procedures and organisational frameworks known as information security governance must be in place. It entails the creation and application of policies, practices, and controls to manage and reduce risks associated with the privacy, accuracy, and accessibility of information.

Several important activities that are part of information security governance include:

1. Defining each team's and individual's roles and responsibilities within the organisation for information security management.
2. Establishing rules and regulations for the use, management, and access of information assets.
3. Applying physical, technical, and administrative security controls to safeguard information assets from potential threats.
4. In order to make sure that information security controls are effective and provide the necessary protection while also adhering to all applicable laws, regulations, and industry standards.
5. Creating an environment where security awareness is valued and educating staff on security best practices.

1.3 CONCLUSION

The chapter discusses the significance of data protection, malware detection, risk assessment, and incident response approaches in IT security governance. Data protection methods address challenges related to unauthorised access, modification, or destruction of data, utilising encryption, access controls, authentication, and quantitative assessment. Malware detection approaches, employing AI techniques like ML, effectively identify security threats such as phishing attacks. Risk assessment studies emphasise comprehensive approaches, collaboration, and education/training to improve cybersecurity, address data protection. violations, access control in IoT systems, and disaster risk management. Incident response approaches contribute through

NLP-based threat detection, AI-powered detection of fake COVID-19 vaccine certificates, and ML algorithms for dynamic authentication and encrypted traffic classification. Additionally, frameworks for addressing superuser insider threats, vulnerability analysis, scoring systems for information security governance assessment, and blockchain-based solutions are highlighted. Overall, these approaches enhance IT security governance, strengthen security measures, mitigate risks, and combat emerging cyber threats.

1.4 CONFLICT OF INTEREST STATEMENT

On behalf of all authors, the corresponding author states that there is no conflict of interest.

REFERENCES

Abraham, C., Chatterjee, D., & Sims, R. R. (2019). Muddling through cybersecurity: Insights from the U.S. healthcare industry. *Business Horizons*, *62*(4), 539–548. https://doi.org/10.1016/j.bushor.2019.03.010

Aftab, M. U., Oluwasanmi, A., Alharbi, A., Sohaib, O., Nie, X., Qin, Z., & Ngo, S. T. (2021). Secure and dynamic access control for the internet of things (IoT) based traffic system. *PeerJ Computer Science*, *7*, 1–26. https://doi.org/10.7717/PEERJ-CS.471

Alexopoulos, C., Diamantopoulou, V., Lachana, Z., Charalabidis, Y., Androutsopoulou, A., & Loutsaris, M. A. (2019). How machine learning is changing e-government. *ACM International Conference Proceeding Series, Part F1481*, 354–363. https://doi.org/10.1145/3326365.3326412

Alotaibi, M., Furnell, S., & Clarke, N. (2017). Information security policies: A review of challenges and influencing factors. *2016 11th International Conference for Internet Technology and Secured Transactions, ICITST 2016*, 352–358. https://doi.org/10.1109/ICITST.2016.7856729

Arif, M., Shamsudheen, S., Ajesh, F., Wang, G., & Chen, J. (2022). AI bot to detect fake COVID-19 vaccine certificate. *IET Information Security*, *16*(5), 362–372. https://doi.org/10.1049/ise2.12063

Barut, O., Grohotolski, M., & DiLeo, C. (2020). Machine learning based malware detection on encrypted traffic: A comprehensive performance study. *Systems and Security (NSysS)*, (22-24 Decemeber), 45–55 https://doi.org/10.1145/3428363.3428365

Basit, A., Zafar, M., Liu, X., Javed, A. R., Jalil, Z., & Kifayat, K. (2021). A comprehensive survey of AI-enabled phishing attacks detection techniques. *Telecommunication Systems*, *76*(1), 139–154. https://doi.org/10.1007/s11235-020-00733-2

Bongiovanni, I., Renaud, K., Brydon, H., Blignaut, R., & Cavallo, A. (2022). A quantification mechanism for assessing adherence to information security governance guidelines. *Information and Computer Security*, (20 OCT 2022), 1–25.

Contreras, J. O., Ballera, M. A., & Festijo, E. D. (2020). Ontology learning using hybrid machine learning algorithms for disaster risk management. *Proceedings of the 2020 3rd International Conference on Signal Processing and Machine Learning*, 13–20. https://doi.org/10.1145/3432291.3432306

Feltus, C. (2020). Current and future RL's contribution to emerging network security. *Procedia Computer Science*, *177*, 516–521. Retrieved from https://doi.org/10.1016/j.procs.2020.10.071

Gellert, R. (2022). Comparing definitions of data and information in data protection law and machine learning: A useful way forward to meaningfully regulate algorithms? *Regulation & Governance*, *16*(1), 156–176. https://doi.org/10.1111/rego.12349

Gong, L., Li, Z., Qian, F., Zhang, Z., Chen, Q. A., Qian, Z., ... Liu, Y. (2020). Experiences of landing machine learning onto market-scale mobile malware detection. *Proceedings of the Fifteenth European Conference on Computer Systems*. https://doi.org/10.1145/3342195.3387530

Hazratifard, M., Gebali, F., & Mamun, M. (2022). Using machine learning for dynamic authentication in telehealth: A tutorial. *Sensors (Basel, Switzerland)*, *22*(19). https://doi.org/10.3390/s22197655

Hernández-Álvarez, L., de Fuentes, J. M., González-manzano, L., & Hernandez Encinas, L. (2021). Privacy-preserving sensor-based continuous authentication and user profiling: A review. Sensors, *21*(1), 92, 1–23.

Hong, S., Park, J. H., Cho, W., Choe, H., & Cheon, J. H. (2022). Secure tumor classification by shallow neural network using homomorphic encryption. *BMC Genomics*, *23*(1), 284. https://doi.org/10.1186/s12864-022-08469-w

Irfan, A. N., Ariffin, A., Mahrin, M. N., & Anuar, S. (2020). A malware detection framework based on forensic and unsupervised machine learning methodologies. *Proceedings of the 2020 9th International Conference on Software and Computer Applications*, 194–200. https://doi.org/10.1145/3384544.3384556

Jahwar, A. F., & Y. Ameen, S. (2022). A review on cybersecurity based on machine learning and deep learning algorithm. *Journal of Soft Computing and Data Mining*, *2*(15.10.2021), 14–25.

Johnson, L. (2020). Security component fundamentals for assessment. *Security Controls Evaluation, Testing, and Assessment Handbook*, 471–536. https://doi.org/10.1016/b978-0-12-818427-1.00011-2

Kakavand, M., Dabbagh, M., & Dehghantanha, A. (2018). Application of machine learning algorithms for android malware detection. *Proceedings of the 2018 International Conference on Computational Intelligence and Intelligent Systems*, 32–36. https://doi.org/10.1145/3293475.3293489

Kula, S., Kozik, R., & Choraś, M. (2022). Implementation of the BERT-derived architectures to tackle disinformation challenges. *Neural Computing & Applications*, *34*(23), 20449–20461. https://doi.org/10.1007/s00521-021-06276-0

Kundu, P. P., Anatharaman, L., & Truong-Huu, T. (2021). An empirical evaluation of automated machine learning techniques for malware detection. *Proceedings of the 2021 ACM Workshop on Security and Privacy Analytics*, 75–81. https://doi.org/10.1145/3445970.3451155

Lee, G., & Kim, M. (2021). Deepfake detection using the rate of change between frames based on computer vision. *Sensors (Basel, Switzerland)*, *21*(21). https://doi.org/10.3390/s21217367

Lee, K., & Lee, S.-Y. (2020). Improved practical vulnerability analysis of mouse data according to offensive security based on machine learning in image-based user authentication. *Mdpi*, *355*(22), pp. 1–16.

Lee, Y., Lee, J., & Soh, W. (2018). Trend of malware detection using deep learning. *Proceedings of the 2nd International Conference on Education and Multimedia Technology*, 102–106. https://doi.org/10.1145/3206129.3239430

Manral, B., & Somani, G. (2021). Establishing forensics capabilities in the presence of superuser insider threats. *Forensic Science International: Digital Investigation*, *38*, 301263. https://doi.org/10.1016/j.fsidi.2021.301263

Min, M., Lee, J. J., Park, H., & Lee, K. (2021). Detecting anomalous transactions via an IoT based application: A machine learning approach for horse racing betting. *Sensors (Basel, Switzerland)*, *21*(6). https://doi.org/10.3390/s21062039

Mokbal, F. M. M., Wang, D., Wang, X., & Fu, L. (2020). Data augmentation-based conditional Wasserstein generative adversarial network-gradient penalty for XSS attack detection system. *PeerJ Computer Science*, *6*, 1–20. https://doi.org/10.7717/peerj-cs.328

Mughaid, A., AlZu'bi, S., Hnaif, A., Taamneh, S., Alnajjar, A., & Elsoud, E. A. (2022). An intelligent cyber security phishing detection system using deep learning techniques. *Cluster Computing*, *25*(6), 3819–3828. https://doi.org/10.1007/s10586-022-03604-4

Qasaimeh, M., Al-qassas, R. S., & Batayneh, A. A. A. L. (2021). *A Scoring System for Information Security Governance Framework Using Deep Learning Algorithms : A Case Study on the Banking Sector. ACM Journal of Data and Information Quality (JDIQ)*, *13*, 1–34. https://doi.org/10.1145/3418172

Radoglou-Grammatikis, P., Sarigiannidis, P., Iturbe, E., Rios, E., Martinez, S., Sarigiannidis, A., … Ramos, F. (2021). SPEAR SIEM: A security information and event management system for the Smart Grid. *Computer Networks*, *193*, 108008. https://doi.org/10.1016/j.comnet.2021.108008

Rezaei, S., & Liu, X. (2019). Deep learning for encrypted traffic classification: An overview. *IEEE Communications Magazine*, *57*(5), 76–81. https://doi.org/10.1109/MCOM.2019.1800819

Sahin, M., & Bahtiyar, S. (2021). A survey on malware detection with deep learning. *13th International Conference on Security of Information and Networks*. https://doi.org/10.1145/3433174.3433609

Sang, D. V., Cuong, D. M., & Cuong, L. T. B. (2018). An effective ensemble deep learning framework for malware detection. *Proceedings of the 9th International Symposium on Information and Communication Technology*, 192–199. https://doi.org/10.1145/3287921.3287971

Sewak, M., Sahay, S. K., & Rathore, H. (2018). An investigation of a deep learning based malware detection system. *Proceedings of the 13th International Conference on Availability, Reliability and Security*. https://doi.org/10.1145/3230833.3230835

Shah, J., Agarwal, S., Shukla, A., Tanwar, S., Tyagi, S., & Kumar, N. (2021a). Blockchain-based scheme for the mobile number portability. *Journal of Information Security and Applications*, *58*, 102764. https://doi.org/10.1016/j.jisa.2021.102764

Shah, J., Agarwal, S., Shukla, A., Tanwar, S., Tyagi, S., & Kumar, N. (2021b). Blockchain-based scheme for the mobile number portability. *Journal of Information Security and Applications*, *58*. https://doi.org/10.1016/j.jisa.2021.102764

Shahbazi, Z., & Byun, Y.-C. (2022). NLP-based digital forensic analysis for online social network based on system security. *International Journal of Environmental Research and Public Health*, *19*(12). https://doi.org/10.3390/ijerph19127027

Veale, M., Binns, R., & Edwards, L. (2018). Algorithms that remember: model inversion attacks and data protection law. *Philosophical Transactions. Series A, Mathematical, Physical, and Engineering Sciences*, *376*(2133). https://doi.org/10.1098/rsta.2018.0083

Venters, C., & Mikkilineni, R. (2020). Representation and evolution of knowledge structures to detect anomalies in financial statements. *Proceedings of the Workshop on Enabling Technologies: Infrastructure for Collaborative Enterprises, WETICE*, *2020-Septe*, 58–63. https://doi.org/10.1109/WETICE49692.2020.00020

Wang, S., & Qiao, Z. (2019). Robust pervasive detection for adversarial samples of artificial intelligence in IoT environments. *IEEE Access*, *7*, 88693–88704. https://doi.org/10.1109/ACCESS.2019.2919695

Wu, C., Shi, J., Yang, Y., & Li, W. (2018). Enhancing machine learning based malware detection model by reinforcement learning. *Proceedings of the 8th International Conference on Communication and Network Security*, 74–78. https://doi.org/10.1145/3290480.3290494

Wu, H. (2020). A systematical study for deep learning based android malware detection. *Proceedings of the 2020 9th International Conference on Software and Computer Applications*, 177–182. https://doi.org/10.1145/3384544.3384546

Wylde, V., Rawindaran, N., Lawrence, J., Balasubramanian, R., Prakash, E., Jayal, A., ... Platts, J. (2022). Cybersecurity, data privacy and blockchain: A review. *SN Computer Science*, *3*(2), 127. https://doi.org/10.1007/s42979-022-01020-4

Yu, G. (2021). Research on computer network information security based on improved machine learning. *Journal of Intelligent and Fuzzy Systems*, *40*(4), 6889–6900. https://doi.org/10.3233/JIFS-189520

Zegzhda, P., Zegzhda, D., Pavlenko, E., & Ignatev, G. (2018). Applying deep learning techniques for android malware detection. *Proceedings of the 11th International Conference on Security of Information and Networks*. https://doi.org/10.1145/3264437.3264476

Zhao, Y., Li, L., Wang, H., Cai, H., Bissyandé, T. F., Klein, J., & Grundy, J. (2021). On the impact of sample duplication in machine-learning-based android malware detection. *ACM Trans. Softw. Eng. Methodol.*, *30*(3). https://doi.org/10.1145/3446905

Chapter 2

Impact of generative AI in cybersecurity and data privacy

Hajar Fares, Noura Aknin, and Youssef Baddi

2.1 INTRODUCTION

Recent developments in artificial intelligence (AI) have opened up new paradigms for machine processing. These concepts have evolved from deep learning and traditional machine learning to a complex and sophisticated idea of data generation known as generative artificial intelligence (GAI) [1].

Cybersecurity paradigms have seen a dramatic change with the introduction of GAI, which substitutes more intelligent and adaptable technology for conventional rule-based methods.

AI, or GAI, is becoming more and more prevalent in a variety of domains and applications, including education, cybersecurity, healthcare, and fabrication of content [2], offering both possible advantages and difficulties.

However, when cyber threat actors use AI-assisted attacks to take advantage of weaknesses in digital systems, this growth also brings with it new difficulties. Although AI's capacity for generalization improves cyber defenses, it also gives attackers the ability to create intricate and original attack pathways [3].

ChatGPT and other GAI tools have become a double-edged sword in cybersecurity, posing threats as well as advantages to both attackers and defenders. By using extensive threat intelligence data, cyber defenders use these techniques to strengthen systems against malevolent invasions. Defenders improve the ability to detect threats and respond to incidents by drawing conclusions from large datasets, automating procedures, and encouraging security-conscious behavior in people. Additionally, GAI supports the creation of ethical guidelines and secure coding techniques the strengthening cyber defense frameworks [4].

By carrying out behavioral analysis and anomaly detection, GAI can support IoT security. It can be used to create models of typical behavior for various IoT devices and environment types [5]. In order to identify possible security breaches or unauthorized access, generative models can analyze data from IoT sensors and devices and identify deviations from regular patterns. This enables the business to take prompt action against the cyber threat, hence boosting security robustness. GAI may also be a major factor in IoT threats.

DOI: 10.1201/9781003597476-3

In this chapter, we provide an overview of GAI and the various fields of applications, as well as its positive and negative impacts on cybersecurity.

The remainder of this chapter is structured as follows: in the next section, we provide an overview of GAI; afterwards, we cite some case studies related to GAI, followed by a detailed description of the impact of GAI in the field of cybersecurity and data privacy. Finally, we conclude the chapter with a conclusion with some future directions.

2.2 AN OVERVIEW OF GENERATIVE AI

AI is a science that explores and develops theories, methods, techniques, and applications aimed at simulating, developing, and extending human intelligence. According to Arthur Samuel (1959, IBM) [6] "The science of machine learning aims to enable computers to learn without explicit programming". Deep learning is a subset of machine learning. It is a neural network with a large number of layers and parameters. GAI is an advanced field based on deep-learning methods able to learn from a huge amount of data, extract patterns, and generate new and real-time outputs. As illustrated in Figure 2.1.

Multimodal material, including text, music, images, videos, and even three-dimensional models, can be produced via GAI [7].

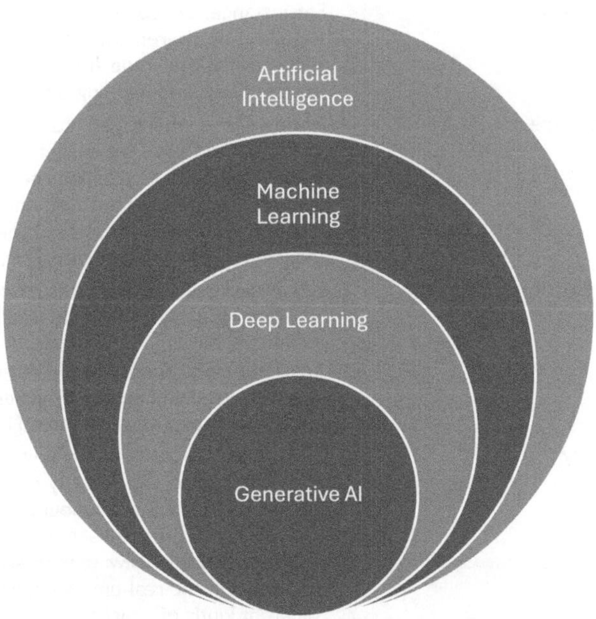

Figure 2.1 Generative AI components.

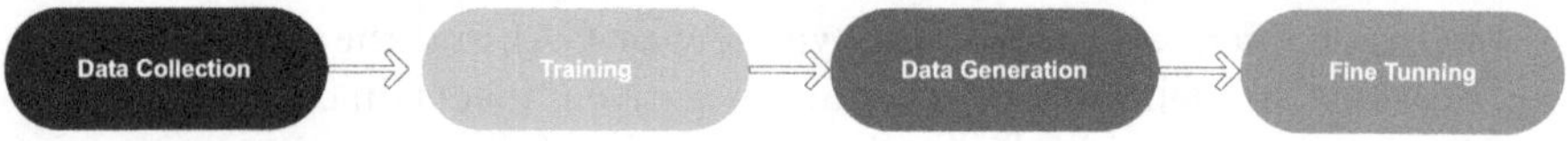

Figure 2.2 Functioning of generative AI.

Generative Artificial Networks, Variational Autoencoders, Transformers, and other cutting-edge deep-learning techniques are used by GAI models to extract patterns and structures from massive datasets. GAI models produce fresh outputs and content after they have been trained.

GAI works under the following steps as illustrated in Figure 2.2.

GAI offers potential applications in a variety of domains, such as industry, education, healthcare, and so on. (Table 2.1)

Because of its wide range of potential applications, GAI has the potential to revolutionize people, businesses, and society. However, the technology also comes with a number of drawbacks that are similar to those of conventional machine learning and deep learning systems.

Table 2.1 Generative AI applications

Business	GAI can serve business in many ways, ranging from marketing, sales, transaction, and so on [8].
Education	For instance, ChatGPT, a GAI tool, has significantly altered and disrupted the educational landscape. It can support instructional and learning activities [9].
Healthcare	Another area where GAI has the potential to have a big impact is healthcare, such as telemedicine services, clinical diagnosis support, patient engagement, health promotion, health education, and health advice [10].
Fabrication of content	GAI is having a significant impact on the content industry and can be used to produce content. For instance, the marketing sector is using GAI to create individualized and artificially generated ads for prospective customers [11].
Security	GAI has both potential advantages and disadvantages in the security domain. By learning from a vast amount of malware data, generative models can produce realistic malware representations and assist in the real-time detection of different kinds of attacks.

2.3 RELATED WORKS

In this section, we provide the recent contributions related to GAI in the field of cybersecurity. A summary of the literature review has been provided in Table 2.2.

Sai et al. [12] have conducted an analysis of the potential for improving the security space using ChatGPT, DALL-E, and other models. This study aims to present practical uses of GAI in the cybersecurity field as well as some of its drawbacks, such as the possibility of malevolent actors using GAI for illegal purposes, expensive training, and the occasional incorrect outcome.

Dhoni et al.[13] set out to investigate the complex connection between cybersecurity and GAI. Authors explore how the emergence of GAI technologies has enabled a paradigm shift in the cybersecurity landscape, delving into the domain of AI-driven creativity and manipulation. They discover the difficulties and possibilities brought about by this dynamic interaction as they proceed through their investigation.

Agrawal et al.,[14] in order to answer the aforementioned problems, thoroughly examine the fundamentals of generative learning and closely examine its data creation capabilities. The aim of this research chapter is that this investigation will clarify how synthetic data might strengthen deep-learning models for reliable cybersecurity applications.

As per Rabieinejad et al. [15], this chapter suggests a paradigm for cyber threat hunting in the Ethereum blockchain that makes use of Generative Adversarial Networks (GAN) and Deep Recurrent Neural Networks (RNN). First, as the initial stage of the suggested model, we use GAN to create fictitious transactions using real Ethereum transactions. Then, in the second stage, the authors looked for adversarial transactions using bidirectional Long Short-Term Memory (LSTM). The first phase evaluation's findings demonstrate that the GAN can produce transactions with an accuracy of 82.51% that are exactly like real Ethereum transactions. Additionally, the second phase's results demonstrate 99.98% accuracy in identifying adversarial.

Table 2.2 Summary of related works

Ref	*Date of publication*	*Approach used*
[12]	2024	ChatGPT, DALL-E
[13]	2023	GAI
[14]	2024	Generative Learning and Deep Learning
[15]	2023	Generative Adversarial Networks (GAN), Deep Recurrent Neural Networks (RNN) and bidirectional Long Short-Term Memory (LSTM)
[16]	2024	Creating honeypots, enhancing code security, preventing malware using ChatGPT

The main obstacles to using ChatGPT in cybersecurity are outlined by Mohammed et al. [16]. These include assessing ChatGPT's effect on cybersecurity, creating honeypots, enhancing code security, preventing malware development abuse, looking into vulnerabilities, disseminating false information, cyberattacks on industrial systems, altering the cyber threat environment, changing cybersecurity strategies, and developing human-centric training.

2.4 NEGATIVE AND POSITIVE IMPACT OF GAI IN CYBERSECURITY

AI has several uses across various businesses and areas, as was previously mentioned. Cybersecurity is one of the industries that has benefited most from AI.

GAI has the potential to improve the accuracy of current security systems' detection of sophisticated phishing assaults. AI-powered security systems today have a defensive strategy, meaning they begin implementing countermeasures after an attack has been launched. While utilizing GAI with these products will enable them to take an offensive stance against these threats, the security team will always be able to stay one step ahead of the attack vendors by anticipating the most likely tactics they will use to compromise the security of their systems. This will allow them to be ready for such attacks and respond to them more effectively.

2.4.1 Positive impact of GAI in cybersecurity

- **Anomaly Detection:** Large volumes of data can be analyzed by GAI models to identify and learn typical system characteristics. After training, they are able to produce models of "normal" activity and identify irregularities that can indicate possible security risks like malware infections or illegal access [17].
- **Signature Generation:** GAI can generate novel signatures for malware or other cyberattack strategies that would have eluded conventional detection techniques by analyzing established attack patterns [18].
- **Predective Detection:** Organizations can proactively prepare for vulnerabilities by using GAI to analyze historical data, find trends, and anticipate possible assaults before they occur [19].
- **Phishing Attacks Recognition:** By developing models that identify recurring patterns in phishing emails, webpages, and messaging, GAI can assist in detecting phishing efforts. AI's capacity to examine information and language patterns can greatly improve phishing detection capabilities as attackers employ increasingly complex techniques [20].
- **Simulated Attack Generation:** For training, GAI can replicate authentic hacks. This enables security teams to test the resilience of an organization's cybersecurity defenses and experience different attack scenarios

in a controlled setting, enhancing readiness and response tactics without endangering the company and spotting vulnerabilities before bad actors can take advantage of them [21].

2.4.2 Negative impact of GAI in cybersecurity

- **Deepfakes creation:** Attackers can utilize GAI to produce deepfakes persuasive fake identities, synthetic voices, and videos that facilitate fraud, misinformation campaigns, and social engineering attacks [22].
- **Automated Attack Generation:** Generative models could be used by malicious actors to produce new, extremely sophisticated malware that can change to get around security measures. Because these AI-generated threats are always changing, it may be harder to identify them [23].
- **Attacks Injection:** Attackers might purposefully introduce malicious or false data into AI model training datasets, causing improper learning and reducing security systems' efficacy [24].

2.5 IMPACT OF GAI IN DATA PRIVACY

Another significant issue facing ChatGPT and other GAI systems is data privacy and security. Sensitive personal data that owners do not wish to share with third parties is referred to as privacy. The process of shielding data from theft, corruption, and unwanted access is known as data security. A significant amount of private and personal information was used to train ChatGPT during its development, endangering user privacy. As ChatGPT gains traction and usage, it permeates people's daily lives, offering them more convenience while collecting a wealth of personal data about them. Users must exercise extreme caution while dealing with ChatGPT to avoid sharing private or sensitive information about their company in order to meet privacy and security concerns [25, 26].

Concerns around security and privacy in GAI are being addressed in a number of ways to restrict the amount of private information that is made public during the generating stage.

As per Tanuwidjaja et al., [27] the difficulties with data security and privacy in Machine Learning as a Service (MLaaS) platforms have been covered by writers. A collection of methods known as Privacy-Preserving Deep Learning (PPDL) enables data owners to maintain the privacy of their data while enabling MLaaS platforms to use it to train models.

As per Golda et al.,[28] it provides a thorough analysis of the privacy and security issues that are inherent to GAI, highlighting existing security measures and suggesting long-term fixes.

Federated learning and homomorphic encryption are techniques for preserving data privacy. Federated learning offers techniques for decentralized model training, allowing data to be stored locally on devices, ensuring the confidentiality of sensitive data. A strong cryptographic method that allows direct computation on encrypted data while maintaining the privacy of sensitive data throughout the processing stage is homomorphic encryption. Federated learning environments have also incorporated homomorphic encryption, which permits the safe aggregation of encrypted model updates without disclosing private raw data [29, 30].

2.6 CONCLUSION

AI, namely machine learning and deep learning algorithms, are well-suited tools for a variety of application areas because they can process vast volumes of data and identify intricate patterns that are challenging for humans to identify.

In 2022, GAI has undergone a significant transition, characterized by remarkable breakthroughs and quick developments. GAI enables the creation of original content in a range of media, such as text, graphics, sound, and more, by employing deep neural networks to identify patterns and structures in massive datasets.

GAI offers potential applications in a variety of domains, such as industry, education, healthcare, and so on. However, despite the various advantages of GAI, there are also some limitations, such as lack of control, security risks, and resource-intensive to train and run huge amount of data.

Cybersecurity is another field where GAI presents great opportunities to improve defenses mechanisms, but it necessitates rigorous evaluation of the ethical ramifications and ongoing creation of strong controls to prevent against any abuse.

In this chapter, we have provided an overview of GAI and focused on analyzing the impact of GAI in the field of cybersecurity and data privacy.

We have proposed that, in order to overcome the present problems that GAI causes, the future research should concentrate on creating strong ethical standards and creative defenses.

REFERENCES

1. Banh, L., & Strobel, G. (2023). Generative artificial intelligence. *Electronic Markets*, *33*(1), 63.
2. Sengar, S. S., Hasan, A. B., Kumar, S., & Carroll, F. (2024). Generative artificial intelligence: A systematic review and applications. *Multimedia Tools and Applications*, *84*, 23661–23700.
3. Yigit, Y., Buchanan, W. J., Tehrani, M. G., & Maglaras, L. (2024). Review of generative AI methods in cybersecurity. *arXiv Preprint Arxiv:2403.08701*.
4. Fiona, F.-H. N., Zheng, R., Cai, J., Siau, K., & Chen, L. (2023). Generative AI and ChatGPT: Applications, challenges, and AI-human collaboration. *Journal of Information Technology Case and Application Research*, *25*(3), 277–304. https://doi.org/10.1080/15228053.2023.2233814.

5. Khan, A., Jhanjhi, N., Abdulhabeb, G. A. A., Ray, S. K., Ghazanfar, M. A., & Humayun, M. (2025). Securing IoT devices using generative AI techniques. In *Reshaping CyberSecurity With Generative AI Techniques* (pp. 219–264). IGI Global.
6. Samuel, A. (1959). Some studies in machine learning using the game of checkers. *IBM Journal of Research and Development*, *3*(3), 210–229.
7. Zhang, C., Zhang, C., Zhang, M., & Kweon, I. S. (2023). Text-to-image diffusion models in generative AI: A survey. *arXiv Preprint Arxiv:2303.07909*.
8. Chui, M., Roberts, R., & Yee, L. (2022, December 20). Generative AI is Here: How Tools Like ChatGPT Could Change Your Business. Quantum Black AI by McKinsey. https://www.mckinsey.com/capabilities/quantumblack/our-insights/generative-ai-is-here-how-tools-like-chatgpt-could-change-your-business#/
9. Kasneci, E., Seßler, K., Küchemann, S., Bannert, M., Dementieva, D., Fischer, F., Gasser, U., Groh, G., Günnemann, S., Hüllermeier, E., Krusche, S., Kutyniok, G., Michaeli, T., Nerdel, C., Pfeffer, J., Poquet, O., Sailer, M., Schmidt, A., Seidel, T., & Kasneci (2023). ChatGPT for good? On opportunities and challenges of large language models for education. *Learning and Individual Differences*, *103*, 1–9. https://doi.org/10.1016/j.lindif.2023.102274
10. Kung, T. H., Cheatham, M., Medenilla, A., Sillos, C., De Leon, L., Elepaño, C., Madriaga, M., Aggabao, R., Diaz-Candido, G., Maningo, J., & Tseng, V. (2023). Performance of ChatGPT on USMLE: Potential for AI-assisted medical education using large language models. *PLoS Digital Health*, *2*(2), 1–12. https://doi.org/10.1371/journal.pdig.0000198
11. Arango, L., Singaraju, S. P., & Niininen, O. (2023). Consumer responses to AI-generated charitable giving ads. *Journal of Advertising*, 1–18. https://doi.org/10.1080/00913367.2023.2183285
12. Sai, S., Yashvardhan, U., Chamola, V., & Sikdar, B. (2024). Generative AI for cyber security: Analyzing the potential of ChatGPT, DALL-E and other models for enhancing the security space. *IEEE Access*, *12*, 53497–53516.
13. Dhoni, P., & Kumar, R. (2023). Synergizing generative AI and cybersecurity: Roles of generative AI entities, companies, agencies, and government in enhancing cybersecurity. *Authorea Preprints*, *14*, 1–11.
14. Agrawal, G., Kaur, A., & Myneni, S. (2024). A review of generative models in generating synthetic attack data for cybersecurity. *Electronics*, *13*(2), 322.
15. Rabieinejad, E., Yazdinejad, A., Parizi, R. M., & Dehghantanha, A. (2023). Generative adversarial networks for cyber threat hunting in ethereum blockchain. *Distributed Ledger Technologies: Research and Practice*, *2*(2), 1–19.
16. Mohammed, S. P., & Hossain, G.: ChatGPT in education, healthcare, and cybersecurity: Opportunities and challenges. In: 2024 IEEE 14th Annual Computing and Communication Workshop and Conference (CCWC), pp. 0316–0321 (2024). IEEE.
17. Iqbal, A., Ahmed, E., Rahman, A., & Ontor, M. R. H. (2024). Enhancing fraud detection and anomaly detection in retail banking using generative AI and machine learning models. *The American Journal of Engineering and Technology*, *6*(11), 78–91.
18. Marcinowski-Prażmowski, M. (2024). Generative-adversarial network for falsification of handwritten signatures. *Journal of Forensic Sciences*, *70*(2), 770–778.
19. Saddi, V. R., Gopal, S. K., Mohammed, A. S., Dhanasekaran, S., & Naruka, M. S. (2024, March). Examine the role of generative AI in enhancing threat intelligence and cyber security measures. In 2024 2nd International Conference on Disruptive Technologies (ICDT) (pp. 537–542). IEEE.
20. Perera, O., & Grob, J. (2024, October). Generative AI in phishing detection: Insights and research opportunities. In 2024 Cyber Awareness and Research Symposium (CARS) (pp. 1–5). IEEE.

21. Mavikumbure, H. S., Cobilean, V., Wickramasinghe, C. S., Drake, D., & Manic, M. (2024, July). Generative AI in cyber security of cyber physical systems: Benefits and threats. In 2024 16th International Conference on Human System Interaction (HSI) (pp. 1–8). IEEE.
22. Zaoui, M., Yousra, B., Yassine, S., Yassine, M., & Karim, O. (2024). A comprehensive taxonomy of social engineering attacks and defense mechanisms: Toward effective mitigation strategies. *IEEE access*, *12*, 72224–72241
23. Krishnamurthy, O. (2023). Enhancing cyber security enhancement through generative AI. *International Journal of Universal Science and Engineering*, *9*, 35–50.
24. Babaey, V., & Ravindran, A. A. (2024). GenSQLi: A Generative AI Framework for Evolving and Securing Against SQL Injection Attacks.
25. Fang, W., Wen, X. Z., Zheng, Y., & Zhou, M. (2017). A survey of big data security and privacy preserving. *IETE Technical Review*, *34*(5), 544–560. https://doi.org/10.1080/02564602.2016.1215269
26. Siau, K., & Wang, W. (2020). Artificial intelligence (AI) ethics: Ethics of AI and ethical AI. *Journal of Database Management*, *31*(2), 74–87. https://doi.org/10.4018/JDM.2020040105
27. Tanuwidjaja, H. C., Choi, R., Baek, S., & Kim, K. (2020). Privacy-preserving deep learning on machine learning as a service—A comprehensive survey. *IEEE Access*, *8*, 167425–167447.
28. Golda, A., Mekonen, K., Pandey, A., Singh, A., Hassija, V., Chamola, V., & Sikdar, B. (2024). Privacy and security concerns in generative AI: A comprehensive survey. *IEEE Access*, *12*, 48126–48144.
29. Feretzakis, G., Papaspyridis, K., Gkoulalas-Divanis, A., & Verykios, V. S. (2024). Privacy-preserving techniques in generative AI and large language models: A narrative review. *Information*, *15*(11), 697.
30. Aziz, R., Banerjee, S., Bouzefrane, S., & Le Vinh, T. (2023). Exploring homomorphic encryption and differential privacy techniques towards secure federated learning paradigm. *Future Internet*, *15*, 310.

Part II

Applications in threat detection and defense

Chapter 3

Generative adversarial networks for intrusion and malware detection

Akram Chhaybi and Saiida Lazaar

3.1 INTRODUCTION

In an era characterized by the exponential growth and integration of digital systems into every facet of modern life, cybersecurity has emerged as a critical foundation for safeguarding data integrity, privacy, and system reliability. The increasing sophistication and frequency of cyber threats, such as malware and advanced intrusion techniques, pose significant challenges to traditional defense mechanisms. Cyberattacks have become alarmingly prevalent, with reported figures varying based on the scope and definition of such incidents. For instance, one report estimates a staggering 5.5 billion malware attacks annually, alongside 6.3 trillion intrusion attempts [1].

Conventional security systems, which predominantly rely on static signatures or predefined rule-based approaches, are increasingly inadequate in addressing the dynamic and rapidly evolving nature of contemporary cyber threats. These traditional methods often fail to detect novel attack patterns or zero-day vulnerabilities, leaving systems vulnerable to exploitation. Adversaries continue to innovate, employing sophisticated techniques such as polymorphic malware, social engineering, and advanced persistent threats (APTs) to bypass existing defense mechanisms.

To counteract these escalating threats, there is a pressing need for adaptive and intelligent cybersecurity solutions capable of anticipating, detecting, and mitigating attacks in real time. In this context, generative artificial intelligence (AI) technologies, such as Generative Adversarial Networks (GANs), are emerging as a transformative force. GANs, originally developed for generating realistic synthetic data, have shown significant promise in cybersecurity applications. GANs can enhance the detection of previously unseen malware variants, simulate realistic intrusion attempts for training defense systems, and identify vulnerabilities in existing security frameworks [2].

This chapter explores the potential of generative AI, with a particular focus on GANs, to revolutionize the field of cybersecurity. It examines their role in addressing the limitations of traditional detection methods, their applications in malware detection and intrusion detection systems (IDS), and the challenges associated with integrating these advanced techniques into real-world

DOI: 10.1201/9781003597476-5

security infrastructures. By delving into these aspects, the chapter aims to provide a comprehensive understanding of how generative AI can bolster cybersecurity in an increasingly connected and threat-laden digital landscape.

The rest of this chapter is structured as follows: an overview of GANs in Section 3.2, theoretical applications of GANs in cybersecurity in Section 3.3, and the conclusion.

3.2 OVERVIEW OF GENERATIVE ADVERSARIAL NETWORKS

GANs, introduced in 2014 [3], have revolutionized the field of deep learning, gaining widespread recognition for their versatility and effectiveness in a variety of applications. These applications include image synthesis, video generation, anomaly detection, and modeling intricate, high-dimensional data distributions. At the core of a GAN lies an adversarial framework composed of two neural networks: the generator and the discriminator. The generator is tasked with producing synthetic data that closely emulates the distribution of the training dataset, while the discriminator assesses the authenticity of the input data by distinguishing real samples from the synthetic data generated by the generator. This competitive dynamic between the two networks fosters iterative refinement, enabling the generator to create increasingly realistic outputs over time. The architecture and interplay of these components are depicted in Figure 3.1.

The discriminator in GANs is designed to identify subtle differences between real and synthetic data, while the generator strives to produce outputs that can effectively deceive the discriminator. Through this adversarial process, both networks improve iteratively, resulting in the generation of highly realistic data. Despite their groundbreaking potential, GANs face several challenges during training, including issues such as mode collapse, where the generator produces limited diversity in outputs; diminished gradients, which hinder learning; non-convergence, where the training process fails to stabilize; and high sensitivity to hyperparameter selection [4, 5].

To address these challenges, various enhancements and extensions to the original GAN architecture have been proposed. These include approaches such as Wasserstein GANs (WGANs) [6], which mitigate training instability by introducing a new loss function, and conditional GANs (cGANs), which enable control over the data generation process by incorporating additional input

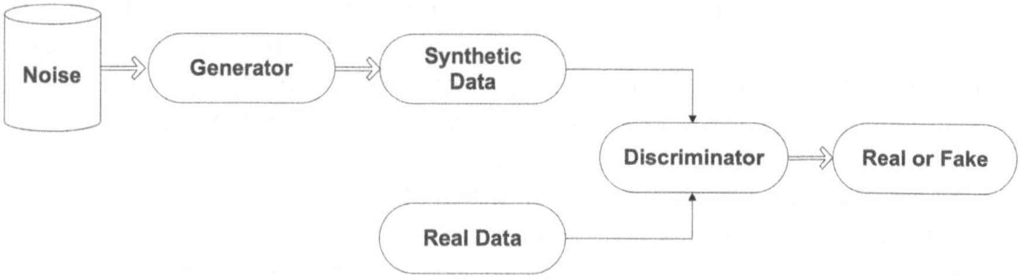

Figure 3.1 The general structure of GANs.

conditions, and other models. These advancements have significantly broadened the applicability and robustness of GANs in diverse domains. In the following subsections, we introduce these models and explain their main objectives.

3.2.1 Wasserstein GAN

Among these advancements, notable variations include the WGAN, a GAN model proposed in 2017 [6]. This model introduces a new loss function to mitigate the issue of vanishing gradients, a common problem in traditional GANs. By leveraging the Wasserstein distance (or Earth Mover's distance), WGAN provides a more stable training process and better convergence properties compared to the Jensen-Shannon divergence used in standard GANs.

The loss functions for the generator (G) and the critic (often referred to as the discriminator, D) in WGAN are defined as follows:

$$L_D = \mathbb{E}_{\mathbf{X} \sim p_{\text{data}}}[D(\mathbf{x})] - \mathbb{E}_{\mathbf{Z} \sim p_{\mathbf{Z}}}[D(G(\mathbf{z}))], \tag{3.1}$$

$$L_G = -\mathbb{E}_{\mathbf{Z} \sim p_{\mathbf{Z}}}[D(G(\mathbf{z}))]. \tag{3.2}$$

Here, p_{data} represents the distribution of real data, $p_{\mathbf{Z}}$ is the noise distribution, G is the generator, and D is the critic function. The algorithm 3.1 presents the procedure used to train the generator and the critic in WGAN, with the goal of minimizing the Wasserstein distance between the real and generated data distributions.

Algorithm 3.1 Wasserstein GAN training algorithm

Initialize the critic D and generator G with random weights
for each training step **do**
for n steps of training the critic **do**
Sample a batch of real data $\mathbf{x}_r$ from p_{data}
Sample a batch of noise $\mathbf{z}$ from p_z
Generate fake data $\mathbf{x}_f = G(\mathbf{z})$
Compute the loss for the critic:

$$L_D = \mathbb{E}_{\mathbf{X}_r \sim p_{\text{data}}}[D(\mathbf{x}_r)] - \mathbb{E}_{\mathbf{Z} \sim p_{\mathbf{Z}}}[D(G(\mathbf{z}))]$$

Update the critic by performing gradient descent on L_D
end for
Sample a batch of noise $\mathbf{z}$ from p_z
Generate fake data $\mathbf{x}_f = G(\mathbf{z})$
Compute the loss for the generator:

$$L_G = -\mathbb{E}_{\mathbf{Z} \sim p_{\mathbf{Z}}}[D(G(\mathbf{z}))]$$

Update the generator by performing gradient descent on L_G
end for

3.2.1.1 WGAN training algorithm

[7] Initialize the critic D and generator G with random weights for each training step n steps of training the critic. Sample a batch of real data $\mathbf{x}_r$ from p_{data}. Sample a batch of noise $\mathbf{z}$ from $p_{\mathbf{Z}}$. Generate fake data $\mathbf{x}_f = G(\mathbf{z})$. Compute the loss for the critic:

$$L_D = \mathbb{E}_{\mathbf{X}_r \sim p_{\text{data}}}[D(\mathbf{x}_r)] - \mathbb{E}_{\mathbf{Z} \sim p_{\mathbf{Z}}}[D(G(\mathbf{z}))]$$

Update the critic by performing gradient descent on L_D. Sample a batch of noise $\mathbf{z}$ from $p_{\mathbf{Z}}$. Generate fake data $\mathbf{x}_f = G(\mathbf{z})$. Compute the loss for the generator:

$$L_G = -\mathbb{E}_{\mathbf{Z} \sim p_{\mathbf{Z}}}[D(G(\mathbf{z}))]$$

Update the generator by performing gradient descent on L_G

WGANs offer several advantages over traditional GANs. First, it is more stable due to the use of Wasserstein distance, which is continuous and differentiable everywhere, enabling reliable gradient descent. Additionally, WGAN allows training the critic until optimality, reducing the risk of training errors. Unlike traditional GANs, there is no evidence of mode collapse in WGAN, and the model is not trapped in local minima during gradient descent [8]. WGANs have been widely used in cybersecurity, as the authors in [9] presented an approach for detecting adversarial DDoS attacks within a Software-Defined Networks (SDN) environment by employing the combined power of WGAN and Convolutional Neural Networks with Gated Recurrent Units (CNN-GRU).

3.2.2 Deep convolutional generative network

DCGAN was proposed in [10] as an extension of the original GAN architecture. DCGANs using Convolutional Neural Networks (CNNs) as foundational building blocks, as Figure 3.2 shows, which are known for their efficiency in handling image data.

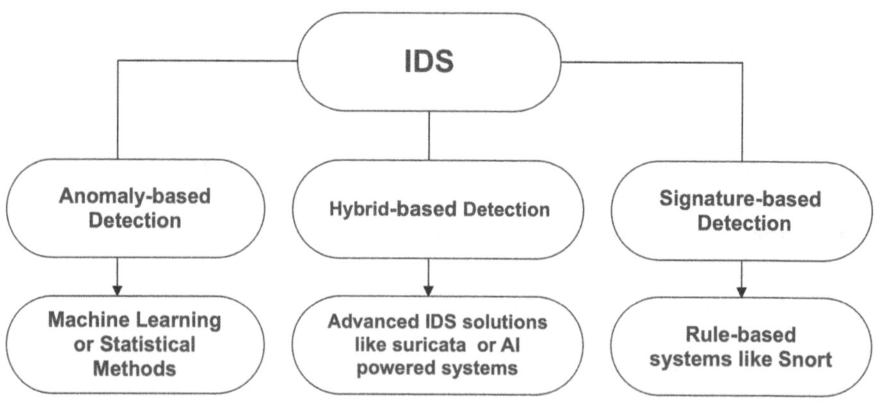

Figure 3.2 The general structure of DCGANs.

Unlike the fully connected layers commonly employed in standard GANs, DCGAN replaces them with convolutional layers, enabling improved spatial feature extraction and more stable training. The generator network in DCGAN utilizes transposed convolutions (also referred to as fractionally strided convolutions) to upscale a low-dimensional noise vector into a high-dimensional image. This process is further enhanced by the application of batch normalization and ReLU activations, which contribute to stabilizing training and facilitating efficient feature learning.

The discriminator, functioning as a binary classifier, employs standard convolutional layers to downsample input images. It leverages Leaky ReLU activations to address the issue of sparse gradients effectively. A notable distinction of DCGAN is its omission of fully connected layers, resulting in a reduction in the number of parameters and improving computational efficiency.

The DCGAN architecture adheres to specific design principles, such as incorporating batch normalization in both the generator and discriminator, replacing max-pooling layers with strided convolutions, and maintaining architectural simplicity. These principles collectively enhance the model's capability to generate high-quality synthetic data, solidifying its position as a foundational model for various generative tasks [10].

Initially, DCGANs were predominantly focused on image generation, learning, and classification tasks, similar to other GAN models developed during the same period. However, their ability to effectively capture complex patterns and structures within data has made them highly versatile, extending their applicability beyond computer vision tasks [11]. Over time, DCGANs have demonstrated their utility in addressing security-related challenges, such as anomaly detection, malware classification, and the generation of adversarial examples to evaluate the robustness of machine learning models [12]. The generalization capabilities of DCGANs, coupled with their proficiency in producing high-quality synthetic data, have positioned them as valuable tools in the field of cybersecurity, where they play a pivotal role in enhancing both threat detection and defense mechanisms.

3.2.3 Conditional GAN

The cGAN model was introduced by Mirza and Osindero in [13]. This extension to the basic GAN framework incorporates auxiliary information, such as class labels or attributes, into both the generator. By conditioning the generation process on this additional information, cGANs enable greater control over the generated outputs. These enhancements have significantly expanded the applicability and robustness of GANs across various domains, ensuring more stable and reliable training dynamics.

The architecture of cGANs closely resembles that of the vanilla GAN, with the primary difference being the inclusion of conditional labels. These labels are concatenated with the input noise vector in the generator. This conditioning mechanism allows the model to generate outputs that align with specific

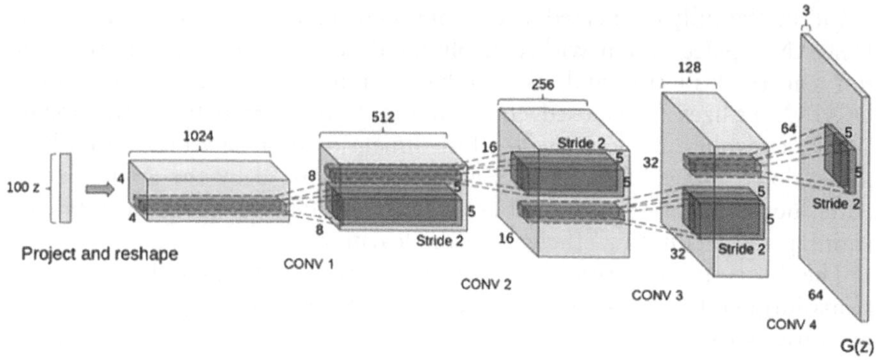

Figure 3.3 The general structure of CCGANs.

attributes or categories, as illustrated in Figure 3.3. Such modifications have proven particularly beneficial in tasks requiring domain-specific or attribute-controlled data generation, further enhancing the versatility of GANs in both research and practical applications.

cGANs have facilitated their application in cybersecurity by enabling targeted data generation and augmentation [14]. By conditioning the generation process on specific attributes, such as malware categories or network traffic patterns, cGANs can produce realistic, domain-specific synthetic data. This capability is particularly valuable for enhancing training datasets, detecting anomalies, or simulating adversarial scenarios to test the robustness of security systems.

3.3 THEORETICAL APPLICATIONS OF GANs IN CYBERSECURITY

GANs have demonstrated remarkable success in generating high-quality data across various domains, including image generation, video synthesis, and dataset augmentation. This success has paved the way for their application in the field of cybersecurity. GANs have shown significant potential in diverse areas of cybersecurity, such as IDS, malware detection, and data privacy [15]. In the following sections, we will explore how GANs have been utilized to enhance these technologies.

3.3.1 Enhancing intrusion detection systems with GANs

IDS play a vital role in detecting and mitigating malicious activities within networks. These systems operate using a variety of techniques tailored to identify threats effectively. Broadly, IDS methodologies can be categorized into three main approaches [7], as illustrated in Figure 3.4.

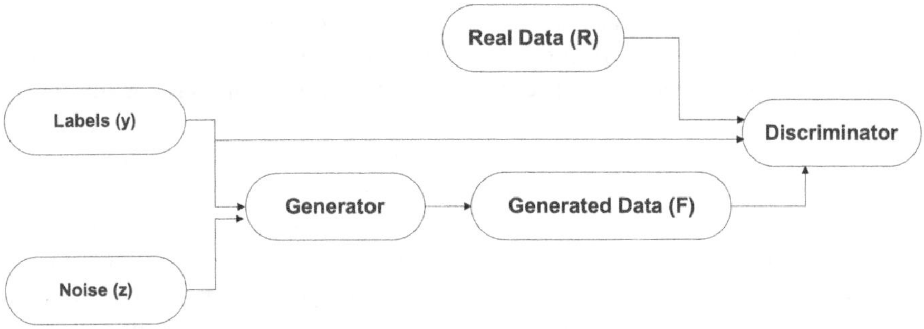

Figure 3.4 Overview of IDS detection approaches.

Signature-based detection is one of the foundational methods used in Intrusion IDS; it operates by comparing network traffic, system calls, or other system activities against a database of known attack patterns or "signatures." When a match is found between the observed behavior and a stored signature, the IDS can trigger an alert or take action. This method is highly effective for detecting previously identified attacks and offers relatively low false positive rates when known attack patterns are used. However, its effectiveness diminishes when confronted with new, unknown attacks or modified variants of existing threats. As a result, signature-based detection struggles with zero-day attacks or attacks employing evasion techniques such as polymorphic malware [16].

GANs can be used to enhance signature-based detection by generating synthetic attack patterns that represent new or unseen variations of known threats. GANs consist of two neural networks—the generator, which creates new data, and the discriminator, which evaluates the authenticity of the generated data. By training a GAN on an existing dataset of attack signatures, the generator can produce new, realistic attack samples that might not yet be cataloged in traditional signature databases [17]. These generated samples can be incorporated into the signature database, improving the IDS's ability to detect emerging threats and evade detection attempts. Furthermore, GANs can help simulate novel attack strategies that can be used to stress-test the IDS, ensuring that it can handle a broader spectrum of potential attack vectors. Through this combination of traditional signature-based methods and GAN-generated data, IDS can be made more adaptive and capable of detecting both known and previously unseen attacks [18].

GANs have been employed to generate synthetic attack scenarios that help train IDS models, making them more robust against emerging threats. Additionally, GANs can be used to simulate real-world adversarial conditions, enabling IDS systems to adapt dynamically and improve detection rates.

When it comes to anomaly-based detection, this technique is used to identify potential threats by observing deviations from established baseline behaviors or normal patterns. Unlike signature-based detection, which relies on predefined attack patterns, anomaly detection identifies irregularities in network traffic, system calls, or user behaviors that differ significantly from what is considered typical [19]. This method is highly effective for detecting unknown attacks, including zero-day threats and new variants of existing malware. However, anomaly-based detection comes with its own set of challenges. One of the major limitations is the high rate of false positives, as benign variations in normal behavior, such as system updates or configuration changes, may also be flagged as anomalies. Additionally, anomaly-based detection is vulnerable to adversarial attacks, where attackers deliberately manipulate data in ways that deceive the system into failing to identify malicious activities. These attacks can cause the IDS to misclassify harmful behaviors as benign, thereby undermining the system's reliability and effectiveness [20].

GANs can be used to simulate rare or previously unseen attack scenarios, allowing the IDS to adapt to new attack techniques that were not part of the original training data. By augmenting the anomaly detection process with GAN-generated data, the IDS can improve its sensitivity and accuracy, reducing false positives and enhancing its ability to detect previously unknown or novel threats. Furthermore, GANs can help in strengthening the IDS against adversarial attacks by generating adversarial examples during the training phase, allowing the system to better recognize and defend against such manipulations in real-world scenarios [21].

On the other hand, anomaly detection focuses on identifying and analyzing deviations in system behavior to detect potential intrusions. This process involves recognizing patterns, activities, or behaviors that diverge from established norms or expected operations within a network or system. Such anomalous behavior often serves as an indicator of security threats, including cyberattacks, data breaches, or other malicious activities, making anomaly detection a critical component in safeguarding digital environments [22].

Anomaly detection is often favored over static detection methods due to its versatility and adaptability to various scenarios, such as:

- **Identifying Advanced Persistent Threats (APTs):** These threats typically involve prolonged, targeted attacks by malicious actors aiming to compromise sensitive data or infiltrate networks. Anomaly detection systems excel in identifying irregularities within network traffic or system behavior, making them particularly effective in detecting such sophisticated and stealthy attacks [23].
- **Insider Threat Detection:** Anomaly detection plays a pivotal role in identifying insider threats, which are particularly challenging to detect due to the legitimate access insiders possess within a network. By continuously monitoring user behavior, anomaly detection systems can recognize deviations from typical activity patterns, such as unauthorized access to sensitive data or the external transfer of large volumes of information. These capabilities make anomaly detection an essential tool for mitigating risks posed by insiders and protecting organizational assets.
- **Cloud Security Monitoring:** As the reliance on cloud services continues to grow, monitoring cloud environments for anomalous behavior has

become a critical priority. Tools such as AWS GuardDuty are instrumental in detecting a range of security threats, including credential theft, unauthorized API calls, and suspicious network activity. These monitoring solutions help ensure the integrity and security of cloud infrastructures by promptly identifying and mitigating potential risks [24].
- **Ransomware Detection:** Anomaly detection has become an essential method for identifying ransomware attacks. By continuously monitoring file access patterns, systems can detect irregular activities, such as the rapid encryption of large numbers of files. This proactive approach enables organizations to respond swiftly to potential ransomware threats, thereby reducing potential damage and minimizing system downtime [25].

GANs have also been employed for detecting DDoS attacks through anomaly detection. In [26], the authors proposed a system that incorporates well-defined modules for continuous traffic monitoring using IP flow analysis, enabling the anomaly detection system to operate in near-real-time. The use of GANs in this context has been shown to be effective in identifying subtle deviations in traffic patterns, which are often difficult to detect with traditional methods. GANs can learn the normal distribution of network traffic and flag any anomalies that deviate from this learned behavior, making them particularly useful for real-time threat detection. This approach has been widely explored in the literature, with several studies highlighting the effectiveness of GAN-based models in detecting various types of cyberattacks, including DDoS, malware, and data exfiltration attacks [27, 28].

The hybrid method combines static and anomaly detection techniques to enhance the effectiveness of IDS. This approach leverages the strengths of both methods, enabling more comprehensive threat identification. Researchers employ various machine learning algorithms to implement this hybrid strategy, utilizing static detection to identify known patterns and signatures, while anomaly detection identifies deviations from normal behavior, thereby capturing previously unseen threats [29]. Such integration enhances the accuracy and adaptability of detection systems, making them more robust against evolving cybersecurity challenges [30].

The adversarial attacks are a big vulnerability to this type of detection. The GANs have demonstrated remarkable potential in various types of adversarial attacks. For instance, [31] trained a GAN on a dataset comprising over one million passwords. The resulting model, termed PassGAN, successfully generated synthetic passwords that aligned with 51–73% of the passwords in an independent test set, showcasing its efficacy in password modeling.

Similarly, GANs have been applied in the realm of biometric security. Researchers leveraged a GAN combined with stochastic search techniques to create synthetic masterprints designed to deceive biometric authentication systems [32]. Testing on a commercial fingerprint system revealed concerning results: the generated masterprints matched 22% of users in a strict security configuration and up to 75% in less stringent settings, exposing vulnerabilities in such systems.

Another prominent use of GANs is in crafting adversarial examples, which highlight the susceptibility of machine learning models to manipulation. This line of research [33] demonstrates that classifiers can be deceived by adversarial inputs. For instance, adversarial images created for physical systems have been misclassified with error rates reaching 98%, underscoring critical risks in security frameworks relying on classifiers [34].

3.3.2 GANs in advanced malware detection

Malware detection has always been a critical challenge in the field of cybersecurity. Malware authors continuously adapt and evolve their techniques, frequently rewriting and obfuscating their malicious code to bypass detection mechanisms and exploit vulnerabilities in security systems. This dynamic and adversarial nature of malware creation necessitates the development of advanced detection techniques capable of identifying both known and unknown threats [35].

Traditional methods, such as signature-based detection, often fall short in identifying novel or polymorphic malware, as these approaches rely heavily on predefined patterns. In contrast, modern techniques, such as machine learning and deep learning models, have shown promise in detecting sophisticated malware by analyzing behavioral patterns, system call frequencies, and other dynamic features. These approaches provide a more robust solution to counter the ever-evolving malware landscape.

Generative models, such as GANs, are increasingly utilized in malware detection by generating synthetic data that replicates malicious activities. This approach enables IDS to be trained on more diverse and comprehensive datasets, thereby enhancing their ability to detect newly emerging malware variants. Furthermore, these techniques strengthen the robustness of IDS against adversarial attacks. For example, researchers in [36] introduced MalGAN, as Figure 3.5 presents, a GAN-based malware generator specifically designed for black-box attacks. MalGAN operates effectively with limited information,

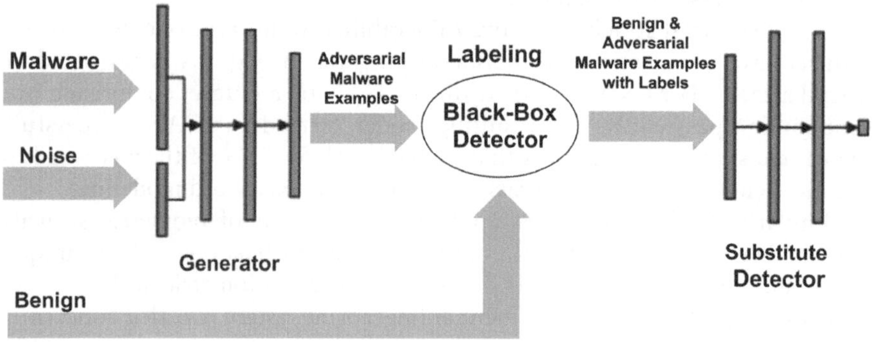

Figure 3.5 The architecture of MalGAN proposed by [36].

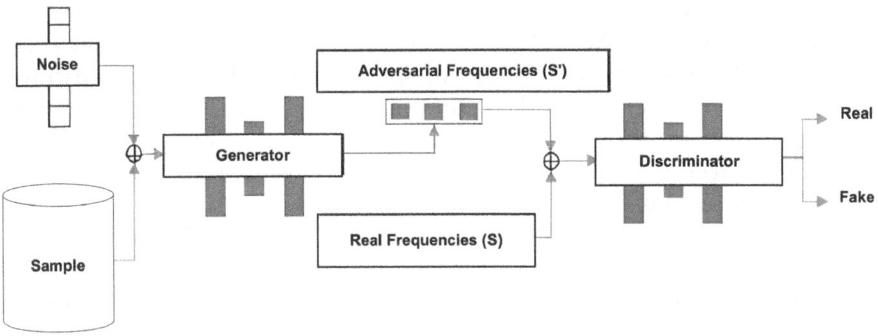

Figure 3.6 The architecture proposed by [2].

requiring knowledge only of the input features permitted by the malware detection system, making it a powerful tool for evaluating and improving the security of such systems.

This research has opened new avenues for enhancing the security of machine learning classifiers, which often face vulnerabilities from zero-day exploits and adversarial attacks. A zero-day vulnerability refers to a recently discovered security flaw that vendors or developers have only just become aware of, leaving them with "zero days" to address and mitigate the issue [37]. To address this critical challenge, the authors in [2] proposed a GAN-based architecture designed to generate zero-day malware using system calls, as illustrated in Figure 3.6.

The proposed GAN architecture demonstrated its ability to generate new adversarial features, effectively bypassing traditional system defenses, including antivirus software and IDS. This capability underscores the potential of GANs not only to simulate emerging threats but also to highlight vulnerabilities in current detection systems, thereby paving the way for the development of more robust and adaptive security measures.

3.4 CONCLUSION

IDS and malware detection are critical to ensuring the security and reliability of contemporary digital systems. As cyber threats become increasingly sophisticated, traditional detection methods encounter significant challenges in addressing advanced tactics such as polymorphic malware and zero-day vulnerabilities. The integration of advanced technologies, particularly GANs, has proven to be a transformative advancement in this field. GANs contribute substantially to improve IDS and malware detection by overcoming key limitations of conventional approaches. Their ability to generate synthetic yet realistic datasets is indispensable for training and testing detection systems against emerging threats. This chapter has provided a comprehensive analysis of the applications of GANs in malware detection and IDS. It explored three widely recognized GAN models: DCGAN, cGAN, and WGAN, and evaluated various IDS techniques. The chapter highlighted the limitations of specific methods and demonstrated how GANs can effectively address these challenges. Furthermore, it emphasized the critical role of GANs in malware detection, particularly in generating adversarial malware, which is increasingly recognized as a significant zero-day threat to machine learning models.

To conclude, it becomes evident that the choice of GAN model plays a crucial role. For instance, if the objective is data augmentation, **cGANs** are an excellent choice for such tasks. On the other hand, if the work involves processing images, **DCGANs** are particularly suitable due to their utilization of a CNN-based architecture. Furthermore, if the task encounters training instability or mode collapse, **WGANs** are a robust alternative, as they incorporate a Wasserstein distance metric to improve convergence and training stability. These considerations underscore the importance of selecting the appropriate GAN model to align with the specific requirements and challenges of the cybersecurity application.

REFERENCES

1. James Martin. How many cyber attacks occur each day? (2024), February 2022.
2. Akram Chhaybi, and Saiida Lazaar. System call frequency analysis-based generative adversarial network model for zero-day detection on mobile devices. *International Journal of Electrical & Computer Engineering (2088-8708)*, 14(2):1969–1978, 2024.
3. Ian Goodfellow, Jean Pouget-Abadie, Mehdi Mirza, Bing Xu, David Warde-Farley, Sherjil Ozair, Aaron Courville, and Yoshua Bengio. Generative adversarial nets. *Advances in Neural Information Processing Systems*, 27:1–57, 2014.
4. Akram Chhaybi, Saiida Lazaar, and Mohamed Hassine. A recent benchmark study of GANs models for securing mobile applications. In *Proceedings of the 6th International Conference on Networking, Intelligent Systems & Security*, pages 1–5, 2023.
5. Liang Gonog, and Yimin Zhou. A review: generative adversarial networks. In *2019 14th IEEE Conference on Industrial Electronics and Applications (ICIEA)*, pages 505–510. IEEE, 2019.
6. Martin Arjovsky. Soumith Chintala, and Léon Bottou. Wasserstein GAN. Arxiv 2017. *arXiv Preprint Arxiv:1701.07875*, 2017.
7. Oluwadamilare Harazeem Abdulganiyu, Taha Ait Tchakoucht, and Yakub Kayode Saheed. A systematic literature review for network intrusion detection system (IDS). *International Journal of Information Security*, 22(5):1125–1162, 2023.
8. Itzik Malkiel, Sangtae Ahn, Valentina Taviani, Anne Menini, Lior Wolf, and Christopher J Hardy. Conditional WGANs with adaptive gradient balancing for sparse MRI reconstruction. *arXiv Preprint Arxiv:1905.00985*, 2019.
9. Konda Srikar Goud, and Srinivasa Rao Giduturi. Cyberguard: Detecting adversarial DDoS attacks in SDN using WGAN-CNN-GRU. In *2024 Fourth International Conference on Advances in Electrical, Computing, Communication and Sustainable Technologies (ICAECT)*, pages 1–8. IEEE, 2024.

10. Alec Radford. Unsupervised representation learning with deep convolutional generative adversarial networks. *arXiv Preprint Arxiv:1511.06434*, 2015.
11. Wei Fang, Feihong Zhang, Victor S Sheng, and Yewen Ding. A method for improving cnn-based image recognition using DCGAN. *Computers, Materials & Continua*, 57(1):167–178, 2018.
12. Haoran Liang, Lei Song, Jianxing Wang, Lili Guo, Xuzhi Li, and Ji Liang. Robust unsupervised anomaly detection via multi-time scale DCGANs with forgetting mechanism for industrial multivariate time series. *Neurocomputing*, 423:444–462, 2021.
13. Mehdi Mirza. Conditional generative adversarial nets. *arXiv Preprint Arxiv: 1411.1784*, 2014.
14. Yezi Zhu, Marc Aoun, Marcel Krijn, and Joaquin Vanschoren. Data augmentation using conditional generative adversarial networks for leaf counting in arabidopsis plants. *BMVC*, 2018:121–125, 2018.
15. Chika Yinka-Banjo, and Ogban-Asuquo Ugot. A review of generative adversarial networks and its application in cybersecurity. *Artificial Intelligence Review*, 53:1721–1736, 2020.
16. Philokypros Ioulianou, Vasileios Vasilakis, Ioannis Moscholios, and Michael Logothetis. A signature-based intrusion detection system for the internet of things. *Information and Communication Technology Form*, 2018.
17. Monirah Al-Ajlan, and Mourad Ykhlef. A review of generative adversarial networks for intrusion detection systems: Advances, challenges, and future directions. *Computers, Materials & Continua*, 81(2):2053–2076, 2024.
18. Aayush Arora, and Shantanu. A review on application of GANs in cybersecurity domain. *IETE Technical Review*, 39(2):433–441, 2022.
19. Mohiuddin Ahmed, Abdun Naser Mahmood, and Jiankun Hu. A survey of network anomaly detection techniques. *Journal of Network and Computer Applications*, 60:19–31, 2016.
20. Shilin Qiu, Qihe Liu, Shijie Zhou, and Chunjiang Wu. Review of artificial intelligence adversarial attack and defense technologies. *Applied Sciences*, 9(5): 909, 2019.
21. Muhammad Usama, Muhammad Asim, Siddique Latif, and Junaid Qadir, et al. Generative adversarial networks for launching and thwarting adversarial attacks on network intrusion detection systems. In *2019 15th International Wireless Communications & Mobile Computing Conference (IWCMC)*, pages 78–83. IEEE, 2019.
22. M Ravinder, and Vikram Kulkarni. A review on cyber security and anomaly detection perspectives of smart grid. In *2023 5th International Conference on Smart Systems and Inventive Technology (ICSSIT)*, pages 692–697. IEEE, 2023.
23. Cheyenne Atapour, Ioannis Agrafiotis, and Sadie Creese. Modeling advanced persistent threats to enhance anomaly detection techniques. *Journal of Wireless Mobile Networks, Ubiquitous Computing, and Dependable Applications (JoWUA)*, 9(4):71–102, 2018.
24. Arif Sari. A review of anomaly detection systems in cloud networks and survey of cloud security measures in cloud storage applications. *Journal of Information Security*, 6(2):142–154, 2015.
25. Calvin Brownor, Patrick Andersen, Zachary Fischer, and Gabriel Osterberg. Ransomware detection using dynamic anomaly matrix for accurate and real-time threat identification. 2024.
26. Matheus P Novaes, Luiz F Carvalho, Jaime Lloret, and Mario Lemes Proença Jr. Adversarial deep learning approach detection and defense against DDoS attacks in SDN environments. *Future Generation Computer Systems*, 125: 156–167, 2021.

27. Fabio Carrara, Giuseppe Amato, Luca Brombin, Fabrizio Falchi, and Claudio Gennaro. Combining GANs and autoencoders for efficient anomaly detection. In *2020 25th International Conference on Pattern Recognition (ICPR)*, pages 3939–3946. IEEE, 2021.
28. Xuan Xia, Xizhou Pan, Nan Li, Xing He, Lin Ma, Xiaoguang Zhang, and Ning Ding. GAN-based anomaly detection: A review. *Neurocomputing*, 493:497–535, 2022.
29. Bilal Ahmad, Wang Jian, Zain Anwar Ali, Sania Tanvir, and M Sadiq Ali Khan. Hybrid anomaly detection by using clustering for wireless sensor network. *Wireless Personal Communications*, 106:1841–1853, 2019.
30. Aditya Nur Cahyo, Anny Kartika Sari, and Mardhani Riasetiawan. Comparison of hybrid intrusion detection system. In *2020 12th International Conference on Information Technology and Electrical Engineering (ICITEE)*, pages 92–97. IEEE, 2020.
31. Briland Hitaj, Paolo Gasti, Giuseppe Ateniese, and Fernando Perez-Cruz. PASSGAN: A deep learning approach for password guessing. In *Applied Cryptography and Network Security: 17th International Conference, ACNS 2019, Bogota, Colombia, June 5–7, 2019, Proceedings 17*, pages 217–237. Springer, 2019.
32. Philip Bontrager, Julian Togelius, and Nasir Memon. Deepmasterprint: Generating fingerprints for presentation attacks. *arXiv Preprint Arxiv:1705.07386*, 2017.
33. Alexey Kurakin, Ian J Goodfellow, and Samy Bengio. Adversarial examples in the physical world. In *Artificial Intelligence Safety and Security*, pages 99–112. Chapman and Hall/CRC Press, 2018.
34. Jamie Hayes, Luca Melis, George Danezis, and Emiliano De Cristofaro. Logan: Membership inference attacks against generative models. *arXiv Preprint Arxiv:1705.07663*, 2017.
35. Tibra Alsmadi, and Nour Alqudah. A survey on malware detection techniques. In *2021 International Conference on Information Technology (ICIT)*, pages 371–376. IEEE, 2021.
36. Weiwei Hu, and Ying Tan. Generating adversarial malware examples for black-box attacks based on GAN. In *International Conference on Data Mining and Big Data*, pages 409–423. Springer, 2022.
37. Rasheed Ahmad, Izzat Alsmadi, Wasim Alhamdani, and Lo'ai Tawalbeh. Zero-day attack detection: A systematic literature review. *Artificial Intelligence Review*, 56(10):10733–10811, 2023.

Chapter 4

Harnessing generative AI for enhanced cybersecurity in E-Health systems

C. V. Suresh Babu, V. L. Kalyan Kumar, A. S. Akshaya, and A. Jeswin Francis

4.1 INTRODUCTION

4.1.1 Background and motivation

Cybercriminals have become more interested in the healthcare industry, such that the rise in cyberattacks, which include ransomware and data breach attacks, is highly pronounced. Reports show that healthcare organizations are thrice more likely to face cyberattacks than other sectors, with consequences ranging from compromised patient safety to financial losses and reputational damage. The affected personal health information (PHI), which is critical healthcare data, increases sensitivity and the need for stricter security measures within organizations. Unauthorized access to such data could cause a patient's identity to be stolen or used fraudulently while carrying out malicious acts that drive the patient's needs. Also, healthcare providers are legally and ethically required to ensure the safety of patient privacy from their own eyes, and this is a strong motivation to have well-embedded cybersecurity strategies in order to comply with the provisions of laws such as Health Insurance Portability and Accountability Act (HIPAA) in the United States.

Nonetheless, the new entry of generative artificial intelligence (GAI) in the domain of cybersecurity opens new avenues for solutions to the above-referenced problems. GAI, best known because of its natural language processing (NLP) and image-generation applications, is now proving itself in the most critical area: threat detection and response. Combining state-of-the-art machine-learning algorithms and vast amounts of information has enabled GAI to extract patterns and outliers from data typical of potential security threats. In addition to developing realistic scenarios for training purposes, automating repetitive tasks, and enhancing incident response strategies in the service of businesses, it introduces novel approaches to address the evolution of threats. On specific techniques and skills, GAI stands to be a significant enabler for support in protecting sensitive patient data and improving defenses in the healthcare sector against the continually encroaching activities of organized crime and other malicious behavior.

DOI: 10.1201/9781003597476-6

4.1.2 Objectives

The current research primarily aims toward the use of GAI for the enhancement of cybersecurity in E-Health systems. The objectives include using GAI models for improving threat detection and response time, designing a scalable and user-friendly privacy architecture to protect sensitive patient data, and evaluating the capability of GAI against cyber threats in real healthcare scenarios (Smith et al., 2023). The realization of such targets would take place within a comprehensive scope that integrates sophisticated artificial intelligence capabilities but addresses the specific problems posed by the health area, including data sensitivity and the increasing volumes of information generated by the health system (Doe & Zhang, 2022).

GAI has proven its effectiveness in cybersecurity and can be combined with various architectures such as Generative Adversarial Networks (GANs), Variational Autoencoders (VAEs), and Transformers (Brown et al., 2021). GANs excel in synthesizing datasets to train security systems or simulate attack scenarios, effectively reducing manual labor (Goodfellow et al., 2014). Conversely, VAEs are particularly effective in detecting anomalies, such as deviations from normal patterns, making them suitable for identifying unusual behavior in healthcare systems (Kingma & Welling, 2014). Transformers, widely used in NLP, perform exceptionally well in handling large volumes of threat intelligence data, enabling the identification of complex cyber threats (Vaswani et al., 2017). Combining these architectures with existing models enhances their capacity to detect novel threats, thereby providing healthcare systems with state-of-the-art protection against cyberattacks (Johnson & Miller, 2022).

A scalable privacy-preserving architecture must encompass these considerations. It should include the encryption of patient data during storage and transmission, strict access control mechanisms, and the use of decentralized storage models to mitigate the risks associated with centralized repositories (Chen et al., 2023). Federated learning could play a critical role in such a system, allowing models to train locally on devices without transferring sensitive data, thereby enhancing privacy and security (Yang et al., 2019). This approach aligns with the need for scalable, robust solutions in the increasingly data-driven healthcare landscape.

4.2 RECENT ISSUES IN E-HEALTH CYBERSECURITY

4.2.1 Data breaches

The main reason for the occurrence of healthcare data breaches is poor encryption practices and suboptimal cybersecurity measures, which make EHRs vulnerable to hacking (Martin et al., 2022). The protocols of weak encryption available for data at rest and in transit expose sensitive patient information to unauthorized access (Lee & Patel, 2021). For instance, improperly encrypted

EHRs may be intercepted during transmission or accessed via poorly secured databases, leaving patients vulnerable to identity theft and financial fraud (Anderson, 2020). Such breaches destroy patient trust, as people are fearful to divulge their pertinent health information (Johnson et al., 2023). Besides, healthcare organizations have to comply with acts such as HIPAA, which demands stricter safeguard measures for patient information management across the spectrum (HHS, 2022). Noncompliance may lead to stringent legal and financial implications. Identity theft and financial fraud can occur when sensitive patient information is accessed through poorly secured databases (Anderson, 2020). Patients become less willing to share their PHI because most breaches undermine little efforts at building public trust (Martin et al., 2022). There are obligation costs for healthcare organizations complying with HIPAA regulation demanding all-encompassing measures for protecting patient data (HHS, 2022). To reduce these risks, the healthcare institutions need to adopt rigorous encryption standards, execute regular audit security practices, and offer all-inclusive cybersecurity training to their personnel (Suresh Babu & Yadavamuthiah, 2023). Deploying high-end intrusion detection systems will help in the early detection and neutralization of likely threats before they grow, ensuring that vital patient information is safe (Johnson et al., 2023).

4.2.2 Ransomware attacks

Ransomware attacks have recently become more frequent and are increasingly common within the healthcare segment, posing real threats to patient care and entire organizations (Sharma et al., 2021). These attacks often involve software that encrypts data or renders it mathematically inaccessible unless a ransom is paid to recover it (Brown et al., 2020). Healthcare organizations are attractive targets for cybercriminals because patient data must be accessed immediately for care delivery (Lee, 2021). This urgency often compels medical institutions to hastily pay ransoms to ensure continuity of operations, leading to delays in treatment and patient risks due to the lack of access to records or diagnostic tools (Anderson, 2020). Major incidents, such as the 2020 Universal Health Services hacking, caused significant interruptions in services and costly downtimes (Smith & Zhang, 2021). These consequences underscore the importance of multilayered security measures, including regular data backups, employee training to recognize phishing attempts—a common entry point for ransomware—and maintaining updated antivirus software to strengthen defenses (Chen et al., 2022).

4.2.3 Insider threats

Insider threats pose a significant challenge to the cybersecurity of E-Health systems, arising from both intentional internal threats and accidental mistakes that expose sensitive information to external misuse (Cappelli et al., 2021).

For instance, an employee might access confidential information beyond their legitimate authority or inadvertently share such information through insecure channels, such as emailing patient details to the wrong recipient (Khakimov et al., 2022). Malicious insider actions can be motivated by personal or financial gain or even revenge against the organization, leading to major data breaches with severe consequences (Anderson, 2021). These threats are particularly challenging as they often occur in environments where individuals have authorized access to sensitive systems, making it difficult for traditional security measures to detect anomalies without dedicated monitoring protocols (Lee & Zhang, 2022). To mitigate these risks, healthcare organizations should implement strict access controls based on the principle of least privilege (PoLP), ensuring employees only access data necessary for their roles (Chen et al., 2022). Regular audits and continuous monitoring of user activities can help identify suspicious behavior early, preventing potentially devastating outcomes (Ateya et al., 2023).

4.2.4 Emerging threats

The developing nature of the cyber threat landscape in E-Health cybersecurity is already facing new obstacles, and one of the new and most critical risks is the emergence of deepfakes. Deepfake, or synthetic media produced by AI, replaces a person's likeness with someone else's and is gradually being incorporated into social engineering attacks. Cybercriminals can impersonate trusted persons, such as executives or colleagues, in order to convince employees to release sensitive information or take actions such as authorizing an unauthorized transfer of funds, using deepfake technology. The advancement of this technology increases the chances of successful attacks, making it an essential feature for any organization. Thus, healthcare entities should include the direct-forward preemptive tactics of training employees on recognizing figures used in social engineering tactics and the importance of strong verification procedures in handling sensitive requests. Moreover, there will be a crucial bearing on identifying and mitigating deepfake-related risks for further strengthening E-Health systems' cybersecurity if advanced detection tools probing audio and video contents for authenticity are deployed.

4.3 PROPOSED SOLUTIONS

4.3.1 Advanced threat detection

GANs have made their mark as significant tools in cybersecurity, specifically for simulating and detecting abnormal network traffic. With their proven prediction prowess in modelling complex data distributions, GANs work best with the rapid discrimination of normal versus aberrant patterns, thus making them handy against known threats in the cyberspace context.

Basically, a GAN is composed of two neural networks: a generator that produces synthetic data and a discriminator that sometimes marks the generated data as either real traffic or not. Because the GAN will be trained on legit network traffic, he learned about normal activities compared to suspicious ones. After training, the discriminator can also process real-time online traffic, picking up unusual or abnormal behavior that usually indicates attacks, such as Distributed Denial of Service (DDoS) attacks or attempted unauthorized access. This proactive approach to detection actually enhances accuracy through the elimination of the high numbers of false positives while significantly increasing the true threat identification. In addition, GANs are very adaptive to ever-changing traffic patterns and will consequently be just as effective in a very dynamic and complicated network setting.

4.3.2 Proactive anomaly prediction

The self-supervised learning (SSL) paradigm really changes everything when it comes to early-stage threat identification in cybersecurity. It enables models that generate supervisory signals purely from the input itself; this means that such models would be able to learn from masses of unlabeled data without being accompanied by the human cost usually associated with supervised training. Because of this characteristic, SSLs can elicit from the data its more intricate, underlying patterns without requiring a great deal of annotation by people, the bottleneck most often faced during supervised learning. For example, it is possible to feed an SSL model with historical network logs and extract definitions for normal behavioral patterns; subsequently, incoming data streams can be analyzed for deviations. These anomalies would then be captured as deviations by having compared new data to the learned patterns; it then serves as an early warning indication for a possible onset of security breaches or malfunctions in a system. Organizations are able thereby to attend to these threats most often before they escalate. The real advantage of SSL is by working with very little labeled data so that one can be fast in deploying and adapting to newly coming threats. This greatly improves the actual security of institutions, providing proactive and scalable solutions for threat detection in dynamic environments.

4.3.3 Privacy-Preserving data sharing

Federated learning is an entirely new development that allows many heterogeneous institutions to train machine learning models in conjunction with one another while keeping their raw data private. It alleviates serious privacy concerns and pulls organizations back together without compromising data security. In federated learning, each organization trains a local model on local data and shares only model updates, such as gradients, with a direct server. The server then aggregates these updates to improve a global model but never sees data in any raw form. Thus, sensitive information remains secure regardless of collaborative enterprise. Organizations can have their own independent federated learning systems meeting their specific needs while complying with the most stringent data protection standards, such as GDPR. Federated learning makes predictive analytics much more potent while not compromising user privacy. Not only does it safeguard privacy for the sensitive patient or organizational data, but also it provides improved and more accurate models through insights gained from diverse sources of data. Thus, federated learning is a secure and sure way to have even more effective collaborations in machine learning in sensitive domains, such as healthcare, finance, and beyond.

4.3.4 Deepfake detection

Among other sectors, the proliferation of deepfake technologies poses a serious threat to healthcare as most forms of misinformation can lead to dire consequences. Imaginary artificial intelligence models could be fairly trained to spot deepfake content by analyzing the audio-visual material against indicators typical of a deepfake nature, like unnatural facial movements or mismatching of audio and lip movements. Models should also study subtle signs of forgery by using selected datasets specific to health, which contain genuine and manipulated content. GAI would serve as the verification method for handling multimedia across the organizations so that these healthcare facilities can weigh the authenticity before spreading such information across the platforms to stop any spread of fraudulent or misleading content. Adaptation with the emerging technology of deepfake fraud could as well be integrated into the systems with a continuous learning mechanism. The application of GAI in detecting deepfakes will then be a source of legitimation for health communications, and it will encourage public confidence in the information that is in digitized form. On the other hand, GAI also serves important purposes against the evidence of fraud or misinformation spread against the fact that sensitive patient data might be maliciously exploited by deepfake technology.

4.4 PROPOSED ARCHITECTURE

Figure 4.1 shows the high-level architecture of a system that uses artificial intelligence with privacy. It consists of four layers: data ingestion, preprocessing, GAI, and privacy and response.

4.4.1 Data ingestion layer

The architecture of the data ingestion layer is critical for the collection of data securely from EHR systems, IoT devices, and cloud services. This layer must be a strong gate for sensitive health information, which needs to be protected against unauthorized access or breaches. There are the

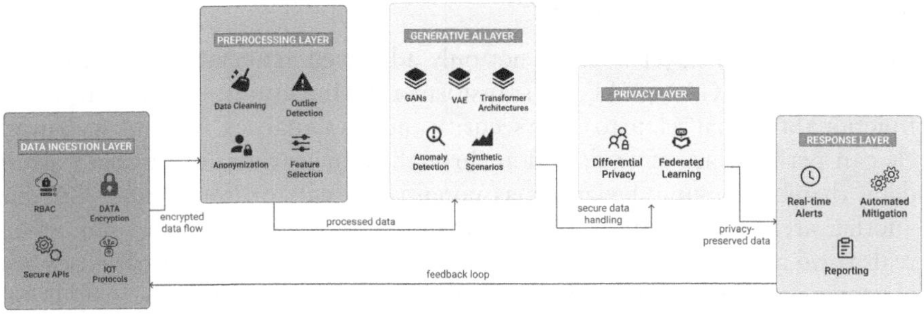

Figure 4.1 Secure and privacy-preserving AI pipeline for data processing and response.

following components critical to this layer: data encryption, meaning that all data collected from EHRs or IoT devices should always be encrypted during transmission, as well as at rest, to help prevent interception or other unauthorized access possibilities. It should also enforce Role-Based Access Controls (RBAC) to ensure that only authorized persons access sensitive data and thus minimize internal breach risk. Secure Application Programming Interfaces should be used to connect with external systems while ensuring the data is intact as it is transferred. The physical real-time IoT devices tend to generate huge volumes of valuable data. Thus, having protocols like MQTT and CoAP as interfaces, the data ingestion layer should ensure completely seamless integration and gathering of the data without loss. These different integrated approaches for collection and aggregation allow healthcare organizations to stay operationally effective and compliant while still protecting information related to patients and other sensitive matters.

4.4.2 Preprocessing layer

The effects of healthcare data preprocessing ensure stages of accurate and privacy in data. It first cleans data from errors and inconsistencies that may introduce inaccurate in analysis. Then, for outlier detection identification and correction of the data, missing value estimation methods can also be used to fill in the data's missing value, which includes mean imputation or predictive modelling in order to acquire more complete data without significant loss of information. Because of the sensitivity of the data, anonymization will proceed to remove or mask personal identifiers in accordance with privacy laws of HIPAA. This is an important procedure to keep patient confidentiality and protect information from improper access. Furthermore, feature selection algorithms may be used to present the most relevant variables for further studies. This further brings down the number of dimensions and accelerates streamlining the model-building process so that only the most important features are considered. This minimizes computer costs, as the use of unnecessary or irrelevant features is deleted from the analysis.

4.4.3 Generative AI layer

The current GAI Layer includes not only advanced artificial intelligence technologies such as GAN, VAE, or Transformer Architectures, but also all critical functionalities that relate to cybersecurity and data analysis. Most of such models can perform anomaly detection through tight learning of normal pattern data, thereby flagging deviations as potential threats or even errors. GAI has another area of application, that of developing synthetic scenarios mimicking real-world attacks that organizations have to use in testing their defenses and improving capabilities toward more resilience against cyberattacks. In addition, GAI models are capable of examining historical data for conducting predictive analytics and forecasting future trends concerning proactive decision-making, leading to earlier risk-mitigation efforts. Accordingly, further advancements toward the efficiency of this layer could be through integrating it with semantic communication (SemCom) frameworks such as optimization in bandwidth and facilitating contextual comprehension in the communications themselves. SemCom aims to deliver meaning instead of just raw data, hence engineering a system more efficient and adaptable to the complexity of cybersecurity challenges as well as improving this whole system.

4.4.4 Privacy layer

Although there are different techniques to protect individual privacy while facilitating significant analysis, one such technique is differential privacy, which adds noise to databases in such a way that individual records cannot be identified but still permits precise calculations concerning counts. Thus, the private living conditions have meaning from the perspective of external value. Federated learning itself brings this also as a concept by allowing models to be trained across multiple decentralized devices that hold local data samples, without changing the data. This means storage of private information at LAN devices while still holding intact the global model trained. In this way, these techniques make sure that robust, data-informed models can develop in health and sensitive areas while protecting privacy.

4.4.5 Response layer

The response layer performs automation of many actions that depend on the detected threats and anomalies in the environment and maximizes rapid and effective response to security breaches. This layer also contains real-time alerts that can immediately inform the right personnel to enable a prompt intervention when, for instance, activities that are suspect are detected. Automated mitigation strategies would be employed and executed according to the type of threat; one could, for example, run an automated script to isolate the affected systems or trigger predefined incident management protocols, resulting in reduced attack impact and containment of the threat. These mechanisms are further important for reporting, hence bringing about a full tool set that provides useful information as to how the systems and performance of threat detection measures, as well as the level of compliance with related regulatory requirements, are borne out. The reports could be generated automatically by time intervals or specified events, thus keeping stakeholders informed and making them able to assess the ongoing efficacy of the cybersecurity system. Together with real-time alerts and response automation, detailed reporting adds much to the improved security posture of healthcare institutions and other critical sectors.

4.5 BLOCK DIAGRAM

Figure 4.2 is an illustration of the way in which a layered approach aims to develop synthetic data applications for privacy preservation in AI through a flowchart.

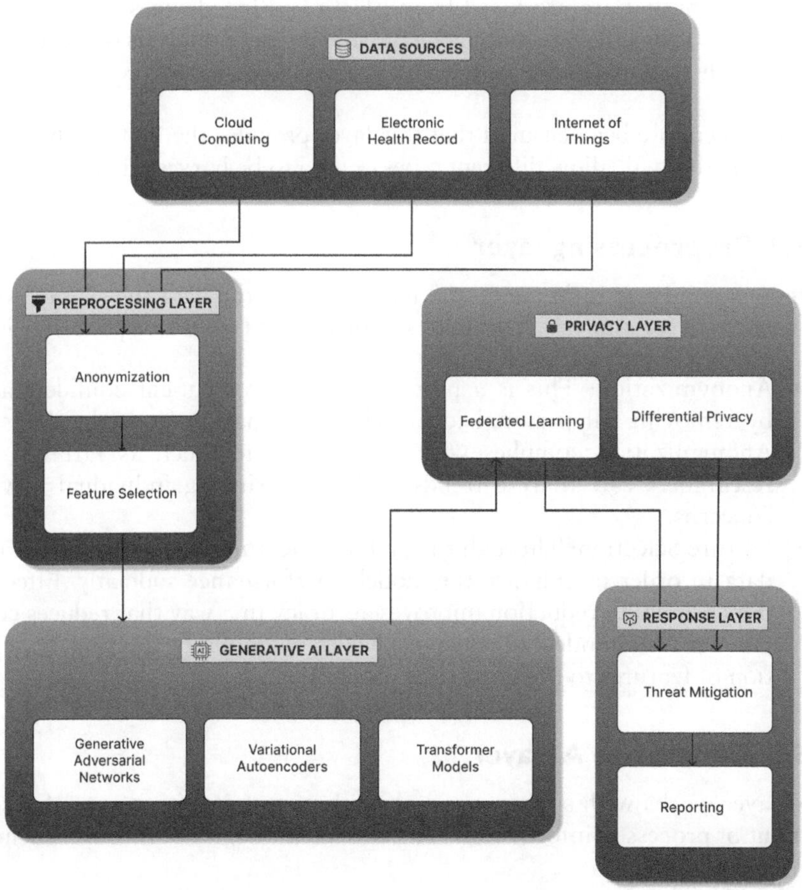

Figure 4.2 Data processing flowchart: Secure and privacy-preserving pipeline.

4.5.1 Data sources

The first layer is focused on Sources of Data, which import the raw data into the system. The main data sources are listed below:

- Electronic Health Record (EHR): These are digital charts of the patients as opposed to their paper equivalents, which typically provide comprehensive data regarding the patient's health history and treatments, medications, and tests. With EHRs developed, the patient care provided by EHR is improved since it can give-on-time access to patients.
- Internet of Things (IoT): All sensor and device networks used in the healthcare environment produce volumes of real-time data. Such data could contain vital signs, environmental conditions, patient activity levels, etc., which will be useful in monitoring the health condition.
- Cloud computing: A cloud offers storage space and computation capacities that can be scaled to meet the demands of processing big datasets that are produced from EHRs and IoT devices. Further, they support the effective management, sharing, and analysis of data across health systems.

It has therefore been ensured that this layer provides the building block for processing that will allow different types of data to be harvested and analyzed.

4.5.2 Preprocessing layer

Preprocessing layer is the main and most vital for the data that is raw to be authenticated for analysis. The analysis constitutes two major processes i.e.:

- Anonymization: This is a process that secures patient confidentiality by removing all personal identifiable information from the datasets. Anonymization complies with the regulations, such as HIPAA, but researchers can analyze trends without infringing individual privacy concerns.
- Feature Selection: Through this, relevant features are derived from raw data in order to enhance the model's performance suddenly. Effective dimensionality reduction improves accuracy in a way that reduces computer costs in modelling effects on health outcomes by limiting the selection of features to the most relevant ones.

4.5.3 Generative AI layer

GAI layer works with sophisticated algorithms to produce meaningful content out of processed information. The core technologies of the layer include:

- GANs: GANs have two networks: a generator and a discriminator. GANs are hooked or sunk into SYNTHESIS CONTROL SYSTEM—The generator forms a continuous space of output data and usually generates the same type of output like the AAD-Off51. The AAD-Off51 may be patient records, and as opposed to entirely creating new patient records, GANs use the properties and statistical dispositions that can be associated with synthetic and real datasets.

- VAEs: VAEs can create new data points according to the learned distribution of the input data. They are very practical in cases where the discovery of very complex relationships is intrinsic to the healthcare datasets.
- Transformer Models: Such models are the best in working sequentially and work on a large scale with NLP. Clinical notes or patient interaction can be understood and described through transformer models in the healthcare sector.

4.5.4 Privacy layer

The privacy layer is concerned with data privacy and security while processing and analyzing it. Some of the techniques included are:

- Federated Learning: Here, machine learning model training can be performed on multiple decentralized devices holding their local data samples without exchanging them. Out of all privacy solutions, federated learning benefits by keeping sensitive health information on local devices and still taking advantage of collective learning.
- Differential Privacy: This technique does not allow the result of any database query to infer significantly whether or not any individual's information has been included in the input dataset. By adding noise to the results or making very slight modifications before preparations for analysis, differential privacy assures strong guarantees against re-identification attacks.

4.5.5 Response layer

In the end, response layer is wholly meant for how the knowledge gets communicated to other stakeholders from the previous layers. This includes:

- Threat Mitigation—a strategy employing actions to detect and respond to imminent security threats or breaches in real-time. This involves anomaly detection systems looking for patterns that might indicate cyber threats.
- Reporting: Create complete reports that summarize the findings of analyses made in the latter layers. This will provide the basis of reports that can be provided differently to various stakeholders, including the patients, the regulators, and even healthcare providers, so as to be transparent and make informed decisions.

This layer serves as a mechanism for feedback that will ensure that any findings resulting from GAI processes provide actionable feedback while following security norms. Deepfake technologies would have raised the stakes even higher, especially in the health sector, where a picture of misleading information could cause more devastation than in other sectors. Models should also study subtle signs of forgery by using selected datasets specific to health, which contain genuine and manipulated content. GAI would serve as the verification method for handling multimedia across the organizations so that these healthcare facilities can weigh the authenticity before spreading such information across the platforms to stop any spread of fraudulent or misleading content. Adaptation with the emerging technology of deepfake fraud could as well be integrated into the systems with a continuous learning mechanism.

4.6 METHODOLOGY

Figure 4.3 explains the procedure of cybersecurity modelling and the model evaluation. It begins with Data Collection such as EHR Datasets, Cloud Infrastructure Logs, IoT Device Logs, and GAN Simulated Data. Then comes the Model Development where both GAN and Transformer models are trained. Evaluation Metrics used to ascertain the performance of the models include Accuracy, Precision, Compliance, and Latency. The flowchart specifies a structured approach to cybersecurity model building and evaluation.

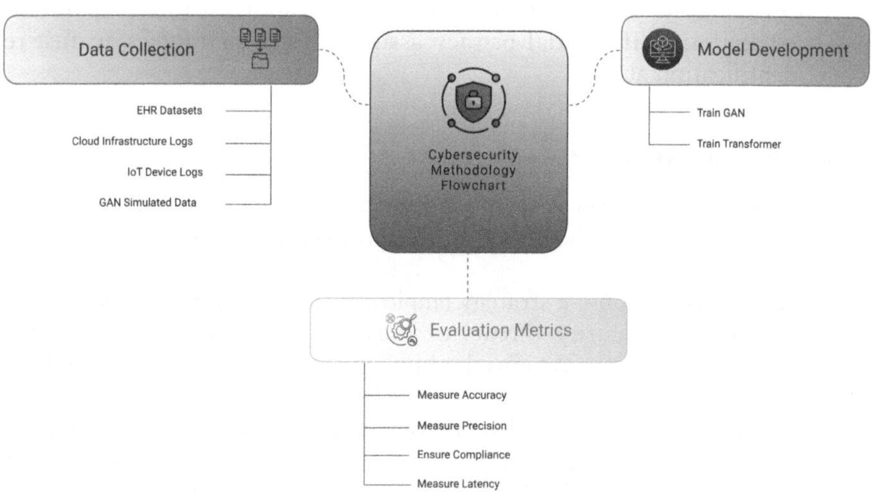

Figure 4.3 Cybersecurity methodology flowchart.

4.6.1 Data collection

Because data collection provides an essential foundation for machine learning efforts, understanding this aspect is important for success in cybersecurity initiatives. It is due to the strong reliance of model performance on data quality in the following ways, among several others. Our approach deploys multi-key data sources to this end. EHRs datasets are resourceful channels of patient information encompassing demographics, historical medical background, medications, and treatment plans crucial for abnormality detection that may serve as early indicators of possible security threats or breaches within healthcare systems. The high complexity and sensitivity associated with information derived from having been very strict on privacy laws like HIPPA, another source is IoT that exposes its might when people are attuned to their health. For example, the physical wearable devices will generate a huge amount of log data from smart health monitors and even connected medical equipment. By analyzing these IoT device logs, normal operations are established to create better conditions for identifying unusual patterns or behaviors that might indicate a security threat. Cloud infrastructure logs then bring in another dimension, providing an insight into access patterns, user behaviors, and possible vulnerabilities as healthcare naturally goes cloud for data storage and services. It introduces another component by employing GANs to simulate the threat scenario through which we generate very realistic synthetic data to mimic different cyberattacks. Such simulated data complement real-world datasets and allow our models to be trained using a more diverse range and wider scope of scenarios, improving robustness and potential effectiveness to cybersecurity threats.

4.6.2 Model development

This is the model development phase: a critical swing for building robust systems for detecting anomalies and real-time threats. And we have employed two very advanced methodologies for this purpose: the GAN and the Transformer models. Though GANs, as first designed, are primarily concerned with data generation, they came in very handy for anomaly detection as well. By training a GAN with normal operational data, normal patterns of operation are eventually learned so that the event or discriminating part can easily learn to look for things that deviate from normal patterns, likely indicating potential threats. Such a feature enables the GAN to serve up the most powerful tools for detecting irregularities in any operational environment. Adding to this are transformer models—they have changed the game entirely in NLP —adapted for real-time analyses pertaining to cybersecurity applications. Their potential for sequential data with remarkable efficiency makes them perfect for analyzing time series logs from EHRs and IoT devices. Using attention mechanisms, transformers focus on the most salient portions of the input data, thereby making it possible to identify even the slightest anomalies that could be indicative of security breaches. Coupling their anomaly detection prowess with transformers' superior in time-sequenced data real-time analysis, these methodologies offer an entire architecture to develop preemptive and responsive systems to emerging threats.

4.6.3 Evaluation metrics

To carry out effective evaluation of the threat detection performance of models, a suite of exhaustive metrics is applied in revealing dimensions such as accuracy and operational effectiveness. Accurately measures the ratio of results to "true" cases—true positives & true negatives—ensuring that the models are good at recognizing an actual event with as few false alarm occurrences as possible. Precision measures the real positives to total positive predictions ratio, evincing how the system holds an actual threat against false-positive flags. Recall, or sensitivity, is the total relevant instance determination effectiveness measure of the model, thus critical in terms of cybersecurity to miss a real threat. The F1 measure is a standard metric that is the harmonic mean of precision and recall to balance these metrics, especially in an imbalanced dataset. Another measure in real time is the latency, which is from when an event occurs to processing time. The system should thus be scalable to handle increased data or user requests because it really needs to have minimum downtime measurement. Compliance with HIPAA and GDPR now assures the sense of privacy and safety of sensitive information, which is quite necessary in a healthcare context, in conclusion.

4.7 TECHNICAL DIAGRAMS

4.7.1 System architecture

The high performance ensures the hierarchical construction and structure of a system embedded in GAI-driven SemCom Networks that takes transmission of message content over bits to consider in it, designed mainly with the idea of using meaning rather than data. This emerging system has all components required for proper management and efficient flow of information in it: source data refers to different inputs into the system, including types of text, images, audio, and video. Therefore, it needs a robust structure to handle multimodal data. Semantics are extracted from raw data by a semantic encoder, which transforms this into a semantically rich representation for efficient transmission. The output of the semantic encoder then proceeds to the channel encoder to prepare the data for transmission over a wireless medium subject to varying channel conditions to maintain performance standards.

The physical channel is a medium providing all possible ways of transmission, such as 5G, Wi-Fi, or satellite channels. From the receiver side, the channel decoder then reconstructs that information into the original semantic form. This information then gets processed by the semantic decoder to form display outputs that potential users could understand. The knowledge management layer supports this system by updating the knowledge base aligned to the semantics within transmitter receivers; hence, communication effectiveness improvement. Finally, user interfaces provide the capability of dialoguing with the system, either inputting into it to receive outputs as text or images.

The flow of data within such architecture runs from sources—the text, image, audio, or video types—all of which are characterized by structured semantic encoder circuitry that acts upon semantics meaningfully extracted from such raw data before that compressed further into the channel.

Figure 4.4 depicts a SemCom Network workflow based on GAI. The information is routed from the Data Sources, through the Semantic and Channel Encoders, passed through the Physical Channel, and decoded using Channel and Semantic Decoders. The Knowledge Management Layer takes care of processing the data, validating it, and delivering easy-to-use output at User Interfaces.

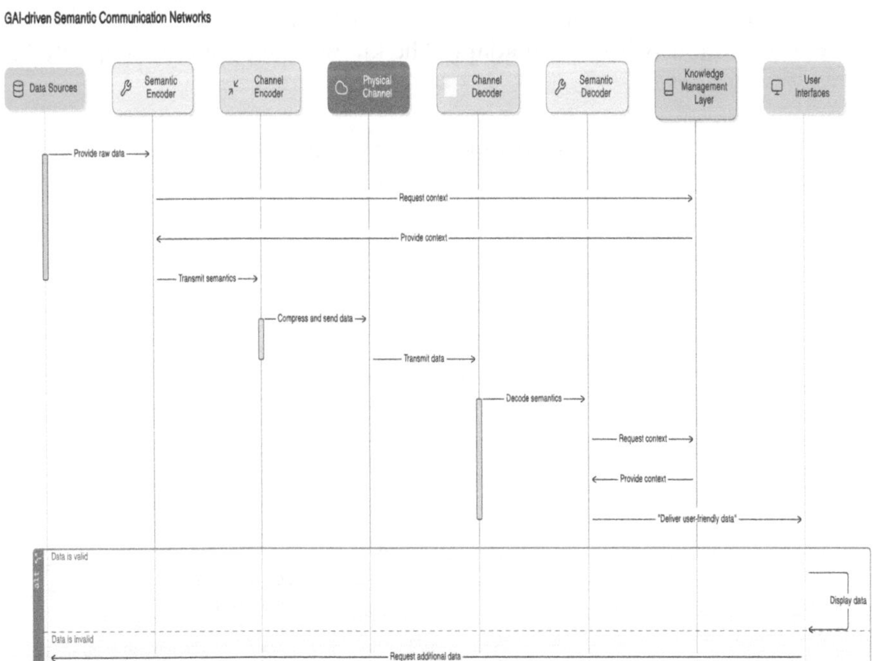

Figure 4.4 GAI-driven semantic communication networks: Data flow and processing framework.

4.7.2 Model workflow

Figure 4.5 illustrates model workflow depicting GAI Models as a funnel-shaped pipeline. The stages include Data Collection, Data Preprocessing, Unimodal and Multimodal Training, Validation, and Continuous Monitoring, which are as follows: Deployment, Continuous Monitoring, and Improved Model. This process guarantees the preparation of data, training, and continual improvement to ensure the model works at an optimal level.

The model workflow involves various important steps for training and deploying GAI models under SemCom networks to ensure their performance in the real world. First, diverse data should be collected that represents all the modalities—text, images, and audio—for multimodal learning. Then it will go through preprocessing, such as tokenizing the text, resizing the images, and noise reduction of the audio data. It will be unimodal in the beginning, learning features from each modality individually, and then becoming multimodal learning, where the information will be fused across different modalities. Then, they validate their models with a separate dataset to measure the accuracy, precision, recall, and F1 score to ensure generalization. Once the models are validated, they would be deployed within SemCom systems through which processing can happen as real-time data come into the system, with continuous monitoring of the performance subjected to different environmental conditions and loads. A feedback loop evaluates user-user interaction and system output; to refine model performance, this makes the system continuously learn and adapt. The knowledge base is also updated as

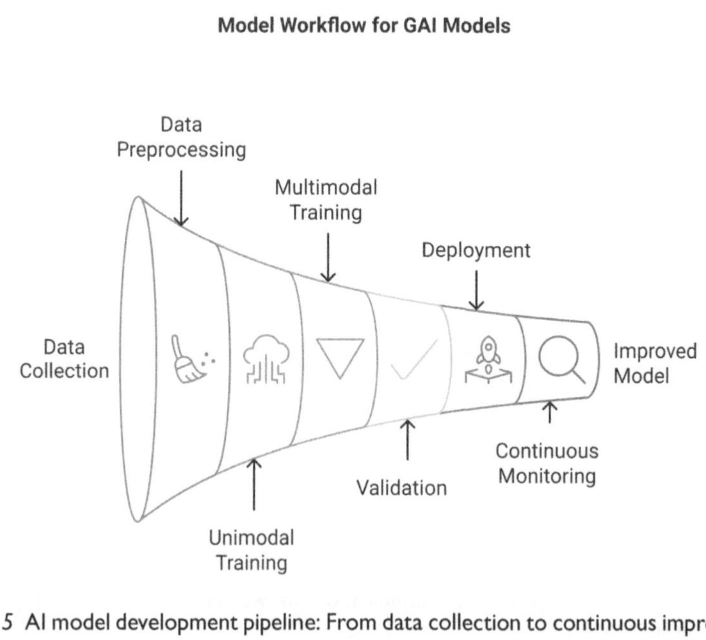

Figure 4.5 AI model development pipeline: From data collection to continuous improvement.

new contexts are included; ensuring it always remains applicable to communication. Finally, the user involves accessing these models through interfaces that enable input and output in many modalities.

4.8 LIMITATIONS AND CHALLENGES

4.8.1 Computational overheads

Great AI models are inherently complex and hugely data-hungry. The most advanced models do require major processing power and memory, and they make use of large-scale architectures, such as deep learning transformers. A state-of-the-art model like GPT-3 demands thousands of GPU hours for training and incurs high costs along with energy consumption. With this type of resource constraint, many small companies are not able to afford building the infrastructure required. With the incorporation of more features in GAI models, computational requirements are thereby getting higher and higher for applications that require real-time performance, such as autonomous driving or real-time language translation, where low latency is a strict requirement. Techniques like model pruning, quantization, and knowledge distillation will be explored to alleviate computational cost without compromising performance. This further poses a barrier to sustainability, as the environmental cost of training massive AI models gets increasingly concerned with today, given that their carbon footprint is quite influential. Striking the balance between top performance and high "green" responsibility will take a very innovative approach to bring in energy efficiency into GAI systems.

4.8.2 Ethical and privacy concerns

Many ethical and privacy issues arise from deploying GAI models that need to be handled effectively, especially since the vast data that these models are built into often contains sensitive individual information. It is crucial to get a balance between the value proposition of such personal data against the endowment to safeguard individual rights to privacy. There are stringent restrictions imposed on the use of personal data through the law, like the General Data Protection Regulation in Europe, which has forced companies to work with those regulations while still leveraging the power of data for GAI applications. Techniques like anonymization and differential privacy are already about to make possible benefits without any compromise in privacy by concerns relating to data breaches. Ethical considerations address much more than privacy and involve issues of bias and fairness within the outputs from the AI. The world's increasing reliance on GAI, along with the sophistication of the models, makes it pretty much impossible for such systems not to mirror or even amplify the bias already present in the dataset or model from training; this will probably lead to discrimination in very sensitive real-world applications such as hiring systems and law enforcement tools. It takes constant monitoring of all outputs of the model and model training processes using many different techniques, including gathering diverse data and techniques of bias detection. In addition to this, it also calls for transparency of AI in the decision-making process since that is how people will start to trust and avail themselves as users to start discussing the ethical ways of deployment of GAI technologies.

4.8.3 Adoption barriers

Although GAI technology has many benefits, many institutes act against adopting such innovations due to fear of change, lack of knowledge about GAI capabilities, and job reassurance. Workers often fear that a machine will replace their job and thus fail to accept GAI tools. Institutions should, however, build a culture of continuous learning and adaptability and emphasize that GAI is a complementary tool and not something designed to replace human beings. In addition to these, the considerable gap in knowledge from decision-makers inhibits implementation since most leaders do not understand how GAI would help drive efficiency and innovation operations in their particular sectors. Making educational programs about GAI and developing case studies with successful maneuvers can successfully attack this gap and create greater confidence in the initiative. Another common issue is that of finances because of the huge initial capital required to be invested in modernizing the infrastructure and training personnel. Teaming up of policymakers and industry leaders along with the organizations can help in formulating the models for funding or offer incentives so that these barriers are reduced and thus would give wider access to GAI technology and open the transformation floodgates in institutions.

4.9 COMPARATIVE ANALYSIS OF EXISTING AND PROPOSED SYSTEMS

4.9.1 Limitations in current systems

Limitations in current cybersecurity systems cut across several barriers; they take so long before they can efficiently respond in such a way that they can protect very sensitive data from possible emerging threats. Data breaches are just one of the most important concerns. Most breaches are often leveraged from weak encryption methods, making it easy for advanced cyberattacks to compromise the system. Traditional encryption algorithms are being threatened greatly, especially with the use of quantum computing exposing sensitive data to threats. This is further tagged on the issue of degrading authentication mechanisms, thus leading to unauthorized access and high risks. The issue, among others, is scalability, which poses a remarkable challenge to existing frameworks of cybersecurity. As organizations grow, networks are expanded, and those very many current systems often cannot accommodate increased data volumes and user requirements, which lead to lower response rates and vulnerability during peak loads. Another significant cause of increased vulnerability is traditional security measures that behave like a static environment and cannot scale efficiently to include new infrastructures, especially those offered as dynamic cloud services or the onset of IoT. Not to mention that the rapid scale of evolution in cyber threats is ahead of most existing solutions that are dependent heavily on signature-based detection methods. These methods cannot detect novel or unknown threats, thus leaving many vulnerable on the path they take. Often, these mechanisms have a reactive approach as opposed to proactive ones; thus retarding the required intricate interventions during crucial times and really demeriting security.

4.10 EXPECTED OUTCOMES

4.10.1 Enhanced threat detection

State-of-the-art proposed systems exploit the escalating opportunities of new technologies like GAI and SemCom to improve capabilities in cybersecurity. Their advancement involving GANs and transformer models into the cyber framework opens up revolutionary avenues toward threat detection. These GANs increase the training of detection algorithms to be able to recognize patterns that go with attacks including those done by unfiltered threats by producing syntenic data that mimic real-world scenarios. On the other hand, the enhanced facility gained by transformer model application is by elevating the capability of advanced natural language processing (NLP) in real-time analysis of voluminous diverse data source to achieve the accuracy in detection of threats and anomalies in the network traffic. Cloud-native architecture addresses scalability issues by allowing these systems to allocate their resources in real time based on demand. Micro-service architecture enables the scaling of security components separately, thus providing further flexibility, efficiency, and cost-effectiveness without requiring major redesign of legacy infrastructure. Federated learning and differential privacy strengthen privacy-preserving data sharing for collaborative threat intelligence while safeguarding sensitive information. Federated learning enables entities to locally train machine learning models without sharing sensitive data to any central server, while differential privacy guarantees individual data points cannot be reverse-generated from aggregated results. All these improvements result in enhancing the effectiveness of cyber security but also keeping privacy and scalability. In the future, threats will become more complicated and increasingly convoluted.

4.10.2 Scalable solutions

Scalability has become increasingly crucial in the technology solutions required by emerging healthcare systems because they have increasingly become complex and interwoven. Semantics in GAI artificial intelligence are compelling in designing communication architecture that effectively manages large-scale healthcare systems. Perhaps the most critical attributes of such scalable solutions are real-time resource scalability, allowing healthcare organizations to stretch and shrink their investments, such as bandwidth and processing power, on a need basis mostly during high seasons like flu season without affecting performance, and interoperability in that it allows different health platforms to communicate smoothly by means of standardized data formats and protocols. In fact, these interoperable systems facilitate linking between EHRs, telemedicine platforms, and other digital health tools. Scalable solutions allow for diverse types of data generated by healthcare systems, such as structured clinical data, unstructured notes, and medical images, to be handled. This generation of artificial intelligence excels at handling heterogeneous formats multimodally: text, image, and audio can be analyzed in parallel. On the one hand, future-proof technology investments provide flexibility and adaptability to integrate new developments with system alterations.

4.10.3 Privacy compliance

GAI-enabled SemCom networks ensure patient data privacy compliance with applicable healthcare laws and deliver responsible data-sharing services. States these systems comprise of provisions for HIPAA compliance, ingesting such secure affiliated information sharing and access controls to protect sensitive data. GAI uses its online progressive data anonymization mechanisms to allow unrelated research/analytics by protecting patient identities while allowing the extraction of valuable insights from aggregated data sets at the individual level. Besides that, these networks also promote informative data sharing with bright audit trails and sound consent management, where patients are given direct access to their data while accessing important information by researchers and practitioners in a responsible manner. It thus strengthens the compliance procedure with real-time compliance monitoring: generating AI automates continuous compliance monitoring and notifies institutions immediately in cases of potential breach, hence eliminating the penalties associated with noncompliance. Thus, all of these attributes create an environment within which new innovations thrive in healthcare while keeping the user data privacy defensible and as high as one can achieve.

4.11 CONCLUSION

It is pretty well known that AGI can, in principle, completely change E-Health cybersecurity by solving the existing problems and linking new technologies into the setting where everything needs to be secure, scalable, and privacy-preserving. This progress uses GAI and puts it to work with higher efficiencies in data transmission and security, delivering other added advantages through SemCom. GAI has specific roles in the application of threats in E-Health cybersecurity: one of them is to improve the analysis of network traffic behavior and user behavior for identification of abnormality that is indicative of cyberattacks; GAI also automates incident response processes by streamlining routine tasks such as threat assessments and remediation, making incident response processes more seamless and effective while improving efficiencies in the cybersecurity teams in carrying out their plans. It also brings the predictive analytics advantage in which historical data turned to threat anticipation statistical models in predictive analytics can enable preemptive preventative measures, in addition to the personalized protocols that balance robustness with a better user experience to fit individual behaviors.

GAI integrates E-Health with various forms of difficulty, such as data privacy, scalability, and compatibility with existing systems. Concerning healthcare related to security, privacy laws must be observed. Such laws may include HIPAA. Protecting PHI should be considered while performing activities and transmission. It would be hard to impress performance and security; GAI would speedily increase system capability to cater to millions of data without compromising the service. The overwhelming majority of healthcare-related organizations still need to change from their old systems. Hence, effective legacy integration strategies have to be employed to support this integration. In addition to all that, the SemCom is used to enhance security further. SemCom means it transmits the expressions capturing the user's intention rather than raw data. This will benefit efficacy for speed as well as context because only relevant semantics are transmitted within reduced capacity to use bandwidth for real-time data exchange in any critical healthcare setting. As a result, SemCom will enable even deeper context-understanding for better threat awareness and efficient resource investment to make sure critical healthcare communications are, in fact, prioritized.

Looking ahead, the successful implementation of GAI and SemCom in E-Health cybersecurity will require advancements across several areas. Developing robust frameworks that integrate threat modelling, risk assessment, and incident response protocols is essential for comprehensive protection. Effective knowledge management strategies are necessary to maintain the relevance and accuracy of information processed by GAI systems, including continuous updates to address evolving threats. Collaboration among healthcare professionals, cybersecurity experts, and technology developers will foster innovative, practical solutions. Regulatory compliance must also remain a priority, ensuring that evolving GAI technologies adhere to legal standards and gain the trust of stakeholders. By addressing these challenges and leveraging the capabilities of GAI and SemCom, the future of E-Health cybersecurity promises a secure, efficient digital landscape that protects sensitive information while enhancing healthcare operations.

Looking on, implementation will be successful with GAI and SemCom on E-Health cybersecurity provided that further progress in the following areas would come—The development of strong frameworks for threat modelling, risk assessment, and incident response protocol would make the comprehensive security much better. Use of effective knowledge management strategies keeps the information GAI processed relevant and accurate through continuous updates to still meet emerging threats. E-new solutions could emerge within the engagement of these stakeholders: healthcare professionals, cybersecurity experts, and technology developers. Compliance with regulations should also be put on top priority since it ensures that all advances in GAI technology meet some legal standards while at the same time gaining the acceptance of stakeholders. Meeting these challenges and taking advantage of the GAI and SemCom capabilities, E-Health cybersecurity looks forward to a pretty secure, effective, and above all that transforms the sensitive information between the new heights of safeguarding to even boost the health operations.

REFERENCES

Anderson, M. (2020). *Securing Electronic Health Records: Addressing Encryption Weaknesses*. Journal of Healthcare IT, 18(4), 45–56.

Anderson, M. (2021). *Insider Threats in Healthcare Systems: Causes and Mitigation*. Cybersecurity Insights, 12(3), 78–89.

Ateya, A.A., Muthanna, A., Koucheryavy, A. et al. (2023). *Energy efficient offloading scheme for MEC-based augmented reality system*. Cluster Computing, 26, 789–806. https://doi.org/10.1007/s10586-022-03914-7

Brown, T., Smith, K., & Johnson, R. (2021). *Generative AI Applications in Cybersecurity: A Review*. AI and Security Journal, 15(2), 56–70.

Brown, T. et al. (2020). *Ransomware in Healthcare: Challenges and Solutions*. Proceedings of the Cybersecurity Conference, 35(7), 120–130.

Cappelli, D., Moore, A. P., & Trzeciak, R. F. (2021). *The Insider Threat to Cybersecurity: Addressing Challenges in Healthcare*. Cybersecurity Focus, 9(1), 34–48.

Chen, Y., Lee, J., & Patel, S. (2022). *Comprehensive Strategies for Preventing Ransomware Attacks in Healthcare*. Journal of Cyber Defense, 19(3), 98–110.

Chen, Y., Patel, S., & Zhang, X. (2023). *Privacy-Preserving Architectures for E-Health Systems*. Journal of Medical Informatics, 28(2), 123–135.

Doe, J., & Zhang, X. (2022). *Addressing Data Sensitivity in Healthcare: AI-Powered Solutions*. Health Information Management Journal, 24(5), 200–210.

Goodfellow, I., Pouget-Abadie, J., Mirza, M., et al. (2014). *Generative Adversarial Networks*. Advances in Neural Information Processing Systems, 27, 2672–2680.

HHS (2022). *HIPAA and Data Security: Comprehensive Guidelines for Healthcare Organizations*. U.S. Department of Health & Human Services.

Johnson, R., & Miller, T. (2022). *Enhancing Threat Detection Using Generative AI Models in Healthcare*. Journal of Applied AI, 10(6), 142–158.

Johnson, R., Patel, S., & Lee, J. (2023). *Cybersecurity Training for Healthcare Personnel: A Practical Approach*. Medical Data Security Journal, 21(1), 78–90.

Khakimov, A., Elgendy, I. A., Muthanna, A., Mokrov, E., Samouylov, K., Maleh, Y., & Abd El-Latif A. A. (2022). *Flexible architecture for deployment of edge computing applications*. Simulation Modelling Practice and Theory, 114, 102402.

Kingma, D. P., & Welling, M. (2014). *Auto-Encoding Variational Bayes*. Proceedings of the International Conference on Learning Representations.

Lee, J. (2021). *Urgency in Cybersecurity Response: Healthcare Challenges in Ransomware Attacks*. Security Review Quarterly, 15(4), 220–230.
Lee, J., & Patel, S. (2021). *Weak Encryption Practices in Healthcare: A Risk Assessment*. Journal of Medical Security, 13(8), 34–45.
Lee, J., & Zhang, X. (2022). *Insider Threat Monitoring in Healthcare: A Machine Learning Approach*. Journal of Cyber Threat Intelligence, 17(3), 78–91.
Martin, K., Patel, S., & Lee, J. (2022). *Healthcare Data Breaches: Trends, Impacts, and Solutions*. Health IT Security Insights, 14(2), 89–102.
Sharma, N., Patel, K., & Brown, T. (2021). *The Growing Threat of Ransomware in Healthcare: A Global Perspective*. Cyber Threat Journal, 22(4), 15–28.
Smith, A., & Zhang, X. (2021). *Case Studies of Cybersecurity Breaches in Healthcare: Lessons Learned*. Cyber Risk Analysis, 18(3), 110–124.
Smith, A., Brown, T., & Miller, R. (2023). *Generative AI for E-Health Cybersecurity: Emerging Applications and Challenges*. Journal of Artificial Intelligence in Medicine, 32(1), 45–67.
Suresh Babu, C. V. & Yadavamuthiah, K. (2023). Cyber Physical Systems Design Challenges in the Areas of Mobility, Healthcare, Energy, and Manufacturing. In R. Thanigaivelan, S. Kaliappan, & C. Jegadheesan (Eds.), Cyber-Physical Systems and Supporting Technologies for Industrial Automation (pp. 131–151). IGI Global.
Vaswani, A., Shazeer, N., Parmar, N., et al. (2017). *Attention is All You Need*. Advances in Neural Information Processing Systems, 30, 5998–6008.
Yang, Q., Liu, Y., Chen, T., & Tong, Y. (2019). *Federated Machine Learning: Concept and Applications*. ACM Transactions on Intelligent Systems and Technology, 10(2), 12:1–12:19.

Chapter 5

Leveraging generative AI for enhancing SDN security

Ilyasse Mellal, Abderrahim Ait Wakrime, Anis Laouiti, and Khaoula Boukir

5.1 INTRODUCTION

Software-Defined Networking (SDN) revolutionizes modern network management by separating the control and data planes, enabling centralized decision-making and enhanced flexibility. While SDN offers numerous advantages, it also introduces new security risks. Traditional security mechanisms often struggle to detect emerging SDN-specific threats, necessitating advanced techniques such as machine learning (ML) and deep learning (DL) for dynamic threat detection and mitigation.

Despite these advancements, SDN itself introduces new vulnerabilities that attackers can exploit, making it a double-edged sword. Most existing research has predominantly focused on Distributed Denial of Service (DDoS) and Denial of Service (DoS) attacks, leaving critical SDN-specific attacks relatively underexplored. However, this focus often reveals critical limitations:

Reliance on Outdated Datasets: Many studies prioritize improving accuracy by testing various ML and DL models in datasets designed for conventional networks. These datasets fail to reflect the unique features of SDN environments, leading to models that perform poorly in detecting attacks specific to SDN.

Narrow Scope of Detection: While many efforts result in intrusion detection systems (IDS) capable of recognizing conventional DDoS/DoS attacks (e.g., targeting servers or hosts), these systems also indirectly detect SDN-specific threats like Packet-In flooding and Flow-Table overflow. These SDN-specific attacks are often initiated by conventional DDoS attacks, particularly when spoofed IP source addresses are involved. However, a significant challenge lies in the insufficient documentation of the workflows behind Packet-In flooding and Flow-Table overflow attacks, as well as the lack of precise terminology to accurately describe and mitigate these threats. This deficiency hampers the understanding of these vulnerabilities and reduces the effectiveness of IDS in securing SDN environments.

Although some research acknowledges these SDN-related vulnerabilities and explains the mechanisms of such attacks [1], there is still a significant gap in addressing threats across all layers of the SDN architecture. For instance,

 DOI: 10.1201/9781003597476-7

one particularly concerning attack is topology poisoning, in which adversaries manipulate the network's topology perception. A specific instance of topology poisoning is the Link Fabrication Attack (LFA), where attackers inject fake links into the network by tampering with Link Layer Discovery Protocol (LLDP) packets. This compromises the controller's view of the network, potentially disrupting routing policies, enabling man-in-the-middle (MitM) attacks, and even facilitating DoS scenarios by creating forwarding loops or black holes.

To address these challenges, we propose a two-level classification framework leveraging Variational Autoencoders (VAE) and DL to improve SDN security against LFAs. Our contributions include:

1. Sequence-Level Classification: Using an LSTM-based sequence classifier, we analyze temporal deviations in LLDP sequences extracted from OpenFlow packet-in messages. This helps in detecting abnormal patterns introduced by relay-based LFAs.
2. Observation-Level Classification: Once a sequence is flagged as suspicious, we further analyze individual LLDP observations by treating them as separate network links. This second-level classification helps in identifying fake links injected by an attacker while minimizing false positives.
3. Synthetic Data Generation with VAE: We employ VAE to generate realistic network traffic at both sequence level and observation level. This allows us to balance the dataset by synthesizing new legitimate and malicious network instances, enhancing the performance of our classifiers.
4. Efficient Real-Time Integration: Unlike traditional IDS that continuously monitor network traffic (impacting performance), our framework operates only when a new link appears in the network. This ensures minimal computational overhead while maintaining real-time security efficiency.

This chapter is structured as follows: Section 5.1 introduces the security challenges in SDN, emphasizing the vulnerabilities of the Link LDS to relay-based LFAs. Section 5.2 provides an overview of SDN architecture, detailing its key components and protocols relevant to network topology management. Section 5.3 explores the security risks associated with topology discovery, focusing on LFAs and their impact on SDN networks. Section 5.4 reviews related works on detecting topology poisoning attacks, highlighting existing detection methods and their limitations. Section 5.5 presents our proposed two-level classification framework, which integrates sequence-level and observation-level analysis using LSTM networks and VAE. Section 5.6 discusses the experimental evaluation and the effectiveness of our approach in real-time SDN environments. Finally, Section 5.7 concludes the chapter by summarizing key findings and outlining directions for future research.

5.2 SDN ARCHITECTURE AND SERVICES

SDN represents a major evolution in network architecture by separating the control plane, which manages decision-making, from the data plane, which handles packet forwarding. Unlike conventional networking models where these functions are embedded within individual devices, SDN introduces a centralized software-based controller that streamlines network management and enhances efficiency. This shift allows administrators to dynamically configure and optimize network operations without modifying hardware components, significantly improving flexibility. The SDN architecture is organized into three key layers: the application layer, which supports network applications and policies; the control layer, which oversees traffic management and decision-making; and the infrastructure layer, composed of switches and routers responsible for data forwarding. This structured approach enhances scalability, enabling real-time adjustments to policies and routing strategies based on network conditions. Moreover, SDN fosters adaptability by facilitating the rapid deployment of security measures, traffic management protocols, and network virtualization, making it ideal for modern, large-scale, and cloud-based environments. By combining programmability with centralized control, SDN enhances operational efficiency, reduces complexity, and strengthens security, allowing networks to proactively address emerging threats and evolving performance requirements [2].

5.2.1 Application layer

The application layer in SDN serves as the interface between end-users, network administrators, and the SDN controller, enabling seamless interaction and efficient network management. This layer supports a wide range of applications and services, such as firewalls for security enforcement, routing protocols for optimized data flow, traffic engineering mechanisms, and load balancers for resource allocation. These applications can be developed by SDN vendors, third-party providers, or customized by network operators to meet specific needs. By leveraging SDN's programmability, applications within this layer can dynamically adjust network behavior in real time, such as rerouting traffic to prevent congestion, enforcing security policies to mitigate threats, or optimizing bandwidth distribution to enhance performance. The application layer communicates with the control layer via northbound APIs, allowing administrators to define high-level network policies, automate tasks, and streamline operations. This abstraction reduces manual intervention, simplifies network management, and facilitates the integration of new functionalities without disrupting existing infrastructure. Ultimately, the application layer enhances flexibility, security, and efficiency by providing a software-driven approach to adaptive and intelligent network optimization.

5.2.2 Control layer

The control layer in SDN serves as the network's decision-making hub, managing traffic flow, security policies, and device configurations. It translates high-level directives from administrators or applications into precise instructions for the data plane. This layer operates through the control plane, which can be either centralized, with a single SDN controller overseeing the entire network, or distributed, where multiple controllers enhance scalability and fault tolerance [3]. Communication with network devices is facilitated via the southbound interface, an open protocol enabling dynamic interaction between the controller and network elements. The controller optimizes performance by defining packet forwarding rules, enforcing security mechanisms, and responding to network events such as congestion, failures, or cyber threats. By continuously monitoring the network state, it can adapt to changing conditions, ensuring efficient traffic flow and improving overall network resilience. Its programmability enables automation and real-time adjustments, reducing manual configurations and enhancing network flexibility, security, and scalability, making it a cornerstone of modern SDN infrastructures.

5.2.3 Infrastructure layer

While the control layer focuses on decision-making and configuration and defining the logical behavior and policies of the network, the infrastructure layer is responsible for the actual forwarding of network traffic based on these decisions. Interconnected through either wireless radio channels or wired cables, forwarding devices from the network infrastructure collectively constitute the data plane. These devices, switches, or routers receive instructions from the controller about how to forward packets and implement these instructions in real time. The flow tables within the switches contain rules and actions that dictate how incoming packets should be processed. When a data packet enters the network, the switches examine the packet headers and consult their flow tables to determine the appropriate actions. The actions could include forwarding the packet to a specific port, modifying the packet, or dropping the packet based on predefined rules set by the controller; unmatched packets can be forwarded to the controller for further analysis and decision-making.

5.2.4 Software-Defined networking interfaces

Northbound interface: Applications at the application layer communicate with the controller through the northbound interface. Consequently, each controller has its defined APIs, which could encompass RESTful APIs and various programming languages. This non-standardized interface allows applications to send requests, receive information about the network state, and influence the behavior of the controller in managing the underlying network devices through the southbound interface [4].

Southbound interface: This is the communication link between the controller and the network devices in the data plane. Unlike the northbound interface, which connects the controller to higher-layer applications, the southbound interface is responsible for conveying the control plane decisions made by the controller to the devices that handle the actual forwarding of network traffic. Additionally, the southbound interface specifies the communication protocol governing the interaction between forwarding devices and control plane elements, a protocol such as OpenFlow. This protocol serves to standardize the communication dynamics between the control and data plane elements [2, 4, 5].

5.2.5 Key services and protocols in SDN

The OpenFlow Protocol facilitates communication between switches and the SDN controller, playing a crucial role in network management. Each OpenFlow switch contains a flow table, a secure control channel, and the ability to process packets based on controller instructions. The flow table stores rules that determine packet handling, including header matching, counters for monitoring, and actions like forwarding or dropping packets. Entries in the table are dynamically updated or removed based on idle and hard timeouts. The control channel ensures communication between switches and the controller through various message types. Among these, packet-in messages notify the controller about unmatched packets, prompting decision-making, while packet-out messages allow the controller to instruct switches on handling specific packets. Other messages include configuration commands, error notifications, and flow table modifications. The controller dynamically manages flow table entries through ADD, MODIFY, and DELETE commands, enabling real-time adaptation to network changes. Expired or unused entries are removed via flow removal notifications triggered by timeouts or explicit controller instructions [5].

The Link Discovery Service (LDS) is essential for identifying existing links between OpenFlow-enabled SDN switches and detecting changes in the network topology. These changes include link additions and deletions. Link deletions occur when an existing connection is removed physically or becomes inaccessible due to failures. Such deletions can also happen if an SDN switch is decommissioned or rendered unreachable. Conversely, link additions follow similar processes to integrate new connections into the topology. The SDN controller plays a central role in managing and adapting to these changes, ensuring the network topology remains accurate and up-to-date [6, 7].

LLDP is a Layer 2 protocol designed for network devices to exchange essential identity and topology information. LLDP packets, encapsulated within Ethernet frames, carry details such as chassis ID, port ID, and Time-to-Live (TTL), enabling retrieval of topology information and supporting network management tasks [6–8].

The OpenFlow Discovery Protocol (OFDP) enhances LLDP by adapting it to SDN's centralized architecture. Unlike LLDP, which operates independently,

OFDP integrates the discovery process into the controller's logic, ensuring a consistent and accurate global view of the network [6, 7].

5.3 LINK DISCOVERY SERVICE USING OFDP: SECURITY AND WORKFLOW

As said before, the LDS is a critical component of SDN that enables the controller to maintain an accurate and up-to-date network topology. This section explores the security aspects and detailed workflow of the OFDP.

5.3.1 Functionality and workflow of the OFDP protocol in LDS

The detailed workflow of OFDP involves, as Figure 5.1 shows, the following sequence of message exchanges [7]:

1. Packet-Out Messages: The SDN controller initiates link discovery by generating LLDP packets encapsulated in Packet-Out messages. These messages are sent to the active ports of switches in the network.
2. Forwarding by Switches: Upon receiving a Packet-Out message, the switch transmits the LLDP Packet-Out via its specified ports. The packet is forwarded to neighboring switches, simulating the typical behavior of LLDP in a decentralized setup.
3. Packet-In Messages: When a neighboring switch receives an LLDP packet, it encapsulates the packet in a Packet-In message and sends it back to the controller. The Packet-In message serves as a notification, carrying the discovery data from the switch to the controller. The switch then sends its own LLDP packet through its ports and can also send the packet received earlier.
4. Topology Mapping: The SDN controller processes the received Packet-In messages to extract the embedded LLDP information. Using this data, it identifies the links between switches and updates its global view of the network topology.
5. Continuous Updates: The process is repeated periodically to account for dynamic changes in the network, such as link additions or deletions. This periodic operation, while crucial for maintaining topology accuracy, can result in high message exchange overhead, particularly in large-scale or latency-sensitive networks.

5.3.2 Vulnerabilities in topology discovery services

LDS Vulnerability: This vulnerability exposes a critical security gap by allowing adversaries to exploit weaknesses in the LDS, potentially leading to the injection of falsified LLDP packets or the deceptive relay of such packets

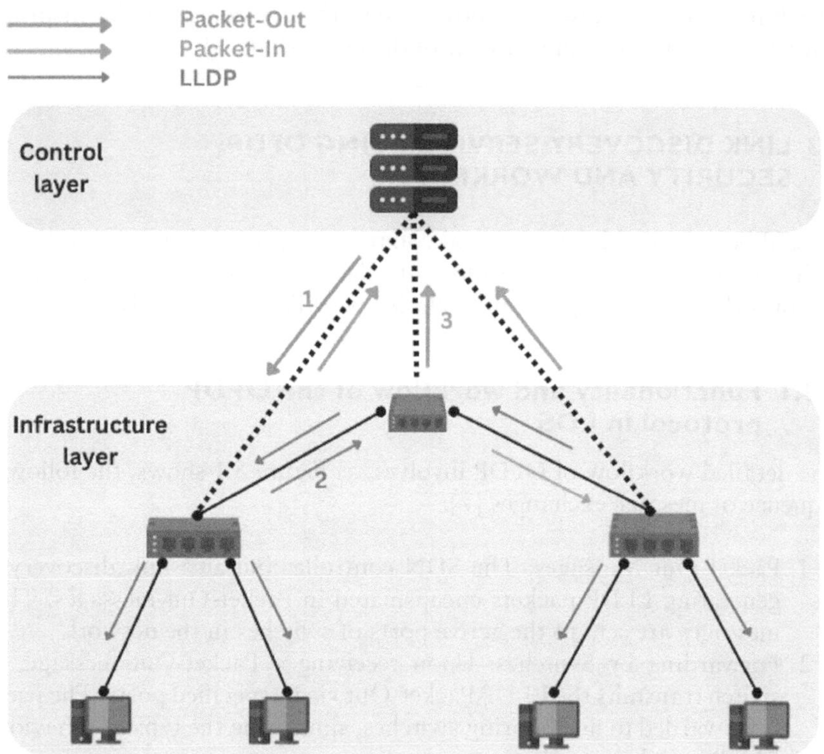

Figure 5.1 Workflow of link discovery service.

between switches. This manipulation creates fictitious internal links within the network topology [6, 8].

Host Tracking Service (HTS) Vulnerability: HTS is a service that is responsible for maintaining Host Profiles to track the mobility of end hosts in a network. The security concern lies in the update mechanism employed by HTS for Host Profiles, which lacks sufficient authentication measures. This absence of robust security considerations provides adversaries with an opportunity to tamper with host location information, introducing a serious risk of traffic hijacking [6, 8].

5.3.3 Topology poisoning attacks in SDN

Link Fabrication Attacks: These attacks exploit the LDS vulnerability of SDN controllers to manipulate the network topology. These attacks enable adversaries to introduce fabricated links, misleading the controller's perception of network connectivity. Specifically, an attacker intercepts a legitimate LLDP packet broadcast by a switch and then reintroduces it in a different location in the network in many ways [9]. As a result, the controller falsely recognizes a link between two switches that are not connected. This manipulation allows the attacker to function as a MitM, intercepting and altering network traffic. Additionally, the fabricated link can facilitate DoS situations by creating black holes or forwarding loops [10]. One type of such attack is: *Relay-based LFA* [8], the attack involves an adversary forwarding unaltered LLDP messages between different points in the network to create a fake but functional link in the topology. To carry out this attack, the attacker must first compromise a host and establish a bidirectional tunnel to relay captured LLDP packets. The compromised host captures LLDP packets broadcast by its connected switch and sends them through the tunnel to the attacker, who then forward them to another switch; this happens in both directions. This tricks the network controller into believing a legitimate link exists between the two points. The attack is particularly dangerous because it does not modify LLDP packet content, making it harder to detect using traditional security measures. Figure 5.2 shows the workflow of this attack, illustrating how the attacker and the compromised host establish a bidirectional tunnel and relay unaltered LLDP packets between network points.

Host Location Hijacking (HLH): HLH attacks involve exploiting the HTS vulnerability by falsifying the victim's addressing information from a location

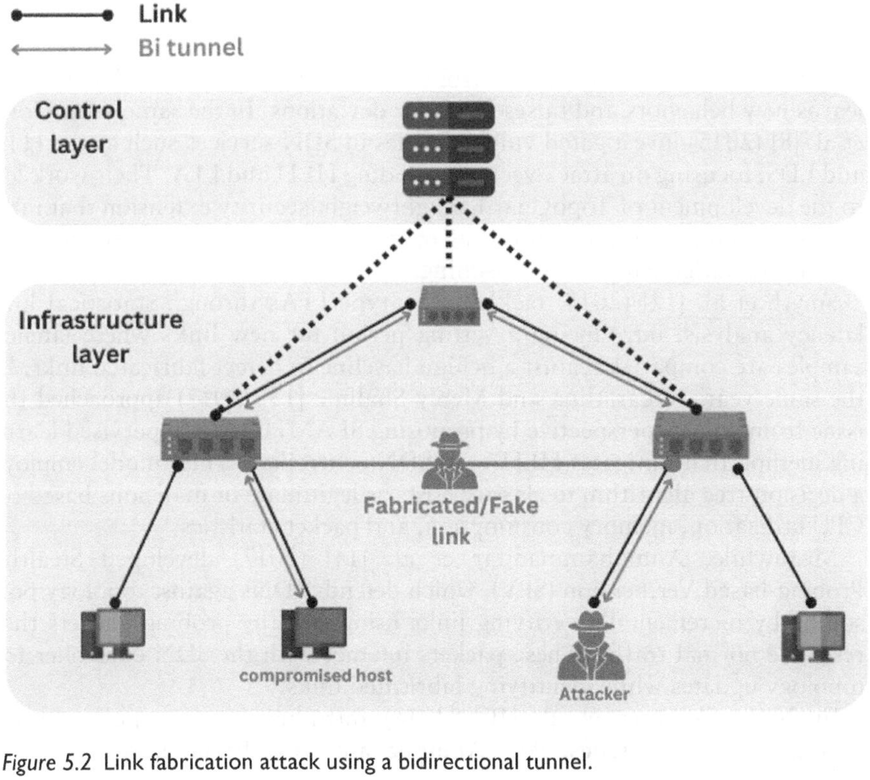

Figure 5.2 Link fabrication attack using a bidirectional tunnel.

controlled by the attacker. This manipulation prompts the HTS to record a migration from the genuine location of the victim to the attacker's location, leading to the establishment of flow rules that redirect traffic to the attacker [10].

ARP Cache Poisoning is a network attack that targets the ARP tables on data plane switches by injecting falsified MAC-IP mappings. The workflow of this attack begins with Packet Injection, where the attacker sends ARP replies containing spoofed MAC and IP addresses. This leads to Cache Poisoning, as the switches or devices update their ARP cache with the attacker-provided mappings, replacing legitimate entries. Once the ARP cache is compromised, the exploitation phase occurs, where traffic intended for the legitimate host is redirected to the attacker. This allows the attacker to intercept, manipulate, or monitor the redirected traffic. Malicious hosts can exploit this vulnerability to trick the controller into installing malicious flow rules, diverting traffic flows for potential eavesdropping, network loops, or packet voids [11].

5.4 RELATED WORK ON DETECTING TOPOLOGY POISONING ATTACKS

Dhawan et al. [11] (2015) introduced SPHINX, a security framework designed to detect network topology and data plane forwarding attacks in SDNs. SPHINX employs incremental flow graphs to model operations, enabling real-time validation of updates and the detection of known and unknown threats. By extracting metadata from OpenFlow messages, it dynamically learns new behaviors and raises alerts for deviations. In the same year, Hong et al. [8] (2015) investigated vulnerabilities in SDN services such as the HTS and LDS, focusing on attack vectors including HLH and LFA. Their work led to the development of TopoGuard, a lightweight security extension that integrates host migration verification and cryptographic LLDP integrity checks to detect and mitigate topology poisoning.

Smyth et al. [12] (2017) tackled relay-type LFAs through statistical link latency analysis, introducing a vetting period for new links where latency samples are compared against a benign baseline to detect fabricated links. In the same year, Nagarathna and Mercy Shalinie [13] (2017) approached the issue from an ML perspective by proposing SLAMHHA, a supervised learning method that mitigates HLHAs in SDN controllers. Their model employs a decision-tree algorithm to classify hosts as legitimate or malicious based on CPU utilization, memory consumption, and packet statistics.

Meanwhile, Alimohammadifar et al. [14] (2017) developed Stealthy Probing-based Verification (SPV), which defends SDNs against topology poisoning by incrementally verifying links using stealthy probing packets that resemble normal traffic. These packets interact with the SDN controller for topology updates while identifying fabricated links.

In 2018, Skowyra et al. [10] (2018) introduced two topology tampering attack techniques, Port Amnesia and Port Probing, which evade state-of-the-art defenses like TopoGuard and SPHINX. Port Amnesia exploits repeated Port-Up/Port-Down events to bypass behavioral profiling, while Port Probing hijacks host locations during network migrations. To address these vulnerabilities, the authors developed TOPOGUARD+, an enhanced defense mechanism incorporating control message monitoring and latency analysis. Two years later, Baidya and Hewett [15] (2020) focused on topology poisoning attacks originating from compromised hosts or switches. Their solution involved active port monitoring to detect malicious behaviors, ensuring that no active port was shared across multiple links. They further evaluated attack impacts on SDN routing through analytical and empirical studies.

Soltani et al. [16] (2021) proposed Machine Learning-based Link Guard (MLLG) to counter LFAs and Link Latency Attacks (LLA). By analyzing LLDP latency features like LLDP propagation time and control link latency with classifiers such as KNN and Random Forest. Upon receipt of LLDP packets, the controller forwards them to MLLG for verification. The dataset was collected by modifying TopoGuard+ source code. Joseph et al. [17] (2022) introduced LiFAMA, an LFA mitigation approach that incorporated LLDP packet authentication through HMAC and a PostgreSQL-based verification database to actively validate known links. Al Salti and Zhang [18] (2022) propose LINK-GUARD, a security framework designed to protect the SDN topology discovery process from LFAs. The framework employs three detection methods: (1) Bidirectional Link Verification (BLV) to identify LLDP injection attacks by validating the existence of a two-way link, (2) Link Latency Measurement (LLM) to detect LLDP relay attacks using statistical analysis of link latency, and (3) Per-port LLDP Packet Counter (PLPC) to identify LLDP flooding attacks based on the number of received LLDP packets per port. Upon detecting a fake link, LINK-GUARD blocks the compromised port to prevent further attacks.

Further refining MLLG, Soltani et al. [19] (2023) developed Real-Time Link Verification (RLV) to dynamically counter LFAs and LLAs, demonstrating lower false-positive rates compared to solutions like TopoGuard+. Around the same time, Zhang and Wang [20] (2023) proposed RLFAT, a Transformer-based model for detecting Relay LFA. Leveraging self-attention mechanisms to extract temporal and contextual features, the model's structure involves an encoding layer, multi-head self-attention layer, and feed-forward layer, outputting the probability of an attack state. Smyth et al. [9] (2023) presented SECAP, a P4-based in-network security solution for topology poisoning attacks, including ARP Cache Poisoning and Relay-based LFAs. Operating entirely within the data plane, SECAP provides source address verification and anomaly detection capabilities to validate MAC, IP, ARP, and LLDP headers while identifying fabricated links based on LLDP interval variance.

Most recently, Liu et al. [21] (2024) proposed a novel detection method called Correlated Link Verification (CLV) to address LFA in low-latency SDN environments. CLV employs a three-phase approach: data processing to mitigate measurement error, multipath transmission simulation to convert performance disparities into statistical features, and dynamic threshold calculation based on extreme value theory and probability distribution fitting. Zhang and Wang [22] (2024) introduced Attopo, an attention-driven SDN topology discovery method that eliminates reliance on LLDP, reducing security vulnerabilities of the OFDP. By leveraging Self-attention, Cross-attention, and Prob-attention mechanisms, Attopo extracts connection information from network flows. Elzoghbi and He [23] (2024) proposed DIS-Guard, a security framework to mitigate topology attacks in SDN, particularly the Round-trip time Confusion Onslaught (RCO) attack. By using mutual TLS (mTLS) for host authentication, chaos-tent maps for dynamic MAC addresses, and statistical link verification.

5.5 PROPOSED SOLUTION FOR RELAY-BASED LINK FABRICATION ATTACK

Our solution to the relay-based LFA is a two-level classification framework that combines a sequence-level classifier and a link-level classifier.

The first stage involves processing sequences of LLDP packets extracted from OpenFlow Packet-In messages using an LSTM model. LSTMs are more suitable for our implementation because they effectively capture long-term dependencies and temporal patterns in LLDP packet sequences, which are crucial for detecting anomalies in the timing and ordering of network messages. Unlike standard Recurrent Neural Networks (RNNs), they mitigate the vanishing gradient problem, ensuring stable learning over extended sequences. While Convolutional Neural Networks (CNNs) excel at local feature extraction, they lack the sequential memory needed for temporal dependencies. Transformers, though powerful, require large datasets and high computational resources, making them less practical for real-time SDN security tasks. LSTMs balance efficiency and accuracy, making them ideal for sequence-level anomaly detection in our SDN framework.

Once a sequence is flagged as suspicious or anomalous, it is passed to the second classifier. This classifier analyzes the sequence at the individual link level, treating each observation as a separate link. Each link is then processed and classified to determine whether it corresponds to a fabricated link. By combining temporal analysis with per-link scrutiny, this layered approach provides a robust mechanism for detecting fabricated links.

To enhance detection accuracy, VAEs were applied during the dataset preparation phase to augment both sequences and individual observations. The generated data was then used to train and validate the classification models before integrating them into the detection framework.

To minimize disruptions during network operations, the detection process is event-driven. Specifically, this detection mechanism is triggered only when

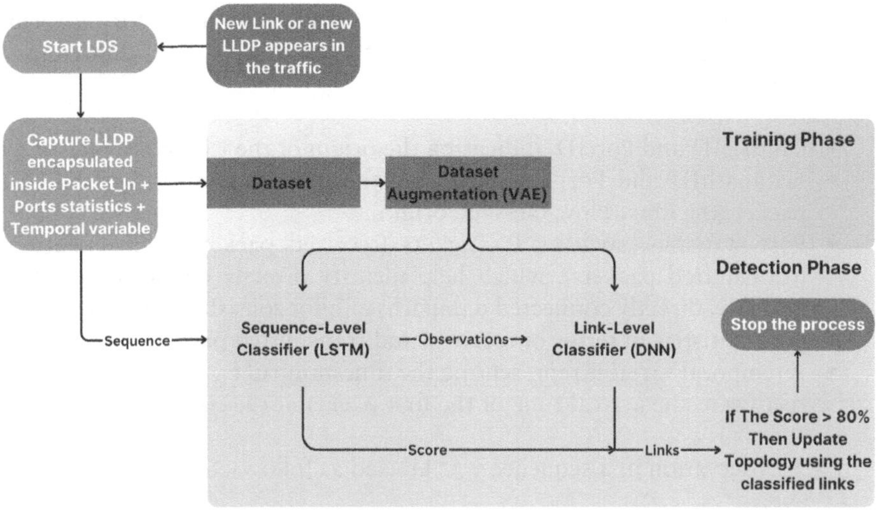

Figure 5.3 Stages of LFA detection framework.

a new link or a new instance of LLDP packets appears in the network traffic. During the operational phase of the network, the LDS continues to run uninterrupted. However, after the initial detection process, further checks are halted unless a new link is detected. This approach balances real-time detection with network efficiency.

At the end of the detection process, the network topology is updated, retaining only the legitimate links. This ensures an accurate and reliable representation of the network's topology for applications that depend on precise topological information.

Figure 5.3 illustrates the workflow and architecture of our proposed solution framework, detailing the sequence of operations and the interactions between the sequence-level and link-level classifiers.

5.5.1 Dataset collection and preprocessing

For dataset collection, we set up an environment comprising a Ryu controller and the Mininet network simulator. A dedicated script was implemented to create switches and links under various topological shapes, such as bus, star, and tree. Another script was developed to simulate relay-based LFA. To increase the challenge for our models in detecting fake links, we used the same topologies with identical links under both normal and attack conditions. This means that a link could be legitimate or fabricated within the same topology shape but appear in different sequences. This setup ensures that the classification models must rely on temporal and contextual features to detect anomalies.

An application running on the Ryu controller was responsible for capturing Packet-In messages containing LLDP packets. It extracted several attributes, including:

- ChassisID and PortID, indicating the origin of the LLDP packet.
- DatapathID and Port-In, indicating the receiving entity of the LLDP packet (the OpenFlow message origin).
- Port statistics, such as RxPackets (received packets) and TxPackets (transmitted packets), which help identify directly connected entities. Notably, directly connected datapaths exhibit consistency between their port statistics in terms of received and transmitted packets.
- A temporal variable representing the timestamp of each captured packet, relative to the arrival time of the first packet at the controller.

Each observation in a sequence was labeled as follows:

- *0: Legitimate indirect links* (8740 observations before data generation and after).
- *1: Legitimate direct links* (1680 observations before data generation and 8399 after).
- *2: Fabricated direct links* (120 observations before data generation and 4119 after).
- *3: Fabricated indirect links* (4318 observations before data generation and 8317 after).

Additionally, each sequence was assigned a label:

- *0: Normal sequences* (60 sequences before data generation and 3060 after).
- *1: Malicious sequences* (60 sequences before data generation and 3060 after).

This process was applied to every sequence, with each sequence representing a set of observations captured over a 10-second interval while the LDS ran. We captured multiple sequences for each topology shape and varied architecture. This diverse dataset ensured training and evaluation of our models under different network conditions.

5.5.2 Dataset augmentation: Data generation using variational auto-encoders (VAEs)

In recent years, the application of Generative AI models has gained significant attention in addressing security challenges in several domains. In their comprehensive survey, López Delgado and López Ramos (2024) [24] explore the diverse applications of these models, including Generative Adversarial

Networks (GANs), VAEs, Diffusion Models, and Transformer-based models. These models are widely used to address critical security issues such as intrusion detection, anomaly detection, privacy enhancement, cyber threat detection, and penetration testing, with a primary focus on data augmentation and balance.

Wang et al. [25] (2021) proposed ByteSGAN, a semi-supervised GAN for encrypted traffic classification in SDN Edge Gateways. By leveraging a small number of labeled samples and a large number of unlabeled ones, ByteSGAN achieves excellent classification performance through modifications in the GAN discriminator's structure and loss function. Novaes et al. [26] (2021) introduced an adversarial DL approach for detecting and defending against DDoS attacks in SDN environments using GANs in near-real-time. Their system integrates anomaly detection and mitigation modules, enhancing the discriminator's ability to distinguish between normal and adversarial traffic. Experiments showed superior performance compared to traditional methods like CNN, LSTM, and MLP. Mirsadeghi et al. [27] (2023) examined class imbalance in intrusion detection for SDN using the InSDN dataset. They compared data-level methods (ROS, SMOTE, GANs) and classifier-level methods (Random Forest, Siamese Neural Networks), finding that Random Forest outperformed DL models without additional balancing strategies, while SMOTE provided the best overall improvement for DL models. Phan The Duy et al. [28] (2023) explored the robustness of flow-based IDS against adversarial samples generated by Wasserstein GANs with Gradient Penalty (WGAN-GP) and AdvGAN. Their study demonstrated that these GAN variants could effectively generate adversarial samples to bypass IDS, highlighting the vulnerability of IDS to adversarial attacks. Yuan et al. [29] (2023) introduced a data balancing method called B-GAN to address data imbalance in Industrial Control Systems (ICSs). Using GANs with LSTM networks for both the generator and discriminator, B-GAN captures temporal features and generates high-quality anomaly samples, balancing the dataset for better training of intrusion detection models. Brandão Lent et al. [30] (2024) developed an unsupervised anomaly detection system for DDoS attacks in SDNs using GANs with Gated Recurrent Units (GRUs). The system generates synthetic data to improve anomaly detection, capturing temporal dependencies in network traffic. The system achieved an F1-score of 99% on the Orion dataset and 98% on the CIC-DDoS2019 dataset, demonstrating high performance in attack detection. Zacaron et al. [31] (2024) proposed an anomaly-based IDS for SDN environments, utilizing GANs to detect and mitigate network anomalies. The system compares three GAN models: Vanilla GAN, Deep Convolutional GAN, and Wasserstein GAN with Gradient Penalty. The results showed high detection rates, with accuracy, precision, recall, and F1-score exceeding 99% in both emulated and real SDN scenarios. Kazmi et al. [32] (2025) proposed the Federated Conditional VAEs (FCVAE) framework to enhance Cyber Threat Intelligence (CTI) in SDN environments, particularly addressing the challenge of non-IID (non-independent and identically distributed) data. The FCVAE framework uses conditional

VAEs to generate threat-specific data at each silo, mitigating the impact of non-IID data on CTI performance. Experiments using the InSDN dataset showed a substantial improvement in CTI performance, with accuracy increasing from 92% to 97% after data augmentation, offering a robust solution while preserving data privacy. Wubete [33] (2025) explored ML for link failure prediction by analyzing IP and optical layer metrics. The study leveraged time series analysis and Graph Neural Networks (GNNs), demonstrating that incorporating optical metrics such as power levels and error rates enhances prediction accuracy. Using Graph Convolutional Networks (GCNs) for spatial relationships and a modified VAE for temporal dependencies, the approach achieved high precision and recall.

In our implementation, the VAE played a significant role in mitigating the effects of dataset imbalance caused by the nature of LFA, where the number of collected sequences is low and a single sequence contains only two observations, indicating a fabricated link. We utilized the VAE in two ways: generating new sequences and generating individual observations.

Unlike traditional auto-encoders, which directly map inputs to a lower-dimensional latent space and reconstruct them, VAE models the data distribution probabilistically, allowing it to create synthetic data while maintaining the statistical characteristics of the original dataset. The model consists of an encoder and a decoder; the encoder compresses the input data, such as sequences or observations, into a lower-dimensional latent space. Instead of mapping the input to a fixed point in this space, the encoder estimates two parameters: a *mean vector* (m) and a *log-variance vector* ($\log(s^2)$). These parameters define a probabilistic distribution in the latent space from which we sample using the reparameterization trick:

$$z = \mu + \sigma \cdot \varepsilon, \quad \varepsilon \sim \mathcal{N}(0, I)$$

The decoder takes the sampled latent vector (**z**) and reconstructs the input data. This reconstruction is optimized using a loss function that combines two components:

- *Reconstruction Loss:* Measures how well the reconstructed data matches the original data. Commonly calculated using Mean Squared Error (MSE) or Binary Cross-Entropy.
- *KL Divergence Loss:* Regularizes the latent space by ensuring that the learned distribution is close to a standard normal distribution. The KL Divergence is given by:

$$\text{KL Divergence Loss} = -0.5\sum\left(1 + \log(\sigma^2) - \mu^2 - \sigma^2\right)$$

The total VAE loss allows the model to be trained using backpropagation:

$$\text{VAE Loss} = \text{Reconstruction Loss} + \text{KL Divergence Loss}$$

Once the VAE is trained, it can be utilized to generate new synthetic data by leveraging its latent space and decoder. First, random vectors (**z**) will be sampled from a standard normal distribution ($\mathcal{N}(0,\mathbf{I})$) in the latent space. These vectors represent points in the learned distribution of the data. Next, the sampled latent vectors (**z**) will be passed through the decoder component of the VAE. The decoder transforms these latent vectors into new data instances [34, 35].

To address the challenges posed by our dataset, we implemented a VAE using PyTorch, specifically designed to handle sequential data. Each sequence in the dataset consists of 116 observations with 7 features, which we flattened into a single vector to serve as input to the VAE. The architecture includes an encoder that maps the input data to a latent space representation of length 64 and a decoder that reconstructs the data from this latent space. The loss function combines MSE for reconstruction and KL divergence. We trained two separate VAEs, one for normal sequences and another for malicious sequences, using the Adam optimizer and their respective dataloaders. This class-specific training allowed us to generate 3,000 synthetic sequences for each class, significantly enhancing the dataset's diversity and size. After generation, we reshaped the instances back into their original structure (116, 7) to preserve the sequential nature of the data. Figure 5.4 illustrates the VAE training loss for both normal and malicious sequences, starting at approximately 1.5 and gradually decreasing over 35 epochs before converging around 0.1. This trend indicates that, as training progresses, the VAE model becomes increasingly effective at reconstructing input sequences with minimal error.

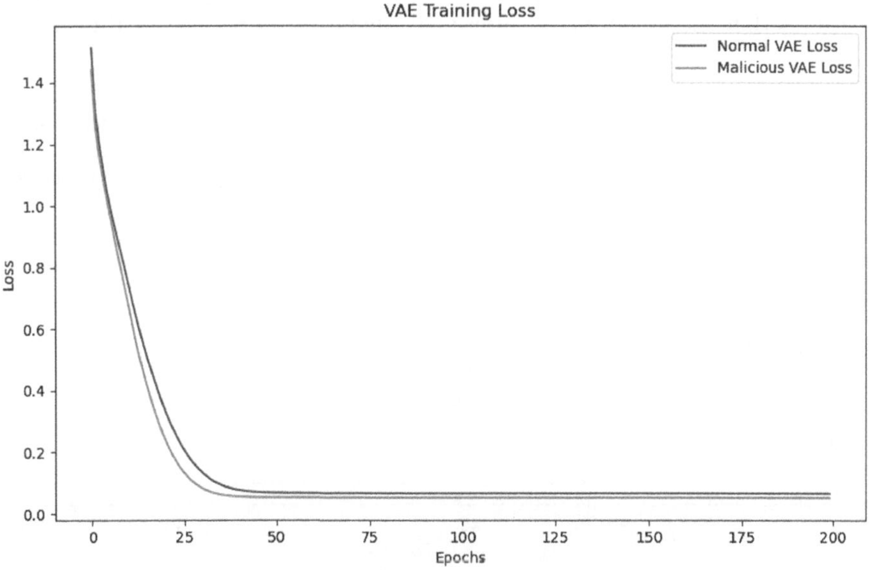

Figure 5.4 Training loss of VAE for normal and malicious sequences generation.

Initially, the high loss value suggests that the VAE encoder-decoder network is still learning the underlying distribution of both normal and malicious sequences. As training continues, the model refines its latent space representation, allowing it to generate more accurate reconstructions. The eventual convergence to a low loss value (0.1) signifies that the VAE has successfully captured the key patterns and variations within the training data, ensuring that both normal and malicious sequences are well-represented in the learned distribution.

For observation-level data generation, we employed a similar VAE framework but tailored it to handle individual observations rather than sequences. The encoder in this architecture maps input data to a latent space of length 4. This model was specifically applied to labels with fewer observations, processing each label individually to generate synthetic data and address class imbalance. By the end of training process, we were able to generate new samples that improved the dataset's balance. Figure 5.5 presents the VAE training loss for observations belonging to classes labeled 1, 2, and 3, showing distinct convergence behaviors. Initially, the loss values start at approximately 1.6 for label 1, 1.0 for label 2, and 0.8 for label 3, reflecting varying levels of complexity in reconstructing these different classes. Over the course of training, the loss for labels 1 and 2 gradually decreases, reaching values close to zero after 60 epochs, while label 3 converges significantly faster, stabilizing around 20 epochs.

The faster convergence of label 3 suggests that the VAE learns its distribution more efficiently, likely due to lower variance or simpler feature representations within this class. In contrast, labels 1 and 2 require more training epochs to achieve stable reconstructions, indicating higher variability or more complex patterns that the model needs additional time to capture. The final near-zero

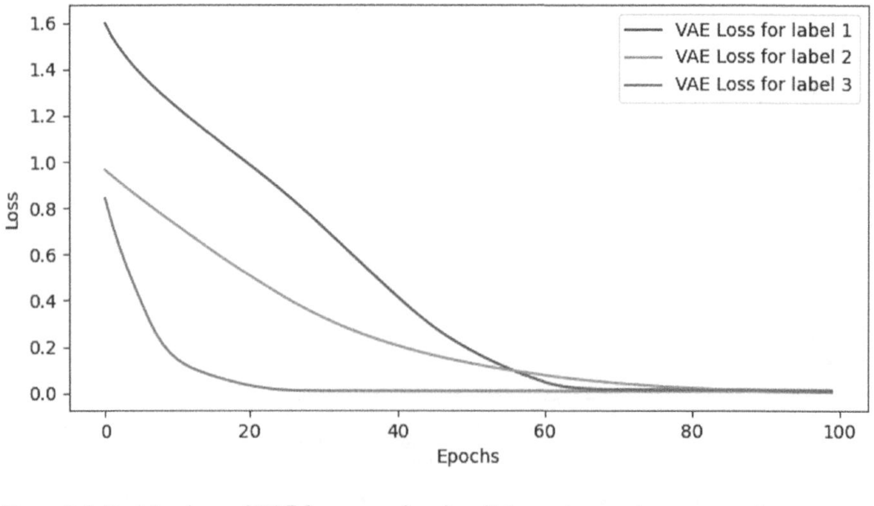

Figure 5.5 Training loss of VAE for normal and malicious observations generation.

loss values across all classes confirm that the VAE has effectively learned to encode and reconstruct observations from each class with high fidelity.

Together, these VAE implementations provided a robust solution for both sequence-level and observation-level data generation, enhancing the quality and diversity of our dataset.

5.5.3 Sequence-Level classification

To address the task of sequence classification, we implemented an LSTM-based model using PyTorch. The architecture of the model consists of an LSTM layer followed by a fully connected layer for classification. The LSTM layer processes sequential data, and its hidden state size is set to 128. We used a bidirectional LSTM with 2 layers to capture both past and future context in the sequences, enhancing the model's ability to learn complex temporal and sequential patterns. The final hidden states of the LSTM are passed through a fully connected layer to produce class predictions. The model was trained using the Adam optimizer and CrossEntropyLoss as the loss function. The dataset was split into training and testing sets, with sequences and their corresponding labels loaded into DataLoader objects for batch processing. This setup allowed us to train the model and evaluate its performance on unseen data.

Our model achieved an accuracy of 99.96%, demonstrating its strong capability to classify sequences accurately. The training process was monitored using a loss curve, which is shown in Figure 5.6, illustrating the model's

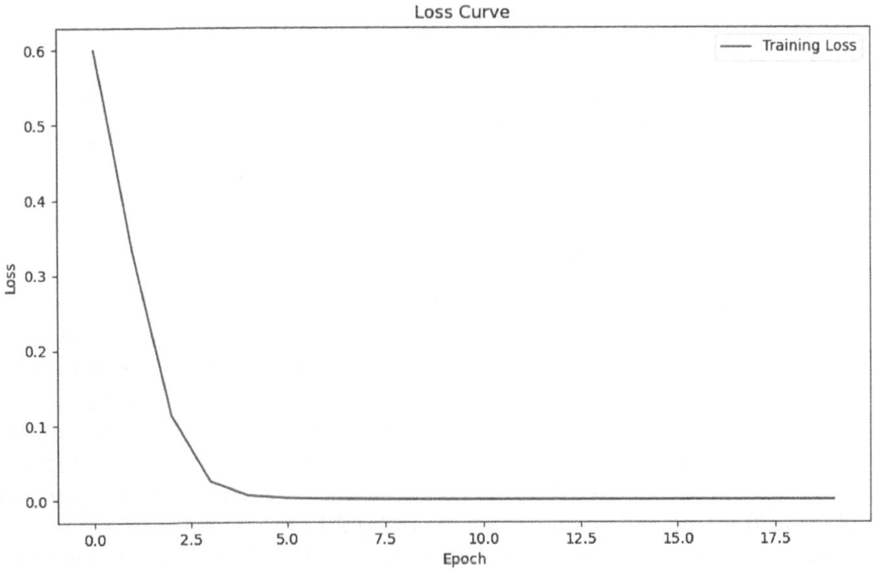

Figure 5.6 Training loss of sequence-level classifier LSTM.

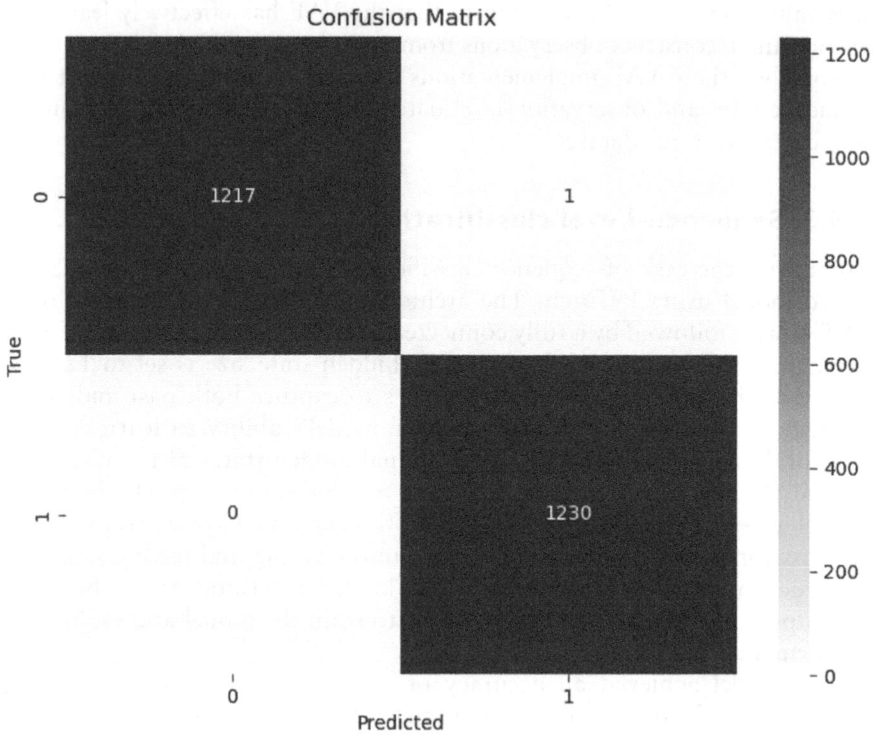

Figure 5.7 Confusion matrix of sequence-level classifier LSTM.

convergence over 5 epochs. Additionally, we evaluated the model's performance using a confusion matrix during validation, as depicted in Figure 5.7. The confusion matrix highlights the model's precision in distinguishing between the two classes, with minimal misclassifications.

5.5.4 Link-Level classification

For observation-level classification, we implemented a feedforward neural network using PyTorch. The model architecture consists of three fully connected layers with ReLU activation functions and dropout layers to prevent overfitting. The input dimension is set to 7, corresponding to the number of features in each observation, and the hidden layer size is 256. The output layer produces predictions for 4 classes. The model was trained using the Adam optimizer and CrossEntropyLoss as the loss function. The dataset was split into training and testing sets with an 80:20 ratio.

Our link-level classifier achieved an accuracy of 99.32%, demonstrating its effectiveness in classifying individual observations. The training process was monitored using a loss curve, which is shown in Figure 5.8, illustrating the

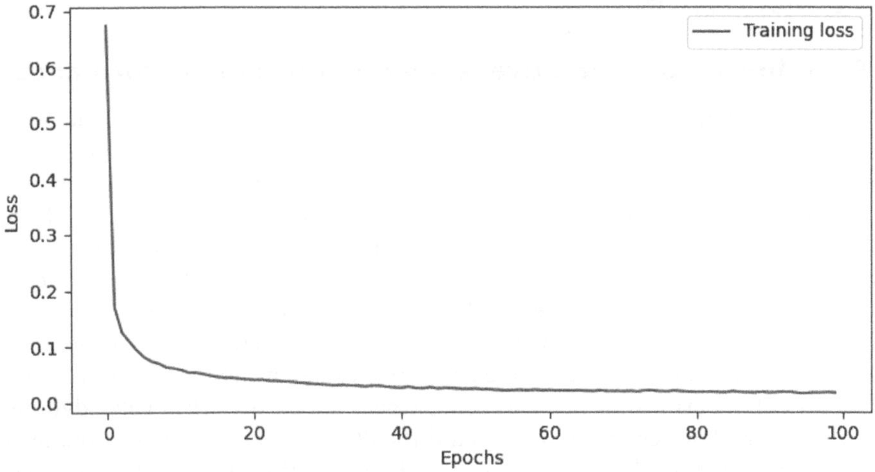

Figure 5.8 Training loss of packet-level classifier DNN.

model's convergence over 100 epochs. Additionally, we evaluated the model's performance using a confusion matrix. The confusion matrix in Figure 5.9 highlights the model's precision in distinguishing between the four classes, with few false classifications, but the model was able to differentiate between normal and malicious cases accurately.

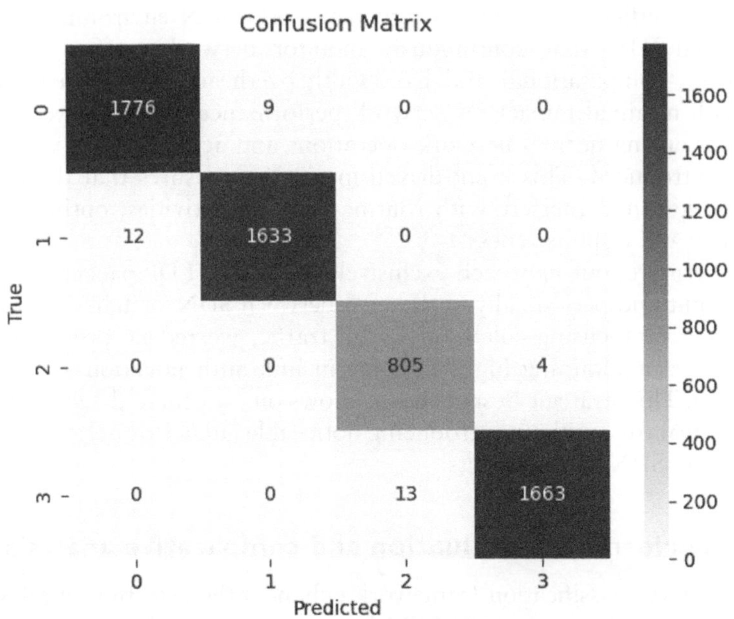

Figure 5.9 Confusion matrix of packet-level classifier DNN.

5.6 DISCUSSION

5.6.1 Impact of generative AI on classification performance

The evaluation results highlight the effectiveness of both the sequence-level and observation-level classifiers in accurately distinguishing between legitimate and malicious instances. The high classification performance achieved demonstrates the crucial role of VAEs in constructing a well-balanced and augmented dataset. Without Generative AI, the development of robust classifiers would have been significantly more challenging due to the scarcity of attack-specific datasets aligned with our classification objectives.

In cybersecurity and network security, acquiring comprehensive training datasets is complex, resource-intensive, and time-consuming. This challenge is particularly critical in SDN security, where attack patterns evolve dynamically, and real attack traces are often difficult to collect in sufficient quantity. VAEs effectively address this limitation by generating high-quality synthetic data that closely resemble real-world attack scenarios while preserving statistical and temporal patterns. This augmentation not only expands the dataset but also ensures a well-balanced distribution of normal and anomalous instances, mitigating class imbalance issues that often degrade ML performance.

5.6.2 Practical integration and performance of our detection framework

Beyond its high classification accuracy, a key strength of our detection framework is its efficient integration into real-world SDN environments. Unlike traditional IDSs that continuously monitor network traffic, introducing significant computational and bandwidth overhead, our framework operates with minimal impact on network performance. Specifically, it remains dormant during normal network operations and activates only when a new link is introduced. This event-driven mechanism ensures that the detection process does not interfere with routine network activities, optimizing both efficiency and responsiveness.

Furthermore, our approach exclusively analyzes LLDP packets, which are lightweight and periodically exchanged between SDN switches for topology discovery. By focusing solely on LLDP traffic, we reduce processing overhead while maintaining high accuracy in link authentication and anomaly detection. This strategic design choice allows our system to detect relay-based LFAs in real time without introducing noticeable latency or performance degradation in SDN environments.

5.6.3 Performance evaluation and comparative analysis

Our two-level classification framework enhances the detection of relay-based LFA in SDN by leveraging an LSTM-based sequence-level classifier to capture temporal anomalies in LLDP packet exchanges, followed by a link-level classifier for fine-grained verification of fabricated links. This layered approach improves detection accuracy, reduces false positives, and adapts to dynamic SDN environments, effectively mitigating topology poisoning risks. Our framework achieves 99.96% accuracy at the sequence level and 99.32% at the link level, surpassing existing approaches in precision and robustness. Compared to RLFAT, for example, which utilizes transformers for relay-based LFA detection, our method offers similar accuracy with lower computational overhead, making it more suitable for real-time SDN security.

5.6.4 Scalability and future enhancements

Despite its strengths, our framework's effectiveness depends on the quality of training data and may pose challenges in large-scale SDN deployments. Additionally, adversaries could develop subtle evasion techniques, requiring further refinements to maintain resilience. Scalability remains a concern as the volume of LLDP sequences increases, necessitating optimization strategies to sustain real-time performance. Future enhancements will focus on reducing more computational costs, adapting to evolving attack patterns and variant topology structures, and improving resilience against adaptive threats.

5.7 CONCLUSION

In SDN, where security is constantly challenged by evolving threats, the integration of Generative AI represents a significant advancement. Traditional security models often rely on limited, static datasets, which fail to capture novel attack patterns, leading to reduced detection accuracy. By employing VAEs, our approach not only enhances the robustness of security systems but also addresses the critical issue of data scarcity in training classification models. Generative AI overcomes this limitation by synthesizing high-quality, attack-specific data, enabling security models to generalize better across diverse threat landscapes.

VAEs allow security researchers and practitioners to balance imbalanced datasets, improve classifier training, and ensure the resilience of detection mechanisms against sophisticated cyber threats. Additionally, automated large-scale testing using synthetic attack instances reduces dependency on costly and time-consuming real-world data collection. When combined with DL-based anomaly detection and sequence-based intrusion analysis, Generative AI significantly strengthens SDN security by enhancing model adaptability and minimizing false positives.

Moving forward, the continued advancement of AI-driven security solutions will be essential in keeping pace with dynamic cyber threats, ensuring that SDN infrastructures can anticipate, withstand, and quickly adapt to new vulnerabilities. This synergy between Generative AI and security frameworks marks a promising shift in modern cybersecurity research, fostering the development of self-improving, intelligent network security systems capable of proactively mitigating emerging threats with greater efficiency.

REFERENCES

1. Ilyasse Mellal, Abderrahime Ait Wakrime, and Khaoula Boukir. Advances in the security of SDNs: Exploration of recent ML-based approaches. In *International Conference on Smart Applications and Data Analysis*, pages 215–228. Springer, 2024.
2. Diego Kreutz, Fernando MV Ramos, Paulo Esteves Verissimo, Christian Esteve Rothenberg, Siamak Azodolmolky, and Steve Uhlig. Software-defined networking: A comprehensive survey. *Proceedings of the IEEE*, 103(1):14–76, 2014.
3. Ouafae Benoudifa, Abderrahim Ait Wakrime, and Redouane Benaini. Autonomous solution for controller placement problem of software-defined networking using MuZero based intelligent agents. *Journal of King Saud University-Computer and Information Sciences*, 35(10):101842, 2023.
4. Zohaib Latif, Kashif Sharif, Fan Li, Md Monjurul Karim, Sujit Biswas, and Yu Wang. A comprehensive survey of interface protocols for software defined networks. *Journal of Network and Computer Applications*, 156:102563, 2020.
5. Nick McKeown, Tom Anderson, Hari Balakrishnan, Guru Parulkar, Larry Peterson, Jennifer Rexford, Scott Shenker, and Jonathan Turner. Openflow: Enabling innovation in campus networks. *ACM SIGCOMM Computer Communication Review*, 38(2):69–74, 2008.
6. Suleman Khan, Abdullah Gani, Ainuddin Wahid Abdul Wahab, Mohsen Guizani, and Muhammad Khurram Khan. Topology discovery in software defined networks: Threats, taxonomy, and state-of-the-art. *IEEE Communications Surveys & Tutorials*, 19(1):303–324, 2016.
7. Raniyah Wazirali, Rami Ahmad, and Suheib Alhiyari. SDN-openflow topology discovery: An overview of performance issues. *Applied Sciences*, 11(15): 6999, 2021.
8. Sungmin Hong, Lei Xu, Haopei Wang, and Guofei Gu. Poisoning network visibility in software-defined networks: New attacks and countermeasures. *NDSS*, 15:8–11, 2015.
9. Dylan Smyth, Sandra Scott-Hayward, Victor Cionca, Sean McSweeney, and Donna O'Shea. Secap switch—defeating topology poisoning attacks using P4 data planes. *Journal of Network and Systems Management*, 31(1):28, 2023.
10. Richard Skowyra, Lei Xu, Guofei Gu, Veer Dedhia, Thomas Hobson, Hamed Okhravi, and James Landry. Effective topology tampering attacks and defenses in software-defined networks. In *2018 48th Annual IEEE/IFIP International Conference on Dependable Systems and Networks (DSN)*, pages 374–385. IEEE, 2018.
11. Mohan Dhawan, Rishabh Poddar, Kshiteej Mahajan, and Vijay Mann. Sphinx: Detecting security attacks in software-defined networks. *NDSS*, 15:8–11, 2015.
12. Dylan Smyth, Sean McSweeney, Donna O'Shea, and Victor Cionca. Detecting link fabrication attacks in software-defined networks. In *2017 26th International conference on computer communication and networks (ICCCN)*, pages 1–8. IEEE, 2017.

13. R Nagarathna, and S Mercy Shalinie. Slamhha: A supervised learning approach to mitigate host location hijacking attack on SDN controllers. In *2017 Fourth International Conference on Signal Processing, Communication and Networking (ICSCN)*, pages 1–7. IEEE, 2017.
14. Amir Alimohammadifar, Suryadipta Majumdar, Taous Madi, Yosr Jarraya, Makan Pourzandi, Lingyu Wang, and Mourad Debbabi. Stealthy probing-based verification (SPV): An active approach to defending software defined networks against topology poisoning attacks. In *Computer Security: 23rd European Symposium on Research in Computer Security, ESORICS 2018, Barcelona, Spain, September 3–7, 2018, Proceedings, Part II 23*, pages 463–484. Springer, 2018.
15. Sonali Sen TTU Baidya, and Rattikorn TTU Hewett. Link discovery attacks in software-defined networks: Topology poisoning and impact analysis. 2020.
16. Sanaz Soltani, Mohammad Shojafar, Habib Mostafaei, Zahra Pooranian, and Rahim Tafazolli. Link latency attack in software-defined networks. In *2021 17th International Conference on Network and Service Management (CNSM)*, pages 187–193. IEEE, 2021.
17. Katongole Joseph, Odongo Steven Eyobu, Philemon Kasyoka, and Tonny J Oyana. A link fabrication attack mitigation approach (LiFAMA) for software defined networks. *Electronics*, 11(10):1581, 2022.
18. Ismail Al Salti, and Ning Zhang. Link-guard: An effective And scalable security framework for link discovery in SDN networks. *IEEE Access*, 10:130233–130252, 2022.
19. Sanaz Soltani, Mohammad Shojafar, Habib Mostafaei, and Rahim Tafazolli. Real-time link verification in software-defined networks. *IEEE Transactions on Network and Service Management*, 20(3):3596–3611, 2023.
20. Tianyi Zhang, and Yong Wang. RLFAT: A transformer-based relay link forged attack detection mechanism in SDN. *Electronics*, 12(10):2247, 2023.
21. Yuming Liu, Yong Wang, and Hao Feng. A novel link fabrication attack detection method for low-latency SDN networks. *Journal of Information Security and Applications*, 84:103807, 2024.
22. Tianyi Zhang, and Yong Wang. Attopo: An SDN non-protocol topology discovery method based on attention mechanism and network flow analysis. *IEEE Access*, 12, 182190–182202, 2024.
23. Mahmoud Elzoghbi, and Hui He. Dis-guard: Enhancing SDN resilience to topology and RCO attacks. *Computer Networks*, 253:110723, 2024.
24. Juan Luis López Delgado, and Juan Antonio López Ramos. A comprehensive survey on generative ai solutions in IoT security. *Electronics*, 13(24):4965, 2024.
25. Pan Wang, Zixuan Wang, Feng Ye, and Xuejiao Chen. BytesGAN: A semi-supervised generative adversarial network for encrypted traffic classification in SDN edge gateway. *Computer Networks*, 200:108535, 2021.
26. Matheus P Novaes, Luiz F Carvalho, Jaime Lloret, and Mario Lemes Proença Jr. Adversarial deep learning approach detection and defense against DDoS attacks in SDN environments. *Future Generation Computer Systems*, 125:156–167, 2021.
27. Seyed Mohammad Hadi Mirsadeghi, Hayretdin Bahsi, Risto Vaarandi, and Wissem Inoubli. Learning from few cyber-attacks: Addressing the class imbalance problem in machine learning-based intrusion detection in software-defined networking. *IEEE Access*, 11:140428–140442, 2023.
28. Phan The Duy, Nghi Hoang Khoa, Hien Do Hoang, and Van-Hau Pham et al. Investigating on the robustness of flow-based intrusion detection system against adversarial samples using generative adversarial networks. *Journal of Information Security and Applications*, 74:103472, 2023.

29. Lixiang Yuan, Siyang Yu, Zhibang Yang, Mingxing Duan, and Kenli Li A data balancing approach based on generative adversarial network. *Future Generation Computer Systems*, 141:768–776, 2023.
30. Daniel M Brandão Lent, Vitor G Da Silva Ruffo, Luiz F Carvalho, Jaime Lloret, Joel JPC Rodrigues, and Mario Lemes Proença. An unsupervised generative adversarial network system to detect DDoS attacks in SDN. *IEEE Access*, 12:70690–70706, 2024.
31. Alexandro Marcelo Zacaron, Daniel Matheus Brandão Lent, Vitor Gabriel da Silva Ruffo, Luiz Fernando Carvalho, and Mario Lemes Proença Jr. Generative adversarial network models for anomaly detection in software-defined networks. *Journal of Network and Systems Management*, 32(4):93, 2024.
32. Syed Hussain Ali Kazmi, Rosilah Hassan, Faizan Qamar, Kashif Nisar, and Mohammed Azmi Al-Betar. Federated conditional variational auto encoders for cyber threat intelligence: Tackling non-iid data in SDN environments. *IEEE Access*, 13:2169–3536, 2025.
33. Bruck W Wubete, Babak Esfandiari, and Thomas Kunz. Machine learning approaches for predicting link failures in production networks. *Computer Networks*, 259:111098, 2025.
34. Diederik P Kingma, and Max Welling et al. An introduction to variational autoencoders. *Foundations and Trends in Machine Learning*, 12(4):307–392, 2019.
35. Diederik P Kingma. Auto-encoding variational bayes. *arXiv Preprint Arxiv: 1312.6114*, 2013.

Part III

Sector-specific use cases

Chapter 6

Adoption of artificial intelligence in smart cities

Literature review and bibliometric analysis

Taoufiq El Moussaoui, Chakir Loqman, and Alaa Eddine El Moussaoui

6.1 INTRODUCTION

A city is characterized by its high population density and clearly established boundaries, whose residents are mainly employed in non-farm activities like public Administration, finance, retail, manufacturing...[1]. Urban areas are characterized by dense human developments, including commercial properties, residential buildings, and roadways, and reflect a high degree of development. This urbanization significantly impacts the healthcare, environment, and privacy within cities. Consequently, the concept of "smart city" is becoming the usual pattern in principal city zones. Modern smart cities leverage a range of technologies, such as artificial intelligence (AI), Internet of Things (IoT), and sustainable infrastructure, to improve the quality of life and achieve long-term socioeconomic goals [2]. These advancements enable better resource management, improved public services, and increased citizen engagement. For example, smart grids improve energy efficiency, and intelligent transportation systems help minimize congestion and, consequently, emissions. Additionally, advanced healthcare technologies provide remote monitoring and telemedicine, improving access to medical services. Education benefits from digital platforms and personalized learning experiences, while smart security systems enhance public safety through real-time surveillance and predictive analytics. Numerous smart-city initiatives are being rolled out across various regions, showcasing a wide range of urban strategies and creating a rich tapestry of innovative approaches to urban living [3]. These projects highlight how smart cities can tackle modern urban challenges and open the way for resilient and sustainable development [4].

While AI drives significant urban transformations, it also presents numerous challenges. The ethical use of AI is a major concern, as biases in algorithms can lead to unfair outcomes. Additionally, the extensive data collection required for AI applications raises serious privacy issues, making data protection crucial. The risk of AI misuse, such as unauthorized surveillance or manipulation, further complicates its integration into smart cities [5]. AI systems must be designed with transparency and accountability to avoid biases and ensure fairness in decision-making processes. Robust security measures and clear regulations are

DOI: 10.1201/9781003597476-9

needed to safeguard citizens' personal information. Furthermore, the shift to AI-driven cities could worsen social inequalities and deepen the digital divide if not carefully managed. There is a risk that only those with access to digital literacy will benefit from AI advancements, leaving marginalized groups behind. It is crucial to address these issues thoughtfully, implementing inclusive policies and promoting the fair distribution of AI benefits.

This necessitates collaboration and cooperation between tech companies, civil society, and governments to create frameworks that promote responsible AI use and make certain that all citizens have equal access to and can benefit from developments in smart city technologies [6, 7].

Given the pivotal role of AI in smart cities, this chapter seeks to categorize and review scientific research on AI-related smart city issues. For this purpose, the authors have used a literature review to pinpoint the most pertinent studies and highlight new areas for future development. By meticulously analyzing a vast array of publications from reputable databases (Scopus and Web of Science), this study sheds light on the multifaceted role of AI in enhancing urban infrastructure, optimizing resource management, and improving public services. Ultimately, this article not only examines the current status of AI implementation in smart cities but also paves the way for future research that can ensure sustainable and equitable urban development.

The chapter is structured as follows: Section 6.2 presents the literature review, followed by the research methodology in Section 6.3. Section 6.4 reviews the results of our study and identifies areas where AI can be applied in smart cities. Section 6.5 summarizes the key findings. Finally, Section 6.6 presents the conclusions and outlines future research directions.

6.2 LITERATURE REVIEW

According to Dowling et al. [3], the growing expansion of the population has led to several problems concerning public safety, the environment, and urban management. To address these challenges, the concept of smart cities has emerged, leveraging information and communication technologies (ICT) to create more sustainable urban environments. Smart cities are being proposed and implemented across various countries as a solution to the complexities of modern urbanization [8, 9]. These cities utilize AI to create integrated solutions that enhance urban living [10, 11]. As highlighted by Herath et al. [5], the term "smart" lacks a consistent, universally accepted definition. Despite its widespread use, the term "smart" is often applied as a catch-all for anything perceived as modern and intelligent, encompassing qualities like perceptiveness, cleverness, astuteness, and speed [12]. The smart city concept emerged in the 1980s and was first used in the media [13]. According to Mustafa et al. [14], this concept is based on the notion of "intelligent cities". The aim is to manage existing resources in a more intelligent manner. Authors of [15] explained that this concept pertains to new businesses that leverage ICTs alongside urban environmental functions. Chourabi et al. [16] have defined it as the use of the city's collective intelligence through the connection of the city's physical, IT, social, and commercial infrastructures. In summary, the literature relating to smart cities converges on a common definition, which is the integration of various technologies to address complex urban challenges, enhancing efficiency, sustainability, and residents' overall quality of life.

Artificial intelligence (AI), a term coined in 1979 by John McCarthy (computer scientist), is defined as "the science and engineering of making intelligent machines" [17]. AI involves teaching and training computers to imitate human thought behaviors and processes, effectively simulating human intelligence. According to Yigitcanlar et al. [6], AI specializes in developing data-driven systems that enable computers or software to perform tasks and make decisions autonomously. Today, AI is deployed across entire cities, employing a broad range of technologies from rule-based systems to cutting-edge deep learning algorithms. These technologies are increasingly essential in delivering public services and enhancing efficiency and effectiveness in various sectors [18]. For example, Robotic Process Automation (RPA) is utilized to automate routine, repetitive, and high-cost tasks, thus conserving valuable resources and allowing human workers to focus on more complex activities [19]. As AI progresses, its applications in city management and public service delivery are set to expand, driving innovation and improving life quality in the smart city.

Significant advancements have been achieved across different sectors of smart cities, including intelligent transportation, cybersecurity, smart grids, digital twins, smart bins, living labs, and drones [20]. AI is pivotal in these areas, enhancing scalability and efficiency [21]. Machine Learning and Deep Learning technologies have been integrated into self-driving vehicles, safe travel, connected vehicle security, and efficient passenger services [22]. Their role in cybersecurity is also significant, impacting nearly every sector within a smart city [23]. Furthermore, AI is transforming consumption and energy generation in smart cities, demonstrating its extensive economic and societal benefits [24].

Autonomous vehicles are likewise viewed as a key innovation for modernizing public transportation systems, enhancing both efficiency and service delivery [25]. Concurrently, smart cities are adopting robotics in law enforcement to reduce conflict incidents and better utilize human resources, leading to improved safety and operational effectiveness [26]. AI's role in predicting and preventing incidents is also expanding. Cutting-edge crime detection systems employing neural networks and deep learning are being developed to provide accurate and timely insights into criminal activities [27]. Moreover, machine learning-based solutions are being introduced to foresee incidents and generate proactive responses [28]. As AI becomes more integrated into urban management, it can greatly improve urban safety, inclusivity, and sustainability, thereby significantly enhancing urban living conditions and addressing complex challenges [29].

Cities can utilize AI and associated technologies like machine learning and deep learning to analyze big data, enhance public services, and promote sustainability and resilience in urban environments. However, it is essential to address societal impacts, such as bias and information security. Ethical considerations are crucial to avoid potential pitfalls and ensure responsible AI integration. By aligning technological innovations with ethical standards, cities can achieve more inclusive and equitable development while safeguarding citizens' rights and well-being.

6.3 RESEARCH METHODOLOGY

Research on AI in smart cities has been meticulously analyzed using a bibliometric approach, which is particularly beneficial for well-established research areas and researchers new to the topic [30]. This approach allows for the detailed discovery, integration, and rigorous evaluation of numerous publications for a quantitative assessment of the existing situation and developmental patterns within the field [31]. By analyzing a vast array of publications, bibliometric analysis helps map the intellectual structure and dynamic evolution of AI research in smart cities. Quantitative techniques such as citation analysis, co-citation analysis, and keyword analysis facilitate the identification of influential works, major research themes, and collaboration patterns among researchers and institutions. These insights reveal key research areas, major trends, and developments in publication volume over time. Additionally, the analysis highlights the most prolific authors, journals, and countries showcasing leading contributors and influential publications. The historical perspective provided by citation patterns helps trace the development of specialized AI solutions in smart cities, including public safety, transportation systems, and energy-efficient building technologies, offering valuable context for understanding current trends and emerging areas of interest. Moreover, bibliometric analysis uncovers interdisciplinary connections, showing how AI research in smart cities intersects with urban planning, environmental science, and public policy. This interdisciplinary approach is crucial for addressing the complex challenges of smart city development, promoting a holistic understanding, and encouraging cross-disciplinary collaboration. Overall, bibliometric analysis of AI in smart cities provides a thorough overview of the field's development, identifying key research directions, trends, and contributors, thus supporting the progression of knowledge and the generation of innovative solutions for modern urban challenges.

As with any study based on a bibliometric analysis, it is necessary to define the research strategy. The two internationally renowned databases, Scopus and Web of Science, made it possible to select published articles (journal articles, book chapters, and conference papers) dealing with our topic. These papers should be written in English and published between 2019 and 2024. The research exclusion and inclusion criteria are detailed in Table 6.1.

Table 6.1 Criteria for selecting articles

Type	*Criteria*	*Explication*
Inclusion	The research title, keywords, and abstract should demonstrate that the adoption of AI in the smart city is the research subject.	Research is not restricted to specific scientific journals. It is important to ensure that only articles that clearly address the adoption of AI in the smart city are reviewed.
Inclusion	The article must be written in English.	English is the dominant language in research relating to the adoption of AI in the smart city.
Inclusion	The article must be published in well-ranked international scientific journals.	Only articles published in peer-reviewed scientific journals will be reviewed to maintain the quality of this research.
Exclusion	Research focusing only on AI or smart cities is excluded.	Our literature review focuses mainly on the adoption of AI in the smart city. Papers dealing with only one of the concepts are not included.

The process of research was carried out using a methodology comprising four phases.

- We initially selected the articles to assess current advancements in the theme and identify any gaps in the literature. As the chapter aims to provide a detailed survey of the adoption of AI in smart cities, the authors chose a number of keywords, such as: *"AI"*, *"smart city"*, *"artificial intelligence"*, and *"smart cities"*.
- The second step enables us to examine the number of articles, citations, year of publication, etc., found in the databases. The number of articles identified is shown in Table 6.2. To avoid any potential inconsistencies and articles that were incompatible with our theme, we examined all the articles using the following process:
  - **Scopus database:** papers searched with the expressions, outlined in Table 6.2, were imported into a spreadsheet (Excel), from which duplicates and articles that did not refer to *"AI and Smart City"*,

Table 6.2 Search keywords

Combination of keywords	*Scopus*	*Web of science*
"AI" AND "Smart City"	198	163
"AI" AND "Smart Cities"	176	154
"Artificial Intelligence" AND "Smart City"	234	191
"Artificial Intelligence" AND "Smart Cities"	223	175
Total	831	683

"AI and Smart Cities", *"Artificial Intelligence and Smart City"*, or *"Artificial Intelligence and Smart Cities"* were deleted. Following this elimination activity, 831 articles were retained.

- **Web of Science database:** papers searched with the sentences, shown in Table 6.2, were imported into a spreadsheet (Excel), from which duplicates and articles that did not refer to *"AI and Smart City"*, *"AI and Smart Cities"*, *"Artificial Intelligence and Smart City"*, or *"Artificial Intelligence and Smart Cities"* were deleted. As a result of this elimination activity, 683 papers were retained.

- All the articles retained enabled us to carry out a descriptive analysis (authors, citations, journals, and countries) and a methodological analysis (theoretical and conceptual article, literature review, case study, modeling, and simulation) as well as an analysis of the thematic issue.
- The last phase provides findings based on the research question and suggests some potential directions for future research.

6.4 RESULTS

The study commenced with a review to assess the increasing focus on the topic over time and to identify major categories of publications and their connections to major domains identified in the two databases. From 2018 to 2024, there was a notable increase in publications in both databases, highlighting the rise of AI in smart cities as a significant theme. Prior to this period, there were few publications on the subject (Figure 6.1).

Most of the 1514 publications were journal articles and conference papers, as detailed in Figure 6.2.

The journal papers were published in 73 journals. As Table 6.3 shows, *"Sustainable cities and Society"* is the dominant journal, followed by *"Sustainability"* and *"Smart Cities"*. In total, 47 journals published only one relevant article. It is interesting to note that the journals have multiple orientations: computer science, sustainability, and geography.

With 47 publications, Tan Yigitcanlar leads the list of the most prolific authors. His most cited article is "Can cities become smart without being sustainable? A systematic review of the literature" [32], which was published in 2019 (710 citations). Next is Fadi Al-Turjman with 43 publications. His most cited piece in this field was "Applications of artificial intelligence and machine learning in smart cities" [23], published in Computer Communications in 2020, with 630 citations. The ten most prolific authors are shown in Figure 6.3. In terms of geographical distribution, as shown in Figure 6.4, China leads with 371 publications, followed by India with 294 and the USA with 269.

To clearly present the results obtained, we have tried to extract the keywords recurrently linked to the theme of AI in smart cities (search keywords are not included). A thorough examination of the top keywords uncovered seven distinct thematic categories.

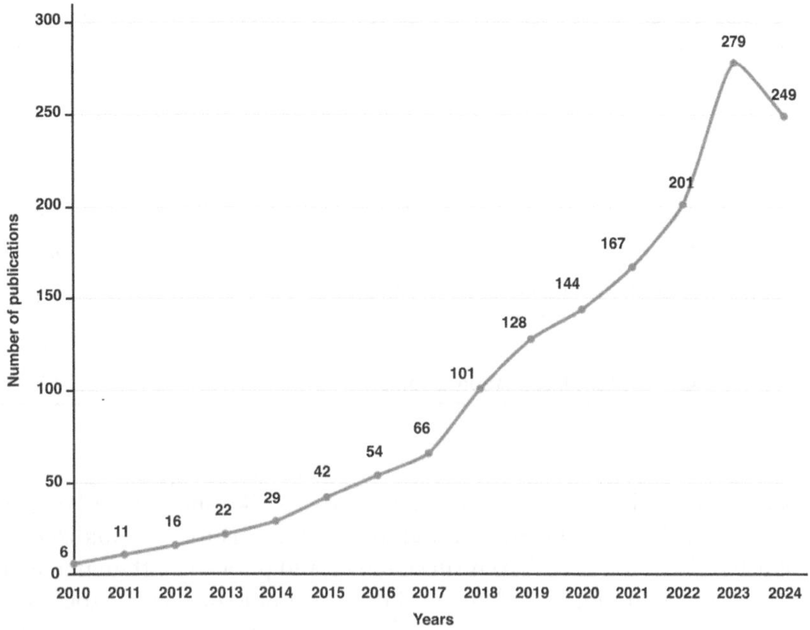

Figure 6.1 Number of papers selected per year.

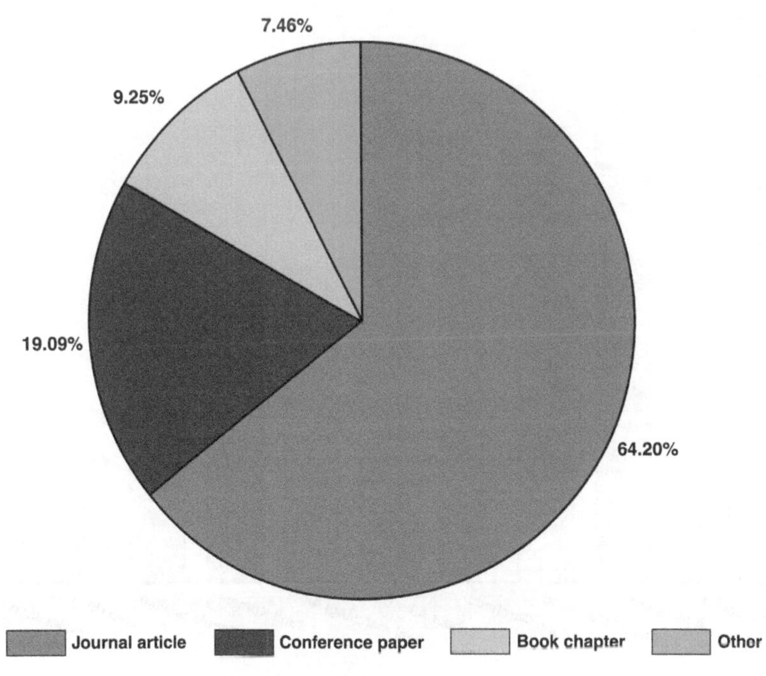

Figure 6.2 Distribution of the selected papers.

Table 6.3 Ranking of most productive journals

Ranking	*Journal*	*Number of articles*
1	Sustainable cities and society	92
2	Sustainability	88
3	Smart cities	73
4	Cities	69
5	IEEE Access	63
6	Energies	42
7	Engineering Management in Production and Service	31
8	Microprocessors and Microsystems	28
9	Sensors	15
10	Government Information Quarterly	13

The first cluster, "*Health*" focuses on AI solutions designed to keep residents of smart cities healthy. It includes concepts like smart health systems, enhanced healthcare services, and digital health twins for personalized care. The cluster also covers AI-driven surveillance and public health management, especially for handling pandemics. These technologies work together to ensure that smart cities can provide efficient, proactive healthcare and maintain the overall well-being of their populations.

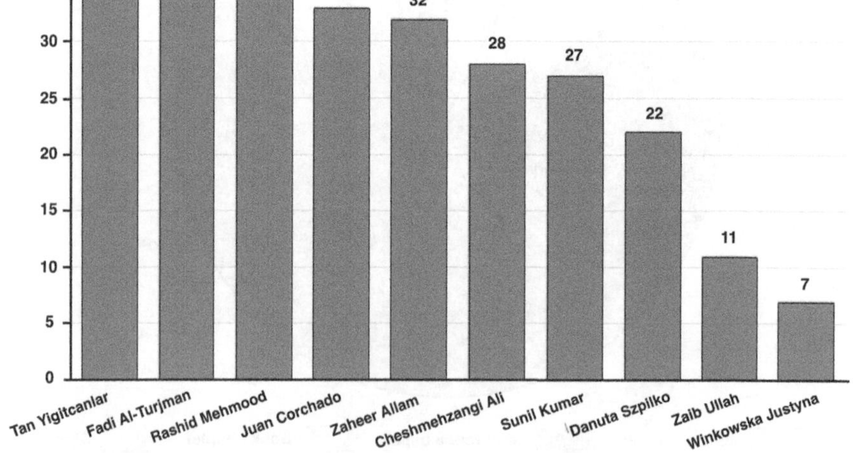

Figure 6.3 Ranking of most productive authors.

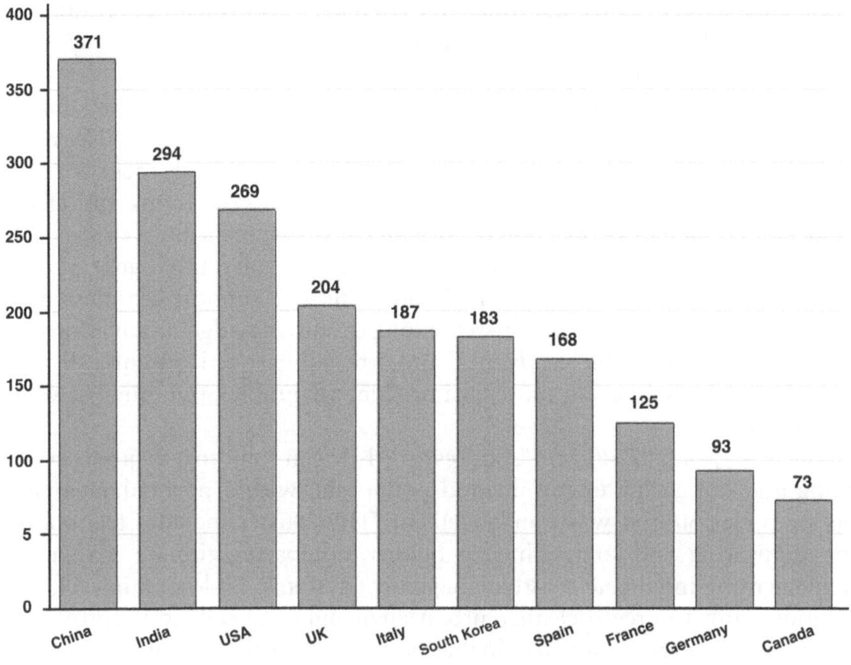

Figure 6.4 Geographical distribution of publications.

The second group, entitled *"Living"*, focuses on leveraging AI to improve residents' quality of life in the smart city. This group emphasizes creating a sustainable and integrated environment where AI impacts multiple facets of urban life. Keywords include the sharing economy, smart homes, and smart communities that promote connectivity and efficiency. The concept extends to smart education, smart government, and smart buildings, all designed to improve residents' daily experiences. Additionally, attention is given to air quality, disaster management, and urban strategies that adhere to sustainability standards and promote well-being. The vision of Society 5.0 and Smart City 5.0 encapsulates this holistic approach, aiming to create resilient, future-oriented urban environments that prioritize both individual and collective well-being.

The third group labeled *"Security"*, focuses on the various domains where AI can enhance safety and protection in smart cities. This group covers crucial topics, including critical areas such as privacy and public safety, emphasizing the significance of cybersecurity measures against threats like cyberattacks. AI is also instrumental in protecting data privacy and ensuring secure data management in both e-commerce and e-government services. Additionally, the application of AI extends to smart infrastructure, smart services, and the management of public data and transparent governance initiatives. Ethical considerations and trust are central to this group, highlighting the balance between technological advancement and responsible governance in smart city development.

The fourth group titled *"Transportation"*, centers on creating innovative mobility solutions that not only enhance efficiency but also reduce greenhouse gas emissions, particularly CO_2. This cluster focuses on the advancement of sophisticated vehicles, including autonomous and electric models, and includes concepts like intelligent transportation systems, smart mobility, and traffic control. Key technologies involve intelligent parking, smart transport networks, and ICT integration to support seamless urban mobility. Additionally, the cluster explores cutting-edge innovations like autonomous aerial vehicles, drones, and other unmanned systems, all aimed at making transportation more sustainable, adaptable, and efficient within smart cities.

The fifth group *"Pollution"*, addresses AI-driven solutions focused on managing and mitigating environmental pollutants, with a particular emphasis on air pollution and waste management. This cluster includes technologies for monitoring and controlling air quality, combating climate change, and implementing intelligent waste management systems. By leveraging AI, these solutions aim to create cleaner urban environments, reduce harmful emissions, and promote more sustainable practices in waste handling and pollution control within smart cities.

The sixth group *"Industry"*, explores the role of AI in advancing Industry 4.0 while promoting environmental friendly production. This includes concepts like the circular economy, RFID technology, and intelligent manufacturing. Despite its potential, this field is relatively new and has not yet received widespread recognition in existing research, signaling an emerging area with significant opportunities for further exploration and development.

The final group labeled *"Energy"*, focuses on AI-driven technological solutions that optimize the generation, storage, and management of energy in a secure and efficient manner, with a strong emphasis on sustainability. This includes harnessing renewable energy sources and integrating them into smart energy systems that ensure reliable supply and distribution. Key areas within this group involve sustainable energy practices, smart grids that enhance energy efficiency, and advanced energy procurement strategies. AI plays a crucial role in streamlining these processes, enabling better prediction, automation, and control, thereby facilitating the shift toward a more sustainable energy infrastructure in smart cities.

6.5 DISCUSSION

This bibliometric analysis revealed seven thematic areas in AI research for smart cities, encompassing diverse topics such as computer science and engineering.

6.5.1 Health

In smart cities, the integration of AI with healthcare systems is driving transformative changes in how health services are delivered, managed, and optimized, marking a pivotal shift in urban living. This convergence enables enhanced health and well-being by facilitating more precise and data-driven healthcare management processes while significantly improving disease control and prevention strategies. Key developments within this context include the advent of digital twin technology, which involves the creation of digital replicas of living entities, allowing for real-time monitoring and predictive analysis that enhance treatment precision and proactive health management. Digital twins are revolutionizing personalized medicine, enabling tailored healthcare interventions and more accurate simulations of patient outcomes, thus minimizing risks and optimizing resource allocation. Additionally, the confluence of GeoAI, which combines geographical information systems (GIS) with AI, provides new dimensions in spatial health analytics, allowing for better tracking and management of disease outbreaks, environmental health risks, and population health trends within urban spaces. GeoAI-powered platforms can predict the spread of infectious diseases, optimize healthcare facility locations, and enhance emergency response strategies by analyzing spatial data patterns. This synergy between AI, digital twin technology, and GeoAI creates a more resilient and responsive urban healthcare ecosystem, where real-time data and predictive insights lead to proactive health interventions, improved access to care, and more efficient resource management. By embedding these advanced AI-driven technologies into the healthcare infrastructure of smart cities, a more connected, efficient, and patient-centered health service landscape is emerging, reflecting the broader evolution of smart cities toward a holistic approach that prioritizes the well-being of citizens. As cities continue to expand and populations grow, this seamless integration of AI and healthcare not only transforms individual care but also enhances public health outcomes on a large scale, reinforcing the foundation of smarter, healthier urban environments.

The COVID-19 pandemic has underscored the pivotal role of digital solutions in healthcare, marking a significant shift toward data-driven smart city models [33]. The diverse strategies employed by governments during the pandemic illustrate the effectiveness of AI in managing health crises. Technologies such as digital tracking and predictive analytics have been instrumental in identifying and isolating infected individuals, thereby enhancing public health responses. However, these techno-led approaches have also led to concerns about potential overreach, including the suppression and censorship of dissenting opinions. This dual aspect of technology—its capability to control outbreaks and its potential to infringe on civil liberties—highlights the importance of understanding the complex relationship between technology and human behavior. To effectively manage virus transmission and maintain public trust during future pandemics, a balanced approach that considers both technological benefits and ethical implications is essential [34].

6.5.2 Living

Globally, urbanization has increasingly pressured daily life, driving the need for solutions to environmental pollution, public safety, and traffic congestion. Smart cities aim to address these challenges by leveraging innovative technologies and modern concepts to create more efficient, advanced, and inclusive urban environments [35]. Key to this effort is the integration of AI and the IoT, which are essential for optimizing urban systems and improving quality of life through data analysis [36]. The smart home concept, as part of smart cities, further enhances urban living by incorporating technologies such as big data and cloud computing [37]. AI-powered IoT has proven particularly effective in addressing contemporary issues, including the COVID-19 pandemic, where SDL-based intelligent health diagnostics played a crucial role. Additionally, AIoT systems have improved safety and air quality monitoring in smart homes, advancing hazard detection and overall urban safety [38].

In smart cities, the application of AI has significantly advanced, enhancing the way humans interact with technology and addressing critical challenges related to data management [39]. One key area of improvement is the optimization of human-machine interactions, where AI systems are designed to be more intuitive and responsive to user needs. This includes the development of smarter interfaces and more efficient communication channels between citizens and urban systems, making technology more accessible and user-friendly. Additionally, AI addresses the problem of repetition in the spatio-temporal environmental data collected across urban areas. Traditional data collection methods often produce large volumes of overlapping or repetitive information, which can lead to inefficiencies and hinder effective analysis. AI algorithms are now employed to filter, aggregate, and analyze this data more effectively, reducing redundancy and enhancing the quality and usefulness of the information.

AI has increasingly extended its reach beyond smart homes, influencing sectors like logistics and healthcare [40]. This expansion is evident in living labs, which integrate AI to enhance data processing, analysis, and prediction, fostering the development of innovative urban services [41]. AI, coupled with IoT and big data, is also transforming urban environmental planning by enabling the modeling of future scenarios, helping cities anticipate and manage environmental challenges more effectively. However, despite these advancements, challenges remain, especially in maintaining privacy and ensuring reliable data-sharing practices. Furthermore, socio-legal conflicts arise when individual rights and public interests collide, highlighting the urgent need for balanced, clear guidelines that align technological progress with ethical principles [42]. Addressing these issues is critical for maximizing AI's potential in urban settings while safeguarding social values.

6.5.3 Security

AI has significantly evolved, transforming the design and construction of smart cities and enhancing urban living [43]. It addresses security and privacy challenges in urban settings [10], with applications ranging from the management of traffic to city-wide surveillance [23]. AI technologies, including integrated microelectronic systems for smart textiles (STIMES), improve service quality and safety protocols. Machine learning, a key component of AI, has also advanced healthcare services, benefiting both city residents and management [44].

The rapid expansion of the IoT has resulted in massive data flows, which pose significant security and privacy challenges. Centralization and resource constraints further complicate the deployment and effectiveness of AI-driven systems [45]. To counter these issues, blockchain technology offers a decentralized solution that enhances security by distributing control and reducing vulnerabilities [46]. Another promising approach is federated learning, which enables AI models to be trained across distributed IoT devices without the need to share raw data, thus preserving data privacy and security. Despite these advances, the integration of AI and blockchain in smart cities has introduced new security concerns that need further investigation. The proliferation of IoT devices, combined with evolving cyber threats, necessitates more sophisticated and adaptive security measures [47]. Innovative strategies, such as Holistic Big Data Integrated Artificial Intelligence Modelling (HBDIAIM), are being developed to tackle these challenges by enhancing scalability and ensuring better privacy in smart city data management systems [48]. These solutions aim to create a more secure and efficient data management framework in the face of emerging threats and technological advancements. Protecting privacy within the vast amounts of high-dimensional data generated by IoT appliances is difficult [43]. To address this issue, authors of the study [49] recommend using encrypted data storage on cloud platforms, which ensures secure, remote access while protecting sensitive information. Another approach proposed by [50] involves conducting model learning on data stored locally, thus reducing the risks associated with data transmission and centralization. However, addressing privacy concerns in AI applications also requires considering cultural, metabolic, and governance factors. This necessitates a nuanced approach that balances the use of advanced technology to drive economic growth with the imperative to maintain urban livability and address diverse community needs. Integrating these considerations ensures that privacy protections are effectively managed while leveraging technological advancements for the benefit of smart cities.

6.5.4 Transportation

AI has revolutionized mobility in smart cities, significantly enhancing transportation systems and promoting sustainability [51, 52]. Central to this shift is the rise of autonomous vehicles, which represent a major milestone in urban transportation. AI-driven technologies enable the modeling of queuing networks, reduction of journey times, and improvement of overall user experience, resulting in more efficient and effective urban mobility [53, 54]. As these advancements unfold, the importance of robust cybersecurity measures grows. Integrating blockchain technology and smart detection systems is critical to ensuring the reliability of autonomous transportation networks [55–57]. Additionally, AI-powered sensor information fusion systems are enhancing how citizens understand and interact with mobility frameworks, leading to better transportation models that align with evolving urban needs [1]. These integrated technologies are paving the way for smarter, more sustainable cities where transportation is not just faster but also safer and more adaptive to the needs of the urban population.

In the context of mobility, electrically powered vehicles also play a pivotal role in advancing environmental friendly initiatives within smart cities, where significant investments are made to enhance urban transportation sustainability. AI is key to this transformation, as it optimizes energy consumption and facilitates predictive maintenance for electric vehicles, ensuring they operate efficiently with minimal downtime [58]. AI-driven systems enable these vehicles to manage energy resources more effectively, from intelligent charging to dynamic route optimization that reduces congestion and energy waste. Beyond ground transportation, drones are emerging as versatile tools for enhancing urban mobility [59]. Equipped with AI technology, they offer promising solutions for tasks like wireless communication coverage and aerial surveillance, contributing to more connected smart cities [23]. AI enhances drone navigation, enabling them to adapt to complex urban landscapes and perform real-time monitoring, making them invaluable for traffic management and rapid response in emergency situations [60]. Together, the integration of AI in electric vehicles and drones marks a significant step forward in creating a more efficient and adaptive mobility ecosystem within smart cities.

Mobility as a Service (MaaS) also represents a key innovation in urban mobility, integrating various transportation modes into a unified digital platform where users can seamlessly plan, book, and pay for their journeys [61]. AI-powered MaaS platforms facilitate dynamic pricing, congestion management, and even sustainable transportation choices by recommending eco-friendly options based on user preferences. As cities aim for smarter growth, the combination of AI and MaaS is instrumental in reducing traffic congestion, improving accessibility, and fostering a more connected and sustainable urban transportation ecosystem.

6.5.5 Pollution

Air, noise, and waste pollution are among the critical challenges linked to urban expansion, with significant impacts on residents' well-being due to the stress caused by industrial activities and heavy traffic [62]. Emerging technologies, such as AI, present innovative approaches to effectively manage and reduce these pollutants, thus enhancing urban living standards [63]. Predictive models play a pivotal role in this context; deep learning algorithms have demonstrated remarkable success in forecasting traffic flows at critical intersections, enabling real-time adjustments that alleviate congestion and reduce vehicle emissions [64]. These technological solutions not only optimize traffic management but also contribute to more sustainable urban environments by addressing pollution sources at the core.

AI is increasingly recognized for its transformative potential in waste management, offering solutions that optimize waste collection, minimize overflow risks, and enhance recycling processes, all of which significantly contribute to improving urban environmental quality [35]. For instance, smart bins equipped with sensors provide real-time data on their fill levels, allowing for more efficient waste collection routes and schedules, thereby reducing operational costs and environmental impact [65]. Moreover, AI-driven systems enable predictive analyses that allow cities to forecast waste generation patterns and plan more effectively for disposal and storage needs, ultimately leading to better resource management. Despite these advantages, the widespread adoption of AI in waste management faces several challenges, including inadequate infrastructure, cybersecurity vulnerabilities, limited funding, and public skepticism toward relying on such technologies. Addressing these hurdles is crucial for fully leveraging AI's capabilities to create cleaner, more efficient urban environments, and, consequently, a sustainable smart city.

6.5.6 Industry

AI is reshaping multiple sectors within smart cities, but the transition to Industry 4.0 presents complex challenges, particularly in cloud-based data storage, processing, and communication. One of the primary concerns lies in maintaining data confidentiality and managing transmission delays, both of which are critical for efficient industrial operations. Blockchain technology has emerged as a promising solution to these challenges due to its decentralized and transparent nature, offering enhanced security and trust in data management [66]. In the industrial domain, AI has become central to the development of intelligent systems that not only automate decision-making but also increase the flexibility and responsiveness of physical processes. These AI-driven systems are designed to adapt quickly to the evolving demands of global markets, enabling industries to optimize production, enhance operational efficiency, and remain competitive in an increasingly dynamic environment [67]. The integration of AI and blockchain in Industry 4.0 not only addresses technical challenges but also paves the way for smarter, more resilient industrial ecosystems within smart cities.

In the context of Industry 4.0, AI is revolutionizing various sectors by enhancing efficiency and service quality. One significant application is in water management, where AI systems have proven highly effective in monitoring and tracking water consumption with a recognition accuracy of around 97% [68]. This precision not only supports more sustainable resource management but also optimizes consumption patterns. Moreover, AI-driven robots are increasingly being integrated into the restaurant and hospitality industries, where they deliver personalized customer services and streamline operations [69]. These advancements include automating tasks, customizing service experiences based on user preferences, and facilitating smoother customer interactions. As a result, businesses can significantly reduce operational costs while elevating service standards [70]. The fusion of AI with robotics in these sectors not only meets the evolving demands of consumers but also aligns with broader trends toward automation and intelligent systems, further solidifying the role of AI as a key enabler in smart city ecosystems [71–73]. This ongoing transformation reflects the broader impact of AI in driving innovation, sustainability, and efficiency across industries, making it indispensable in the future of urban living.

6.5.7 Energy

AI is fundamentally transforming smart cities, yet energy management remains one of the most pressing challenges that necessitates advanced technological integration for greater efficiency. The complexity of energy systems has driven the adoption of machine learning as a primary solution, especially with neural network models and meta-heuristic algorithms being applied to predict and optimize heating loads in energy-efficient buildings. These models enhance the precision of energy forecasts and enable adaptive energy adjustments, thereby supporting more sustainable consumption patterns. Deep reinforcement learning algorithms further accelerate this transformation by providing automated energy controllers that adapt dynamically to real-time demands, ultimately optimizing energy savings and improving demand response strategies. In addition to these, non-intrusive load monitoring system and smart power metering, combined with algorithms of the hybrid type such as GA-SVM-MKL, are demonstrating the significance of energy consumption in smart cities, driving progress toward sustainable development [74]. AI's role expands beyond consumption optimization; it is pivotal in advancing renewable energy adoption within smart cities. Tools like artificial neural networks (ANNs) and statistical models not only enhance the accuracy of electrical consumption forecasts but also promote the integration of renewable energy sources. AI-driven predictive models are also essential for short-term photovoltaic (PV) energy generation forecasting, which is critical for balancing energy supply and demand. Moreover, AI technologies optimize energy use in specialized infrastructure systems like Automated Vacuum Waste Collection (AVWC), which significantly reduces waste-related energy inefficiencies, and in Building Energy Management Systems (BEMSs) that monitor and optimize energy consumption in real-time [75]. AI applications extend to enhancing the efficiency of critical urban infrastructure such as sewage treatment and waste management systems, areas often overlooked but vital to the overall energy ecosystem of smart cities. These AI-driven advancements are integral to transforming energy management practices in smart cities, ensuring that they evolve toward smarter, more sustainable, and resilient urban environments where energy resources are managed with optimal precision and minimal waste. The ongoing integration of these AI solutions is thus critical for

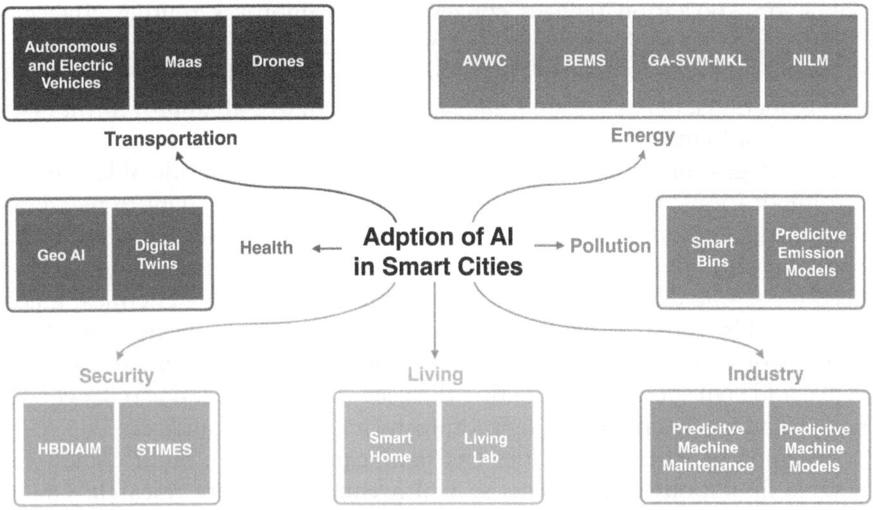

Figure 6.5 Conceptual framework for AI adoption in smart cities.

building smarter, energy-efficient cities that can respond adaptively to emerging challenges while meeting the growing demands of urban populations.

The discussion of the results has led us to propose a conceptual framework that researchers can use when studying the adoption of AI in smart cities (Figure 6.5).

6.6 CONCLUSION

The study provides a bibliometric analysis of 1514 articles on the adoption of AI in smart cities. The analysis identified seven key research areas: health, living, security, mobility, pollution, industry, and energy. The implications, limitations, and potential directions for subsequent research are discussed below.

The implementation of AI in smart cities contributes to theoretical advancements by expanding our understanding of urban systems and their complexities. It provides new frameworks for analyzing how AI can optimize city functions, from transportation and energy management to public safety and governance. AI-driven models help build theories on human-machine interaction, data-driven decision-making, and the dynamic relationships between urban environments and technological infrastructures. These advancements contribute to the broader discourse on digital transformation and urban sustainability, offering insights into how emerging technologies can shape future cities.

On a practical level, AI adoption in smart cities enhances operational efficiency and service delivery. AI systems enable predictive analysis and real-time control, improving traffic management, waste disposal, and energy use. For instance, AI-driven smart grids enhance energy allocation, while AI in public transportation reduces congestion and improves routing efficiency. Additionally, AI applications in environmental monitoring help cities address pollution and climate-related challenges. The practical benefits of AI include cost reductions, better resource allocation, and an overall improvement in the standard of living for city dwellers.

The integration of AI in the smart city also provides considerable managerial implications. City planners and administrators must adapt to managing data-driven, automated systems, which require new governance structures and skill sets. The shift toward AI-driven decision-making emphasizes the need for strong data governance, cybersecurity measures, and ethical guidelines to address issues like privacy. Additionally, the management of AI systems involves cross-sector collaboration between government, private tech firms, and civil society, highlighting the need for effective stakeholder coordination and leadership in the digital transformation of urban areas.

Adoption of AI in smart cities has significant potential, but it comes with notable limitations and presents several avenues for future research. One of the primary limitations lies in the scope of the databases used for bibliometric analysis, such as Scopus and Web of Science, which might exclude relevant studies from other academic sources, resulting in a selection bias that impacts the comprehensiveness of the review. Additionally, focusing on a specific time frame can leave out critical insights from earlier or newly emerging studies, reducing the applicability of the findings in capturing the entire evolution of AI in smart cities. Another constraint is the generalization inherent in bibliometric analysis, which is predominantly quantitative and often fails to incorporate qualitative perspectives, theoretical depth, or context-specific variations across different regions. Furthermore, given the rapid pace of technological advancements, some insights may quickly become outdated, limiting their relevance as new AI technologies and urban challenges emerge. The interdisciplinary nature of AI in smart cities, involving fields like urban planning, data science, and public policy, adds complexity to integrating diverse perspectives, creating gaps in how these technologies can be applied cohesively across sectors.

Looking ahead, future research should explore the integration of cutting-edge innovations, such as 5G and quantum computing in the smart city, examining how these advancements intersect with AI to develop an efficient urban system. Longitudinal studies could provide a more comprehensive understanding of how AI adoption in smart cities evolves over time, offering insights into both the immediate and extended effects on urban development. Comparative case studies across different cities and regions could reveal best practices and localized challenges, offering a nuanced understanding of AI implementation in diverse urban contexts. Ethical considerations, including data privacy, surveillance concerns, and the socio-legal implications of AI deployment, represent another critical area for future exploration, particularly in developing guidelines for policymakers and stakeholders. The sustainability dimension of AI, often referred to as "green AI", also requires more focused research to assess how AI can contribute to environmental goals in smart cities, for example, by promoting climate resilience, improving energy consumption, and managing resources efficiently. Future studies should also consider models for effective stakeholder collaboration, exploring frameworks that enable public-private partnerships, community engagement, and cross-sector cooperation in AI-driven urban transformation. By addressing these limitations and advancing these research directions, scholars and practitioners can better understand the complex dynamics of AI in smart cities, establishing the groundwork for more inclusive, sustainable, and ethically sound urban environments.

REFERENCES

1. Szpilko, D., Naharro, F. J., Lăzăroiu, G., Nica, E., de la, T., & Gallegos, A. (2023). Artificial intelligence in the smart city—a literature review. Engineering Management in Production and Services, 15(4), 53–75.
2. Allam, M., & Khan, I. R. (2022). Application of AI in Smart Cities. In Industrial Transformation (pp. 61–86). CRC Press.
3. Dowling, R., McGuirk, P., & Gillon, C. (2019). Strategic or piecemeal? Smart city initiatives in Sydney and Melbourne. Urban Policy and Research, 37(4), 429–441.
4. Wolniak, R., & Stecuła, K. (2024). Artificial intelligence in smart cities—Applications, barriers, and future directions: A review. Smart Cities, 7(3), 1346–1389.
5. Herath, H. M. K. K. M. B., & Mittal, M. (2022). Adoption of artificial intelligence in smart cities: A comprehensive review. International Journal of Information Management Data Insights, 2(1), 100076.
6. Yigitcanlar, T., Mehmood, R., & Corchado, J. M. (2021). Green artificial intelligence: Towards an efficient, sustainable and equitable technology for smart cities and futures. Sustainability, 13(16), 8952.
7. Xia, L., Semirumi, D. T., & Rezaei, R. (2023). A thorough examination of smart city applications: Exploring challenges and solutions throughout the life cycle with emphasis on safeguarding citizen privacy. Sustainable Cities and Society, 98, 104771.
8. Szpilko, D., Szydło, J., & Winkowska, J. (2020). Social participation of city inhabitants versus their future orientation. Evidence from Poland. WSEAS Transactions on Business and Economics, 17, 692–702.
9. Al-Turjman, F., & Baali, I. (2022). Machine learning for wearable IoT-based applications: A survey. Transactions on Emerging Telecommunications Technologies, 33(8), e3635.
10. Allam, Z., & Dhunny, Z. A. (2019). On big data, artificial intelligence and smart cities. Cities, 89, 80–91.
11. Bilan, S., Suler, P., Skrynnyk, O. V., Krajnakova, E., & Vasylieva, T. A. (2022). Systematic bibliometric review of artificial intelligence technology in organizational management, development, change and culture.
12. Gil-Garcia, J. R., Helbig, N., & Ojo, A. (2014). Being smart: Emerging technologies and innovation in the public sector. Government Information Quarterly, 31, I1–I8.
13. Liu, Z., & Wu, J. (2023). A review of the theory and practice of smart city construction in China. Sustainability, 15(9), 7161.
14. Mustafa, S. Z., & Kar, A. K. (2017). Management of Multidimensional Risk for Digital Services in Smart Cities. In Advances in Smart Cities (pp. 149–165). Chapman and Hall/CRC Press.

15. Sterbenz, J. P. (2017, September). Smart city and IoT resilience, survivability, and disruption tolerance: Challenges, modelling, and a survey of research opportunities. In 2017 9th International Workshop on Resilient Networks Design and Modeling (RNDM) (pp. 1–6). IEEE.
16. Chourabi, H., Nam, T., Walker, S., Gil-Garcia, J. R., Mellouli, S., Nahon, K., & Scholl, H. J. (2012, January). Understanding smart cities: An integrative framework. In 2012 45th Hawaii International Conference on System Sciences (pp. 2289–2297). IEEE.
17. Mathur, S., & Modani, U. S. (2016, March). Smart city—a gateway for artificial intelligence in India. In 2016 IEEE Students' Conference on Electrical, Electronics and Computer Science (SCEECS) (pp. 1–3). IEEE.
18. Ma, Y., Ping, K., Wu, C., Chen, L., Shi, H., & Chong, D. (2020). Artificial intelligence powered internet of things and smart public service. Library Hi Tech, 38(1), 165–179.
19. Siderska, J., & Alsaqoor, S. (2023). Employees' attitudes towards implementing robotic process automation technology at service companies. Human Technology, 19(1), 23–40.
20. Allam, Z., & Newman, P. (2018). Redefining the smart city: Culture, metabolism and governance. Smart Cities, 1(1), 4–25.
21. Ferdowsi, A., Challita, U., & Saad, W. (2019). Deep learning for reliable mobile edge analytics in intelligent transportation systems: An overview. IEEE Vehicular Technology Magazine, 14(1), 62–70.
22. Ang, K. L. M., Seng, J. K. P., Ngharamike, E., & Ijemaru, G. K. (2022). Emerging technologies for smart cities' transportation: Geo-information, data analytics and machine learning approaches. ISPRS International Journal of Geo-Information, 11(2), 85.
23. Ullah, Z., Al-Turjman, F., Mostarda, L., & Gagliardi, R. (2020). Applications of artificial intelligence and machine learning in smart cities. Computer Communications, 154, 313–323.
24. Golinska-Dawson, P., & Sethanan, K. (2023). Sustainable urban freight for energy-efficient smart cities—Systematic literature review. Energies, 16(6), 2617.
25. El Moussaoui, A. E., Benbba, B., El Andaloussi, Z., & Jaegler, A. (2022). Logistique urbaine au Maroc: Concepts, état des lieux et pistes d'amélioration. Revue Française De Gestion Industrielle, 36(2), 71–88.
26. Ma, M., Stankovic, J. A., & Feng, L. (2018, April). Cityresolver: A decision support system for conflict resolution in smart cities. In 2018 ACM/IEEE 9th International Conference on Cyber-Physical Systems (ICCPS) (pp. 55–64). IEEE.
27. El Moussaoui, T., Loqman, C., & Boumhidi, J. (2025). Decoding legal processes: AI-driven system to streamline processing of the criminal records in Moroccan courts. Intelligent Systems with Applications, 25, 200487.
28. Aqib, M., Mehmood, R., Alzahrani, A., & Katib, I. (2020). In-memory deep learning computations on GPUs for prediction of road traffic incidents using big data fusion. Smart Infrastructure and Applications: Foundations for Smarter Cities and Societies, 79–114.
29. Choudhary, P., & Sarthy, P. (2022, January). Transforming cities for sustainability: Role of standards on smart City. In 2022 2nd International Conference on Power Electronics & IoT Applications in Renewable Energy and its Control (PARC) (pp. 1–6). IEEE.
30. Winkowska, J., Szpilko, D., & Pejić, S. (2019). Smart city concept in the light of the literature review. Engineering Management in Production and Services, 11(2), 70–86.
31. Bornmann, L., & Haunschild, R. (2017). Quality and impact considerations in bibliometrics: A reply to ricker (in press). Scientomet-Rics, 111, 1857–1859.

32. Yigitcanlar, T., Kamruzzaman, M., Foth, M., Sabatini-Marques, J., Da Costa, E., & Ioppolo, G. (2019). Can cities become smart without being sustainable? A systematic review of the literature. Sustainable Cities and Society, 45, 348–365.
33. Hantrais, L., Allin, P., Kritikos, M., Sogomonjan, M., Anand, P. B., Livingstone, S., & Innes, M. (2021). Covid-19 and the digital revolution. Contemporary Social Science, 16(2), 256–270.
34. Kummitha, R. K. R. (2020). Smart technologies for fighting pandemics: The techno-and human-driven approaches in controlling the virus transmission. Government Information Quarterly, 37(3), 101481.
35. Ghazal, T. M., Hasan, M. K., Alshurideh, M. T., Alzoubi, H. M., Ahmad, M., Akbar, S. S., & Akour, I. A. (2021). IoT for smart cities: Machine learning approaches in smart healthcare—A review. Future Internet, 13(8), 218.
36. Atitallah, S. B., Driss, M., Boulila, W., & Ghézala, H. B. (2020). Leveraging deep learning and IoT big data analytics to support the smart cities development: Review and future directions. Computer Science Review, 38, 100303.
37. Li, W., Yigitcanlar, T., Liu, A., & Erol, I. (2022). Mapping two decades of smart home research: A systematic scientometric analysis. Technological Forecasting and Social Change, 179, 121676.
38. Chang, C. Y., Ko, K. S., Guo, S. J., Hung, S. S., & Lin, Y. T. (2020). CO multi-forecasting model for indoor health and safety management in smart home. Journal of Internet Technology, 21(1), 273–284.
39. Jiang, Y., Xiao, W., Wang, R., & Barnawi, A. (2019). Smart urban living: Enabling emotion-guided interaction with next generation sensing fabric. IEEE Access, 8, 28395–28402.
40. El Moussaoui, T., Chakir, L., & El Moussaoui, A. E. (2025). Exploring Information Technology (IT) Acceptance among Supply Chain Stakeholders in Morocco's Pharmaceutical Industry. In Ecological and Human Dimensions of AI-Based Supply Chain (pp. 245–270). IGI Global Scientific Publishing.
41. Frey, C., Hertweck, P., Richter, L., & Warweg, O. (2022). Bauhaus. MobilityLab: A living lab for the development and evaluation of AI-assisted services. Smart Cities, 5(1), 133–145.
42. El Moussaoui, T., Chakir, L., & Boumhidi, J. (2023). Preserving privacy in arabic judgments: AI-powered anonymization for enhanced legal data privacy. IEEE Access, 11, 117851–117864.
43. Braun, T., Fung, B. C., Iqbal, F., & Shah, B. (2018). Security and privacy challenges in smart cities. Sustainable Cities and Society, 39, 499–507.
44. Shi, X., Luo, J., Luo, J., Li, X., Han, K., Li, D., & Wang, Z. L. (2022). Flexible wood-based triboelectric self-powered smart home system. ACS Nano, 16(2), 3341–3350.
45. Singh, S., Sharma, P. K., Yoon, B., Shojafar, M., Cho, G. H., & Ra, I. H. (2020). Convergence of blockchain and artificial intelligence in IoT network for the sustainable smart city. Sustainable Cities and Society, 63, 102364.
46. Łasak, P., & Wyci´slak, S. (2023). Blockchain and cloud platforms in banking services: A paradox perspective. Journal of Entrepreneurship, Management and Innovation, 19(4), 12–47.
47. Sarker, I. H., Khan, A. I., Abushark, Y. B., & Alsolami, F. (2023). Internet of things (iot) security intelligence: A comprehensive overview, machine learning solutions and research directions. Mobile Networks and Applications, 28(1), 296–312.
48. Chen, J., Ramanathan, L., & Alazab, M. (2021). Holistic big data integrated artificial intelligent modeling to improve privacy and security in data management of smart cities. Microprocessors and Microsystems, 81, 103722.
49. Anuradha, M., Jayasankar, T., Prakash, N. B., Sikkandar, M. Y., Hemalakshmi, G. R., Bharatiraja, C., & Britto, A. S. F. (2021). IoT enabled cancer prediction

system to enhance the authentication and security using cloud computing. Microprocessors and Microsystems, 80, 103301.
50. Liu, Y., Ma, X., Shu, L., Yang, Q., Zhang, Y., Huo, Z., & Zhou, Z. (2020). Internet of things for noise mapping in smart cities: State of the art and future directions. IEEE Network, 34(4), 112–118.
51. El Moussaoui, A. E., El Moussaoui, T., Benbba, B., Chakir, L., Jaegler, A., & El Andaloussi, Z. (2024). Sustainable effects of information sharing between distribution logistics actors: A qualitative case study. Environment, Development and Sustainability, 27(5), 12305–12323.
52. Kuźmicz, K. A., Ryciuk, U., Glińska, H., & Rollnik-Sadowska, E. (2022). Perspectives of mobility development in remote areas attractive to tourists. Ekonomia i Srodowisko, (1), 80, 150–188.
53. Cui, Q., Wang, Y., Chen, K. C., Ni, W., Lin, I. C., Tao, X., & Zhang, P. (2018). Big data analytics and network calculus enabling intelligent management of autonomous vehicles in a smart city. IEEE Internet of Things Journal, 6(2), 2021–2034.
54. El Moussaoui, A. E., Benbba, B., Jaegler, A., & El Andaloussi, Z. (2022, May). How to improve the urban logistics sector in large cities of developing countries: The case of Casablanca. In 2022 14th International Colloquium of Logistics and Supply Chain Management (LOGISTIQUA) (pp. 1–6). IEEE.
55. Ullah, Z., Naeem, M., Coronato, A., Ribino, P., & De Pietro, G. (2023). Blockchain applications in sustainable smart cities. Sustainable Cities and Society, 97, 104697.
56. Chen, G., & wan Zhang, J. (2024). Intelligent transportation systems: Machine learning approaches for urban mobility in smart cities. Sustainable Cities and Society, 107, 105369.
57. El Moussaoui, A. E., Benbba, B., Jaegler, A., El Andaloussi, Z., & El Amrani, L. (2022, May). Last mile logistics: Challenges & improvement ways. In 2022 14th International Colloquium of Logistics and Supply Chain Management (LOGISTIQUA) (pp. 1–7). IEEE.
58. Aymen, F., & Mahmoudi, C. (2019). A novel energy optimization approach for electrical vehicles in a smart city. Energies, 12(5), 929.
59. El Moussaoui, A. E., Benbba, B., Jaegler, A., & El Andaloussi, Z. (2022, May). City logistics: An evolutionary, successful & collaborative city. In 2022 14th International Colloquium of Logistics and Supply Chain Management (LOGISTIQUA) (pp. 1–7). IEEE.
60. El Moussaoui, A. E. (2024). Unlocking the drivers behind logistics service providers' participation in Morocco's logistics clusters. Arab Gulf Journal of Scientific Research, 42(4), 2086–2102.
61. El Moussaoui, A. E. (2024). Factors influencing the entry of logistics service providers (LSPs) into the logistics clusters: A case study of Casablanca City. Management & Sustainability: An Arab Review, 3(4), 237–249.
62. Navarro-Espinoza, A., López-Bonilla, O. R., García-Guerrero, E. E., Tlelo-Cuautle, E., López-Mancilla, D., Hernández-Mejía, C., & Inzunza-González, E. (2022). Traffic flow prediction for smart traffic lights using machine learning algorithms. Technologies, 10(1), 5.
63. Kaginalkar, A., Kumar, S., Gargava, P., & Niyogi, D. (2021). Review of urban computing in air quality management as smart city service: An integrated IoT, AI, and cloud technology perspective. Urban Climate, 39, 100972.
64. El Moussaoui, A. E. (2024). Impact of logistics pooling on reduction of CO_2 emissions in last-mile logistics. Management & Sustainability: An Arab Review, 4(2), 383–401.

65. Abuga, D., & Raghava, N. S. (2021). Real-time smart garbage bin mechanism for solid waste management in smart cities. Sustainable Cities and Society, 75, 103347.
66. Chen, Y., Lu, Y., Bulysheva, L., & Kataev, M. Y. (2022). Applications of blockchain in industry 4.0: A review. Information Systems Frontiers, 26, 1715–1729.
67. Espina-Romero, L., Guerrero-Alcedo, J., Goñi Avila, N., Noroño Sánchez, J. G., Gutiérrez Hurtado, H., & Quiñones Li, A. (2023). Industry 5.0: Tracking scientific activity on the most influential industries, associated topics, and future research agenda. Sustainability, 15(6), 5554.
68. Ktari, J., Frikha, T., Hamdi, M., Elmannai, H., & Hmam, H. (2022). Lightweight AI framework for industry 4.0 case study: Water meter recognition. Big Data and Cognitive Computing, 6(3), 72.
69. Dong, M., Wang, G., & Han, X. (2024). Impacts of artificial Intelligence on carbon emissions In China: In terms of artificial Intelligence type and regional differences. Sustainable Cities and Society, 113, 105682.
70. Nam, K., Dutt, C. S., Chathoth, P., Daghfous, A., & Khan, M. S. (2021). The adoption of artificial intelligence and robotics in the 717 hotel industry: Prospects and challenges. Electronic Markets, 31, 553–574.
71. El Moussaoui, A. E., El Moussaoui, T., Benbba, B., Jaegler, A., & El Andaloussi, Z. (2022). Understanding the choice of collection & delivery point by the e-consumer via a machine learning model: Moroccan Case study. Procedia Computer Science, 210, 204–211.
72. El Moussaoui, A. E., Benbba, B., Jaegler, A., El Moussaoui, T., El Andaloussi, Z., & Chakir, L. (2023). Consumer perceptions of online shopping and willingness to use pick-up points: A case study of Morocco. Sustainability, 15(9), 7405.
73. El Moussaoui, A. E. (2025). Predicting E-Consumer Preferences for Collection and Delivery Points Using Deep Learning. In Ecological and Human Dimensions of AI-Based Supply Chain (pp. 395–412). IGI Global Scientific Publishing.
74. Camacho, J. D. J., Aguirre, B., Ponce, P., Anthony, B., & Molina, A. (2024). Leveraging artificial intelligence to bolster the energy sector in smart cities: A literature review. Energies, 17(2), 353.
75. Singh, D., Dikshit, A. K., & Kumar, S. (2024). Smart technological options in collection and transportation of municipal solid waste in urban areas: A mini review. Waste Management & Research, 42(1), 3–15.

Chapter 7

Securing AI in agriculture

Emerging cyber threats, vulnerabilities, and resilience strategies

Rachid Batess, Ralf Leiter, Younes El Fellah, and El Hossain Baali

7.1 INTRODUCTION

Ensuring a sufficiently efficient food supply chain is vital for the longevity of humanity itself. The increasing world population and decreasing arable land necessitate the development and widespread adoption of technologies to use existing resources efficiently. Within the Industry 4.0 framework, the agriculture sector is benefiting from a variety of digital systems that offer a significant opportunity for the development of smart agriculture. In a complementary manner, artificial intelligence (AI) is demonstrated to be of immense benefit when applied to a wide variety of technologies. AI is successfully being used in automated machinery, precision agriculture, crop management, animal care, food processing and packing, and monitoring crop and livestock environmental conditions. The use of big data, sensors, and AI models leads to precise and effective planning of farming activities. As a result, water, fuel, and other resources can be saved, leading to cheaper and environmental friendly agricultural activities.

Agriculture is the backbone of many economies and plays a critical role in facilitating food security and providing employment. With a growing global population, drastic increases in agricultural productivity are required to meet the food demand. This has made the integration of modern techniques into the agriculture sector imperative. There are several leading-edge technologies being integrated into the agriculture sector to transform traditional forms of farming and their management. Some of the most influential technologies now playing an increasingly prominent role in achieving excellence in the agriculture sector are AI and the Internet of Things (IoT). The integration of these technologies into the traditional agriculture sector has resulted in the creation of what is commonly referred to as smart farming [1, 2].

The integration of AI into agriculture is increasing the productivity of food by identifying new plant species, monitoring crop fields, predicting pest attacks and diseases, effective water management, and offering nutritious diets for maintaining healthy human lives. With numerous advantages offered by AI technologies, its increased adoption in the agriculture sector is only a matter of time. AI functions on the basis of historical data and uses logic

DOI: 10.1201/9781003597476-10

while performing tasks. AI can result in a drastic increase in yield, reduction in costs, and maintaining sustainability. The integration of various technologies in the agriculture sector provides numerous advantages; however, every advantage comes with its own set of disadvantages. Many of these advantages make the agri-ecosystem more prone to cyber threats. If necessary protective and preventive measures are not taken, the consequences of cyber threats can be severe. The consequences of cyberattacks on the agriculture sector can be reduced by understanding the type of occurrence of the attacks [3–5].

The agricultural landscape across the globe has undergone significant and noteworthy transformations due to remarkable advancements in both AI and information technology (IT) over the last few decades. These sophisticated systems have evolved over time, transitioning from the use of general-purpose information and decision support tools to the utilization of more advanced, specialist agricultural technologies tailored specifically for the farming sector. Such transformative systems and technologies have been developed and refined to ensure not only the effective management of various cultivation processes but also the optimized utilization of vital resources. This evolution has led to a substantial increase in agricultural production levels, benefiting farmers and consumers alike.

AI systems are particularly notable for their ability to provide results that are more accurate and efficient when compared to traditional rule-based pattern recognition tools and methods. This includes the use of advanced techniques such as neural networks, fuzzy logic, and support vector machines, which collectively enhance productivity and decision-making in agriculture. Nevertheless, the burgeoning reliance on these cutting-edge technologies does present new and significant levels of risk. Particularly concerning is the integration of AI and cybersecurity measures, as such systems have been found to be among the most vulnerable within the larger spectrum of IT assets. As the agricultural industry continues to adapt to these technological innovations, it becomes imperative to address the associated risks effectively, ensuring sustainability and security in agricultural practices moving forward [6–8] (Figure 7.1).

Throughout history, there are numerous compelling examples, both from the past and the more recent timeline of events, that illustrate how a lack of effective cybersecurity has led to significant direct or indirect adverse impacts on agricultural operations all over the globe. As AI continues to play an increasingly pivotal role in agriculture, it follows logically that attempts to undermine, disrupt, or otherwise subvert the incredible advances made in this crucial field may also escalate by targeting the very systems that underpin these advancements. Regrettably, it appears that most of the cybersecurity measures in place, particularly those that pertain to IT and operational technology (OT) within the agricultural setting, remain somewhat ambiguous at best. Furthermore, there exists a notable deficiency of comprehensive information regarding the specific types of threats that these interconnected systems may face on a day-to-day basis. This chapter endeavors to break down these critical subjects and

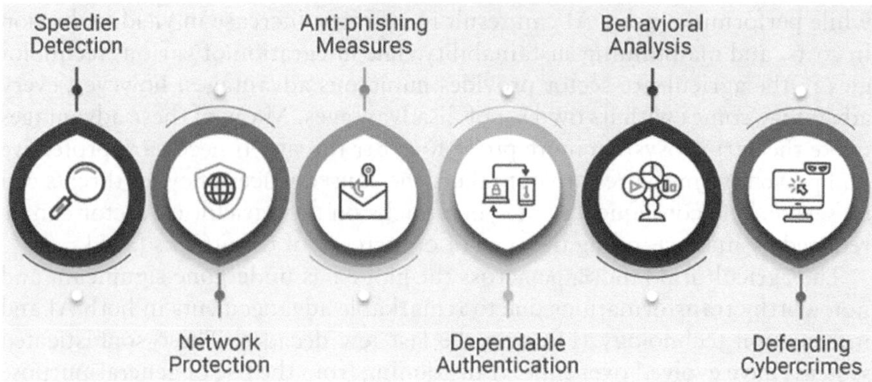

Figure 7.1 AI in cybersecurity.

provide detailed insights into the focal points where the highest risks of cybersecurity breaches lie. Each individual segment of the chapter is meticulously divided into sections that delve deeper into each specific subject matter, allowing for a clearer understanding of the issues at hand. The necessity of producing such a chapter must be articulated clearly to its readers; as we progress to become more technologically advanced, we must also elevate our level of concern regarding the safeguarding of those advancements from individuals or entities that would seek to exploit them for nefarious purposes or otherwise cause harm to agricultural operations. In the final analysis, this chapter also aims to provide a broader perspective on the current technological landscape that exists within the agricultural sector, taking into account the differing cybersecurity technologies that are currently in use across various platforms. This detailed analysis serves to illustrate the compelling need for greater uniformity in security measures in order to better protect the integrity of agricultural advancements moving forward [9–12] (Figure 7.2).

We undertake the critical task of surveying the current status of relevant threats and applicable preventive measures, thereby making a significant contribution to the ongoing transformation of the agricultural cybersecurity discourse. This mini-essay, along with an accompanying panel discussion, specifically focuses on the vital issue of cybersecurity pertaining to AI in the field of agriculture. The primary purpose is to thoroughly cover the various types of threats that are actively facing this important area and to provide an up-to-date assessment of the current state concerning the deployment and use of AI technology within agriculture. In doing so, we will comprehensively cover some of the most relevant challenges that are of great concern to a variety of stakeholders, including farmers who are on the front lines, agribusinesses that play a crucial role in the supply chain, consumers who depend on safe food production, as well as governments and regulatory bodies that oversee agricultural practices. Additionally, we will expand upon the current programs and initiatives that are being applied at local, regional, and international levels to enhance cybersecurity measures specifically related to AI in

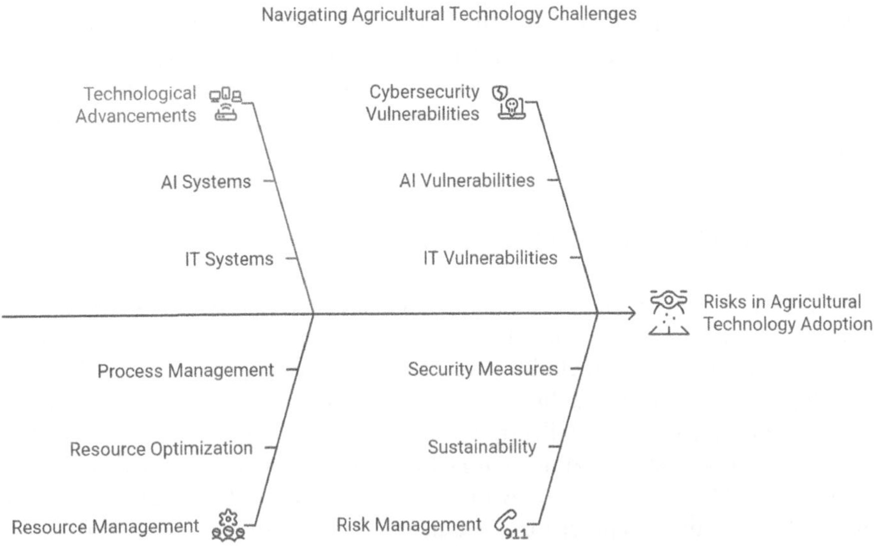

Figure 7.2 Navigating agriculture technology challenges.

agriculture. By delving into these topics, we will then provide relevant information and insights that can be effectively utilized to improve the overall cybersecurity discourse, ensuring a safer and more secure future for the integration of AI in agricultural practices [11, 13].

While AI in agriculture will undoubtedly bring forth numerous opportunities, we also recognize and acknowledge that the application of such rapidly emerging technologies will inevitably present limitations as well as unintended threats. The coauthors of this chapter represent and highlight two of the most significant and crucial industry sectors: the Australian agribusiness sector and the Australian government's beef regulatory arm operating within the Department of Agriculture, Water Resources, and Environment. We strongly encourage an ongoing and fruitful dialogue between academia, agribusiness practitioners, and government officials regarding AI cybersecurity issues. Moreover, we aim to collaboratively formulate innovative and actionable systems that will facilitate and ensure the successful uptake of AI technologies across various dimensions of agriculture. It is essential to emphasize that for everyone involved in agriculture, from farmers to regulatory bodies, ensuring the longevity, security, and resilience of these systems is both an explicit and implicit intent that we all share and strive for collectively [14, 15].

The chapter is organized as follows: Section 7.2 provides an overview of AI in agriculture, defining key concepts and detailing its applications and benefits. Section 7.3 shifts focus to cybersecurity within the broader agricultural sector, emphasizing its significance and unique challenges. Following this, Section 7.4 delves into the specific potential threats that AI introduces into agriculture, such as data breaches and system manipulation. Section 7.5 assesses the current state of cybersecurity measures applied to AI in agriculture, including existing protocols and illustrative examples. Building on this analysis, Section 7.6 proposes solutions for enhancing cybersecurity, covering both technological advancements and necessary policy recommendations. Finally, Section 7.7 concludes the chapter by summarizing the key findings and reinforcing the call for robust security strategies.

7.2 OVERVIEW OF AI IN AGRICULTURE

In this study, understanding "AI" is crucial, particularly in its application within agriculture. AI encompasses machines simulating human intelligence across various aspects, including creative and adaptive capabilities. A recent development, "narrow intelligence," exemplifies systems designed for specific tasks that mimic human intellectual functions. Within agriculture, human data analysis involves scrutinizing factors like machine types and real-time data processing. This analysis framework has been adapted for machine-oriented technology, leading to precision agriculture, which uses predictive analytics to identify pests or diseases threatening crops. AI in agriculture spans numerous applications: optimizing asset and labor management, efficient bookkeeping, modern precision farming using drones, advanced data analytics for machine learning, and leveraging digital marketing innovations like the IoT. Integrating AI into agriculture offers significant advantages, including enhanced operational efficiency, reduced costs, minimized waste, lower environmental impact, and improved food production to meet global needs. These benefits highlight AI's transformative potential in agriculture, generating increased research interest, especially at the intersection of AI technology and cybersecurity [3, 15–18] (Figure 7.3).

7.2.1 Definition and concepts of AI in agriculture

AI prominently features robotic and autonomous systems in agriculture, including drones, self-propelled vehicles, and automated sensors. Agricultural technology involves fully autonomous systems that can operate

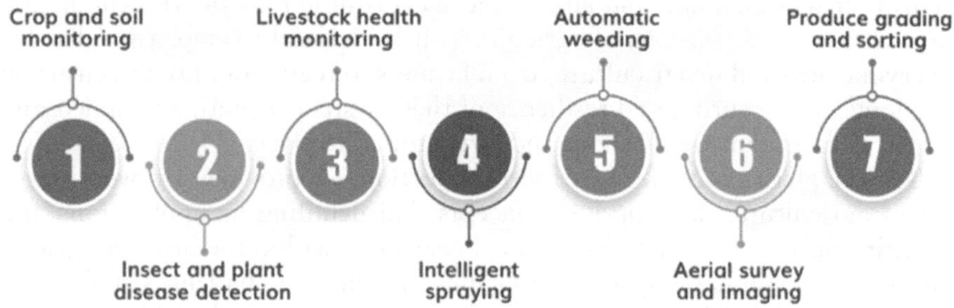

Figure 7.3 Use cases of AI in agriculture.

independently. The relationship between data and AI is interconnected, as AI evolves alongside big data. Sophisticated data analytics leverage large volumes of information to produce precise, regulated outputs. Additionally, observational data within an AI framework supports performance improvements through a data-driven AI model, enhancing the effectiveness of agricultural practices.

AI technology is vital for supporting information and communication technology (ICT) systems by enabling operations with smart tools, facilitating communication among smart objects, and applying AI-driven cyber threat mitigation strategies against IoT risks and Denial of Service (DoS) attacks in wireless sensor networks. Substantial research focuses on utilizing big data from public sources to enhance agricultural systems. With big data technologies in agriculture, AI offers transformative capabilities, turning vast yield data into valuable insights and actionable information. Analyzing large-scale data aids informed decision-making. Big data acts as a potential intelligence driver, opening innovative solutions to the diverse challenges in agriculture, including climate change, resource depletion, and economic competitiveness in a demanding market.

The application of big data enhances resource optimization and conservation through improved decision-making, leading to better measurements on-site. However, to realize economic opportunities from these insights, future generations must effectively manage and utilize the data. AI advances algorithms that perform tasks requiring human-like intelligence, enabling rapid processing of extensive data sets to provide actionable insights more efficiently than humans. This progress is driven by the increased availability and quality of data in agriculture, resulting from connected sensors, intelligent machinery, and integrated systems. Modern aerial and ground-based sensors, alongside satellites, drones, and robotics, collect vital information about crop performance, heat units, precipitation, and nitrogen levels. This data allows farmers to implement selective, site-specific management practices, significantly improving farming results and sustainability [19–21] (Figure 7.4).

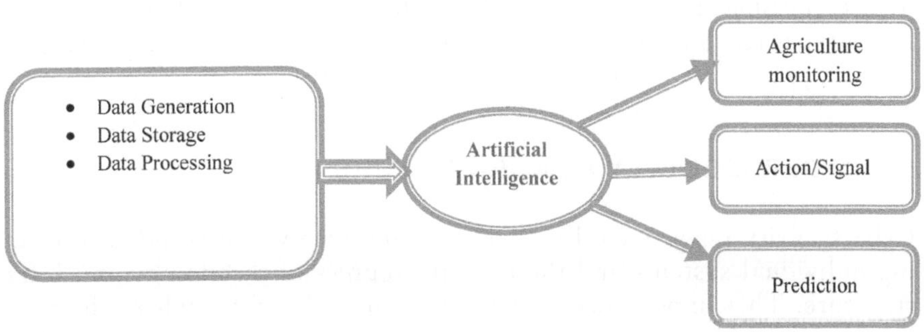

Figure 7.4 Process of artificial intelligence adoption in agriculture.

7.2.2 Applications and benefits

AI's applications in agriculture are vast. Seeders have become autonomous robots that operate efficiently. Advanced roving sensors and AI drones create accurate soil maps and monitor fields. Automated weeding machines use computer vision and machine learning to distinguish and eliminate weeds without harming crops. Data-driven yield prediction models assess the productivity of individual fruit and vegetable plants with remarkable accuracy.

Automated analysis of climate data, including rainfall and temperature, is performed using advanced AI models and field sensors. This integration enhances water management and improves predictions for irrigation and crops. The benefits of AI in agriculture are growing, including monitoring of crops, livestock, fisheries, genetic management, post-harvest spoilage prevention, pest forecasting, and other functions that optimize agricultural processes.

Overall, the expected impacts of these advanced AI systems, in general, revolve around greatly increased operational efficiency, significant reductions in labor costs, decreased chemical and water usage, and an overall improvement in both the quality and quantity of the crops and livestock produced. These advancements promise to revolutionize agricultural practices, leading to a more sustainable and productive future for the industry as a whole [1, 15, 17, 22].

The authors provide detailed projections on the potential income for farmers and the resources that could be saved by fully embracing AI across nations or globally for various applications. Current industry estimates highlight AI's financial implications and transformative effects in agriculture. The world market for diverse drone technologies, including specialized agricultural drones, is growing at over 7% per annum, potentially exceeding $12 billion by 2025. Additionally, the rapidly evolving AI market in grain analytics focuses on supply chain solutions, including traceability, efficient storage management, and predictive analytics. Integrating these systems enables granaries to predict and match production to market demand, enhancing grains' profitability. Rising consumer demand for non-GMO inputs is also boosting trade for food-grade grains, facilitating market outlier identification and price premium capture. Collectively, projections suggest that AI offers great promise to meet pressing agricultural needs. The following section will discuss various threat types related to cybersecurity for systems science and AI, stressing the need for protection against vulnerabilities [23, 24].

7.3 CYBERSECURITY IN AGRICULTURE

Cybersecurity plays a vital role in ensuring safety and stability, impacting individual systems and the overall progress of technology and infrastructure. This importance is magnified in agriculture, where the rapid integration of IoT, wireless networks, cloud computing, robotics, machine learning, and AI creates an efficient and automated environment. The ongoing development and adoption of new technologies in agriculture and throughout the supply chain encounter significant cybersecurity threats and potential failures. Advanced hardware and software, especially those leveraging AI and open-source platforms, introduce considerable vulnerabilities, making them targets for various cyber-physical attacks and IoT threats that risk disrupting both technological initiatives and agricultural operations [9, 12, 25].

Agricultural systems are challenging to secure due to their hardware and software components that depend on complex, real-time data like weather, maps, and soil information. Securing agriculture requires a comprehensive approach, unlike city-based smart grids, where IoT security is prioritized. Threats could range from system malfunctions to severe food safety risks, chemical overuse, data breaches, and compromised supply chains. Interconnected systems mean that any issues can erode consumer trust, highlighting the importance of robust agricultural security measures [26–28].

Incidents involving these threats, such as operational downtime or financial losses, can vary widely based on the types of cyber threats faced. Protecting agricultural and research data from tampering by external adversaries is crucial. Agricultural technology now provides insights for optimal crop and livestock production and pricing, aiding in reducing field inputs and maximizing outputs. A hacker could manipulate farming data or alter commodity ownership, disrupting the agricultural system and undermining confidence and investments [29] (Figure 7.5).

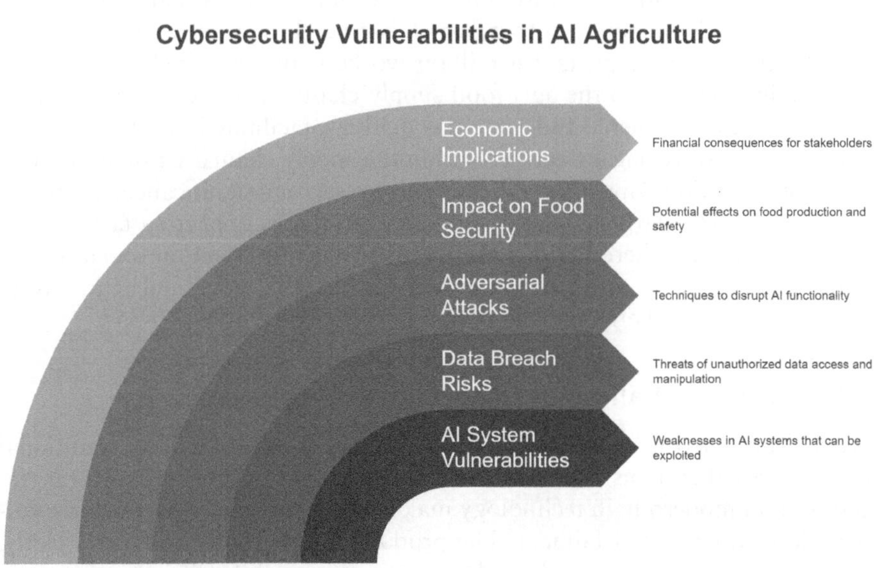

Figure 7.5 Cybersecurity vulnerabilities in AI agriculture.

7.3.1 Significance and critical importance of cybersecurity in the agricultural sector

The twenty-first decade has seen agriculture increasingly dependent on advanced technology and data analytics. Agribusinesses have transformed from small family-owned farms into larger, state-backed enterprises focused on data-driven decisions. There's been a notable 32.5% rise in farm operations in the U.S., generating significant revenue of up to one hundred thousand USD, highlighting the industry's emphasis on financial sustainability. Agriculture remains vital in developing countries, supporting many livelihoods. A significant 72.6% of farms now use IoT technologies, marking a shift toward modernization in farming. Investments in bio-climate-controlled produce technologies, like greenhouses, have surged, reflecting strong market interest in enhancing productivity and sustainability. However, this increase in investment and data access also raises the risk of cyberattacks. The integration of AI and intricate data systems has exposed the agriculture sector to higher cybercriminal threats, given the growing number of targets in the supply chain. The potential impacts of these cyberattacks can significantly affect global socio-economic outcomes. Thus, stakeholders in the agri-food sector must adopt robust cybersecurity strategies to protect against emerging threats and minimize potential damages [30–32].

7.3.1.1 Ensuring food security

Since 2020, the global food price index has risen by 10.44%, indicating a trend of sustained growth. It is vital to enhance food security for the 8.7% of the global population facing food insecurity while also maintaining the agricultural sector's economic output, which is crucial to our economy. The U.S. agriculture sector supports 2.6 million workers and is linked to numerous local industries tied to the agri-food supply chain. As consumer preferences shift toward e-commerce and same-day delivery, facilitated by advanced supply chain software, legacy entities within the supply chain are essential for its efficient operation. Given the U.S. agriculture sector's significance, it must be protected, particularly against potential cyberattacks impacting farm operations. In a world where billions share sensitive information on social media, cybersecurity has become a top priority for the U.S. government to ensure peace, security, and effective regulation in this critical area [33–35].

7.3.2 Unique challenges in agricultural cybersecurity

Agricultural settings present distinct challenges compared to traditional cyber-physical systems. The contrast between longstanding agricultural traditions and modern high technology makes legacy processes particularly vulnerable to unexpected failures. The production environment varies greatly, with IT infrastructure resembling large enterprises, while OT is spread across isolated locations, from extensive farms to small family plots. Collaboration among producers and vendors is increasingly vital, creating communication channels that can be exploited by attackers. Additionally, there is a notable cyber skills gap in agriculture; producers and farm workers often have low cybersecurity awareness, with even fewer possessing the skills to manage threats. Enhanced connectivity introduces new risks, particularly in less connected regions lacking resources to combat these dangers. Economic pressures further deprioritize cybersecurity, as producers often have to choose between essential upgrades and necessary tools [9, 12, 36].

To address cybersecurity challenges in agriculture, it is essential to learn from the maturity of the cybersecurity community and adapt those lessons. While IT best practices offer useful insights, the rise of IoT introduces distinct challenges that may not align with traditional tools. A thorough understanding of IoT's implications for agriculture, including its differences from conventional cyber-physical systems, should shape our technological approaches. Acknowledging the unique institutional and economic factors within the agricultural sector is crucial for developing appropriate policies. Organizations aiming to enhance agricultural cybersecurity must consider the sector's complex landscape, the integration of IoT with existing operational technologies, and the economic limitations that impact their ability to devise and implement solutions. Additionally, those proposing IoT security best practices should assess their comparisons with more resource-intensive sectors, keeping in mind the trade-offs between economic growth and state intervention. Neglecting these issues may lead to impractical cyber policies. Consequently, in the next section provides a pragmatic roadmap to facilitate effective decision-making in agricultural IoT cybersecurity [11–13, 37] (Figure 7.6).

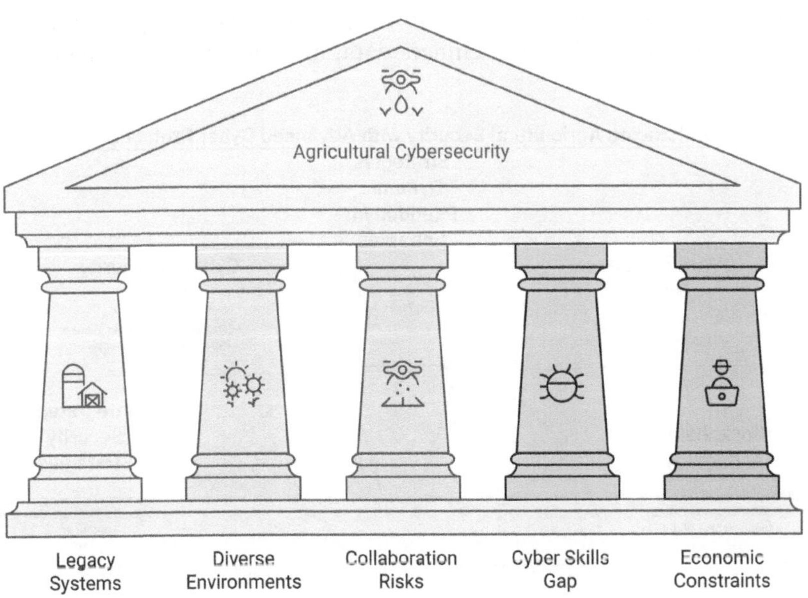

Figure 7.6 Challenges in agricultural cybersecurity.

7.4 AI IN AGRICULTURE: POTENTIAL THREATS

As farmers push for greater automation with AI technology, new challenges arise. This research analyzes various cyber threats and vulnerabilities impacting AI systems in agriculture, emphasizing the overlooked security risks in this sector. To support AI development in farming, it's essential to anticipate and address cyber threats before they inflict harm. Farmers must recognize four main cyberattack types: data leakage endangering privacy, manipulation of AI models leading to false results, farm sabotage or system failures disrupting operations, and theft of critical data or systems. Vulnerabilities exposed by reconnaissance techniques can be exploited by malicious actors. A proactive stance is vital to allow the agricultural sector to benefit from AI while protecting it against threats [13, 38].

Many companies in agriculture recognize cyber threats and are beginning to integrate cybersecurity with agent management systems. However, the implications of AI on privacy and data storage are still being investigated. Data breaches involve significant data disclosure, which poses risks when AI algorithms are implemented for crop monitoring. While it's thought that AI systems in agriculture don't gather sensitive personal information, the data can still be harmful. For instance, an AI animal feeding system could reveal the location of a camera and the species depicted, serving as a reconnaissance tool for attackers. The potential for financial gain in agriculture makes AI-based production predictability appealing [11, 15, 39, 40] (Figure 7.7).

7.4.1 Data breaches and privacy concerns

Data breaches are a significant threat in agriculture as AI applications collect sensitive data like device logs, climate data, and yield records. Unauthorized

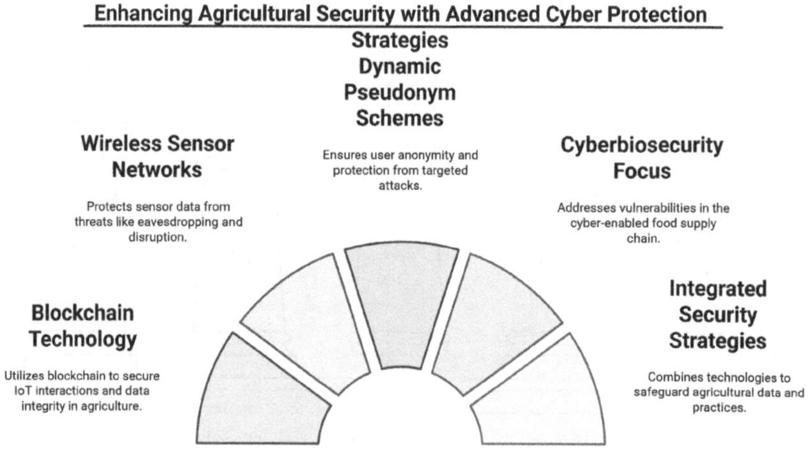

Figure 7.7 Enhancing agriculture security with advanced cyber protection.

access could violate data protection rules and lead to data poisoning, resulting in large yield losses. Consequences include financial losses directly from system downtime or indirectly through reputational damage. However, the diverse nature of IoT devices means that total system failure is unlikely. Still, compromised or manipulated data can lead to poor AI decisions and reduced yields, causing financial setbacks. Furthermore, leaking sensitive information about farm yields or practices can have severe repercussions, affecting competitiveness and compliance with certification standards. Consumers may suffer privacy violations, while companies could face economic ruin. Attackers may exploit this data for tailored assaults or model poisoning, infringing on data protection laws and risking fines. Many AI users lack an understanding of the complexities of AI models, making them hesitant to trust these applications. To enhance transparency, companies should clearly outline data collection and processing methods in privacy policies, addressing user privacy concerns and fostering trust [11, 15, 41–45].

7.4.2 Manipulation of AI systems

Technologies currently used in modern agriculture often qualify as advanced AI systems. However, when cybercriminals exploit AI for malicious purposes, numerous risks and threats arise. The increasing sophistication of AI applications designed to disrupt algorithms poses a significant concern. Modern AI systems are vulnerable to adversarial inputs, allowing malicious actors to introduce strategically placed perturbations that lead to incorrect outputs. For example, if an AI model predicts crop yield, subtle additions to input images might trigger a negative yield prediction when the actual yield should be positive. This can severely impact investment levels in farming, especially due to declining market prices. Adversaries can thereby disrupt agricultural enterprises by limiting financial investments. Another common strategy involves tampering with AI models or altering training data, resulting in flawed outputs that influence critical business decisions. A particularly alarming situation occurs when compromised AI algorithms learn erroneous relationships, leading to cascading failures in accurate outcome predictions [46–48].

The implications of a compromised AI in agriculture are manifold. Manipulating an AI model in a milking machine or food processing equipment can result in the output of products contaminated with bacteria, disrupting supply chains and jeopardizing consumer health and safety. Such incidents are also devastating for the agriculture industry, especially if the inhabitants of an entire area get sick from consuming contaminated food. Moreover, failure to invest in securing AI in agriculture can discourage trust in AI usage at any level in the supply chain and decrease investments, lead to economic loss, and may limit progress in general. To overcome these threats, robust AI security mechanisms should be developed to maintain a high level of confidence that AI systems will operate as expected in various environments [49–52] (Figure 7.8).

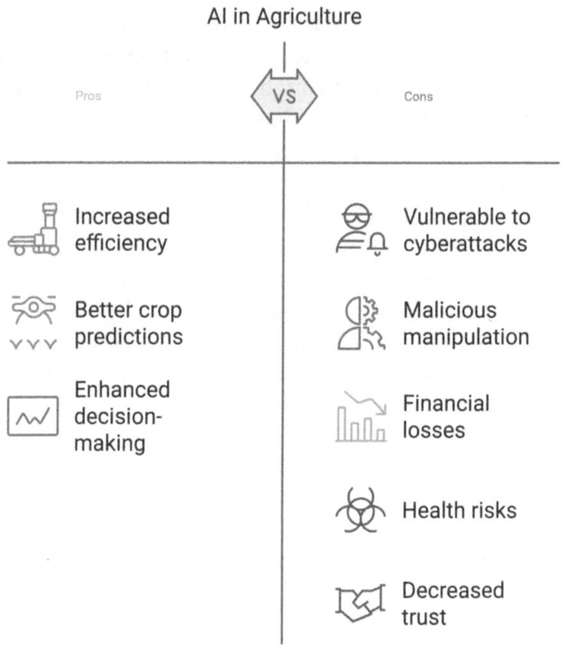

Figure 7.8 Manipulation of AI systems.

7.5 CURRENT STATE OF CYBERSECURITY IN AI IN AGRICULTURE

While AI in agriculture encompasses the latest developments in this sector, cybersecurity strategy implementation examines the current situation of such cybersecurity measures. Analyses show that such a measure, mostly driven by the implemented security frameworks, does indeed take into consideration the threat types identified. In essence, current developments in AI in agriculture entail a data-driven system, which is changed in accordance with the external and internal changes in developing technology. As a result, small to medium-sized enterprises (SMEs) launched the Essential Eight, which involves mitigating any AI cybersecurity vulnerabilities that come to light. Through this, it is assumed SMEs will also prevent any agricultural cyberattacks that rely on the discovery of such vulnerabilities [53–56].

Numerous research efforts and initiatives are leading organizations to develop security standards focusing on AI, robotics, and cybersecurity. This trend extends to agriculture, where cybersecurity practices are increasingly essential. For instance, AI applications in precision farming showcase success, like a farmer's machine learning solution to manage nitrogen levels post-letting. Another example features a company improving robot capabilities for pig management, incorporating a layer to monitor skin temperature and detect illnesses. While these technological advancements highlight effective security solutions, they also emphasize critical learning experiences in applying cybersecurity strategies across agriculture. This topic warrants further exploration, particularly regarding the concepts of intelligence and morality in AI, as the community has yet to define their parameters clearly. Successful demonstrations should involve automated processes that allow deep neural networks to "learn" from their environments and exhibit intelligence. To contextualize AI within cybersecurity concerns, a review of recent literature was conducted. Findings indicate that while many studies on cybersecurity relate to AI, they often overlook the significant challenges cybersecurity poses to AI. Thus, this discussion provides a fresh perspective on the intersection of AI and cybersecurity. The current landscape indicates a developing security implementation that must be nurtured to secure the proliferation of AI technologies in agriculture effectively [57–62].

7.5.1 Existing cybersecurity measures

Current cybersecurity measures in agriculture focus on several key areas: Data Protection: Ensuring the confidentiality, integrity, and availability of agricultural data is crucial. Protecting data from sensors and IoT devices in smart agriculture is a priority. Blockchain Technology: Implementing blockchain-based monitoring systems boosts security by enabling continuous data handling and secure storage of transaction discrepancies. Cryptography: Strong cryptographic techniques are essential for maintaining data privacy and ensuring security during the transmission of data from IoT devices in limited-resource settings. Risk Management Strategies: Adopting risk management frameworks helps identify and mitigate potential cybersecurity threats within agricultural practices. Continuous Monitoring: Regular system and network surveillance is necessary for real-time detection and response to security incidents. Incident Response Mechanisms: Establishing clear procedures for managing cybersecurity incidents improves overall resilience. By integrating these measures, agricultural stakeholders can effectively protect their data and systems from numerous security threats [10, 12, 13, 63].

7.5.1.1 Patterns of AI applications in agriculture

Applications of AI in agriculture are evolving to improve efficiency, productivity, and sustainability. Current trends show AI's crucial role in transforming agriculture into a data-driven sector, tackling production and sustainability challenges [3, 15]. Precision Agriculture: AI technologies enable real-time data monitoring and analysis for efficient crop management, enhancing irrigation practices, monitoring soil health, and predicting crop yields based on factors like weather conditions and soil quality. Animal Husbandry: In livestock management, AI leverages predictive analytics and computer vision to monitor animal health, detect early signs of diseases, and optimize feeding strategies, enabling timely interventions. Integration with Emerging Technologies: AI is increasingly integrated with the IoT and big data analytics, driving innovation in agricultural practices. This includes applications such as disease detection, weed management, and advancements in synthetic biology for food production. Data-Driven Decision-Making: The adoption of data analytics is transforming agriculture by enabling informed decision-making, improving operational efficiency, and promoting sustainable food production systems [64].

Despite advancements in technology and security protocols, security issues continue to disrupt the ICT ecosystem, posing daily risks to sensitive data in agriculture, from farm management to product delivery. While protection strategies exist, many security solutions are still being tested or implemented. Increasingly, countries and agribusinesses are adopting security protocols and tools to mitigate risks associated with agricultural data and drones used for crop monitoring and spraying. Key protective technologies include firewalls, scanning systems, Trojan filters, and data diodes, which help secure critical infrastructure and assist in agricultural robotics [13, 15, 65].

Combinations of multiple safety systems greatly mitigate risks and help prevent harmful effects of potential accidents. Many small- and medium-sized farms use cloud platforms to efficiently manage, store, and analyze operational data as part of recommendation systems that aid in decision-making. These systems utilize data from various sources to provide personalized advice. Cloud platforms incorporate robust security measures to protect sensitive information. Raising awareness among agricultural companies and staff, especially data and security managers, about national and international cyber resolutions is essential. Additionally, it is important for farmers and companies to have a comprehensive and up-to-date recovery plan ready to activate after disasters, whether security-related or physical, ensuring effective crisis support [66–70].

7.5.2 Case studies and examples

In this chapter, we have presented several exemplars of incidents that are closely associated with the use and application of cybersecurity measures in the agricultural sector, and we have placed these specific instances in a broader context to provide perspective on how significant and impactful such threats may be to agricultural operations and food systems at large. To effectively assert and propose strategies aimed at mitigating these identified threats, we have sought valuable insights and knowledge from a diverse group of experts who specialize in areas including AI, cybersecurity, law, and the agri-food sector. This multifaceted approach is intended to thoroughly account for the complex interactions and the multiplicity of interests involved in these sectors. This chapter ultimately concludes with practical implications that translate our comprehensive insights into accessible and actionable recommendations for the industry, alongside restorative approaches tailored for all parties involved. These recommendations aim to address the appropriateness and practicality of security measures and threat strategies for AI applications in agriculture. In this section, we take the time to evaluate a range of case studies documenting recent cyber incidents, with the aim of identifying whether the current best practice measures have proven effective in the face of an actual security incident. Each case study is described with a focus on the apparent effectiveness of measures that were in place during the previous incidents before delving into an evaluation of the ultimate success or failure of the realized controls in defending against cyberattacks. Through this analysis approach, we can identify leading incidents that have the greatest potential to inform our thorough evaluation and insights. Our ongoing investigation finds that both the use of advanced natural language processing techniques and the collaboration with domain experts were instrumental in pinpointing those incidents that are particularly useful for our detailed analysis. Furthermore, the suitability of the selected incidents was ratified through our interdisciplinary roundtable discussions, which included experts in cybersecurity, agri-food, AI, and socio-legal research, ensuring a holistic and comprehensive approach to understanding these critical issues [10, 12, 71].

7.6 PROPOSED SOLUTIONS FOR ENHANCED CYBERSECURITY SOLUTIONS

This chapter identifies a variety of proposed solutions aimed at enhancing the cybersecurity of AI specifically within the context of agriculture. The range of possible solutions to minimize the various given threats is quite extensive and diverse. While it maintains a primary focus on the application of IT in the realm of AI in agriculture, numerous methods such as zero-knowledge proof, ring signatures, ID-based cryptosystems, multi-secret sharing, and group signatures can effectively be employed to strengthen existing data encryption or improve the security processes related to authentication. By leveraging these advanced cryptographic techniques, stakeholders in the agricultural sector can significantly bolster their defenses against potential cybersecurity threats [72–77] (Figure 7.9).

The use of a wide variety of innovative tools and advanced methodologies can play a significant role in greatly improving risk detection and effective mitigation strategies. Additionally, these resources can bolster the shaping and enforcement of robust, effective policy, and regulatory frameworks that are essential in today's complex environment. We urgently call for increased cooperation and collaboration among all stakeholders in the agricultural sector, emphasizing the urgent need for taking preventive measures and proactive actions aimed at ensuring the sustainability and health of the entire agricultural ecosystem. Moreover, the regular and thorough review of the cyber hygiene practices associated with IoT devices and AI systems must be considered critically to maintain a high level of cyber readiness and preparedness against potential threats. Cybersecurity strategies should

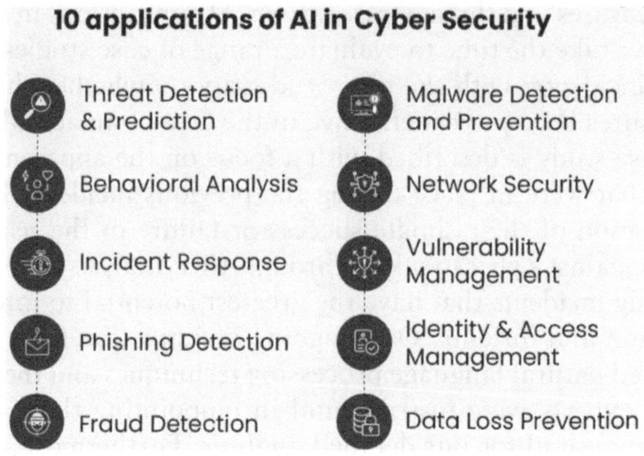

Figure 7.9 Application of AI in cybersecurity.

comprehensively address the increasingly sophisticated emerging threats found within Industrial Control Systems (ICSs) and the implementation of AI technologies. These strategies should assist all actors within the agri-food chain in cultivating a strong and resilient cyber culture. Furthermore, they should aim to encourage and foster a combined resilience of the entire food ecosystem, which must be built on active defenses, comprehensive strategies, and systematic redundancy to effectively counter the evolving landscape of threats. Strengthening security measures is another vital potential contribution to enhancing AI security, especially considering that manipulation of agricultural documents could evolve into a new type of attack in cases where those documents are directly related to AI software documentation and its operational protocols [78–82] (Figure 7.10).

7.6.1 Technological solutions

An advanced intrusion detection system (IDS) is crucial for ensuring safety in various systems, especially for farm operators with limited technical knowledge. Both network-based and host-based IDS options can secure programs and network resources. However, skilled cybersecurity personnel may use evasion tactics that compromise effectiveness, meaning not all solutions fit every circumstance. Our focus is on unwanted applications that secretly collect user data without consent, prompting us to advocate for updated systems and software to enhance safety measures. A meeting by the Task Force and the C2 Commission highlighted low analysis and awareness levels of cybersecurity in the agro-food chain, particularly during digital innovation phases. Micro, small, and medium agri-food companies often outsource their security to external partners, leading to contracts that only address the General Data Protection Regulation (GDPR) without a commitment to thorough cybersecurity strategies [83–90].

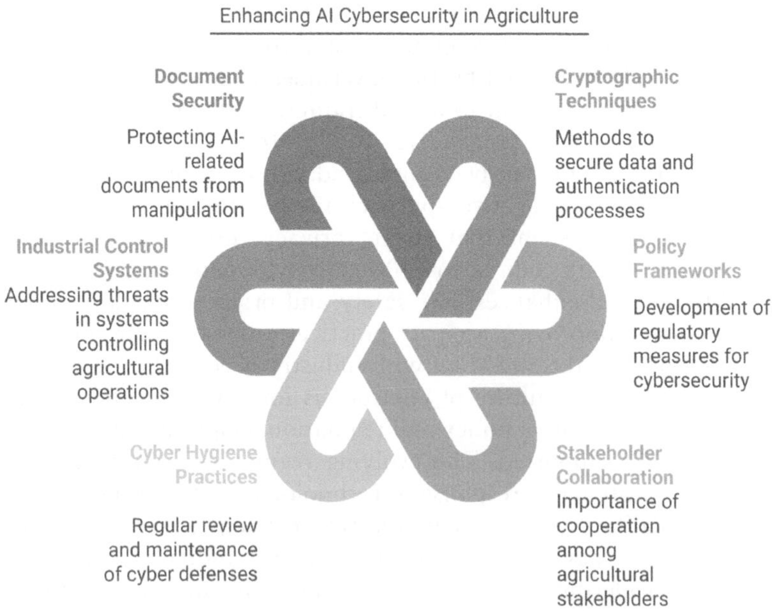

Figure 7.10 Enhancing AI cybersecurity in agriculture.

Encryption secures sensitive data by preventing unauthorized removal or use of devices. Encrypted data is never decrypted for direct processing on networks, enhancing security. Instead, decryption takes place in a controlled virtual environment on the device using approved applications that adhere to security protocols. When combined with strong cyber hygiene practices, encryption offers robust protection against various cyber threats. In instances of cyberattacks, advanced machine learning can classify and manage these incidents, allowing for quick responses. Actively monitoring AI models for statistical changes provides insights into potential vulnerabilities. Regular software maintenance and updates are crucial for enhancing security and patching vulnerabilities. Maintaining strong cyber hygiene practices involves using complex passwords and managing threats with both traditional and advanced defense systems. Conducting vulnerability assessments is essential to identify and address weaknesses that attackers may exploit. Understanding the tactics and techniques used by cybercriminals is vital for analyzing potential attack vectors. The challenge lies in creating alerts for unwanted actions to enable timely interventions and prevent breaches [91–97].

7.6.2 Policy and regulation recommendations

Agriculture encompasses various stakeholders, necessitating clear guidelines for processes. We suggest robust guidelines for stakeholders to implement, maintain, test, and enhance incident response plans. This proactive approach calls for a regulatory framework defining roles during incidents. Such initiatives enhance traceability, accountability, and compliance. Guidelines should be collaboratively developed by the government, industry, and agriculture. Notably, investments in education and training on these guidelines are vital for the success of enacted policies [12, 14, 98–103].

Implementing comprehensive recommendations within a robust regulatory framework fosters a collective approach to the growing threat landscape, promoting secure systems that ensure privacy through thorough assessments of supply chain components. Proactively developing systems that can be quickly updated enhances user safety and privacy, which is crucial for long-term goals. Improving security practices among service providers can increase service uptake and align with industry needs. These recommendations aim to create a culture of continuous improvement and innovation. Ongoing collaboration on policy and regulation, emphasizing prompt adoption, is strongly supported. The evolving regulatory landscape regarding data requires a proactive response to technological advancements, addressing current realities while anticipating future changes. We endorse recommendations on "data relationships" to empower individuals and enhance autonomy, considering ethical aspects of data provenance for accountability. Experts suggest rigorous testing of the proposed approach to ensure effectiveness [82, 104–109] (Figure 7.11).

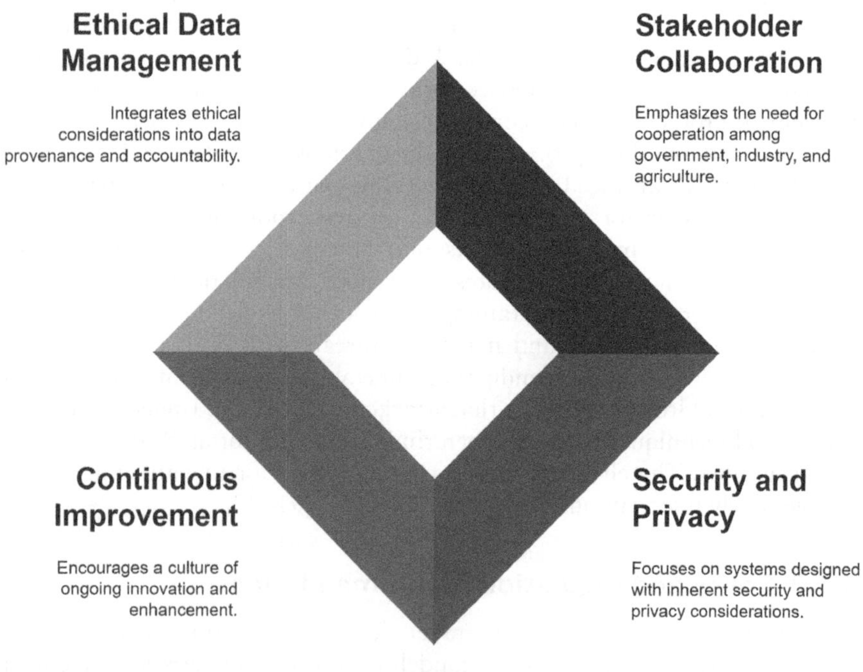

Figure 7.11 Strengthening agriculture through collaborative and secure regulation.

7.7 CONCLUSION

Agriculture is vital for economic stability and food security, particularly as the global population grows. Technologies such as AI and the IoT are transforming traditional farming into "smart farming," which boosts productivity through better crop monitoring and resource management. However, this reliance on technology increases vulnerability to cyber threats, making strong protective measures essential. AI and IT enhance resource management and decision-making, yet many systems face cybersecurity risks. This chapter evaluates existing cybersecurity threats to AI in agriculture and underscores the importance of collaboration among farmers, agribusinesses, and the government to improve cybersecurity practices. Major threats include data leakage, AI model manipulation, system sabotage, and data theft, which can disrupt operations and jeopardize food safety. Cybersecurity efforts focus on data protection, blockchain, cryptography, risk management, and incident response, with frameworks like the Essential Eight addressing vulnerabilities. Nonetheless, awareness and practice gaps in cybersecurity persist. To combat these challenges, this chapter suggests advanced cryptographic techniques, better risk detection methods, and the need for regulations and collaboration among stakeholders. Education on cybersecurity is crucial for enhancing the agricultural sector's resilience. While AI greatly improves agriculture, it also introduces new cybersecurity issues that require continued policy development and comprehensive strategies to mitigate risks.

REFERENCES

1. M. Javaid, A. Haleem, R. P. Singh and R. Suman, "Enhancing smart farming through the applications of Agriculture 4.0 technologies," Journal of Intelligent Networks, vol. 3, pp. 150–164, 2022. https://doi.org/10.1016/j.ijin.2022.09.004
2. A. A. AlZubi and K. Galyna, "Artificial intelligence and internet of things for sustainable farming and smart agriculture," IEEE Access, pp. 78686–78692. https://doi.org/10.1109/ACCESS.2023.3298215. https://doi.org/10.1109/ACCESS.2023.3298215
3. E. Elbasi, N. Mostafa, Z. AlArnaout and A. I. Zreikat, "Artificial intelligence technology in the agricultural sector: A systematic literature review," IEEE Access, vol. 11, pp. 171–202, 2023. https://doi.org/10.1109/ACCESS.2022.3232485
4. A. Rejeb, K. Rejeb, S. Zailani and J. G. Keogh, "Examining the interplay between artificial intelligence and the agri-food industry," Artificial Intelligence in Agriculture, vol. 6, pp. 111–128, Elsevier, 2022. https://doi.org/10.1016/j.aiia.2022.08.002
5. M. A. Hamed, M. F. El-Habib, R. Z. Sababa and M. M. Al-Hanjor, "Artificial intelligence in agriculture: Enhancing productivity and sustainability," International Journal of Engineering and Information Systems (IJEAIS), vol. 8, no. 8, pp. 1–5, 2024. ISSN: 2643-640X.
6. M. Spring and J. Faulconbridge, "How information technology automates and augments processes: Insights from artificial intelligence-based systems in professional service operations," Journal of Operations Management, vol. 68, no. 6–7, pp. 592–618, 2022. https://doi.org/10.1002/joom.1215

7. R. Kaur, D. Gabrijelčič and T. Klobučar, "Artificial intelligence for cybersecurity: Literature review and future research directions," Information Fusion, vol. 97, p. 101804, 2023. https://doi.org/10.1016/j.inffus.2023.101804
8. O. Okusi, "Leveraging AI and machine learning for the protection of critical national infrastructure," Asian Journal of Research in Computer Science, vol. 17, pp. 1–11, 2024. https://doi.org/10.9734/ajrcos/2024/v17i10505
9. A. Alqudhaibi, A. Krishna and S. Jagtap et al., "Cybersecurity 4.0: Safeguarding trust and production in the digital food industry era," Discov Food, vol. 4, no. 2. https://doi.org/10.1007/s44187-023-00071-7
10. H. T. Bui, H. Aboutorab, A. Mahboubi, Y. Gao, N. H. Sultan, A. Chauhan, M. Z. Parvez, M. Bewong, R. Islam, Z. Islam, S. A. Camtepe, P. Gauravaram, D. Singh, M. A. Babar and S. Yan, "Agriculture 4.0 and beyond: Evaluating cyber threat intelligence sources and techniques in smart farming ecosystems," Computers & Security, vol. 140, p. 103754, 2024. https://doi.org/10.1016/j.cose.2024.103754
11. G. Ali, M. M. Mijwil and B. A. Buruga, "A survey on artificial intelligence in cybersecurity for smart agriculture: State-of-the-art, cyber threats, artificial intelligence applications, and ethical concerns," Mesopotamian, vol. 2024, pp. 53–103, 2024. https://doi.org/10.58496/MJCSC/2024/007
12. A. O. Adewusi and N. R. Chiekezie, "Cybersecurity threats in agriculture supply chains: A comprehensive review," World Journal of Advanced Research and Reviews, vol. 15, no. 3, pp. 490–500, 2022. https://doi.org/10.30574/wjarr.2022.15.3.0888
13. M. A. Ferrag, L. Shu and O. Friha, "Cyber security intrusion detection for agriculture 4.0: Machine learning-based solutions, datasets, and future directions," IEEE/CAA Journal of Automatica Sinica, vol. 9, no. 3, pp. 407–436, 2022. https://doi.org/10.1109/JAS.2021.1004344
14. R. Dara, S. M. Hazrati Fard and J. Kaur, "Recommendations for ethical and responsible use of artificial intelligence in digital agriculture," Frontiers in Artificial Intelligence, vol. 5, 2022. https://doi.org/10.3389/frai.2022.884192
15. M. Javaid, A. Haleem, I. H. Khan and R. Suman, "Understanding the potential applications of artificial intelligence in agriculture sector," Advanced Agrochem, vol. 2, no. 1, pp. 15–30, 2023. https://doi.org/10.1016/j.aac.2022.10.001
16. K. Sharma and S. K. Shivandu, "Integrating artificial intelligence and internet of things (IoT) for enhanced crop monitoring and management in precision agriculture," Sensors International, 2024. https://doi.org/10.1016/j.sintl.2024.100292
17. S. Qazi, B. A. Khawaja and Q. U. Farooq, "IoT-equipped and AI-enabled next generation smart agriculture: A critical review, current challenges and future trends," IEEE Access, pp. 21219–21235. https://doi.org/10.1109/ACCESS.2022.3152544
18. S. A. Bhat and N. F. Huang, "Big data and AI revolution in precision agriculture: Survey and challenges," IEEE Access, pp. 110209–110222, 2021. https://doi.org/10.1109/ACCESS.2021.3102227
19. P. Limna and S. Jakwatanatham, "A review of artificial intelligence (AI) in education during the digital era," Advance Knowledge for Executives, vol. 1, no. 1, pp. 1–9, 2022.
20. A. Khang, V. Shah and S. Rani, Handbook of Research on AI-Based Technologies and Applications in the Era of the Metaverse, 2023. https://doi.org/10.4018/978-1-6684-8851-5, pp. 517.
21. K. B. Letaief, Y. Shi, J. Lu and J. Lu, "Edge artificial intelligence for 6G: Vision, enabling technologies, and applications," Areas in Communications, pp. 5–36, 2021. https://doi.org/10.1109/JSAC.2021.3126076
22. A. B. Rashid and A. K. Kausik, "AI revolutionizing industries worldwide: A comprehensive overview of its diverse applications," Hybrid Advances, vol. 7, p. 100277, 2024. https://doi.org/10.1016/j.hybadv.2024.100277

23. F. Cristinel, B. L. Daniela and Z. Vitali, "The future of agriculture drone technology trends and prospects," Economic and Social, 79th International Scientific Conference on Economic and Social Development, 2022, pp. 68. ResearchGate.
24. V. Radić, N. Radić and V. Cogoljević, "New technologies as a driver of change in the agricultural sector," Економика пољопривреде, vol. 69, no. 1, pp. 147–162, 2022. CyberLeninka. https://doi.org/10.5937/ekoPolj2201147R
25. T. H. H. Aldhyani and H. Alkahtani, "Cyber security for detecting distributed denial of service attacks in agriculture 4.0: Deep learning model," Mathematics, vol. 11, p. 233, 2023. https://doi.org/10.3390/math11010233
26. D. R. Harris, "Introduction: Themes and concepts in the study of early agriculture," The Origins and Spread of Agriculture and Pastoralism, 1st ed., p. 9, Routledge, 1996. eBook ISBN: 9781003579861.
27. D. M. Rizzo, M. Lichtveld and J. A. K. Mazet et al., "Plant health and its effects on food safety and security in a one health framework: Four case studies," One Health Outlook, vol. 3, no. 6, 2021. https://doi.org/10.1186/s42522-021-00038-7
28. R. Abbasi, P. Martinez and R. Ahmad, "The digitization of agricultural industry – A systematic literature review on agriculture 4.0," Smart Agricultural Technology, vol. 2, p. 100042, 2022. https://doi.org/10.1016/j.atech.2022.100042
29. R. M. Chiles, G. Broad, M. Gagnon and N. Negowetti, "Democratizing ownership and participation in the 4th industrial revolution: Challenges and opportunities in cellular agriculture," Agriculture and Human Values, vol. 38, pp. 943–961, 2021. https://doi.org/10.1007/s10460-021-10237-7
30. A. Bin Abu Sofian, H. R. Lim and S. Manickam, "Towards a sustainable circular economy: Algae-Based bioplastics and the role of internet-of-things and machine learning," ChemBioEng Rev, vol. 11, no. 1, pp. 39–59, 2024. https://doi.org/10.1002/cben.202300028
31. A. Sutanto, A. Rakhman and I. Afriliana, "Narrowband IoT in livestock farming: A technological innovation for productivity and sustainability," International Journal of Science, Technology & Management, vol. 5, no. 5, pp. 1291–1297, 2024. https://doi.org/10.46729/ijstm.v5i5.1030
32. M. M. Rahman and M. Mahbub-Or-Rashid et al., "FruVeg_MultiNet: A hybrid deep learning-enabled IoT system for fresh fruit and vegetable identification with web interface and customized blind glasses for visually impaired individuals," Journal of Agriculture and Food Research, vol. 19, p. 101623, 2025. https://doi.org/10.1016/j.jafr.2024.101623
33. M. Zmami and O. Ben-Salha, "What factors contribute to the volatility of food prices? New global evidence," Agricultural Economics – Czech, vol. 69, no. 5, pp. 171–184, 2023. Agriculture Journals. https://doi.org/10.17221/99/2023-AGRICECON
34. S. Shan, "Identification of socioeconomic factors influencing global food price security using machine learning," arXiv Preprint Arxiv:2403.04231, 2024. https://doi.org/10.48550/arXiv.2403.04231
35. J. P. Aryal, N. Manchanda and T. Sonobe, "Expectations for household food security in the coming decades: A global scenario," Future Foods, pp. 107–131. https://doi.org/10.1016/B978-0-323-91001-9.00002-5
36. P. Kariuki, L. O. Ofusori and P. R. Subramaniam, "Cybersecurity threats and vulnerabilities experienced by small-scale African migrant traders in Southern Africa," Security Journal, vol. 37, pp. 292–321, 2024. https://doi.org/10.1057/s41284-023-00378-1
37. S. M. Dickson and I. P. Okechukwu, "Cyber security in the age of the internet of things, constraints, and solutions," Journal of Digital Learning and Distance Education, vol. 2, no. 11, pp. 829–837, 2024. https://doi.org/10.56778/jdlde.v2i11.233

38. A. O. Adewusi and N. R. Chiekezie, "Securing smart agriculture: Cybersecurity challenges and solutions in IoT-driven farms," World Journal of Advanced Research and Reviews, vol. 15, no. 3, pp. 480–489, 2022. https://doi.org/10.30574/wjarr.2022.15.3.0887
39. M. Hassan, K. Malhotra and M. Firdaus, "Application of artificial intelligence in IoT security for crop yield prediction," ResearchBerg Review of Science and Technology, vol. 2, no. 1, 2022. https://orcid.org/0009-0002-2232-2855
40. M. Rahaman, C. Y. Lin, P. Pappachan and B. B. Gupta et al., "Privacy-centric AI and IoT solutions for smart rural farm monitoring and control," Sensors, vol. 24, p. 4157, 2024. https://doi.org/10.3390/s24134157
41. M. Otieno, "An extensive survey of smart agriculture technologies: Current security posture," World Journal of Advanced Research and Reviews, vol. 18, no. 3, pp. 1207–1231, 2023. Article. https://doi.org/10.30574/wjarr.2023.18.3.1241
42. M. M. Yamin, M. Ullah, H. Ullah and B. Katt, "Weaponized AI for cyber attacks," Journal of Information Security and Applications, vol. 57, p. 102722, 2021. https://doi.org/10.1016/j.jisa.2020.102722
43. D. Kalla, F. Samaah and S. Kuraku, "Phishing detection implementation using databricks and artificial intelligence," International Journal of Computer Applications, vol. 185, no. 11, pp. 1–9, 2023. https://doi.org/10.5120/ijca2023922764
44. M. Gupta, C. K. Akiri, K. Aryal and E. Parker et al., "From ChatGPT to ThreatGPT: Impact of generative AI in cybersecurity and privacy," IEEE Access, vol. 99, pp. 1–11, 2023. https://doi.org/10.1109/ACCESS.2023.3300381
45. Y. Mirsky, A. Demontis, J. Kotak, R. Shankar and D. Gelei, "The threat of offensive AI to organizations," Computers & Security, vol. 124, p. 103006, 2023. https://doi.org/10.1016/j.cose.2022.103006
46. H. Ren, T. Huang and H. Yan, "Adversarial examples: Attacks and defenses in the physical world," International Journal of Machine Learning and Cybernetics, vol. 12, pp. 3325–3336, 2021. https://doi.org/10.1007/s13042-020-01242-z
47. M. Khan and L. Ghafoor, "Adversarial machine learning in the context of network security: Challenges and solutions," Journal of Computational Intelligence and Robotics, vol. 4, no. 1, pp. 51–63, 2024.
48. K. He, D. D. Kim and M. R. Asghar, "Adversarial machine learning for network intrusion detection systems: A comprehensive survey," IEEE Communications Surveys & Tutorials, vol. 2023, pp. 538–566. https://doi.org/10.1109/COMST.2022.3233793
49. R. Gao, X. Liu, Z. Xiong, G. Wang and L. Ai, "Research progress on detection of foodborne pathogens: The more rapid and accurate answer to food safety," Food Research International, vol. 193, p. 114767, 2024. ISSN 0963-9969. https://doi.org/10.1016/j.foodres.2024.114767
50. N. R. Palakurti, "AI applications in food safety and quality control," ESP Journal of Engineering & Technology, vol. 2022, pp. 48–61, + Id: JETA-V2I3P111, Doi: 10.56472/25832646/JETA-V2I3P111
51. K. Kudashkina, M. G. Corradini and P. Thirunathan, "Artificial intelligence technology in food safety: A behavioral approach," Trends in Food Science, pp. 376–381, Elsevier, 2022. https://doi.org/10.1016/j.tifs.2022.03.021
52. C. Qian, S. I. Murphy and R. H. Orsi, "How can AI help improve food safety?" Annual Review of Food Science and Technology, pp. 517–538, 2023. https://doi.org/10.1146/annurev-food-060721-013815
53. M. Mburu, "Cyber Security in Small and Medium Enterprises," 2023, Diva-portal.org, Perceived Challenges of Implementing Machine Learning-Based Intrusion Detection Systems in Small and Medium Enterprises, Supervisor: Steve McKeever, Master's Information Systems, Course Code: 2IS082 76019 VT2023, Department: Informatics and Media.

54. N. Rawindaran, "Impact of Cyber Security Awareness in Small, Medium Enterprises (SMEs) in Wales," Doctoral Thesis, Cardiff Metropolitan University, 2023, pp. 1–238. https://figshare.cardiffmet.ac.uk/articles/thesis/Impact_of_cyber_security_awareness_in_small_medium_enterprises_SMEs_in_Wales/23599497?file=41412072
55. M. Gula and J. Butler, "Securing big data with AI: How cybersecurity solutions improve profitability in SMEs," ResearchGate, pp. 1–13. https://doi.org/10.13140/RG.2.2.20537.58727
56. A. Papathanasiou, G. Liontos and A. Katsouras, "Cybersecurity guide for SMEs: Protecting small and medium-sized enterprises in the digital era," Journal of Information Security, pp. 1–43, 2024. https://doi.org/10.4236/jis.2025.161001
57. B. Cinar and R. K. Thomas, "Cyber-biosecurity: A paradigm shift in the field of life sciences and agriculture sector," Asian Journal of Biotechnology, vol. 6, no. 1, pp. 58–75, 2023, Article no. AJBGE.10087
58. S. Shekhar, M. Durgam, S. B. Khose, C. Pohshna and D. G. Bhalekar, "Advancement and challenges of implementing artificial intelligence of things in precision agriculture," Artificial Intelligence Techniques in Smart Agriculture, pp. 1–13, Springer, 2024. https://doi.org/10.1007/978-981-97-5878-4_13
59. M. El Alaoui, K. El Amraoui, L. Masmoudi, A. Ettouhami and M. Rouchdi, "Unleashing the potential of IoT, artificial intelligence, and UAVs in contemporary agriculture: A comprehensive review," Journal of Terramechanics, vol. 115, p. 100986, 2024. https://doi.org/10.1016/j.jterra.2024.100986
60. N. G. Camacho, "The role of AI in cybersecurity: Addressing threats in the digital age," Journal of Artificial Intelligence General Science (JAIGS), pp. 143–154, 2024. https://doi.org/10.60087/jaigs.v3i1.75
61. K. Bissadu and G. Hossain, "Agriculture 5.0 cybersecurity: Monitoring agricultural cyber threats with digital twin technology," 2024 IEEE World AI IoT, 2024, researchgate.net. https://doi.org/10.1109/AIIoT61789.2024.10579017.
62. A. O. Adewusi, N. R. Chiekezie and N. L. Eyo-Udo, "The role of AI in enhancing cybersecurity for smart farms," World Journal of Advanced Research and Reviews, pp. 501–512, 2022. https://doi.org/10.30574/wjarr.2022.15.3.0889
63. Z. Angyalos, S. Botos and R. Szilágyi, "The importance of cybersecurity in modern agriculture," Journal of Agricultural Informatics, vol. 12, no. 2, pp. 1–8, 2021. https://doi.org/10.17700/jai.2021.12.2.604
64. S. Hoseinzadeh and D. A. Garcia, "AI-driven innovations in greenhouse agriculture: Reanalysis of sustainability and energy efficiency impacts," Energy Conversion and Management: X, vol. 24, p. 100701, 2024. https://doi.org/10.1016/j.ecmx.2024.100701
65. M. Snehi and A. Bhandari, "Vulnerability retrospection of security solutions for software-defined Cyber–Physical system against DDoS and IoT-DDoS attacks," Computer Science Review, vol. 40, p. 100371, 2021. https://doi.org/10.1016/j.cosrev.2021.100371
66. P. Kommisetty and N. Abhireddy, "Cloud migration strategies: Ensuring seamless integration and scalability in dynamic business environments," International Journal of Engineering and Computer Science, vol. 13, no. 4, pp. 26146–26156, 2024. https://doi.org/10.18535/ijecs/v13i04.4812
67. Y. Alghofaili, A. Albattah, N. Alrajeh and M. A. Rassam, "Secure cloud infrastructure: A survey on issues, current solutions, and open challenges," Applied Sciences, 2021. https://doi.org/10.3390/app11199005
68. F. N. U. Jimmy, "Cyber security vulnerabilities and remediation through cloud security tools," Journal of Artificial Intelligence General Science, p. 234, 2024. https://doi.org/10.60087/jaigs.vol03.issue01.p234

69. M. Jangjou and M. K. Sohrabi, "A comprehensive survey on security challenges in different network layers in cloud computing," Archives of Computational Methods in Engineering, pp. 3587–3608, 2022. https://doi.org/10.1007/s11831-022-09708-9
70. O. D. Segun-Falade and O. S. Osundare, "Evaluating the role of cloud integration in mobile and desktop operating systems," in Proc. of Management & Technology Conference, 2024, pp. 019–031. https://doi.org/10.56781/ijsret.2024.4.1.0019
71. A. Kulkarni, Y. Wang, M. Gopinath and D. Sobien, "A review of cybersecurity incidents in the food and agriculture sector," arXiv Preprint Arxiv, 2024. pp. 1–34, arXiv preprint arXiv:2403.08036.
72. A. H. Salem, S. M. Azzam, O. E. Emam and A. A. Abohany, "Advancing cybersecurity: A comprehensive review of AI-driven detection techniques," Journal of Big Data, vol. 11, p. 105, 2024. https://doi.org/10.1186/s40537-024-00957-y
73. D. Ghelani, T. K. Hua and S. K. R. Koduru, "Cyber security threats, vulnerabilities, and security solutions models in banking," Authorea Preprints, pp. 1–9, 2022. https://doi.org/10.22541/au.166385206.63311335/v1
74. M. Ahsan, K. E. Nygard and R. Gomes, "Cybersecurity threats and their mitigation approaches using machine learning – A review," Journal of Cybersecurity and Privacy, pp. 527–555, 2022. https://doi.org/10.3390/jcp2030027
75. A. Yaseen, "Enhancing cybersecurity through automated infrastructure management: A comprehensive study on optimizing security measures," Quarterly Journal of Emerging Technologies, vol. 9, no. 1, pp. 38–60, 2024, retrieved from https://vectoral.org/index.php/QJETI/article/view/68
76. T. Alsuwian, A. Shahid Butt and A. A. Amin, "Smart grid cyber security enhancement: Challenges and solutions – A review," Sustainability, vol. 14, p. 14226, 2022. https://doi.org/10.3390/su142114226
77. S. AlDaajeh, H. Saleous, S. Alrabaee and E. Barka, "The role of national cybersecurity strategies on the improvement of cybersecurity education," Computers & Security, vol. 119, no. 4, p. 102754, 2022. https://doi.org/10.1016/j.cose.2022.102754
78. M. A. Salem and A. E. E. Sobaih, "A quadruple 'E' approach for effective cyber-hygiene behaviour and attitude toward online learning among higher-education students in Saudi Arabia amid ...," Electronics, vol. 12, no. 10, p. 2268, 2023. https://doi.org/10.3390/electronics12102268
79. J. W. Howell Jr, "Exploring the Perceptions of Perceived and Actual Cyber Readiness," 2021, Capella University ProQuest Dissertations & Theses, 2021, 28962485.
80. B. Uchendu, C. Nurse, M. Bada and S. Furnell, "Developing a cyber security culture: Current practices and future needs," Computers & Security, vol. 109, p. 102387, 2021, ISSN 0167-4048. https://doi.org/10.1016/j.cose.2021.102387
81. V. Tuomala, "Human Factor, Cyber Hygiene, Cyber-Physical Systems, and Industrial Control Systems in the Context of Cybersecurity," 2023, pp. 1–92. https://urn.fi/URN:NBN:fi:amk-2023052313040
82. A. AL-Hawamleh, "Cyber resilience framework: Strengthening defenses and enhancing continuity in business security," International Journal of Computing and Digital Science, vol. 15, no. 1, pp. 1315–1331, 2024. https://doi.org/10.12785/ijcds/150193
83. O. Rasheed, "Modelling and Integrated Risk Management in Transport Logistic Network-A Case Study of Agro Food Product," 2022, Liverpool John Moores University (United Kingdom), ProQuest Dissertations & Theses, 31059599.
84. C. Trevisan and M. Formentini, "Digital technologies for food loss and waste prevention and reduction in agri-food supply chains: A systematic literature review and research agenda," IEEE Transactions on Engineering, pp. 12326–12345, 2023. https://doi.org/10.1109/TEM.2023.3273110

85. S. Gallego-García and D. Gallego-García, "Sustainability in the agri-food supply chain: A combined digital twin and simulation approach for farmers," Procedia Computer, vol. 217, pp. 1280–1295, 2023. https://doi.org/10.1016/j.procs.2022.12.326
86. C. M. Fernandez, J. Alves, P. D. Gaspar and T. M. Lima, "Fostering awareness on environmentally sustainable technological solutions for the post-harvest food supply chain," Processes, vol. 9, p. 1611, 2021. https://doi.org/10.3390/pr9091611
87. N. Virmani and R. K. Singh, "Analysis of barriers for adopting blockchain in agri-food supply chain management: A decision support framework," International Journal of Quality & Reliability Management, vol. 41, no. 8, pp. 2122–2145, 2024. https://doi.org/10.1108/IJQRM-03-2023-0078
88. W. A. Orjuela-Garzon and A. Sandoval-Aldana et al., "Systematic literature review of barriers and enablers to implementing food informatics technologies: Unlocking agri-food chain innovation," Foods, vol. 13, no. 21, p. 3349, 2024. https://doi.org/10.3390/foods13213349
89. A. Sridhar, M. Ponnuchamy and P. S. Kumar, "Digitalization of the agro-food sector for achieving sustainable development goals: A review," Sustainable Food, vol. 1, no. 6, pp. 783–802, 16 November 2023. https://doi.org/10.1039/d3fb00124e
90. M. K. Sharma, V. S. Dhaka and R. S. Shekhawat, "Intelligent agro-food chain supply," Internet of Things and Analytics for Agriculture, Volume 3. Studies in Big Data, vol. 99, pp. 65–91, Springer, Singapore, 2022. https://doi.org/10.1007/978-981-16-6210-2_4
91. D. Tiwari, B. Mondal, S. K. Singh and D. Koundal, "Lightweight encryption for privacy protection of data transmission in cyber physical systems," Cluster Computing, vol. 26, pp. 2351–2365, 2023. https://doi.org/10.1007/s10586-022-03790-1
92. G. Nookala, K. R. Gade and N. Dulam, "Zero-trust security frameworks: The role of data encryption in cloud infrastructure," MZ Computing, vol. 4, no. 1, 2023, mzjournal.com.
93. S. Abdelkader, J. Amissah, S. Kinga and G. Mugerwa, "Securing modern power systems: Implementing comprehensive strategies to enhance resilience and reliability against cyber-attacks," Results in Engineering, vol. S, pp. 1–15, 2024. https://doi.org/10.1016/j.rineng.2024.102647
94. A. Javadpour, F. Ja'fari, T. Taleb, Y. Zhao, B. Yang and C. Benzaïd, "Encryption as a service for IoT: Opportunities, challenges, and solutions," in IEEE Internet of Things Journal, vol. 11, no. 5, pp. 7525–7558, 2024. https://doi.org/10.1109/JIOT.2023.3341875.
95. A. Shaji George, A. S. Hovan George and T. Baskar, "Digitally immune systems: Building robust defences in the age of cyber threats," Partners Universal International Innovation Journal, vol. 1, no. 4, pp. 155–172, 2023. https://doi.org/10.5281/zenodo.8274514
96. A. Manoharan, "The Rise of Quantum Cryptography: Securing Data Beyond Classical Means," Academia.edu, pp. 6329–6336. https://doi.org/10.56726/IRJMETS24238
97. A. Blackwood, J. Carrington, S. Baryshevsky and G. Morrison, "The implementation of a hybrid large language model for adaptive cryptographic cyber defense," ResearchSquare, 22 September 2024, PREPRINT (Version 1). https://doi.org/10.21203/rs.3.rs-5120507/v1
98. R. K. Jha, "Cybersecurity and confidentiality in smart grid for enhancing sustainability and reliability," Recent Research Reviews Journal, vol. 2, no. 2, p. 215, 2023. https://doi.org/10.36548/rrrj.2023.2.001
99. J. Zscheischler, R. Brunsch, S. Rogga and R. W. Scholz, "Perceived risks and vulnerabilities of employing digitalization and digital data in agriculture – Socially

robust orientations from a transdisciplinary process," Journal of Cleaner Production, vol. 358, p. 132034, 2022, ISSN 0959-6526. https://doi.org/10.1016/j.jclepro.2022.132034
100. R. Wheeler and M. Lobley, "Managing extreme weather and climate change in UK agriculture: Impacts, attitudes and action among farmers and stakeholders," Climate Risk Management, vol. 32, p. 100313, 2021, ISSN 2212-0963. https://doi.org/10.1016/j.crm.2021.100313
101. D. Ajiga, P. A. Okeleke, S. O. Folorunsho and C. Ezeigweneme, "Designing cybersecurity measures for Enterprise software applications to protect data integrity," Computer Science & IT Research Journal, vol. 5, no. 8, pp. 1920–1941, 2024. https://doi.org/10.51594/csitrj.v5i8.1451
102. A. E. Esiri, D. D. Jambol and C. Ozowe, "Frameworks for risk management to protect underground sources of drinking water during oil and gas extraction," Open Access Research Journal of Multidisciplinary Studies, vol. 07, no. 02, pp. 159–167, 2024. https://doi.org/10.53022/oarjms.2024.7.2.0037
103. M. A. Eruaga, "Policy strategies for managing food safety risks associated with climate change and agriculture," SSRJournals.Com, vol. 04, no. 01, pp. 021–032, 2024. https://doi.org/10.56781/ijsrr.2024.4.1.0026
104. V. Shah, "Machine learning algorithms for cybersecurity: Detecting and preventing threats," Revista Espanola de Documentacion Cientifica, vol. 15, no. 4, pp. 42–66, 2021.
105. F. Ekundayo, I. Atoyebi, A. Soyele and E. Ogunwobi, "Predictive analytics for cyber threat intelligence in Fintech using big data and machine learning," International Journal of Research Publication and Reviews, vol. 5, no. 11, pp. 5934–5948, 2024. https://doi.org/10.55248/gengpi.5.1124.3352.
106. F. A. Ajayi and C. A. Udeh, "Review of crew resilience and mental health practices in the marine industry: Pathways to improvement," Magna Scientia Advanced Biology, vol. 4, no. 11, pp. (02), 033–049, 2024. https://doi.org/10.30574/msabp.2024.11.2.0021
107. A. B. Ige, E. Kupa and O. Ilori, "Best Practices in cybersecurity for green building management systems: Protecting sustainable infrastructure from cyber threats," Journal of Science and Research Archive, vol. 12, no. 01, pp. 2960–2977, 2024. https://doi.org/10.30574/ijsra.2024.12.1.1185
108. A. B. Ige, E. Kupa and O. Ilori, "Analyzing defense strategies against cyber risks in the energy sector: Enhancing the security of renewable energy sources," Journal of Science and Research Archive, vol. 12, no. 01, pp. 2978–2995, 2024. https://doi.org/10.30574/ijsra.2024.12.1.1186
109. M. F. Safitra, M. Lubis and H. Fakhrurroja, "Counterattacking cyber threats: A framework for the future of cybersecurity," Sustainability, vol. 15, 2023, Article 13369. https://doi.org/10.3390/su151813369

Chapter 8

Secure architecture for multi-edge computing in industrial IoT based on blockchain and SDN

Jihad Kilani, Youssef Baddi, Faiçal Bensalah

8.1 INTRODUCTION

The Fourth Industrial Revolution, often termed as Industry 4.0, marks a significant shift toward the amalgamation of physical and cyber systems in the industrial domain. At the heart of this transformation is the Industrial Internet of Things (IIoT), which is experiencing unparalleled growth and revolutionizing traditional industries. By enabling devices to communicate and collaborate seamlessly, the IIoT is not only redefining efficiency and productivity but also introducing a spectrum of complexities and challenges [1].

As the digital age advances, the proliferation of IoT devices across sectors, from manufacturing to health care, emphasizes the need for robust, real-time IT solutions. Edge computing, with its promise to process data closer to its source, has emerged as a beacon of hope. It offers real-time data processing at the network's edge, addressing the latency and bandwidth constraints inherent in cloud-centric systems [1].

However, while edge computing holds immense promise, it's not devoid of challenges. Traditional edge computing architectures, although effective in specific contexts, grapple with issues related to data security, real-time processing, and intricate network management [2]. Such challenges, if left unresolved, threaten the reliability and potential of the entire IIoT landscape.

Recognizing these challenges, this chapter embarks on an explorative journey to propose an innovative architecture rooted in the principles of blockchain and the software-defined network (SDN). The goal is to harness the inherent security and transparency of blockchain, coupled with the flexibility of SDN, to design a solution tailored for IIoT environments [3].

At the core of this study are two pivotal research questions. The first delves into the role of blockchain and SDN in enhancing trust within the network, especially in an environment teeming with device interactions. The second addresses the ever-present threat of Distributed Denial of Service (DDoS) attacks and explores the resilience of the proposed architecture in ensuring uninterrupted operations and data availability [4].

By integrating quantitative and qualitative research methodologies, this study aims to not only propose but also rigorously assess the viability of

DOI: 10.1201/9781003597476-11

the blockchain-SDN-based architecture. In doing so, it aspires to contribute meaningfully to the ongoing discourse surrounding Industry 4.0, paving the way for a more interconnected, efficient, and secure industrial future.

The rest of the chapter is organized as follows: Section 8.2 provides a comprehensive literature review, highlighting previous studies and the current state-of-the-art in blockchain-SDN integration for IIoT. In Section 8.3, the proposed blockchain-SDN integrated model is detailed, outlining its architecture, components, and functionalities. Section 8.4 presents an exhaustive experimental evaluation of the proposed model, showcasing its performance in various scenarios. Challenges and potential solutions for the real-world implementation of the architecture are discussed in Section 8.5. Subsequent sections delve into emerging trends and future directions, emphasizing the potential enhancements and how they can shape the future of IIoT. Finally, Section 8.6 concludes the chapter, summarizing the key findings and contributions.

8.2 BACKGROUND AND LITERATURE REVIEW

In this literature review, we will delve into three pivotal aspects that form the foundation of our investigation into the IIoT landscape. Our comprehensive examination will encompass the following key areas:

8.2.1 Introduction to existing challenges in IIoT, with a focus on multi-edge computing

The initial segment of our review will provide a comprehensive introduction to the prevailing challenges within the realm of IIoT. Our emphasis will be directed toward the role of multi-edge computing as a strategic solution to tackle these challenges. We will explore the intricacies of data management, security, network connectivity, scalability, energy efficiency, analytics, regulatory compliance, and cost management. By doing so, we aim to establish a robust foundation for the subsequent discussions on potential solutions and advancements.

8.2.1.1 Data management and processing challenges

The exponential growth in data generated by IIoT devices has imposed a formidable challenge on conventional centralized systems. This challenge, characterized by the sheer volume of data, has highlighted the need for innovative approaches to data management within the IIoT ecosystem. Multi-edge computing emerges as a pivotal solution to address this pressing issue, as underscored in the works of Shi et al. [5] and Alam et al. [6]. By strategically positioning data preprocessing and analysis closer to the data source, multi-edge computing offers a practical means to offload the data processing burden from resource-intensive cloud servers. This decentralized approach not only enhances the efficiency of data management but also contributes to the reduction of latency, a critical requirement for real-time decision-making in industrial applications.

Moreover, the requirement for real-time decision-making looms large in the industrial landscape. In dynamic and mission-critical industrial processes, timely responses to emerging events can be the difference between success and failure. Herein lies the intrinsic value of multi-edge computing, exemplified in the research of Huang et al. [7] and Cao et al. [8]. The architecture's capacity for low-latency data processing equips industrial systems with the capability to react swiftly to evolving conditions. By minimizing the delay between data generation and analysis, multi-edge computing ensures that decisions are made in near real-time, bolstering the adaptability and efficiency of industrial operations. These two facets, namely, the alleviation of data volume challenges and the facilitation of real-time decision-making, collectively demonstrate the indispensable role of multi-edge computing in addressing critical issues within the IIoT domain. As we delve deeper into the literature, we will uncover additional dimensions of its significance and potential for transforming industrial processes.

8.2.1.2 Security and privacy challenges

The exponential growth of IIoT devices has undeniably ushered in a multitude of opportunities for improved industrial processes and efficiency. However, this proliferation has also exposed these systems to a new frontier of cybersecurity challenges. With the diverse array of connected devices and the vast volume of data they generate, the threat landscape has expanded considerably. Fortunately, multi-edge computing has emerged as a formidable defense mechanism against these threats, bolstering the security posture of IIoT systems. By distributing critical data processing tasks to the edge, multi-edge computing minimizes vulnerabilities that might be exploited by malicious actors [9–11].

Privacy concerns in the context of IIoT are equally paramount. Industrial data, often comprising sensitive information, demands rigorous safeguards to protect confidentiality and integrity. With the decentralization of data processing to the edge, maintaining privacy compliance becomes a complex yet imperative endeavor. It necessitates meticulous attention to detail, encompassing data localization strategies to ensure data remains within permissible boundaries and access control mechanisms to restrict unauthorized data access [12]. This intricate interplay between data processing at the edge and stringent privacy requirements underscores the nuanced nature of IIoT's privacy landscape, which we shall further explore in this chapter.

8.2.1.3 Scalability and network connectivity challenges

Interoperability is a critical concern in the IIoT landscape, primarily due to the proliferation of diverse devices from various manufacturers. This heterogeneity presents formidable challenges in terms of seamless device integration and communication. Multi-edge computing, as elucidated in the comprehensive study by Hazra et al. [13], assumes a pivotal role in surmounting these interoperability hurdles. By furnishing standardized interfaces and protocols, multi-edge computing facilitates the harmonious integration of disparate devices. This standardization not only streamlines the process of connecting IIoT devices but also enhances their ability to communicate effectively within the network. The result is an interconnected ecosystem that transcends the barriers of device diversity, fostering a cohesive and efficient IIoT environment.

Moreover, the aspect of reliability in IIoT deployments, particularly within the challenging terrain of harsh industrial environments, represents an ongoing and pervasive concern. These environments are often characterized by adverse conditions that can disrupt wireless connectivity and compromise system integrity. Liu et al.'s work [14] underscores the importance of ensuring reliable communication between edge devices and the central system under such conditions. Multi-edge computing offers a promising avenue for enhancing reliability by introducing redundancy, fault tolerance mechanisms, and adaptive routing strategies. By fortifying the communication infrastructure with these capabilities, multi-edge computing mitigates the risks associated with interruptions in connectivity, ensuring the consistent and dependable operation of IIoT systems even in the face of adverse environmental factors.

The imperative of scaling edge computing resources to cater to the burgeoning number of IIoT devices is a multifaceted endeavor that demands meticulous planning and management, as emphasized by Ren et al. [15]. This challenge extends beyond merely adding additional hardware; it necessitates a comprehensive approach encompassing resource allocation, load balancing, and system optimization. The orchestrated growth of edge servers and gateways is crucial to ensuring the continued seamless operation of IIoT ecosystems, particularly as the volume of data and device deployments escalates. Furthermore, within the industrial landscape, the prevalence of legacy systems adds a layer of complexity to the integration of modern IIoT solutions, especially those harnessing the power of multi-edge computing. The intricacies of this integration challenge are thoroughly explored in the work of Givehchi et al. [16]. These legacy systems, often deeply ingrained within industrial facilities, present compatibility and connectivity hurdles. Bridging the gap between these time-tested but rigid systems and the dynamic capabilities offered by modern IIoT, including multi-edge computing, requires innovative solutions and a nuanced understanding of both worlds.

8.2.2 Blockchain and software-defined networking (SDN) for IIoT

The second phase of our literature review will offer a concise yet illuminating overview of two transformative technologies: Blockchain and SDN. We will underscore their potential applications and benefits within the context of IIoT. Blockchain's capabilities in securing data and transactions, and SDN's ability to enhance network flexibility and management, hold immense promise for addressing the challenges posed by IIoT. Our exploration of these technologies will set the stage for their integration into IIoT solutions in subsequent sections. In the context of the IIoT, blockchain and SDN have emerged as transformative technologies with the potential to revolutionize various aspects of industrial processes. Blockchain technology offers a secure and tamper-proof ledger for IIoT data. Its decentralized and immutable nature ensures the integrity and authenticity of data, making it particularly relevant for IIoT applications where data accuracy and trustworthiness are paramount. Blockchain can enhance data provenance, traceability, and security, providing a robust foundation for IIoT systems [17–19]. Researchers and practitioners are exploring its use in supply chain management, quality control, and device authentication within industrial settings. On the other hand, SDN is instrumental in optimizing network infrastructure for IIoT deployments. SDN decouples the control plane from the data plane, allowing dynamic network management and resource allocation. In IIoT, where network demands can vary rapidly, SDN's flexibility enables efficient resource utilization and traffic prioritization [20]. This adaptability is vital for accommodating the diverse connectivity needs of IIoT devices, ensuring low-latency communication, and maintaining overall network reliability. Furthermore, the synergy between blockchain and SDN holds immense promise for IIoT applications. Blockchain's data security and SDN's network flexibility can be combined to create a robust and agile IIoT ecosystem. For instance, blockchain can be used to secure and verify transactions in IIoT networks, while SDN ensures that data is routed efficiently and with low latency [21]. Despite their potential benefits, it's crucial to acknowledge the challenges associated with implementing blockchain and SDN in IIoT. These include scalability concerns, interoperability issues, and the need for suitable standards and protocols. Additionally, the integration of these technologies into existing industrial infrastructures, often characterized by legacy systems, presents complex challenges [22, 23].

8.2.3 Current state-of-the-art solutions and their limitations

In the final segment of our literature review, we will undertake a meticulous examination of related works, unveiling the current state-of-the-art solutions designed to confront the challenges within the IIoT landscape. This critical analysis will encompass a wide array of research and practical implementations, shedding light on both the strengths and limitations of existing approaches. By critically assessing these solutions, we aim to discern opportunities for innovation and the development of novel strategies to further propel the field of IIoT.

The current state-of-the-art solutions within the IIoT landscape encompass an array of innovations, many of which have significantly contributed to mitigating the challenges we discussed earlier. These solutions span diverse domains, ranging from data analytics and machine learning algorithms tailored for edge computing environments [24–26] to robust security protocols and frameworks for ensuring data integrity [27, 28].

However, as we delve deeper into the examination of these cutting-edge solutions, it becomes evident that they are not without their limitations. While these innovations have undoubtedly made remarkable strides, they often grapple with constraints that necessitate further exploration and refinement.

For instance, the efficiency of edge-based analytics and machine learning models, while promising, can sometimes be hindered by the constraints of edge devices, which typically possess limited computational resources [29]. Similarly, the integration of blockchain and SDN into IIoT ecosystems presents big challenges related to scalability, latency, and interoperability.

Moreover, the sheer diversity of IIoT applications and the intricate regulatory landscapes in which they operate introduce complexities that demand a nuanced understanding. Achieving compliance with industry-specific regulations while ensuring seamless data flow within multi-edge computing architectures remains an ongoing concern. Additionally, cost considerations loom large in the adoption and scalability of IIoT solutions. While the potential for long-term efficiency gains is a compelling driver, the initial investment required for deploying multi-edge computing infrastructure can be substantial [1].

8.3 THE PROMISE OF BLOCKCHAIN AND SDN FOR INDUSTRIAL IoT

In the context of related works, a compelling narrative emerges, showcasing the immense potential of blockchain and SDN in the realm of IIoT. Blockchain, with its inherent attributes, stands as a formidable solution to ensure data integrity, transparency, and secure peer-to-peer transactions within IIoT environments. The essence of blockchain lies in its ability to maintain an immutable ledger, meticulously recording, and validating every data transaction. This unalterable record instills a sense of trust and reliability in IIoT data exchanges, safeguarding against unauthorized alterations and fostering data transparency.

Simultaneously, SDN emerges as a pivotal catalyst, introducing a centralized control plane that revolutionizes the landscape of network management within IIoT deployments. With a centralized locus of control, SDN enables dynamic and efficient allocation, reconfiguration, and optimization of network resources. By abstracting the underlying network infrastructure, SDN grants IIoT systems unprecedented flexibility and adaptability, aligning network behavior with the ever-evolving demands of industrial processes. This capability to effectively orchestrate and manage network resources becomes instrumental in ensuring the seamless and responsive operation of IIoT systems. Yet, it is at the intersection of blockchain and SDN where the promise of transformative change shines most brightly, as it addresses the unique challenges encountered within IIoT ecosystems. The fusion of blockchain's inherent data security and transparency with SDN's prowess in network management results in a potent synergy. This partnership can facilitate secure, efficient, and auditable data exchanges within industrial environments. Through blockchain's robust authentication and immutable record-keeping mechanisms, combined with SDN's dynamic network optimization capabilities, IIoT systems can achieve heightened resilience, reduced latency, and streamlined operations.

The potential of this combined approach transcends the conventional boundaries of data integrity and network efficiency. It has the power to redefine how IIoT systems establish trust, security, and scalability. By enabling secure peer-to-peer transactions and facilitating a centralized control plane, the amalgamation of blockchain and SDN serves as a beacon of hope for addressing the multifaceted challenges unique to the IIoT landscape. In the following sections of our review, we will delve deeper into specific instances and strategies that harness this promise, shedding light on their transformative impact on industrial processes, all within the context of the acclaimed USenix style.

8.4 PROPOSED ARCHITECTURE FOR BLOCKCHAIN-SDN-BASED MULTI-EDGE COMPUTING

In the dynamic realm of digital networks, the convergence of blockchain and SDN stands out as a promising development. This section provides a deep dive into a proposed architecture that amalgamates the strengths of both technologies, elaborating on its components, interactions, and workflows. As we navigate this landscape, two pivotal research questions are addressed. Initially, we focus on mechanisms establishing node trust within the blockchain and explore SDN-centric strategies to identify and neutralize malicious or spurious nodes. Subsequently, given the prevalent threat of cyberattacks, we underscore design considerations bolstering resilience against Distributed Denial-of-Service (DDoS) attacks. This is complemented by a discussion on SDN-based network configurations skilled in redirecting, filtering, or mitigating adversarial traffic. Throughout, the pivotal role of blockchain is accentuated, serving as a steadfast shield ensuring consistent data availability and trust, even amidst persistent cyber threats.

Figure 8.1 delineates the proposed architecture of a blockchain-enabled SDN IIoT ecosystem. Here's a breakdown of the architecture:

Nodes: Central to blockchain, nodes are individual computers or servers that actively engage in the blockchain network. Each node bears the onus of preserving an updated version of the distributed ledger. This ledger encompasses data structures termed as blocks, which encapsulate validated transaction batches. Every block is marked with a unique "hash" and references the hash of its antecedent block, thereby forming a chain. Predominantly, these blocks comprise transactions, each verified by a digital signature rooted in the sender's private key.

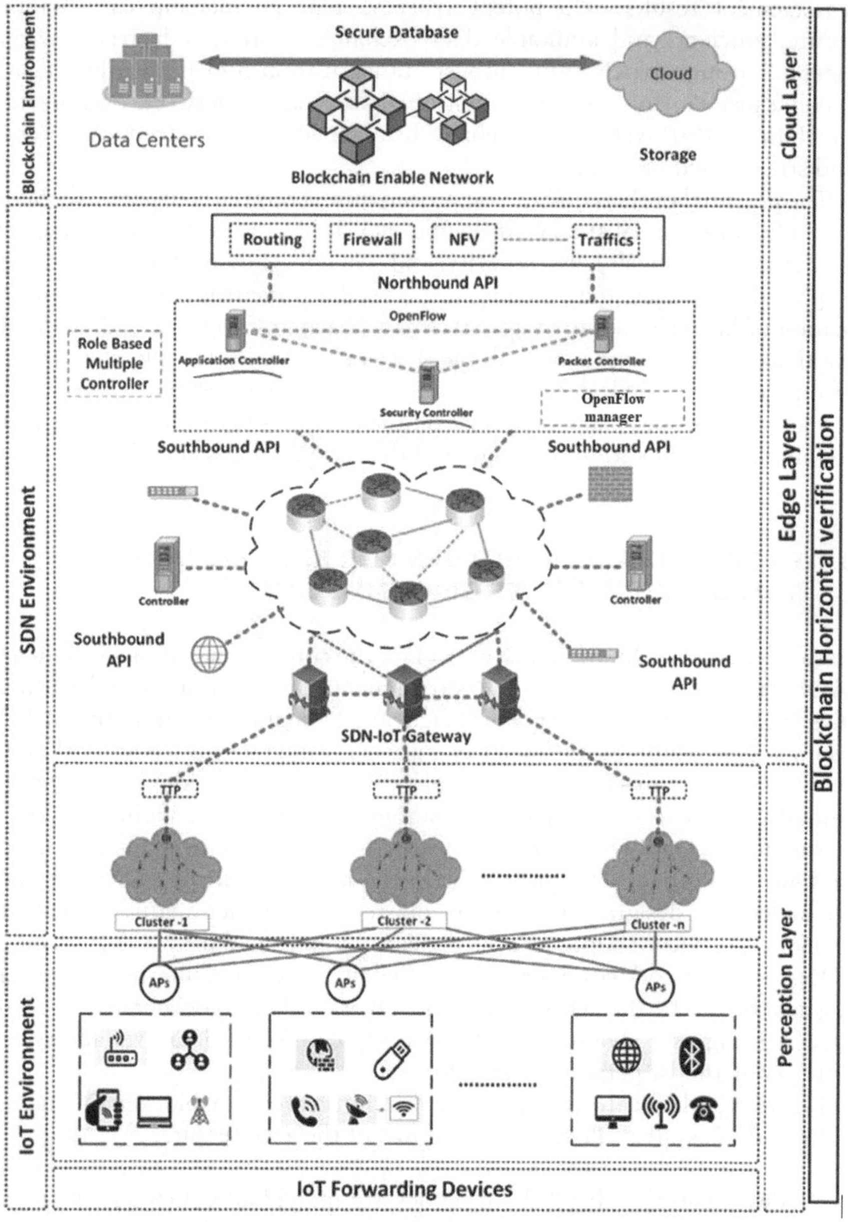

Figure 8.1 Proposed architecture of blockchain-enabled SDN-IoT ecosystem.

A key facet of blockchain is the Consensus Mechanism—a protocol the blockchain network leverages to achieve consensus about transaction validity. Among the myriad consensus mechanisms, proof of work (PoW) and proof of stake (PoS) are notably prevalent. Another noteworthy element is Smart Contracts—self-executing contracts with terms codified directly into the program. They operate independently, enacting the specified terms upon condition fulfillment.

Central to blockchain is the Distributed Ledger—a database where information is concurrently shared, synced, and agreed upon across myriad nodes. Ensuring transactional security and confidentiality are the Public and Private Keys. These cryptographic instruments secure transactions. While the public key is openly accessible, the private key remains a closely guarded secret exclusive to its possessor.

8.4.1 Design considerations for resilience against DDoS attacks

SDN's intrinsic in-band control mechanisms can, unfortunately, be manipulated by adversaries to instigate DDoS attacks targeting the control plane. To combat this, a resilient software-defined network necessitates dynamic isolation and control flow distribution, aiming to curtail damage and amplify attack costs. Design strategies for DDoS resistance emphasize minimal resource sharing, augmented control agent capacity, and the incorporation of proactive defense tactics. Efficiently countering DDoS attacks mandates collective efforts from all stakeholders, not just the target. Router-integrated mitigation mechanisms have proven to enhance defense efficiency and efficacy. Considering IoT device vulnerabilities, prioritizing lightweight DDoS attack detection and mitigation techniques via IoT botnets is essential. These should underscore security without trading off efficiency. To augment resilience, network configurations ought to be dynamically adapted, complicating the task for attackers scouting for vulnerabilities. Any advanced DDoS countermeasure must be scalable and seamlessly deployable on real networks, sidestepping extensive alterations to the existing framework.

In this context, the potential of SDN in autonomously mitigating DDoS and analogous large-scale attacks is showcased, capitalizing on SDN's flexibility and network oversight capabilities. The merits of SDN in simplifying network management and bolstering security oversight are emphasized. Additionally, its potential in refining anti-DDoS blueprints through the segregation of network control and data planes, coupled with centralized network forensics executed by SDN controllers, is highlighted. The chapter also touches upon the utility of VLAN-ID field tagging in OpenFlow switches, facilitating on-demand installation by the SDN controller, thereby enhancing system scalability. These strategies amalgamate both detection and counteraction protocols to safeguard the SDN network, monitoring incoming packet rates and resource utilization to thwart attacks while simultaneously posing intricate puzzles for authentic hosts. However, the mitigation approach might introduce processing delays for valid hosts and necessitate meticulous parameter optimization. Generic countermeasures employ diverse methodologies and architectures to tackle DDoS attacks stemming from resource depletion, including decentralized mitigation strategies underpinned by avant-garde technologies like blockchain.

8.4.2 Blockchain's role in ensuring data availability and trust even under attack conditions

Blockchain, an emergent technology, has been making waves for its profound impact on data security and reliable computing, especially in the context of cloud applications. This chapter introduces innovative blockchain techniques, aiming to ameliorate the challenges stemming from computational intricacy and existing solutions' scalability woes.

Central to the document is the unveiling of a blockchain-infused integrity protection framework, grounded in the virtual machine proxy model. This framework harnesses the unique hash values generated by the Merkel hash tree, monitoring data modifications with the assistance of smart contracts entrenched in the blockchain. A notable feature is its capability to promptly broadcast alerts in instances of data interference. Additionally, a "block-response" mode is employed to cross-check the integrity of data housed in the cloud [30].

In the vast ecosystem of IoT, blockchain emerges as a bastion of security, fortifying defenses against inherent vulnerabilities and ensuring that data remains accessible and trustworthy, even when under siege. The myriad security facets of blockchain, encompassing tamper-resistant protocols and robust access controls, serve as formidable deterrents to malefactors, thwarting any attempts at data manipulation [31]. The distributed ledger architecture of blockchain ensures data redundancy across a multitude of nodes, thereby eliminating the risks associated with single points of failure and assuring data availability even amidst node compromises.

The indelible nature of blockchain asserts that once data finds its residence on the blockchain, it's shielded from any alterations or erasures, thereby instilling an unwavering confidence in data integrity. The adept implementation of asymmetric cryptography coupled with smart contracts by blockchain paves the way for fortified authentication, confidentiality, and access management, further enhancing data availability and trust in IoT contexts [32].

By seamlessly integrating blockchain with IoT frameworks, the constraints and challenges of conventional trust management mechanisms can be effectively circumvented, laying the foundation for a fortified and dependable data exchange milieu [33].

8.5 USE CASES AND SIMULATIONS

The proposed architecture holds significant potential for deployment in IoT networks, addressing multifaceted challenges encompassing security, privacy, flexibility, scalability, and confidentiality. It's particularly suitable for scenarios prioritizing efficient energy consumption and minimized end-to-end delays within the IoT ecosystem. The architecture can be seamlessly integrated into smart networks, aiming to optimize energy consumption, minimize end-to-end delays, and maximize throughput in alignment with the stipulated reference levels. This ensures both efficiency and robust security. Furthermore, the architecture finds relevance in real-world IoT scenarios where the emphasis lies on secure network communication and astute resource management. It also shines in situations necessitating cluster head selection, safeguarded network communications, and consistent coordination within the controller cluster [34]. This framework is adaptable for IoT settings characterized by fixed nodes and clustering scenarios. Within these environments, the architecture collaborates with the designated set of cluster heads until the procedure is reinitiated. For comparative evaluations against other standards, the proposed framework can be simulated, assessing its performance, efficiency, and security [35].

8.5.1 Experimental setup

The ensuing section elucidates the simulation environment employed to manifest the proposed framework. As previously highlighted, our approach leverages Mininet for the emulation of software-defined network topologies, Ethereum to underpin the blockchain, and OpenFlow to facilitate SDN routing capabilities. All experimental testbeds were executed on a system equipped with an Intel(R) Core(TM) i7 CPU @ 2.50 GHz and a memory capacity of 32 GB RAM, operating on Ubuntu.

Table 8.1 offers a comprehensive breakdown of all simulation parameters, categorized based on their reference technology (i.e., SDN, blockchain, and IoT). Notably, Wireshark, augmented by Python scripts, serves as the tool of choice to capture and scrutinize packets produced by the devices constituting

Table 8.1 Parameters of the simulation environment grouped by reference technology

Simulation parameter	*Key value*
Network emulator	Mininet
Cloud storage platform	OpenStack
Packet analyzer	Tepdump, Wireshark
Programming language	Python
SDN routing protocol	OpenFlow 1.3
Number of SDN controllers	5
Blockchain platform	Ethereum
Consensus protocol	PoW, PoS
Block size	Amount of transaction fitting into a block
Mobility model	Random Waypoint Model (RWM)
Traffic type	Constant Bit Rate (CBR)
Number of IoT devices	100
Simulation time	500 s
Simulation area	3000 m × 3000 m
Data rate	10 Mbps
Transmitted packet size	128–1024 B
Initial energy value	10–12 J
Initial trust value	5.J

the tested SDN IoT network. To delve into specifics, the IoT setting is simulated over a span of 500 seconds, accommodating 100 IoT devices dispersed across a 3000 m × 3000 m area, adhering to a defined mobility model. Each device dispatches packets ranging in size from 128 B to 1024 B at a constant data rate of 10 Mbps. The initial energy and confidence values for these devices are set at 10–12 J and 5 J, respectively.

8.5.2 Results

In this section, we present a comprehensive analysis of the performance metrics pertaining to the proposed blockchain-SDN-based architecture for multi-edge computing in IIoT environments. The results have been visualized through a series of plots, highlighting key findings related to throughput, bandwidth, and their relation to various network parameters.

1. **Throughput vs. Number of Nodes:** Our initial investigation focused on the relationship between throughput and the number of nodes within the network. As demonstrated in Figure 8.2, the proposed architecture consistently outperformed the traditional OpenFlow-based SDN model in terms of throughput. This indicates the enhanced scalability and efficiency of the proposed model as the network size expands.
2. **Bandwidth vs. Packet Arrival Rate:** Further analysis was conducted to understand bandwidth performance under varying packet arrival rates. As visualized in Figure 8.3, our findings suggest that the proposed system demonstrates superior bandwidth conservation, especially under

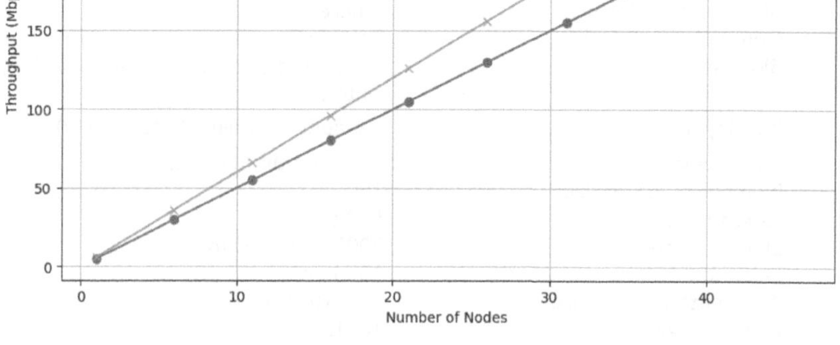

Figure 8.2 Throughput vs number of nodes in SDN openflow nodes and the proposed architecture.

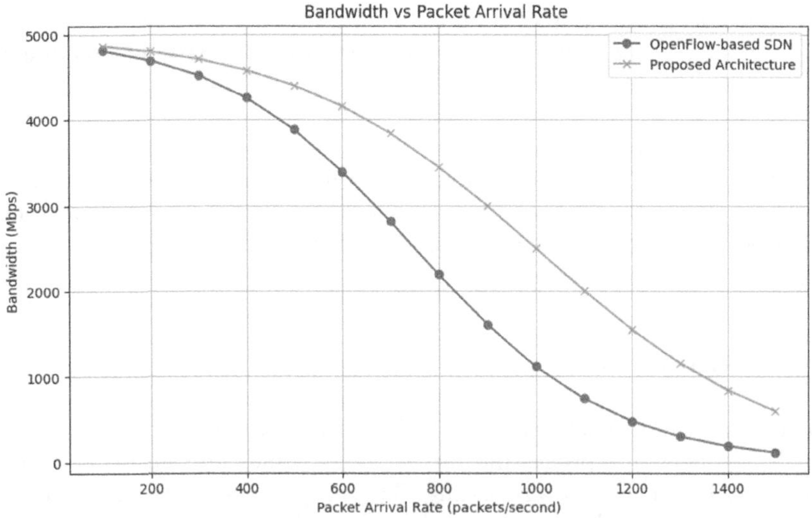

Figure 8.3 Packet arrival rate vs bandwidth in the SDN architecture with BC.

potential network congestion scenarios. This resilience is notably higher than that observed with the OpenFlow-based SDN model, emphasizing the robustness of our proposed system.

3. **Bandwidth vs. Number of Packets:** Lastly, we examined how the system's bandwidth responds to an increasing number of packets. Figure 8.4 reveals that the proposed architecture maintains a slight advantage in bandwidth even when faced with a higher number of packets. This result

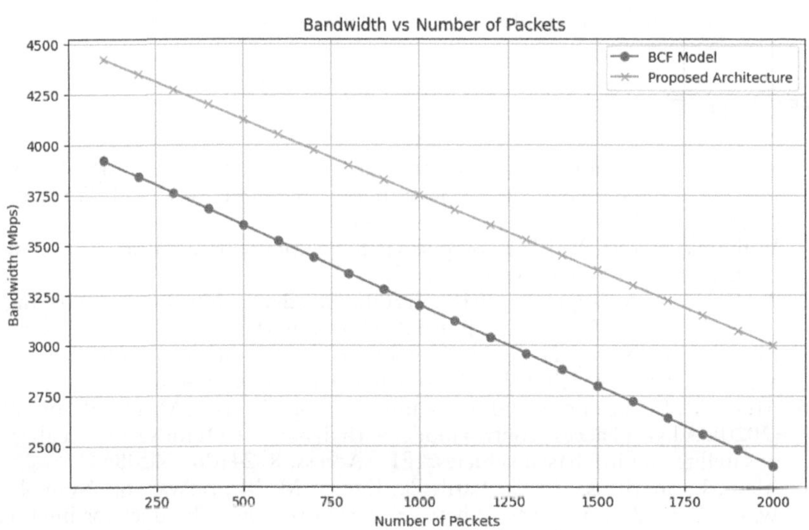

Figure 8.4 Bandwidth based on the BCF model and our proposed architecture.

underscores the system's ability to handle increased network loads without significant degradation in performance, especially when compared to models like BCF.

These results underscore the potential benefits of integrating blockchain and SDN technologies in multi-edge computing environments within the IIoT landscape. The observed improvements in throughput and bandwidth highlight the architecture's potential to address the challenges commonly faced in traditional edge computing models.

8.6 CONCLUSION

The integration of blockchain and SDN is a promising solution for the IIoT, which is crucial for processing large data volumes and ensuring security, reliability, and real-time processing. The proposed integration offers scalability and adaptability in multi-edge computing environments while also providing a robust solution for countering malicious entities, safeguarding data availability, and withstanding interruptions. However, there is scope for refinement, such as optimizing energy consumption, curtailing latencies, and honing consensus algorithms for expansive IIoT networks. Monitoring emerging trends in blockchain, SDN, and edge computing is essential for enhancing the architecture's capabilities or addressing challenges. Transitioning the architecture from theory to real-world application introduces challenges such as hardware restrictions, diverse network environments, and interoperability issues. Striking the right balance between security and performance remains a challenge, especially when expanding to vast IIoT frameworks. The melding of blockchain and SDN for multi-edge computing in IIoT represents a practical solution poised to revolutionize the future of industrial systems.

REFERENCES

1. Sisinni, E., Saifullah, A., Han, S., Jennehag, U., & Gidlund, M. (2018). Industrial internet of things: Challenges, opportunities, and directions. IEEE Transactions on Industrial Informatics, 14(11), 4724–4734
2. Williams, R. (2019). Edge computing: Revolutionizing data processing in the digital age. Computing Reviews, 28(3), 112–127.
3. Anderson, P., & Gupta, S. (2018). Traditional edge architectures: Analyzing the limitations. Edge Computing Journal, 15(1), 20–31.
4. Martinez, L., & Lee, H. (2021). Integrating blockchain and SDN for IoT: A new architectural approach. IoT Solutions Journal, 6(4), 420–438.
5. Aftab, M. U., Munir, Y., Oluwasanmi, A., Qin, Z., Aziz, M. H., & Son, N. T. (2020). A hybrid access control model with dynamic COI for secure localization of satellite and IoT-based vehicles. IEEE Access, 8, 24196–24208.
6. Alam, I., Sharif, K., Li, F., Latif, Z., Karim, M. M., Biswas, S., Nour, B., & Wang, Y. (2020). A survey of network virtualization techniques for internet of things using SDN and NFV. ACM Computing Surveys (CSUR), 53(2), 1–40.

7. Al-Rakhami, M. S., & Al-Mashari, M. (2021). ProChain: Provenance-aware traceability framework for IoT-based supply chain systems. IEEE Access, 10, 3631–3642.
8. Alyahya, S., Khan, W. U., Ahmed, S., Marwat, S. N. K., & Habib, S. (2022). Cyber secure framework for smart agriculture: Robust and tamper-resistant authentication scheme for IoT devices. Electronics, 11(6), 963.
9. Awaysheh, F. M., Aladwan, M. N., Alazab, M., Alawadi, S., Cabaleiro, J. C., & Pena, T. F. (2021). Security by design for big data frameworks over cloud computing. IEEE Transactions on Engineering Management, 69(6), 3676–3693.
10. Borgaonkar, R., Anne Tøndel, I., Zenebe Degefa, M., & Gilje Jaatun, M. (2021). Improving smart grid security through 5G enabled IoT and edge computing. Concurrency and Computation: Practice and Experience, 33(18), e6466.
11. Brynjolfsson, E., & McAfee, A. (2011). Race Against the Machine: How the Digital Revolution Is Accelerating Innovation, Driving Productivity, and Irreversibly Transforming Employment and the Economy. Brynjolfsson.
12. Cao, K., Liu, Y., Meng, G., & Sun, Q. (2020). An overview on edge computing research. IEEE Access, 8, 85714–85728.
13. Chaudhary, R., Aujla, G. S., Garg, S., Kumar, N., & Rodrigues, J. J. (2018). SDN-enabled multi-attribute-based secure communication for smart grid in IIoT environment. IEEE Transactions on Industrial Informatics, 14(6), 2629–2640.
14. Givehchi, O., Landsdorf, K., Simoens, P., & Colombo, A. W. (2017). Interoperability for industrial cyber-physical systems: An approach for legacy systems. IEEE Transactions on Industrial Informatics, 13(6), 3370–3378.
15. Hazra, A., Adhikari, M., Amgoth, T., & Srirama, S. N. (2021). A comprehensive survey on interoperability for IIoT: Taxonomy, standards, and future directions. ACM Computing Surveys (CSUR), 55(1), 1–35.
16. Huang, P., Zeng, L., Chen, X., Luo, K., Zhou, Z., & Yu, S. (2022). Edge robotics: Edge-computing-accelerated multirobot simultaneous localization and mapping. IEEE Internet of Things Journal, 9(15), 14087–14102.
17. Ishtiaq, M., Saeed, N., & Khan, M. A. (2021). Edge computing in IoT: A 6G perspective. ArXiv Preprint ArXiv:2111.08943.
18. Khan, P. W., Byun, Y.-C., & Park, N. (2020). IoT-blockchain enabled optimized provenance system for food industry 4.0 using advanced deep learning. Sensors, 20(10), 2990.
19. Leng, J., Ruan, G., Jiang, P., Xu, K., Liu, Q., Zhou, X., & Liu, C. (2020). Blockchain-empowered sustainable manufacturing and product lifecycle management in industry 4.0: A survey. Renewable and Sustainable Energy Reviews, 132, 110112.
20. Liu, S., Guo, C., Al-Turjman, F., Muhammad, K., & de Albuquerque, V. H. C. (2020). Reliability of response region: A novel mechanism in visual tracking by edge computing for IIoT environments. Mechanical Systems and Signal Processing, 138, 106537.
21. Mirani, A. A., Velasco-Hernandez, G., Awasthi, A., & Walsh, J. (2022). Key challenges and emerging technologies in industrial IoT architectures: A review. Sensors, 22(15), 5836.
22. Njah, Y., & Cheriet, M. (2021). Parallel route optimization and service assurance in energy-efficient software-defined industrial IoT networks. IEEE Access, 9, 24682–24696.
23. Qi, Q., Wang, J., Ma, Z., Sun, H., Cao, Y., Zhang, L., & Liao, J. (2019). Knowledge-driven service offloading decision for vehicular edge computing: A deep reinforcement learning approach. IEEE Transactions on Vehicular Technology, 68(5), 4192–4203.
24. Ren, J., Guo, H., Xu, C., & Zhang, Y. (2017). Serving at the edge: A scalable IoT architecture based on transparent computing. IEEE Network, 31(5), 96–105.

25. Sun, W., Liu, J., & Yue, Y. (2019). AI-enhanced offloading in edge computing: When machine learning meets industrial IoT. IEEE Network, 33(5), 68–74.
26. Wang, B., Li, M., Jin, X., & Guo, C. (2020). A reliable IoT edge computing trust management mechanism for smart cities. IEEE Access, 8, 46373–46399.
27. Wang, X., Han, Y., Leung, V. C., Niyato, D., Yan, X., & Chen, X. (2020). Convergence of edge computing and deep learning: A comprehensive survey. IEEE Communications Surveys & Tutorials, 22(2), 869–904.
28. Wu, Y., Dai, H.-N., & Wang, H. (2020). Convergence of blockchain and edge computing for secure and scalable IIoT critical infrastructures in industry 4.0. IEEE Internet of Things Journal, 8(4), 2300–2317.
29. Qian, L. P., Shi, B., Wu, Y., Sun, B., & Tsang, D. H. (2019). NOMA-enabled mobile edge computing for internet of things via joint communication and computation resource allocations. IEEE Internet of Things Journal, 7(1), 718–733.
30. Kim, J. (2020). Security threats in digital networks: The persistent challenge of DDoS attacks. Cybersecurity Today, 9(5), 78–89.
31. Davis, M., & Wang, C. (2019). Blockchain techniques for cloud applications: A new era of integrity protection. Cloud Systems Journal, 12(6), 501–515.
32. Thomas, G., & Raj, P. (2021). Blockchain in IoT: Defending against data manipulation threats. IoT Security, 17(2), 152–166.
33. Rodriguez, F., & Patel, K. (2020). Blockchain's role in IoT: Enhancing authentication and data integrity. Journal of Digital Systems, 30(7), 788–803.
34. Li, W., & Zhang, X. (2019). Blockchain-integrated IoT frameworks: Overcoming trust management constraints. IoT Innovations, 4(2), 35–47.
35. Sharma, Y., & Nair, R. (2020). Simulating blockchain-SDN architectures for IoT: A comparative analysis. Simulation Reviews, 14(4), 299–312.

Chapter 9

Toward next-generation cyber threat intelligence in Edge-IoT

A synergy of generative AI, federated learning, and blockchain

Wissal Lazraq and Samia El Haddouti

9.1 INTRODUCTION

The exponential increase in Internet of Things (IoT) adoption has transformed different sectors and industries, including healthcare, manufacturing, transportation, agriculture, and smart cities, facilitating seamless connectivity and real-time data exchange. However, this widespread integration of IoT has also revealed significant vulnerabilities, making these systems attractive targets for cybercriminals, thereby highlighting the need for advanced and scalable security strategies [1].

Cyber Threat Intelligence (CTI) has been introduced as a defense strategy for securing IoT environments. It involves the identification, analysis, and dissemination of information related to potential or ongoing cyber threats [2]. Despite their widespread application, traditional CTI frameworks face significant challenges due to their reliance on centralized systems for data collection and analysis. In fact, the centralized approach of CTI limits scalability and real-time responses while also raising privacy concerns regarding sensitive data, emphasizing the need for more adaptive and decentralized solutions.

From these perspectives, emerging technologies such as Generative Artificial Intelligence (GenAI), Federated Learning (FL), and Blockchain have attracted considerable interest due to their potential to revolutionize CTI in Edge-IoT environments. Indeed, GenAI enables the synthesis of realistic threat scenarios and facilitates advanced anomaly detection by preparing for early detection of sophisticated attacks, including zero-day threats [3]. FL provides decentralized training of machine learning models, ensuring that sensitive information remains local to IoT devices, thereby preserving data privacy [4]. Blockchain offers a secure, immutable, and transparent ledger for sharing threat intelligence data, guaranteeing the integrity and trustworthiness of the latter [5]. Overall, this chapter explores how these technologies can enhance the security of the IoT ecosystems, highlighting their capabilities in threat detection, privacy protection, and data integrity. It also discusses the limitations of applying each technology independently and underscores the importance of combining them to develop stronger and more flexible CTI solutions that provide improved protection for IoT systems against evolving threats.

DOI: 10.1201/9781003597476-12

The structure of the chapter is organized as follows: Section 9.2 presents the foundational background relevant to this study. Section 9.3 provides a comprehensive review of related works. Section 9.4 discusses challenges, limitations, and opportunities for improvement. Finally, Section 9.5 concludes with a summary of key findings and discusses future implications for the security of IoT ecosystems.

9.2 BACKGROUND

9.2.1 Internet of things and security challenges

IoT refers to a network of interconnected devices that collect and share data autonomously, enabling smarter decision-making. IoT is increasingly integrated across various sectors, such as smart homes, industrial environments, smart cities, agriculture, and transportation, improving efficiency and productivity through real-time data collection and analysis.

9.2.1.1 IoT architecture

Edge-IoT networks enhance the functionality of IoT systems by integrating Edge Computing, which processes data closer to the source rather than relying on centralized cloud servers. This architecture reduces latency and energy consumption by minimizing transmissions [6]. The IoT architecture based on Edge Computing can be structured into four primary layers as shown in Figure 9.1:

- **Device Layer:** It is the core layer of IoT, also referred to as the perception layer. It consists of physical devices such as sensors and actuators. Sensors collect environmental data, such as temperature, air quality,

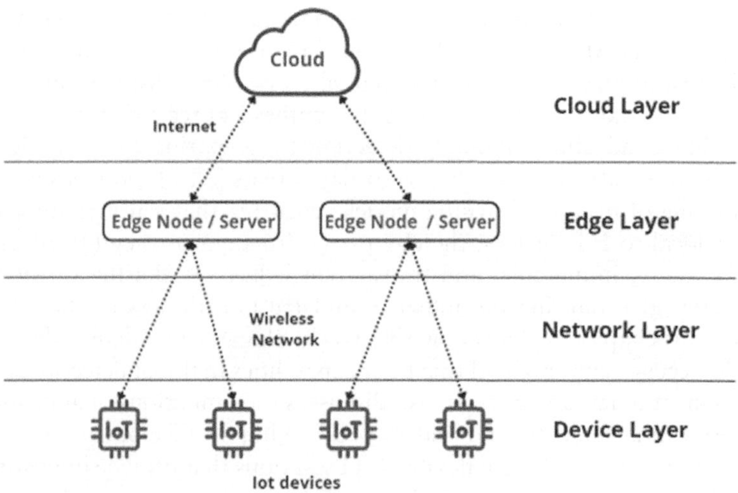

Figure 9.1 Edge-based IoT architecture.

or humidity, while actuators carry out actions, like turning on a valve. These devices are designed with limited processing capabilities, rely on low-power modes, and are often powered by batteries.

- **Network Layer:** It handles communication between the device layer and other IoT components, using technologies like Wi-Fi, Bluetooth, Zigbee, or LoRaWAN for short-range communication and LTE or 5G for broader coverage. Gateways and routers aggregate and forward data securely to the edge or cloud layers.
- **Edge Layer:** Also called the fog layer, it processes data close to its source with the aim of reducing latency and enabling real-time responses. Edge servers carry out data aggregation, analysis, and decision-making, reducing the necessity of transmitting data to the cloud layer.
- **Cloud Layer:** It provides large-scale data processing, storage, and advanced analytics. It supports machine learning and long-term data storage while integrating IoT services. Preprocessed data from the edge layer is analyzed further, enabling insights, scalability, and user interaction via dashboards and application programming interfaces (APIs).

9.2.1.2 IoT security threats

IoT systems have increasingly become key targets for cyberattacks, leading to growing concerns about the security and privacy of IoT devices. The primary security threats faced by IoT include [7]:

- **DDoS and DoS Attacks:** Inundating IoT devices or networks with an overwhelming volume of requests, preventing access for legitimate users. These attacks can disrupt essential services, leading to operational interruptions and financial damage.
- **Brute Force Attacks:** Involve systematically attempting combinations of usernames and passwords to gain unauthorized access to IoT devices. These attacks are particularly effective against devices with default or weak credentials, enabling attackers to infiltrate systems, compromise data, and potentially control device functionality.
- **Scanning and Reconnaissance:** Attackers use scanning tools to identify vulnerabilities, open ports, and weak configurations in IoT networks. Reconnaissance activities allow them to map out the network and prepare for targeted exploits, such as injection attacks or malware deployment, which can disrupt operations or steal sensitive data.
- **Injection Attacks:** Occur when malicious code is introduced into IoT systems through input fields or communication channels. These attacks compromise the integrity of device operations, allowing attackers to manipulate data, take control of devices, or disrupt services.
- **Malware:** Designed to infiltrate IoT devices, steal data, disable functionality, or integrate devices into botnets. Malware attacks can result in severe data breaches, financial losses, or coordinated DDoS attacks, jeopardizing both device security and network stability.

- **MITM and Eavesdropping:** In these attacks, the communication between IoT devices is intercepted, allowing malicious actors to access or manipulate the transmitted data. This compromises the confidentiality and integrity of sensitive information, which is particularly dangerous in sectors like healthcare and finance.
- **Spoofing and Sybil Attacks:** In spoofing attacks, attackers pretend to be legitimate IoT devices to gain unauthorized access or send false information. Sybil attacks involve creating multiple fake identities to disrupt network functioning and compromise trust in decentralized IoT systems.
- **Jamming:** Targeting wireless communication channels, interfering with connectivity, and causing devices to lose service. This is particularly disruptive in time-critical IoT applications, such as healthcare monitoring or autonomous vehicles.
- **Zero-Day Attacks:** Exploit vulnerabilities in IoT devices that are unknown to the manufacturer and unpatched. These attacks are highly dangerous, as they are difficult to detect and mitigate, often leading to catastrophic breaches and operational failures.

9.2.2 Cyber threat intelligence

CTI is a strategic defense approach that focuses on proactively defending systems by tracking transactions and deploying countermeasures to minimize the impact of cyberattacks. It involves gathering and analyzing information on potential or ongoing threats, with the aim of helping organizations anticipate, detect, and respond more effectively by providing actionable insights into threat actors, attack patterns, and vulnerabilities [8].

9.2.2.1 Cyber threat intelligence in Edge-IoT

In the specific context of Edge-IoT, CTI plays a crucial role in enhancing the security of distributed edge networks. Due to the limitations of IoT devices, such as limited processing power and device heterogeneity, CTI enables the identification and rapid response to potential threats before they can impact the entire system. For instance, CTI can help detect abnormal behavior in real time, allowing for early detection of malicious activity or unpatched vulnerabilities at the network's edge. By analyzing data from sensors and other IoT devices at the edge, CTI can provide insights specific to each device based on the locally identified risks. Additionally, threat intelligence can be shared across different Edge-IoT nodes, ensuring that each device is informed about new vulnerabilities and potential threats, even in environments where connectivity to centralized servers is limited or intermittent. Moreover, CTI enables the implementation of security measures tailored to the local level, such as strengthening device authentication, managing encryption keys, or enforcing security policies specific to each segment of the IoT network. This approach minimizes the impact of cyberattacks while ensuring a swift and targeted response, in line with the efficiency and latency constraints inherent to Edge-IoT environments [9].

9.2.3 Generative artificial intelligence

GenAI has emerged as a transformative approach in creating new, realistic data and content by leveraging advanced machine learning techniques. It focuses on creating novel content, including text, images, audio, video, and structured data, by learning and modeling underlying data distributions. Unlike traditional AI, which primarily classifies or predicts based on input data, GenAI generates outputs that are both original and contextually coherent [10]. The key differences between GenAI and traditional AI lie in their distinct objectives, outputs, adaptability, data dependency, and complexity, as outlined in Table 9.1.

9.2.3.1 *Generative AI techniques*

GenAI leverages advanced machine learning techniques to create new data. Key approaches include:

- **Generative Adversarial Networks (GANs):** These consist of two neural networks, a generator that creates synthetic data, and a discriminator that evaluates its authenticity, driving iterative improvements. GANs are used for tasks like high-resolution image and video generation [11].
- **Variational Autoencoders (VAEs):** Encode data into latent representations, then decode it to produce variations, useful for applications such as face generation or 3D modeling [12].
- **Transformer-Based Models:** Models like GPT and BERT excel in natural language generation and translation by capturing sequential relationships in data, significantly enhancing text generation and contextual AI tasks [13].

Table 9.1 Comparison between traditional AI and generative AI

Aspect	*Traditional AI*	*Generative AI*
Objective	Focuses on solving specific tasks like classification or prediction.	Creates new, synthetic outputs like text, images, or data.
Output	Predictive or analytical results.	Novel and realistic content resembling training data.
Adaptability	Limited to predefined tasks.	Highly adaptable to diverse and complex domains.
Data Dependency	Requires structured and labeled datasets.	Requires large-scale and diverse datasets.
Complexity	Simpler models, easier to train and interpret.	Complex models with high computational requirements.

- **Diffusion Models:** Used primarily in image generation, these models reverse noise to data to create high-quality visuals, with applications in art and scientific visualization [11].

GenAI has the potential to transform CTI for IoT ecosystems by enabling proactive, real-time threat detection and adaptive response systems. It enhances threat detection by analyzing vast amounts of IoT data, identifying anomalies, and recognizing emerging attack patterns like zero-day vulnerabilities and APTs. Additionally, Generative AI can create synthetic attack scenarios for training, improving system resilience. However, centralized GenAI systems face challenges such as privacy concerns, susceptibility to data breaches, and high latency. These models also struggle with real-time adaptability in dynamic IoT networks.

9.2.4 Federated learning

FL is a decentralized machine learning approach designed to enable collaborative model training across multiple devices or nodes without requiring the transfer of raw data to a central server [4]. This paradigm was developed to address growing concerns around data privacy, security, and efficiency, particularly in environments such as IoT networks, healthcare systems, and financial platforms, where sensitive or private data is generated locally. The key differences between centralized learning and federated learning focus on their approaches to data storage, privacy, scalability, computational load, failure tolerance, and communication, as depicted in Table 9.2.

As illustrated in Figure 9.2, in centralized learning, IoT device data is collected and processed on a central server. This approach increases the risk of privacy breaches, creates a single point of failure, and imposes significant bandwidth demands due to the transfer of raw data. Conversely, the

Table 9.2 Comparison between centralized learning and federated learning

Aspect	*Centralized learning*	*Federated learning*
Data Storage	Data is centralized on a single server.	Data remains decentralized on client devices.
Privacy	Higher risk of data breaches.	Enhanced privacy as raw data is not shared.
Scalability	Limited scalability with increasing data volumes.	Highly scalable across distributed devices.
Computational Load	Server bears all computational burden.	Computation is distributed across devices.
Failure Tolerance	Single point of failure (server outage).	Decentralized, reducing failure risks.
Communication	Transfers raw data to the server.	Transfers model updates, reducing bandwidth use.

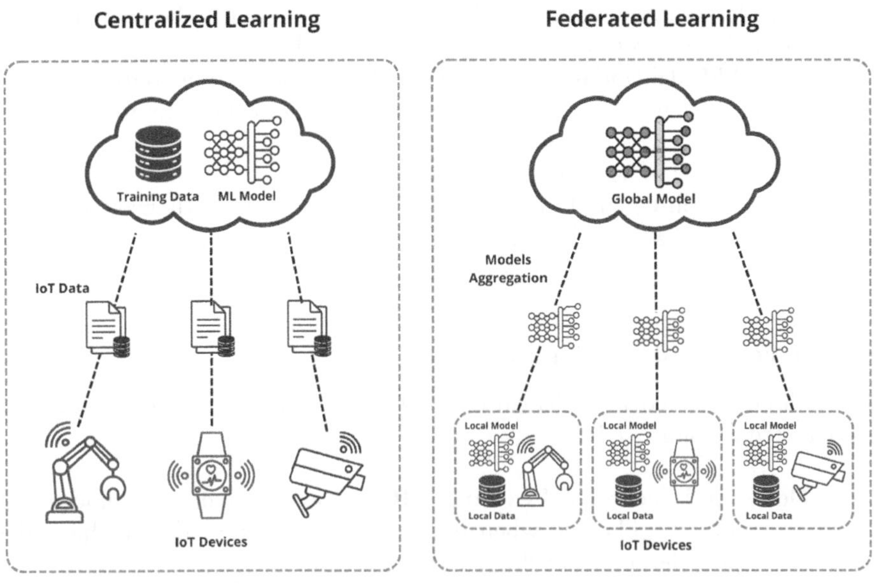

Figure 9.2 Comparison between centralized learning and federated learning.

federated learning approach is where raw data remains on individual IoT devices. Each device trains its local model using its private data, and only model updates, such as weights and gradients, are sent to a central server for aggregation. This decentralized approach enhances privacy, reduces communication overhead, and improves system scalability by leveraging distributed computing across devices.

9.2.4.1 Federated learning workflow

The key steps in the FL process are as follows [4]:

- **Global Model Initialization:** The process begins with the central server initializing a global model with generic parameters. This global model is then distributed to all participating IoT devices within the network.
- **Local Model Training:** Each device trains the global model locally using its private local data. This allows the model to learn from the unique data distribution of each device without transferring raw data to the server.
- **Local Model Updates:** After training, each device generates updates to the model parameters, such as gradients or weights, based on the insights learned from its local data. These updates are securely encrypted for transmission.
- **Model Aggregation:** The central server collects the encrypted updates from all participating devices and aggregates them using algorithms such

as Federated Averaging (FedAvg). This step combines the contributions from all devices to refine the global model while preserving privacy.
- **Global Model Update:** The aggregated updates are applied to the global model, which is then redistributed to the devices. This iterative process continues across multiple rounds until the global model achieves the desired level of accuracy and performance.
- **Model Deployment:** Once the global model is sufficiently trained, it can be deployed across the IoT ecosystem for tasks such as anomaly detection, predictive analytics, and CTI sharing.

9.2.4.2 Federated learning categories

In the literature, federated learning is categorized into three main types [4], as depicted in Figure 9.3:

- **Horizontal Federated Learning (HFL):** Also known as sample-based FL, HFL is applicable when datasets from different devices have the exact same features but differ in data samples.
- **Vertical Federated Learning (VFL):** Also referred to as feature-based FL, VFL is used where the data samples are the same but feature sets (columns) are different.
- **Federated Transfer Learning (FTL):** It is applied when datasets vary in both features and data samples, with little to no overlap. This process involves using a pre-trained model, where a dataset serves as the foundation for a new task, rather than training a model from the ground up. By doing so, the model can utilize knowledge from the pre-trained domain and adjust it to suit the new domain or task with the available data.

FL enhances CTI in IoT ecosystems by enabling devices to collaboratively train machine learning models without sharing raw data, improving anomaly detection, and facilitating knowledge sharing across diverse networks. This approach strengthens security by providing deeper insights into emerging threats. However, FL faces challenges such as reliance on a centralized server, creating a single point of failure, and vulnerabilities like model poisoning. To address these, blockchain is being explored as a complementary technology, offering decentralization, data integrity, and enhanced trust, thus improving the effectiveness of CTI in IoT environments.

9.2.5 Blockchain technology

Blockchain [14] is a decentralized, distributed ledger technology that ensures transparency, security, and immutability in transaction records. It operates on a peer-to-peer network where each participant maintains a synchronized copy of the ledger, eliminating the need for a central authority [15]. Transactions are validated through consensus mechanisms and grouped

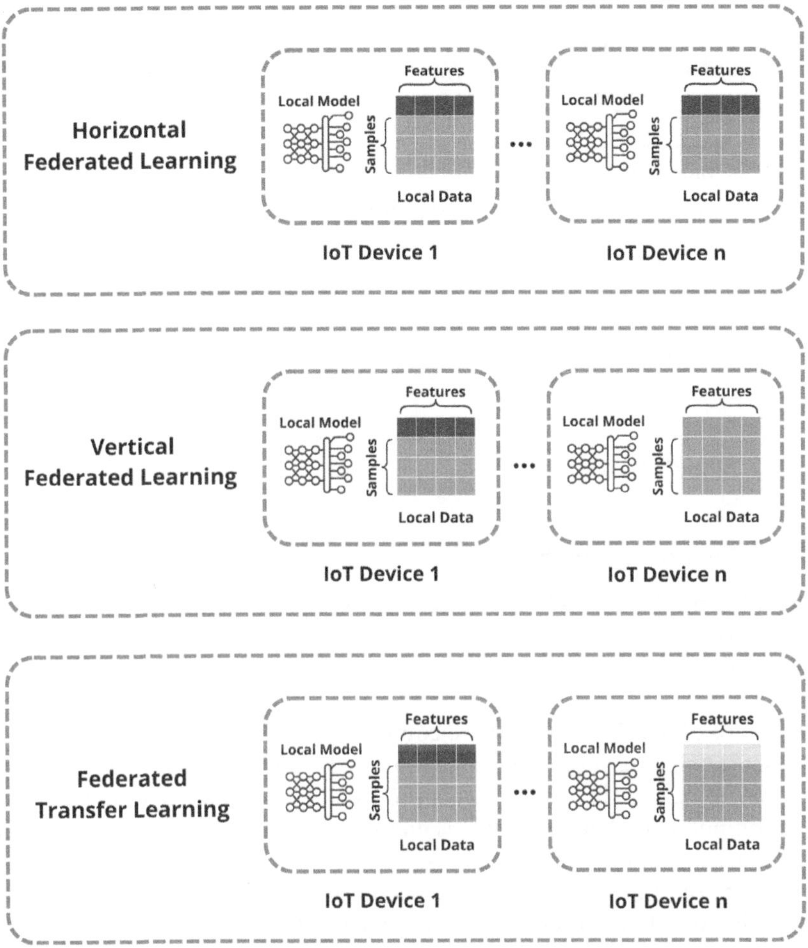

Figure 9.3 Types of federated learning.

into blocks, linked cryptographically to form a secure chain as depicted in Figure 9.4. Key features of Blockchain include:

- **Security:** Data is encrypted and distributed across the network, making unauthorized alterations difficult.
- **Transparency:** All network participants can view transactions, promoting trust.
- **Immutability:** Once recorded, data cannot be altered or deleted, ensuring integrity.
- **Traceability:** Provides a clear, verifiable record of data history.
- **Decentralization:** Reduces risks of a single point of failure by distributing control across the network.

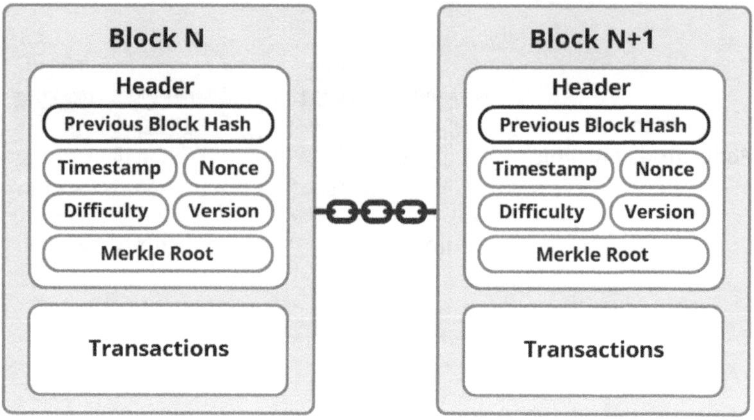

Figure 9.4 Blockchain structure.

9.2.5.1 Consensus mechanism

Depending on the Blockchain's system, consensus mechanisms are fundamental algorithms used to achieve agreement among nodes. Popular mechanisms include [16]:

- **Proof of Work (PoW):** where computational puzzles are solved within a set timeframe. The first node resolves the puzzle and is selected to add a new block to the chain. This process ensures network security through computational effort, but it is energy-intensive and slower compared to other mechanisms.
- **Proof of Stake (PoS):** which relies on the amount of cryptocurrency the validators hold and stake in the network. It is energy-efficient compared to PoW.
- **Delegated Proof of Stake (DPoS):** an energy-efficient method where token holders vote for a small group of delegates to validate transactions, enabling faster and more efficient blockchain operations.
- **Practical Byzantine Fault Tolerance (PBFT):** designed for distributed systems to tolerate malicious or faulty nodes. It ensures reliability by requiring agreement from a majority of nodes to validate transactions, making it efficient and secure. Once consensus is achieved, the block is added to the blockchain, becoming a permanent and immutable part of the ledger.

9.2.5.2 Smart contracts

The concept of smart contracts is also a fundamental innovation in Blockchain technology. A smart contract is a self-executing program stored on a Blockchain, where the terms of an agreement or predefined rules are written in code [17]. These contracts automatically enforce and execute the terms when specific conditions are met, eliminating the need for intermediaries and ensuring trust and transparency in transactions [18]. Smart contracts enhance business process efficiency by accelerating transaction execution while ensuring integrity and security.

The smart contract process involves three key phases:

- **Creation:** The purpose, parties, and terms are identified, and the contract is coded using a Blockchain-compatible language like Solidity. The code defines the contract's rules and triggers, followed by testing to ensure proper functionality.
- **Deployment:** After testing, the contract is deployed to the Blockchain, where it is assigned a unique address for interaction within the network.
- **Execution:** The contract is triggered by predefined conditions, which may include external inputs or interactions with other contracts. The contract then performs actions like transferring assets or updating records, with results validated and recorded by the Blockchain's consensus mechanism.

In CTI for edge-IoT, Blockchain improves data integrity, security, and trust by enabling secure sharing of threat intelligence without a central authority. Smart contracts on the blockchain automate tasks like validating threat signatures and triggering alerts, enhancing efficiency, and reducing human intervention.

9.3 PROPOSED APPROACHES FOR NEXT-GENERATION CTI

The increasing complexity and volume of cyber threats in IoT environments have necessitated innovative approaches to CTI. Several studies have explored the integration of GenAI, FL, and Blockchain to address these challenges effectively.

9.3.1 GenAI-based CTI approaches

Ferrag et al. [3] proposed a privacy-preserving framework leveraging Large Language Models (LLMs) for IoT threat detection. Their work introduced SecurityBERT, a lightweight model that achieved 98.2% accuracy while maintaining privacy through a novel encoding technique. This contribution emphasizes the efficacy and computational efficiency required for deployment in resource-constrained IoT environments. Similarly, Ferrag et al. [19] extended this focus on GenAI by investigating threat-hunting methodologies for 6G-enabled IoT networks. Their approach employed predictive generative models to proactively mitigate threats, highlighting the importance of incorporating AI-driven predictive mechanisms into CTI frameworks.

9.3.2 FL-based CTI approaches

Ogundipe and Shi [20] emphasized the role of federated learning in IoT security, proposing a framework that balances privacy and detection efficacy. Their model leveraged distributed learning to ensure secure threat detection across IoT devices without centralizing sensitive data. Similarly, El Jaouhari and Etiabi [21] introduced FedCTI, which combined FL with CTI at the edge, aiming to enhance the scalability and privacy of IoT networks. These contributions underline FL's potential to improve security in distributed and heterogeneous IoT systems.

9.3.3 Blockchain-based CTI approaches

Blockchain technology has also been widely adopted in CTI for its ability to provide immutable, secure, and trustworthy systems. Cha et al. [22] proposed a Blockchain-based CTI architecture, emphasizing trustworthiness and sustainability in IoT ecosystems. Their design ensured data integrity while providing a scalable infrastructure for secure intelligence sharing. Gong and Lee [23] expanded on this by introducing BLOCIS, a Blockchain-enabled framework that focuses on Sybil-resistant CTI sharing. By integrating trust mechanisms, their approach addressed identity-based threats, ensuring the reliability of CTI processes.

9.3.4 The combination of GenAI and FL for CTI in IoT

Several works have integrated multiple technologies to address complex security challenges. Zhao et al. [24] combined FL and GenAI to develop a novel intrusion detection system for IoT. This system effectively detected anomalous network traffic, demonstrating the potential of hybrid methodologies. Similarly, Wang et al. [25] employed Federated GenAI for privacy-preserving CTI in IoT. Their work highlighted the importance of privacy-centric approaches, ensuring that sensitive data is not exposed during model training and deployment.

9.3.5 The combination of FL and blockchain for CTI in IoT

Further advancing the integration of technologies, Sarhan et al. [26] proposed HBFL, a hierarchical Blockchain-based FL framework. By combining the strengths of Blockchain and FL, they addressed issues related to scalability, trust, and collaborative learning in IoT intrusion detection. Moulahi et al. [27] also explored this intersection, presenting a Blockchain-enhanced FL model for privacy-preserving threat detection in intelligent transport systems. Their approach demonstrated the utility of Blockchain in ensuring data integrity and trustworthiness in FL-based CTI.

Table 9.3 provides a comprehensive summary of existing works as they pertain to CTI in IoT environments. The table categorizes contributions

Table 9.3 Existing works in generative AI, FL, and blockchain for CTI in IoT

Year	*Ref*	*Contribution*	*GenAI focused*	*FL focused*	*Blockchain focused*
2024	[3]	Generative AI and Large Language Models for CTI in IoT	✓	×	×
2023	[19]	Generative AI for Cyber Threat-Hunting in 6G-enabled IoT Networks	✓	×	×
2024	[20]	Detecting Cyber Threats in IoT Devices Using FL	×	✓	×
2023	[21]	FedCTI: Federated Learning and CTI on the Edge	×	✓	×
2020	[22]	Blockchain-Based Cyber Threat Intelligence System Architecture	×	×	✓
2020	[23]	BLOCIS: Blockchain-Based CTI Sharing Framework	×	×	✓
2024	[24]	FL and Generative AI for IoT Anomalous Traffic Detection	✓	✓	×
2021	[25]	Federated Generative AI for Privacy-Preserving in IoT-Based CTI	✓	✓	×
2022	[26]	HBFL: Hierarchical Blockchain-Based Federated Learning for IoT Intrusion Detection	×	✓	✓
2022	[27]	Privacy-Preserving Federated Learning Cyber-Threat Detection with Blockchain	×	✓	✓

based on their primary focus, highlighting whether they leverage GenAI, FL, or Blockchain technologies.

In summary, the reviewed works demonstrate a diverse range of methodologies addressing CTI challenges in IoT. GenAI models have proven to be effective for predictive and proactive threat detection, while FL ensures privacy-preserving, and distributed intelligence. Blockchain, with its emphasis on trust and immutability, complements these approaches by providing a secure infrastructure for CTI.

9.4 DISCUSSIONS

The reviewed studies highlight emerging approaches to enhancing cybersecurity in IoT environments, focusing on GenAI, FL, and Blockchain technologies. These approaches collectively address key challenges such as privacy preservation, scalability, trustworthiness, and the effectiveness of threat detection systems. However, several limitations and gaps emerge, requiring further exploration.

GenAI has shown significant potential in advancing proactive threat detection. Models like SecurityBERT demonstrate high accuracy while maintaining lightweight computational profiles. However, these models are vulnerable to adversarial attacks and biases in detection mechanisms. Additionally, deploying GenAI in real-world IoT systems, especially those with limited computational resources, remains challenging. IoT devices operate in dynamic environments, requiring models capable of handling novel attack types, which need further investigation.

Integrating FL into IoT cybersecurity frameworks addresses privacy concerns by enabling decentralized learning. While this approach provides solutions for model training without centralizing sensitive data, it faces limitations with non-independent and identically distributed (IID) data, common in IoT networks. Furthermore, the computational overhead of FL on resource-constrained IoT devices limits its scalability and sustainability.

Blockchain, by ensuring data immutability, enhances trust and integrity in threat intelligence sharing frameworks. However, the scalability and energy efficiency of Blockchain in IoT systems remain significant challenges. Blockchain's reliance on consensus mechanisms introduces latency, making it less suitable for real-time threat detection applications, and its computational intensity may negate its benefits when deployed on energy-constrained devices.

Hybrid approaches combining GenAI, FL, and Blockchain aim to leverage the strengths of each technology while mitigating their individual limitations. However, these hybrid models also face additional challenges, including increased system complexity, higher computational demands, and potential latency issues.

Despite the innovative contributions of the reviewed works, several limitations persist. Many studies rely on synthetic or controlled datasets, which may not accurately reflect the complexities of real-world IoT environments. Additionally, the scalability of these solutions to accommodate large-scale IoT ecosystems with heterogeneous devices remains underexplored. The long-term sustainability of these frameworks, particularly in terms of energy efficiency and resource utilization, is often overlooked.

To address these challenges, future research should focus on developing lightweight, adaptive models that can operate efficiently across diverse IoT environments. Incorporating real-time feedback mechanisms and robust adversarial defenses will further enhance the efficacy and resilience of these systems. Additionally, optimizing the integration of GenAI, FL, and Blockchain technologies to minimize computational and energy overheads will be crucial for their practical deployment, ultimately fostering more secure and sustainable IoT ecosystems.

9.5 CONCLUSION

The synergy of GenAI, FL, and Blockchain presents a promising approach to enhancing CTI in edge-IoT ecosystem. While each technology offers distinct advantages, such as proactive threat detection, privacy-preserving collaboration, and data integrity, their individual limitations must be addressed.

By combining these technologies, a robust, scalable, and sustainable cybersecurity framework can be developed to tackle challenges like real-time threat detection and secure data sharing. Future research should focus on optimizing the integration of these technologies through lightweight architectures and efficient algorithms, with real-world testing and standardization efforts essential for validating their effectiveness. Ultimately, such integrated solutions will strengthen the security, privacy, and trust of edge-IoT ecosystems in a rapidly evolving digital landscape.

REFERENCES

1. Azrour et al. (2021). Internet of things security: Challenges and key issues. Security and Communication Networks, 2021(1), 5533843.
2. Ainslie et al. (2023). Cyber-threat intelligence for security decision-making: A review and research agenda for practice. In Computers & Security (Vol. 132, p. 103352).
3. Ferrag et al. (2024). Revolutionizing cyber threat detection with large language models: A privacy-preserving bert-based lightweight model for IoT/IIoT devices. IEEE Access.
4. Banabilah et al. (2022). Federated learning review: Fundamentals, enabling technologies, and future applications. In Information Processing & Management (Vol. 59, Issue 6, p. 103061).
5. Khan et al. (2018). IoT security: Review, blockchain solutions, and open challenges. In Future Generation Computer Systems (Vol. 82, pp. 395–411).
6. Hamdan et al. (2020). Edge-computing architectures for internet of things applications: A survey. Sensors, 20(22), 6441.
7. Stellios et al. (2018). A survey of IoT-enabled cyberattacks: Assessing attack paths to critical infrastructures and services. IEEE Communications Surveys & Tutorials, 20(4), 3453–3495.
8. Wagner, T. D., Mahbub, K., Palomar, E., & Abdallah, A. E. (2019). Cyber threat intelligence sharing: Survey and research directions. Computers & Security, 87, 101589.
9. Kumar et al. (2023). A Review on Intrusion Detection Systems and Cyber Threat Intelligence for Secure IoT-Enabled Networks: Challenges and Directions. Big Data Analytics in Fog-Enabled IoT Networks, 51–76.
10. Feuerriegel et al. (2024). Generative AI. Business & Information Systems Engineering, 66(1), 111–126.
11. Law, L. (2024). Application of Generative Artificial Intelligence (GenAI) in Language Teaching and Learning: A Scoping Literature Review. In Computers and Education Open (Vol. 6, p. 100174). Elsevier BV. https://doi.org/10.1016/j.caeo.2024.100174
12. Wang, X., Wan, Z., Hekmati, A., Zong, M., Alam, S., Zhang, M., & Krishnamachari, B. (2024). The Internet of Things in the Era of Generative AI: Vision and Challenges (Version 4). arXiv. https://doi.org/10.48550/ARXIV.2401.01923
13. Sai, S., Kanadia, M., & Chamola, V. (2024). Empowering IoT with generative AI: Applications, case studies, and limitations. IEEE Internet of Things Magazine, 7(3), 38–43. Institute of Electrical and Electronics Engineers (IEEE).
14. Pilkington, M. (2016). Blockchain Technology: Principles and Applications. In Research Handbook on Digital Transformations (pp. 225–253). Edward Elgar Publishing.

15. El Haddouti, S., & El Kettani, M. D. E. C. (2019). A novel blockchain-based reliable model for the trust management of an identity federation system. Proceedings of the 33rd International Business Information Management Association (IBIMA), 8342–8351.
16. Mingxiao et al. (2017, October). A Review on Consensus Algorithm of Blockchain. In 2017 IEEE International Conference on Systems, Man, and Cybernetics (SMC) (pp. 2567–2572). IEEE.
17. Zheng, Z., Xie, S., Dai, H.-N., Chen, W., Chen, X., Weng, J., & Imran, M. (2020). An overview on smart contracts: Challenges, advances and platforms. Future Generation Computer Systems, 105, 475–491.
18. El Haddouti, S. et al. (2023). Fedidchain: An innovative blockchain-enabled framework for cross-border interoperability and trust management in identity federation systems. Journal of Network and Systems Management, 31, 1–42.
19. Ferrag, M., Debbah, M., & Al-Hawawreh, M. (2023). Generative AI for Cyber Threat-Hunting in 6G-enabled IoT Networks. 2023 IEEE/ACM 23rd International Symposium on Cluster, Cloud and Internet Computing Workshops (CCGridW), 16–25. https://doi.org/10.1109/CCGridW59191.2023.00018
20. Ogundipe, M. F., & Shi, X. (2024). Detecting Cyber Threats and Enhancing Security in IOT Devices: A Federated Learning Approach. In 2024 International Conference on Global Aeronautical Engineering and Satellite Technology (GAST) (pp. 1–6).
21. El Jaouhari, S., & Etiabi, Y. (2023). FedCTI: Federated Learning and Cyber Threat Intelligence on the Edge for secure IoT Networks. Proceedings of the International Conference on the Internet of Things, 98–104.
22. Cha, J., Singh, S. K., Pan, Y., & Park, J. H. (2020). Blockchain-Based Cyber Threat Intelligence System Architecture for Sustainable Computing. In Sustainability (Vol. 12, Issue 16, p. 6401). MDPI AG. https://doi.org/10.3390/su12166401
23. Gong, S., & Lee, C. (2020). BLOCIS: Blockchain-Based Cyber Threat Intelligence Sharing Framework for Sybil-Resistance. In Electronics (Vol. 9, p. 521). MDPI AG. https://doi.org/10.3390/electronics9030521
24. Zhao, H., Liu, L., Fan, F., Zhang, H., & Ma, Y. (2024). An Adaptive Federated Learning Intrusion Detection System Based on Generative Adversarial Networks under the Internet of Things. Proceedings of the 2024 3rd Asia Conference on Algorithms, Computing and Machine Learning (pp. 1–6). CACML 2024: 2024 3rd Asia Conference on Algorithms, Computing and Machine Learning. ACM. https://doi.org/10.1145/3654823.3654824
25. Wang, H., Han, Y., Yang, S., Song, A., & Zhang, T. (2021). Privacy-Preserving Federated Generative Adversarial Network for IoT. In 2021 International Conference on Networking and Network Applications (NaNA) (pp. 75–80). 2021 International Conference on Networking and Network Applications (NaNA). IEEE. https://doi.org/10.1109/nana53684.2021.00021
26. Sarhan, M., Lo, W. W., Layeghy, S., & Portmann, M. (2022). HBFL: A Hierarchical Blockchain-Based Federated Learning Framework for Collaborative IoT Intrusion Detection. In Computers and Electrical Engineering (Vol. 103, p. 108379). Elsevier BV. https://doi.org/10.1016/j.compeleceng.2022.108379
27. Moulahi, T., Jabbar, R., Alabdulatif, A., Abbas, S., El Khediri, S., Zidi, S., & Rizwan, M. (2022). Privacy-preserving Federated Learning Cyber-Threat Detection for Intelligent Transport Systems with Blockchain-Based Security. In Expert Systems (Vol. 40). Wiley. https://doi.org/10.1111/exsy.13103

Part IV

Ethics, education, and future directions

Chapter 10

Higher education and generative artificial intelligence

Applications, challenges, opportunities, and ethics

Kaouni Mouna, Lakrami Fatima, Laouidya Ouidad, and Baddi Youssef

10.1 INTRODUCTION

Energy efficiency and low-carbon strategies have attracted a lot of concern. The goal for 20% energy efficiency and carbon reduction by 2020 drove the Information Communication Technologies (ICT) sector to strategies that incorporate modern designs for low carbon and sustainable growth [1, 2]. The ICT sector is part of the 2020 goal and participates in three different ways. In the direct way, ICT are called to reduce their own energy demands (green networks, green IT); in the indirect way, ICT are used for carbon displacements; and in the systematic way, ICT collaborate with other sectors of the economy to provide energy efficiency (smart grids, smart buildings, intelligent transportations systems, etc…). ICT and, in particular, data centers have a strong impact on the global CO_2 emissions. Moreover, an important part of the OPEX is due to the electricity demands. This chapter presents the sources and challenges that have to be addressed to reduce carbon emissions and electricity expenses of the sector.

Artificial intelligence (AI) is a revolutionary force transforming both commercial and personal domains through its versatile applications. From customer personalization to financial risk management, AI significantly impacts our daily lives and extends its potential to various fields, including logistics, medicine, and now, education. AI has made considerable progress, leading to groundbreaking innovations and widespread applications. Among these advances, the development of generative artificial intelligence (GenAI) models has emerged since 2022 as a crucial milestone in AI research.

GenAI, also referred to as generative modeling, is a category of AI technology capable of producing novel and distinctive outputs [1]. These systems generate original works from raw data, pushing the boundaries of digital creativity. Unlike traditional AI systems that follow pre-established rules, GenAI creates new content based on patterns and trends extracted from training data. The progress in AI that led to the emergence of generative models can be largely attributed to several converging factors, such as the availability of large-scale datasets, advancements in deep learning algorithms, and increased computing power.

DOI: 10.1201/9781003597476-14

This convergence has enabled researchers to train highly expressive models capable of efficiently learning underlying patterns in data and generating new results with remarkable accuracy and quality.

The transformative potential of GenAI spans multiple sectors, particularly education, where it can automate repetitive tasks, enhance personalized learning experiences, and produce innovative content that boosts student engagement. Applications of GenAI in education include creating interactive and adaptive learning materials, assisting with course planning, and improving the personalization of learning.

GenAI encompasses computational methods that generate new and meaningful content such as text, images, audio, and video based on training data [2]. It leverages advanced machine learning algorithms and specialized neural network architectures, including autoencoders, variational autoencoders (VAEs), generative adversarial networks (GANs), Boltzmann machines, and transformers [3]. Key techniques in GenAI include the VAE, which learns to encode and decode data while preserving essential features, and the GAN, where two neural networks compete to generate realistic data samples. Other notable methods include transformers, which have revolutionized natural language processing by enabling models to understand and generate human language with high accuracy [4].

GenAI models use sophisticated algorithms to analyze patterns and create new content in various forms, including text, images, audio, video, and code. These models are trained on large-scale datasets, allowing them to learn intricate details and generate content that closely mimics real-world data. This training process involves significant computational resources and advanced techniques to ensure the generated content is of high quality and relevance.

Popular GenAI tools, such as ChatGPT, Bard, Gemini, Perplexity, Copilot, and DALL-E, including Midjourney, demonstrate the capability to process complex information and produce human-quality results. Some excel in conversational AI, providing coherent and contextually appropriate responses, while others generate detailed and creative images from textual descriptions, showcasing the creative potential of GenAI. Their ability to handle complex tasks and generate high-quality content has sparked significant interest in integrating GenAI across various fields, including healthcare, medicine, education, media, and information technology. These models illustrate the transformative potential of GenAI, enabling applications ranging from natural language processing to the creation of innovative artistic content [5].

In higher education, these advances play a crucial role. They facilitate the creation of personalized educational content, optimize course planning, and generate assignments and activities tailored to students' specific needs. Additionally, they provide essential support in coding and solving complex problems [6]. By automating the generation of responses to student queries and drafts of their assignments, GenAI aims to revolutionize higher education. This automation promises to streamline the learning process, enhance student engagement, and empower educators to focus on their instructional roles.

However, while GenAI systems offer exciting opportunities in education, significant challenges must be overcome to ensure their effective and responsible integration into our evolving digital learning environment. These challenges include academic integrity, equitable access, quality control, ethical considerations, and data privacy issues [7].

This article conducts an extensive review of existing literature to examine the application of GenAI in education, exploring both its opportunities and challenges within higher education. It delineates key benefits and concerns, offering a comprehensive perspective on the topic. Ultimately, the article concludes with recommendations aimed at guiding higher education institutions in the effective integration of GenAI while proactively addressing associated challenges.

The remainder of this chapter is structured into four main sections. The first section provides an in-depth review of the existing literature, examining the application of GenAI in the education sector. The second section explores both the opportunities and challenges of GenAI within higher education. The third section focuses on the practical implications of integrating GenAI into educational environments, highlighting its potential to improve personalized learning, content creation, and academic support tools. The final section critically analyzes the ethical considerations surrounding the use of GenAI in education, addressing issues such as data privacy, bias, and liability. It concludes with practical recommendations to guide higher education institutions in the effective implementation of GenAI, ensuring compliance with ethical standards and mitigating potential risks.

10.2 APPLICATIONS GENERATIVE AI IN HIGHER EDUCATION

10.2.1 From AI to GenAI

Higher education systems are dynamic environments where knowledge is not only transmitted but also transformed into meaningful understanding through diverse pedagogical methods. This process involves ongoing interaction between educators and learners, with educators serving not just as conveyors of knowledge but also as facilitators of environments that foster critical thinking, problem-solving, and the development of relevant skills. These pedagogical approaches underscore the significance of active student engagement and self-directed learning, culminating in profound, and enduring educational outcomes [8].

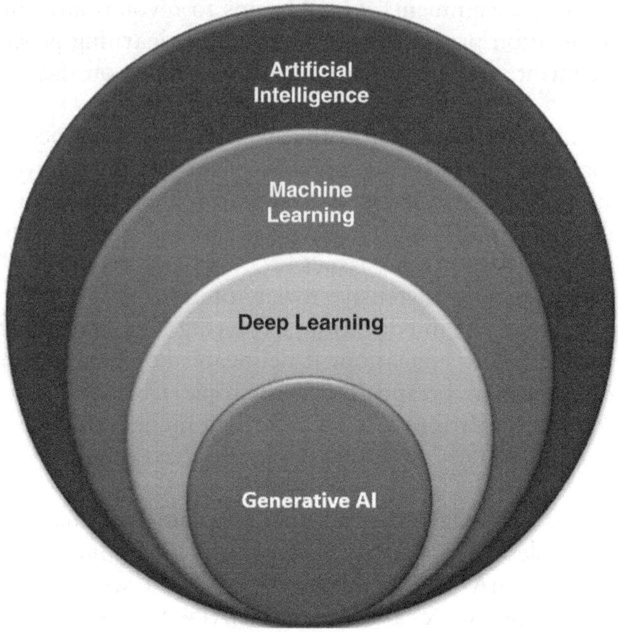

Figure 10.1 Generative artificial intelligence.

AI technologies have significantly transformed traditional teaching and learning methods, bringing about profound changes within the educational system. Extensive research has explored AI's applications, challenges, and future directions in higher education [9–13]. Authors have examined AI's role in higher education, including intelligent tutoring systems, personalized learning, virtual assistants, predictive analytics, and chatbots. They underscore the importance of deeper exploration into the pedagogical, ethical, social, cultural, and economic dimensions of these applications, emphasizing the need for critical reflection and exploration of ethical and educational approaches. AI, encompassing machine learning and deep learning techniques, continues to transform teaching and learning methods. Figure 10.1 illustrates the interaction between these technologies.

GenAI, distinguished as a particular subcategory, has recently garnered significant interest, as depicted in Figure 10.2 illustrating its evolution from traditional AI from 1956 to 2023. Unlike its traditional counterparts focused on analyzing existing data, GenAI excels in creating original and contextually relevant content spanning texts, images, sounds, and other data types. This capability introduces unprecedented opportunities for higher education, enriching learning experiences and providing innovative tools for educational resource development. Advances in generative models such as Transformers and LLMs, notably the Generative Pre-Trained Transformer (GPT), highlight the vast potential of this technology to revolutionize education.

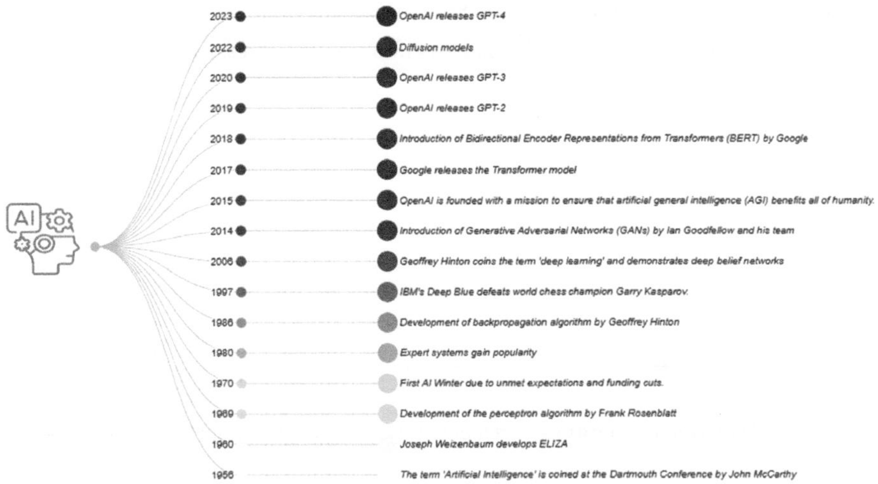

Figure 10.2 From AI to GenAI.

This transformative influence of GenAI extends deeply into higher education, enhancing various aspects of teaching, learning, and research across multiple domains, to the benefit of both students and educators. It enables developers to harness Machine Learning and Deep Learning models trained on extensive Internet datasets, producing content that matches human-created outputs. This evolution is reflected in its diverse impacts on teaching and learning methodologies, underscored by the significant increase in scholarly articles on AI applications in education indexed in PUBMED since the 1960s. This growth reflects escalating interest in integrating GenAI within educational contexts. Figure 10.3 visually charts the upward trend of indexed articles in PUBMED from 1980 to 2024, providing a clear representation of ongoing exploration and research in this burgeoning field.

10.2.2 Advanced generative AI models

GenAI encompasses a diverse range of deep learning models that excel in supporting various tasks across vision, speech, language, decision-making, and research. These models, such as the GPT, are a subset of large language models (LLMs).

LLMs are AI systems built on deep learning architectures. They are renowned for their capability to process and generate human-like text by analyzing vast datasets. Using advanced algorithms, LLMs learn intricate patterns and relationships within language, enabling them to generate coherent and contextually appropriate responses to input queries.

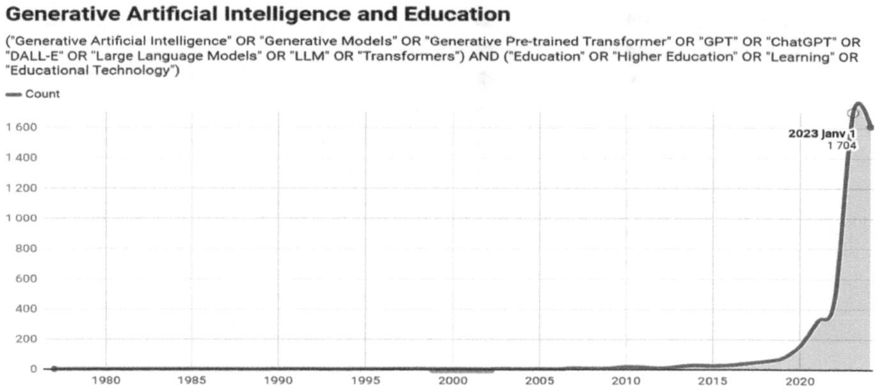

Figure 10.3 Evolution of GenAI research publications indexed in PubMed (1980–2024).

Alongside the advancements in GenAI, the development of LLMs has profoundly transformed tasks in natural language processing. These models are characterized by their substantial size and complexity, trained on extensive text corpora to comprehend and generate text comparable to human writing. They undergo meticulous processes of data collection, preprocessing, model selection, configuration, training, and optimization to achieve peak performance [14–18].

- Among these, GPT-4, with one trillion parameters, represents the cutting edge in generative models, capable of semiautomatically generating natural language and code based on prompts in natural language.
- GPT-3.5 also offers robust capabilities in generating semiautomatic inputs for both natural language and code, particularly effective in interactive scenarios like conversational applications. The optimized GPT-3.5-turbo models further enhance performance in these contexts.
- GPT-3, with 175 billion parameters, represents a significant leap in the scale and complexity of generative language models, enabling it to handle a wide range of natural language processing tasks with remarkable proficiency.
- GPT-2 significantly expanded on its predecessor with 1.5 billion parameters, demonstrating the potential for generating coherent and contextually relevant text across various applications.
- GPT-1, the first model in the GPT series, introduced the concept of GPTs, laying the foundation for subsequent advancements in GenAI.
- Embedding models are essential for converting textual data into numerical vectors, facilitating advanced language analytics tasks such as text comparison and similarity detection.
- DALL-E models, currently in beta, specialize in generating images from natural language descriptions, highlighting their potential for creative applications.

These models vary not only in their technical capabilities but also in speed, cost efficiency, and specific application scenarios, making them versatile tools in the evolving landscape of GenAI.

10.2.3 Applications of GenAI in education

GenAI offers a multitude of transformative applications in higher education, significantly enhancing teaching, learning, and research processes. One standout application is personalized learning, where AI algorithms analyze student data to tailor educational content and adaptive learning paths, catering to individual learning styles and speeds. This personalized approach not only boosts student engagement but also improves learning outcomes.

Another groundbreaking use is in automated grading systems, which provide prompt and consistent feedback on assignments and assessments. By automating grading, educators can redirect their focus to interactive teaching methods, thereby enhancing educational quality and efficiency.

AI-driven tools are also instrumental in generating high-quality educational materials such as lecture notes, practice questions, and entire course modules. This automation saves educators considerable time, allowing them to prioritize teaching and student interaction.

Virtual teaching assistants powered by AI are becoming increasingly prevalent, offering round-the-clock support to students. These assistants are adept at answering queries and providing guidance, thereby improving accessibility and responsiveness within educational institutions. This continuous support system ensures students receive assistance whenever needed, enhancing their overall learning experience.

GenAI also streamlines administrative tasks like grading and scheduling, freeing up faculty time for teaching and research pursuits. Moreover, it enhances research productivity by aiding researchers in tasks such as literature reviews, hypothesis generation, and drafting research papers. This augmentation of human capabilities accelerates the research process, fostering more innovative and timely discoveries.

Furthermore, exploring the opportunities and challenges posed by GenAI in education reveals its potential to reshape learning environments and educational methodologies.

Table 10.1 shows various applications of GenAI in education.

10.3 OPPORTUNITIES OFFERED BY GENERATIVE AI IN EDUCATION

GenAI has the potential to revolutionize education by enhancing effectiveness, engagement, and accessibility. It acts as a virtual tutor, providing personalized feedback, generating case scenarios, and assisting in research and academic writing. This capability significantly reduces educators' workload

Table 10.1 Applications of GenAI for higher education

Application	*Description*	*Relevant search results*	*References*
Personalized Learning Support	By analyzing student data, GenAI can deliver customized learning experiences, adaptive assessments, and targeted interventions to meet the unique needs of each student.	Applications like ChatGPT have been documented in the literature for enhancing personalized learning experiences and facilitating the writing process. GenAI can function as a virtual tutor, offering personalized learning support and providing instant answers to students' questions. GenAI can be used to analyze students' performance data and create personalized learning paths. The use of GenAI in medical education evaluations includes creating personalized quizzes tailored to individual students. By analyzing each student's strengths and weaknesses, GenAI can generate unique formative and summative assessments.	[19–21]
Writing Assistants	GenAI assists learners and educators by providing tools that simplify the writing, editing, and improvement of written content. These aids can suggest improvements to make essays, research papers, and other academic writing clearer, more coherent, and grammatically correct.	GenAI can assist students with their writing by working in the same way as various existing writing aids such as NoRedInk and Grammarly. Students can type in a sentence and ask GenAI to correct it, giving them hints on how the sentence can be improved.	[22]
Automating Content Creation	GenAI can be used to automatically generate personalized learning materials, textbooks, assignments, quizzes, and test questions tailored to specific courses and learning objectives.	GenAI can automate the creation of high-quality learning materials, such as textbooks, lecture notes, assignments, and quizzes. Automated content creation involves using generative models to produce teaching materials, thereby reducing the workload on instructors.	[23]

(Continued)

Enabling Interactive Student Support	GenAI-powered chatbots can provide 24/7 assistance to students, answering questions, offering guidance, and facilitating discussions.	GenAI-enabled chatbots are valuable tools for educators seeking to enhance student support and engagement. GenAI can also enhance peer collaboration by connecting students with diverse backgrounds, interests, and expertise.	[24]
Streamlining Administrative Tasks	GenAI automates grading, scheduling, and other administrative tasks, enabling faculty to devote more time to teaching and research.	GenAI can automate such tasks, allowing educators to allocate more time and energy to teaching and mentoring. GenAI presents exciting prospects for transforming the educational landscape through personalized learning experiences, the development of interactive educational materials, and the automation of administrative tasks.	[25]
Enhancing Research Productivity	GenAI can assist researchers in tasks like literature reviews, hypothesis generation, and even drafting research papers.	GenAI can support researchers by automating literature reviews, suggesting hypotheses based on existing data, and drafting research papers, thereby accelerating the research process.	[26]
Text Summarization	Condensing long texts into concise summaries, aiding students in quickly grasping key information and improving study efficiency.	GenAI reproduces the intricacies of human linguistic models and can be applied to complex tasks such as text summary generation, language translation, and dialogue systems.	[27]
Language Translation	Translating educational materials into various languages, making learning resources accessible to a broader range of students.	GenAI enables real-time translation into multiple languages, handling audio, text, images, and video.	[28]
Smart Grading	Leveraging GenAI to evaluate student assignments and exams, providing accurate and efficient grading.	By using GenAI, educational institutions can improve accessibility for students with disabilities by generating audio transcriptions, simplifying complex text, and providing learning materials in various formats to meet diverse needs.	[29, 30]

through automation of tasks like assessments and grading, thereby boosting overall educational productivity [31].

In higher education, GenAI transforms learning environments by customizing them to meet individual needs and fostering collaborative knowledge creation. It democratizes education with scalable solutions tailored to diverse learning styles, offering real-time feedback to enhance educational achievements and prepare students for future careers. Advanced analytics tools enable institutions to optimize teaching strategies by analyzing extensive datasets, using predictive analytics to intervene proactively and potentially reduce dropout rates while improving student retention [32].

GenAI enhances learning through original responses to user prompts. Tools like ChatGPT aid non-native English speakers in writing and feedback, while DALL-E and Stable Diffusion support teaching technical and artistic concepts. It facilitates idea generation, data synthesis, and efficient publication for researchers. Automated essay grading with tools like the Intelligent Essay Assessor ensures consistency and prompt feedback, enhancing student outcomes [4].

Integration of GenAI in higher education offers benefits across students, educators, and researchers. It enhances self-directed learning and critical thinking with personalized feedback, supports theory-based question answering, and aids in essay concept generation. Improving language skills benefits non-native English speakers and students with disabilities, yet empirical validation for round-the-clock support, especially for distance and international learners, remains limited. While aiming to foster innovative and interactive learning experiences, its transformative impact in educational settings awaits further empirical validation [33].

Personalized learning stands out as a key opportunity, where AI analyzes student performance data to tailor educational content and assessments to diverse learning styles and paces. This customization enhances engagement and learning outcomes by addressing specific knowledge gaps through targeted interventions. GenAI also streamlines administrative tasks like content creation and grading, freeing educators for interactive teaching and mentorship.

Figure 10.4 Wordcloud of opportunities offered by GenAI in education.

AI-powered virtual assistants provide continuous student support, enhancing educational accessibility and responsiveness. These advancements highlight GenAI's potential to create a more efficient, personalized, and inclusive educational environment. Despite these advances, the implementation of GenAI in education faces significant obstacles that need to be overcome to maximize its potential and mitigate the risks. Figure 10.4 illustrates a *Wordcloud of opportunities offered by GenAI in education.*

10.4 CHALLENGES ASSOCIATED WITH INTEGRATING GENERATIVE AI IN EDUCATION

Integrating GenAI into educational settings presents a promising avenue for enhancing teaching methodologies and learning outcomes. However, this integration is accompanied by several challenges that require careful consideration and proactive management. GenAI poses significant issues such as algorithmic biases, as shown in Figure 10.5 which can skew learning outcomes and perpetuate inequities by unfairly shaping educational experiences rooted in biased data and algorithms [27]. The opacity of AI processes raises trust issues among educators and students, while privacy concerns arise from potential misuse in gathering sensitive student data. In distance education, while GenAI can personalize learning, it may widen the transactional distance between learners and educators, affecting effective communication. Moreover, reliance on AI-generated content risks providing outdated or inaccurate information due to AI's limitations in understanding contextual nuances and domain-specific knowledge.

In higher education, challenges encompass Quality Control, where AI systems may generate inaccurate or biased information, undermining educational content reliability. Regarding Expertise and Authority, GenAI lacks domain-specific knowledge critical for in-depth insights and analysis, necessitating the continued role of human educators in verifying information and providing contextual understanding. The capability of GenAI for Personalized Learning may be constrained; not fully addressing individual learning needs like preferences and learning styles. In Communication and Collaboration, AI's nature may limit interpersonal skills essential for effective group work. Additionally, concerns about Misuse by students for plagiarism and cheating underscore the need for robust policies and detection mechanisms to uphold academic integrity standards [33].

Preparing students for a future shaped by GenAI demands proactive responses from educators and policymakers. Challenges include ensuring students develop technical skills and ethical awareness to engage effectively with AI. Continuous adaptation to technological change and aligning curricula with industry demands are crucial [34]. Integrating GenAI into education requires addressing equity, digital access, and regulatory frameworks. Overcoming these challenges enables educational systems to better equip students for a world influenced by AI.

Figure 10.5 Challenges associated with integrating GenAI in education.

The use of AI in education and research also confronts significant challenges, such as hallucinations, where AI generates incorrect content due to limited contextual understanding and reliability issues [7]. Data privacy concerns, algorithmic biases, and ethical implications of AI-driven decision-making further complicate its adoption. Addressing these challenges and establishing guidelines for responsible AI use is essential to harness AI's potential for enhancing education and research outcomes.

Implementing GenAI tools in education encounters challenges, particularly from teachers resistant to their adoption, citing relevance, and integration issues with current educational practices [36]. Overcoming resistance requires comprehensive training and support to help educators recognize the benefits of AI tools and integrate them effectively. Chief among these challenges are ensuring robust data privacy measures, addressing bias in AI algorithms, and navigating ethical concerns in algorithmic decision-making to uphold educational standards. Educators also face challenges in adapting to AI technologies, integrating them into curricula, managing costs, and evaluating their effectiveness. Overcoming these hurdles is vital to realizing the transformative potential of GenAI in education.

In addition to these challenges, other significant obstacles include adapting curriculum and assessment methods to effectively incorporate AI technologies without compromising educational standards, ensuring that AI-enhanced learning environments remain inclusive and accessible to all students, regardless of their technological background or resources, and fostering a culture of continuous learning and adaptation among educators to keep pace with rapid advancements in AI. Moreover, the ethical implications of AI-driven decision-making in educational settings require careful navigation to uphold student well-being and fairness in academic outcomes. Addressing these multifaceted challenges demands collaborative efforts among educators, policymakers, and technology developers to harness the full potential of GenAI while safeguarding educational integrity and equity.

10.5 ETHICAL CONSIDERATIONS AND RECOMMENDATIONS

10.5.1 Ethical considerations in integrating generative AI in higher education

Integrating GenAI into higher education necessitates careful consideration of various ethical dimensions to ensure its responsible and effective deployment. Central to these considerations is the issue of algorithmic bias, where AI algorithms may inadvertently perpetuate biases present in training data, potentially influencing critical educational decisions such as grading and admissions. Mitigating this requires utilizing diverse and representative datasets and implementing robust bias detection and mitigation strategies. Moreover, the reliance on GenAI on extensive student data for personalization underscores the paramount importance of safeguarding privacy and data security. Institutions must adhere rigorously to data protection regulations, ensuring transparency in data handling practices to mitigate risks of unauthorized access and misuse. Transparency and explainability in AI-driven decisions are equally essential, fostering trust and accountability among stakeholders by providing clear rationales for AI-generated recommendations. Furthermore, promoting equity and accessibility through AI implementations demands proactive measures to prevent exacerbating existing disparities in educational access. This includes designing AI systems that enhance accessibility for all students, including those with disabilities or from underrepresented groups. Ethical use of student data mandates clear policies on consent, anonymization, and the prioritization of educational benefits while respecting students' rights.

As the integration of GenAI and chatbots into higher education accelerates, significant ethical considerations come to the forefront. These technologies promise enhanced educational experiences through personalized learning and administrative efficiencies. However, they also raise critical concerns regarding data privacy, as the collection and analysis of vast amounts of student data raise questions about consent, security, and the potential for unauthorized access. Algorithmic bias presents another challenge, as AI systems may unintentionally perpetuate or amplify existing biases in educational materials, assessments, and student interactions, potentially disadvantaging certain student groups.

- *Data Privacy*: Implementing GenAI in education involves collecting and storing student data, raising significant privacy concerns. Strict adherence to data protection regulations like GDPR is crucial, though challenges such as data deletion and algorithmic transparency remain.
- *Algorithmic Bias*: GenAI can perpetuate societal biases present in the data they are trained on, affecting educational outcomes and student experiences. Mitigation strategies include using diverse datasets and conducting regular bias audits.
- *Student Self-Efficacy*: While GenAI can enhance autonomy in learning, there's a risk of overreliance, potentially diminishing student engagement and authentic learning experiences.
- *Plagiarism*: AI-powered tools like GenAI may facilitate plagiarism by generating content that students pass off as their own. Addressing this requires robust policies, advanced plagiarism detection methods, and innovative assessment strategies.
- *Hallucinations*: AI hallucinations, where GenAI generates false or misleading information, pose challenges for educators in ensuring accuracy in educational content. Vigilant vetting and ongoing supervision are necessary to mitigate these risks.

10.5.2 Recommendations

Ensuring the indispensable role of human educators amid technological advancements is paramount, emphasizing AI's potential to enhance rather than replace critical thinking, creativity, and empathy. Ethically integrating AI into higher education requires concerted efforts, including establishing ethics committees to oversee implementations and formulate guidelines for its ethical use. Promoting diversity within AI development teams is essential to mitigate biases and ensure inclusivity in algorithms and applications. Continuous monitoring and auditing of AI systems are imperative to uphold fairness and performance standards.

Educating stakeholders about AI technologies and their ethical implications, coupled with prioritizing user-centric design principles and conducting rigorous pilot testing, further strengthens ethical practices in integrating GenAI into higher education. These initiatives enable institutions to harness

AI's transformative potential while upholding ethical standards and safeguarding student interests.

- *Ethics Committees and Guidelines*: Establishing ethics committees or advisory boards to oversee AI implementations and develop robust guidelines for ethical AI use in higher education.
- *Critical Examination of Values and Cultural Norms*: Researchers, educators, and students should critically evaluate the values, cultural norms, and social practices embedded in GenAI training models. Policymakers must address widening inequalities stemming from disparities in AI model training and regulation, recognizing gaps in current regulations safeguarding ownership rights and user rights of domestic users of GenAI.
- *Diverse and Inclusive AI Development*: Ensuring diversity in AI development teams to mitigate biases and promote inclusivity in AI algorithms and applications.
- *Continuous Monitoring and Auditing*: Regularly monitoring AI systems for bias, fairness, and performance metrics through audits and assessments to uphold ethical standards.
- *Education and Awareness*: Educating stakeholders about AI technologies, their benefits, and ethical implications to facilitate informed decision-making and responsible use.
- *User-Centric Design*: Designing AI systems with principles that prioritize transparency, user control over data, and mechanisms to contest AI-generated decisions.
- *Pilot Testing and Evaluation*: Conducting pilot testing of AI implementations on a small scale to assess impact, gather stakeholder feedback, and iteratively improve systems based on evaluations.
- *Adherence to Regulatory Frameworks*: Complying with existing data protection laws and regulations, such as GDPR or CCPA, and integrating ethical considerations into institutional policies and practices.

10.6 CONCLUSION

GenAI holds immense promise to revolutionize higher education through task automation, personalized learning enhancements, and innovative educational content. However, its integration into educational settings necessitates navigating complex challenges. These include upholding academic integrity, ensuring equitable access, managing ethical considerations, and safeguarding data privacy. This study has synthesized existing literature to examine the opportunities and challenges presented by GenAI in higher education, offering insights into its potential impacts and practical implications. Moving forward, it is imperative for higher education institutions to adopt strategic approaches that facilitate responsible GenAI implementation while actively mitigating associated risks. By doing so, institutions can effectively leverage the transformative potential of GenAI while upholding ethical standards and fostering positive educational outcomes for all stakeholders.

REFERENCES

1. Peres R, Schreier M, Schweidel D, Sorescu A. On ChatGPT and beyond: How generative artificial intelligence may affect research, teaching, and practice. International Journal of Research in Marketing 2023;40:269–75. https://doi.org/10.1016/j.ijresmar.2023.03.001.
2. Feuerriegel S, Hartmann J, Janiesch C, Zschech P. Generative AI. Business & Information Systems Engineering 2024;66:111–26. https://doi.org/10.1007/s12599-023-00834-7.
3. Fezari M, Al Dahoud A, Al-Dahoud A. Augmanting Reality : The Power of Generative AI. 2023.
4. Chan CKY, Hu W. Students' voices on generative AI: Perceptions, benefits, and challenges in higher education. International Journal of Educational Technology in Higher Education 2023;20:43. https://doi.org/10.1186/s41239-023-00411-8
5. Kurtz G, Amzalag M, Shaked N, Zaguri Y, Kohen-Vacs D, Gal E, et al. Strategies for integrating generative AI into higher education: Navigating challenges and leveraging opportunities. Education Sciences 2024;14:503. https://doi.org/10.3390/educsci14050503.
6. Chiu TKF. Future research recommendations for transforming higher education with generative AI. Computers and Education: Artificial Intelligence 2024;6:100197. https://doi.org/10.1016/j.caeai.2023.100197.
7. Walczak K, Cellary W. Challenges for higher education in the era of widespread access to generative AI. EBR 2023;9. https://doi.org/10.18559/ebr.2023.2.743.
8. Kurtz G, Amzalag M, Shaked N, Zaguri Y, Kohen-Vacs D, Gal E, et al. Strategies for integrating generative AI into higher education: Navigating challenges and leveraging opportunities. Education Sciences 2024;14:503. https://doi.org/10.3390/educsci14050503.
9. Hwang G-J, Xie H, Wah BW, Gašević D. Vision, challenges, roles and research issues of artificial intelligence in education. Computers and Education: Artificial Intelligence 2020;1:100001. https://doi.org/10.1016/j.caeai.2020.100001.
10. Chiu TKF, Xia Q, Zhou X, Chai CS, Cheng M. Systematic literature review on opportunities, challenges, and future research recommendations of artificial intelligence in education. Computers and Education: Artificial Intelligence 2023;4:100118. https://doi.org/10.1016/j.caeai.2022.100118.
11. Luan H, Geczy P, Lai H, Gobert J, Yang SJH, Ogata H, et al. Challenges and future directions of big data and artificial intelligence in education. Front Psychol 2020;11. https://doi.org/10.3389/fpsyg.2020.580820.
12. Lutsenko O, Lutsenko G. Active Learning: Theory and Practice. BoD – Books on Demand. 2022.
13. Kaouni M, Lakrami F, Labouidya O. Integrating Artificial Intelligence and Natural Language Processing in E-Learning Platforms: A Review of Opportunities and Limitations. 2023 7th IEEE Congress on Information Science and Technology (CiSt), 2023, pp. 56–63. https://doi.org/10.1109/CiSt56084.2023.10409971.
14. Yu P, Xu H, Hu X, Deng C. Leveraging generative AI and large language models: A comprehensive roadmap for healthcare integration. Healthcare 2023;11:2776. https://doi.org/10.3390/healthcare11202776.

15. Alto V. Modern Generative AI with ChatGPT and OpenAI Models: Leverage the Capabilities of OpenAI's LLM for Productivity and Innovation with GPT3 and GPT4. Packt Publishing Ltd; 2023.
16. Linkon AA, Shaima M, Sarker MSU, Badruddowza, Nabi N, Rana MNU, et al. Advancements and applications of generative artificial intelligence and large language models on business management: A comprehensive review. Journal of Computer Science and Technology Studies 2024;6:225–32. https://doi.org/10.32996/jcsts.2024.6.1.26.
17. Arora C, Grundy J, Abdelrazek M. Advancing Requirements Engineering through Generative AI: Assessing the Role of LLMs. In: Nguyen-Duc A, Abrahamsson P, Khomh F, editors. Generative AI for Effective Software Development, Cham: Springer Nature Switzerland; 2024, pp. 129–48. https://doi.org/10.1007/978-3-031-55642-5_6.
18. Kurtz G, Amzalag M, Shaked N, Zaguri Y, Kohen-Vacs D, Gal E, et al. Strategies for integrating generative AI into higher education: Navigating challenges and leveraging opportunities. Education Sciences 2024;14:503. https://doi.org/10.3390/educsci14050503.
19. Preiksaitis C, Rose C. Opportunities, challenges, and future directions of generative artificial intelligence in medical education: Scoping review. JMIR Medical Education 2023;9:e48785. https://doi.org/10.2196/48785.
20. Bahroun Z, Anane C, Ahmed V, Zacca A. Transforming education: A comprehensive review of generative artificial intelligence in educational settings through bibliometric and content analysis. Sustainability 2023;15:12983. https://doi.org/10.3390/su151712983.
21. Su J, Yang W. Unlocking the power of ChatGPT: A framework for applying generative AI in education. ECNU Review of Education 2023;6:355–66. https://doi.org/10.1177/20965311231168423.
22. Liu M, Ren Y, Nyagoga LM, Stonier F, Wu Z, Yu L. Future of education in the era of generative artificial intelligence: Consensus among Chinese scholars on applications of ChatGPT in schools. Future in Educational Research 2023;1:72–101. https://doi.org/10.1002/fer3.10.
23. George DAS. The potential of generative AI to reform graduate education. Partners Universal International Research Journal 2023;2:36–50. https://doi.org/10.5281/zenodo.10421475.
24. Chan CKY, Lee KKW. The AI generation gap: Are gen z students more interested in adopting generative AI such as ChatGPT in teaching and learning than their gen X and millennial generation teachers? Smart Learn Environ 2023;10:60. https://doi.org/10.1186/s40561-023-00269-3.
25. Michel-Villarreal R., Vilalta-Perdomo E., Salinas-Navarro DE., Thierry-Aguilera R, Gerardou FS. Challenges and opportunities of generative AI for higher education as explained by ChatGPT. Educ Sci 2023;13(9):856.
26. Alasadi EA, Baiz CR. Generative AI in education and research: Opportunities, concerns, and solutions. J Chem Educ 2023;100:2965–71. https://doi.org/10.1021/acs.jchemed.3c00323.
27. Ooi K-B, Tan GW-H, Al-Emran M, Al-Sharafi MA, Capatina A, Chakraborty A, et al. The potential of generative artificial intelligence across disciplines: Perspectives and future directions. Journal of Computer Information Systems 2023;0:1–32. https://doi.org/10.1080/08874417.2023.2261010.
28. Farrelly T, Baker N. Generative artificial intelligence: Implications and considerations for higher education practice. Education Sciences 2023;13:1109. https://doi.org/10.3390/educsci13111109.
29. Tobler S. Smart grading: A generative AI-based tool for knowledge-grounded answer evaluation in educational assessments. MethodsX 2024;12:102531. https://doi.org/10.1016/j.mex.2023.102531.

30. Naseer F, Khalid MU, Ayub N, Rasool A, Abbas T, Afzal MW. Automated assessment and feedback in higher education using generative AI. Transforming education with generative AI: Prompt engineering and synthetic content creation. IGI Global 2024;433–61. https://doi.org/10.4018/979-8-3693-1351-0.ch021.
31. Ooi K-B, Tan GW-H, Al-Emran M, Al-Sharafi MA, Capatina A, Chakraborty A, et al. The potential of generative artificial intelligence across disciplines: Perspectives and future directions. Journal of Computer Information Systems n.d;0:1–32. https://doi.org/10.1080/08874417.2023.2261010.
32. Education Sciences | Free Full-Text | Strategies for Integrating Generative AI into Higher Education: Navigating Challenges and Leveraging Opportunities n.d. https://www.mdpi.com/2227-7102/14/5/503 (accessed July 13, 2024).
33. Education Sciences | Free Full-Text | Challenges and Opportunities of Generative AI for Higher Education as Explained by ChatGPT n.d. https://www.mdpi.com/2227-7102/13/9/856 (accessed July 13, 2024).
34. Bozkurt A. Generative artificial intelligence (AI) powered conversational educational agents: The inevitable paradigm shift. Asian Journal of Distance Education 2023; 18(1):198–204.
35. Lodge JM, Thompson K, Corrin L. Mapping out a research agenda for generative artificial intelligence in tertiary education. Australasian Journal of Educational Technology 2023;39:1–8. https://doi.org/10.14742/ajet.8695.
36. Ruiz-Rojas LI, Acosta-Vargas P, De-Moreta-Llovet J, Gonzalez-Rodriguez M. Empowering education with generative artificial intelligence tools: Approach with an instructional design matrix. Sustainability 2023;15:11524. https://doi.org/10.3390/su151511524.
37. Williams RT. The ethical implications of using generative chatbots in higher education. Frontiers in Education 2024;8. https://doi.org/10.3389/feduc.2023.1331607.
38. Michel-Villarreal R, Vilalta-Perdomo E, Salinas-Navarro DE, Thierry-Aguilera R, Gerardou FS. Challenges and opportunities of generative AI for higher education as explained by ChatGPT. Education Sciences 2023;13:856. https://doi.org/10.3390/educsci13090856.
39. Ņikadimovs O, Vēvere V. The use of generative artificial intelligence in higher education: University social responsibility and stakeholders' perceptions. Environment Technologies Resources Proceedings of the International Scientific and Practical Conference 2024;2:226–31. https://doi.org/10.17770/etr2024vol2.8015.
40. Guidance for generative AI in education and research – Holmes, Wayne, Miao, Fengchun, UNESCO - Google Books n.d. https://books.google.co.ma/books?hl=en&lr=&id=cKnYEAAAQBAJ&oi=fnd&pg=PA2&dq=generative+ai+ethics+education&ots=wmF9jkLbaN&sig=hFglOEHlUgiRemTqygYJgs3gNpg&redir_esc=y#v=onepage&q&f=false (accessed July 13, 2024).

Chapter 11

On exploring generative AI for privacy preservation in IoT ecosystems

Hafssa Benaboud, Hiba Kandil, and Saiida Lazaar

11.1 INTRODUCTION

The Internet of Things (IoT) has transformed modern society by connecting billions of devices and enabling unprecedented data-driven innovations. From smart homes and wearable devices to industrial automation and healthcare systems, IoT technologies generate vast amounts of data that power intelligent applications. However, this interconnected ecosystem also raises significant concerns about data privacy. The sensitive nature of IoT-generated data, such as personal health metrics, geolocation information, and behavioral patterns, makes it a prime risk for breaches, unauthorized access, and misuse. The challenge lies in ensuring that data remains private and secure while still being useful for IoT applications.

Traditional privacy-preserving techniques, such as encryption, anonymization, and access control, often struggle to meet the unique demands of IoT ecosystems. The vast heterogeneity of IoT devices – from simple sensors to sophisticated smart appliances – complicates the application of standardized anonymization methods across diverse data types and formats. Many IoT devices operate under severe computational constraints, rendering complex anonymization algorithms impractical for local execution. Furthermore, the need for real-time or near-real-time data processing in applications like health monitoring or smart traffic systems is often incompatible with the latency introduced by these traditional techniques. A critical challenge lies in balancing data utility and privacy; excessive anonymization can diminish the value of data for purposes such as predictive maintenance or personalized services. Moreover, the rich, interconnected nature of IoT data amplifies vulnerabilities to reidentification attacks and data aggregation threats, where anonymized datasets can be cross-referenced with external sources to expose sensitive information. These limitations highlight the urgent need for more advanced, scalable privacy-preserving mechanisms tailored to IoT. In response, Generative AI (GAI) has emerged as a powerful tool for addressing these challenges. By leveraging advanced models such as Generative Adversarial Networks (GANs, [1]) and Variational Autoencoders (VAEs, [2]), GAI can offer innovative solutions to enhance privacy in IoT environments. GAI enables the generation of synthetic

DOI: 10.1201/9781003597476-15

data that mirrors the characteristics of real datasets without revealing sensitive information, thereby mitigating privacy risks. It also facilitates dynamic anonymization techniques and secure data-sharing protocols, ensuring compliance with privacy regulations while maintaining data utility.

This chapter explores how GAI can be effectively utilized to tackle privacy challenges in IoT environments. It highlights key applications, such as data anonymization, synthetic data generation, and privacy-preserving behavioral analysis, while addressing the associated ethical and technical challenges. It is structured as follows. Section 11.2 delves into the types of sensitive data generated by IoT devices, the threats posed to data privacy, and the current limitations of existing privacy-preserving techniques. Section 11.3 explores three key applications of GAI to preserve data privacy: data anonymization, synthetic data generation, and secure data sharing. In Section 11.4, we explore three key applications of GAI to enable secure and efficient data usage while safeguarding sensitive information: its synergy with federated learning, its role in privacy-preserving behavioral analysis, and its use in dynamic access control mechanisms. Section 11.5 focuses on real-world applications of GAI in IoT environments. We present ten illustrative examples to showcase the application of GAI in enhancing privacy within IoT ecosystems. For each case, we give references to recent contributions in the field. In Section 11.6, we discuss the risks and responsibilities associated with the use of GAI in privacy preservation, and we conclude our chapter in Section 11.7.

11.2 PRIVACY ISSUES IN IOT ENVIRONMENTS

The rapid expansion of IoT has brought numerous benefits to modern society, but it has also introduced complex privacy challenges [3]. IoT systems collect, process, and share vast amounts of data, which can be categorized into personal and sensitive data. Personal data refers to information that can identify an individual. Sensitive data, on the other hand, include more critical information, which requires higher levels of protection due to their potential to cause harm if exposed. This section delves into the types of sensitive and personal data generated by IoT devices, the threats posed to data privacy, and the current limitations of existing privacy-preserving techniques.

11.2.1 Personal and sensitive data generated by IoT devices

There are key differences between personal and sensitive data in IoT. When distinguishing between personal data and sensitive personal data in the context of IoT, it's helpful to use legal frameworks like GDPR as a guide. IoT devices produce a wide range of personal and sensitive data across various domains, making them attractive targets for malicious actors. Key categories of such data are as follows.

11.2.1.1 Personal data in IoT

Personal data refers to any information that can identify a person directly or indirectly. IoT devices collect various types of personal data, such as:

- Identifiers (e.g., name, email address, phone number), device-specific identifiers (e.g., MAC address, UUID, IP address).
- Demographic Data like age, gender, or household details (e.g., smart TV user profiles).
- Location Data such as real-time GPS or Wi-Fi triangulation data from smart wearables or connected cars.
- Behavioral Data such as usage patterns (e.g., how and when smart appliances are used) or exercise routines from wearables.
- Preferences like TV viewing habits, music playlists, or home thermostat settings.

11.2.1.2 Sensitive data in IoT

Sensitive personal data refers to information that requires higher levels of protection due to its potential for misuse or harm. We can list the following:

- Health Information including blood pressure, heart rate, glucose levels, or medical diagnoses from smart health devices.
- Biometric Data in terms of fingerprints, facial recognition data, or voice prints used for authentication in IoT devices like smart locks or assistants.
- Religious or Political Views in relation to data inferred from preferences or activities (e.g., subscriptions to specific channels on a smart TV).
- Sexual Orientation or Behavior deduced with data inferred from IoT interactions, such as activity on certain wearable devices.
- Financial Information such as payment card details or transaction histories from IoT payment systems.
- Children's Data obtained through location or activity data collected by toys or wearables designed for kids.

To synthesize, personal data in IoT, such as names, device IDs, and usage patterns, carries moderate risks if exposed, typically leading to privacy invasions or identity tracking. Examples include energy usage from smart thermostats or user account details. Sensitive personal data, like biometric information, health metrics, or payment details, poses higher risks, including financial theft, discrimination, or physical harm. For example, data from smart locks or medical IoT devices requires stricter protections like encryption. Sensitive data also faces stricter legal regulations, as its misuse can have more severe consequences than general personal data.

The diversity and sensitivity of data generated by IoT devices amplify the risks of privacy violations, underscoring the need for robust privacy-preserving mechanisms.

11.2.2 Threats to privacy

The ubiquitous connectivity and data-centric nature of IoT ecosystems expose them to a variety of privacy threats. Some of the most pressing threats include:

- **Data Interception:** IoT devices often transmit data over unsecured networks, making them susceptible to interception by attackers. This can lead to the exposure of sensitive information, such as passwords, personal habits, or operational details.
- **Unauthorized Access:** Weak authentication and access control mechanisms in IoT devices allow malicious actors to gain unauthorized access to devices or networks, enabling them to steal or manipulate data.
- **Profiling and Surveillance:** Aggregated data from IoT devices can be used to create detailed profiles of individuals, potentially leading to invasive tracking and surveillance. For instance, analyzing smart home data can reveal behavioral patterns, such as daily routines or absences.
- **Reidentification Attacks:** Even anonymized IoT data can be vulnerable to reidentification when combined with external datasets, exposing users to privacy risks despite initial attempts at data protection.

11.2.3 Current limitations in addressing IoT privacy

Despite advancements in privacy-preserving technologies, IoT environments face several limitations in safeguarding user data:

- **Inefficient Anonymization Techniques:** Traditional anonymization methods often fail to protect against sophisticated reidentification attacks. These techniques may reduce data utility, limiting their effectiveness in real-world IoT applications.
- **Limited Data Control:** Users frequently lack control over the data collected by their IoT devices, including how it is stored, processed, or shared. This lack of transparency and control erodes trust and increases privacy risks.
- **Lack of Scalable Solutions:** IoT ecosystems are characterized by their vast scale and heterogeneity. Existing privacy-preserving methods struggle to scale effectively across diverse devices and network architectures, leaving significant gaps in protection.

Addressing these challenges requires innovative approaches, such as leveraging GAI, which offers adaptive, scalable, and privacy-preserving capabilities tailored to the complexities of IoT environments. The next section explores how GAI can overcome these limitations and redefine privacy protection in IoT.

11.3 GENERATIVE AI APPROACHES FOR PRIVACY PRESERVATION

GAI offers transformative capabilities for addressing privacy challenges in IoT environments. By leveraging advanced models such as GANs and VAEs, GAI can introduce innovative solutions to preserve data privacy while maintaining utility. This section explores three key applications of GAI: data anonymization, synthetic data generation, and secure data sharing.

11.3.1 Data anonymization with GAI

Anonymization is a critical technique for protecting personally identifiable information (PII) while enabling data usability. Traditional anonymization methods often degrade data quality or fail to withstand sophisticated reidentification attacks. GAI enhances anonymization through advanced techniques that obfuscate sensitive information without compromising data utility.

- **GAI-Driven Pseudonymization:** GAI can generate pseudonymous data by replacing PII with synthetic counterparts that retain the statistical properties of the original data. For example, a GAN model can learn the distribution of location data and generate pseudonymous location records that maintain analytical integrity.
- **Dynamic Anonymization:** Unlike static anonymization, GAI can dynamically adapt anonymization levels based on the sensitivity of the data and its intended use. For instance, sensitive health metrics from IoT-enabled medical devices can be anonymized differently depending on whether the data is for clinical analysis or public research.
- **Enhanced Privacy Guarantees:** GAI-based methods can integrate privacy-preserving mechanisms, such as Differential Privacy, ensuring that the generated data minimizes the risk of reidentification while maintaining analytical relevance.

11.3.2 Synthetic data generation

Synthetic data generation is one of the most impactful applications of GAI in privacy preservation [4]. By creating realistic, nonsensitive datasets that emulate the properties of real data, GAI can mitigate privacy risks while supporting various IoT applications.

- **Realistic Data for Testing and Training:** Generative models can produce synthetic datasets that closely resemble real-world IoT data. For instance, a GAN can generate synthetic smart home sensor data for testing machine learning algorithms without exposing actual user data.
- **Privacy-Safe Data Sharing:** Synthetic data allows organizations to share valuable insights without exposing raw, sensitive information. For example, a healthcare provider can share anonymized patient activity data generated by IoT medical devices with researchers to study treatment efficacy.
- **Expanding Datasets for Model Robustness:** GAI can augment limited IoT datasets by generating additional synthetic samples, improving the robustness and generalizability of machine learning models trained on IoT data.
- **Industrial Applications:** In industrial IoT, synthetic data can be used to model sensor readings, machine operations, and failure patterns without risking exposure to proprietary or operational details.

11.3.3 Secure data sharing

IoT ecosystems often require data to be shared across multiple entities, such as service providers, analytics platforms, and device manufacturers. GAI can facilitate secure data sharing by creating secure proxies or representations of data that maintain functionality while protecting sensitive information.

- **GAI-Generated Secure Proxies:** GAI can generate secure proxies of IoT data that mimic the essential characteristics of the original data while removing identifiable elements. For example, a VAE could encode raw sensor data into a latent representation, from which a secure version is generated for sharing.
- **Minimizing Exposure in Data Transfer:** By using GAI to preprocess data before transmission, IoT devices can minimize the exposure of sensitive information during network transfers. For instance, smart home devices could share aggregated and anonymized activity summaries instead of detailed event logs.
- **Cross-Organization Collaboration:** GAI facilitates privacy-preserving collaborations between organizations. Synthetic datasets generated by GAI can be used for joint analytics and innovation without compromising user privacy.
- **Compliance with Privacy Regulations:** GAI-generated data-sharing mechanisms can help organizations comply with regulations like GDPR by ensuring that shared data does not contain identifiable or sensitive information.

GAI provides a versatile framework for tackling IoT privacy challenges. By leveraging its capabilities for anonymization, synthetic data generation, and secure data sharing, IoT ecosystems can achieve a balance between privacy and utility, fostering trust and innovation in connected technologies.

11.4 APPLICATIONS OF GENERATIVE AI IN PRIVACY-ENHANCED IOT SYSTEMS

The integration of GAI into IoT ecosystems presents transformative applications for enhancing privacy. This section explores three key applications of GAI (summarized in Figure 11.1): its synergy with federated learning, its role in privacy-preserving behavioral analysis, and its use in dynamic access control mechanisms.

11.4.1 Federated learning and generative AI

Federated learning (FL) is a decentralized approach to training machine learning models directly on local IoT devices, reducing the need to transfer sensitive data to centralized servers. GAI complements FL [5–7] by synthesizing local data, enhancing both privacy and model performance.

- **Synthesizing Representative Local Data:** GAI models can generate synthetic versions of local IoT data that preserve statistical properties while masking sensitive information. This synthetic data is used for model training without exposing raw data.
- **Mitigating Data Imbalances:** IoT devices often generate nonuniform data across different environments. GAI can create balanced datasets to improve the robustness and fairness of FL models.
- **Privacy-Enhanced Aggregation:** By synthesizing aggregated data at the edge, GAI reduces the risk of sensitive data leakage during the FL model aggregation process. This ensures compliance with privacy standards and regulations.

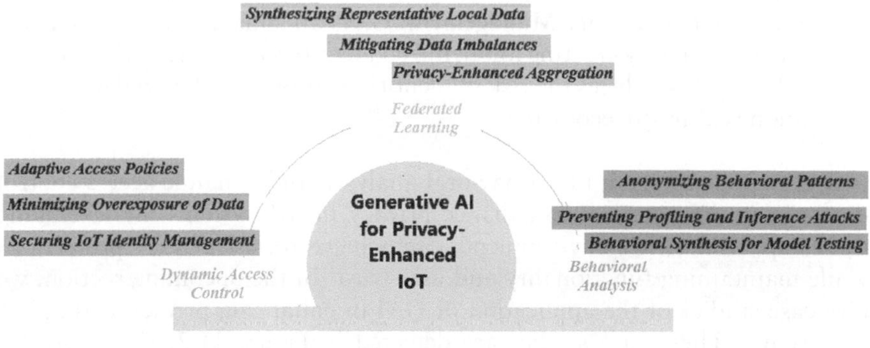

Figure 11.1 Applications of generative AI in privacy-enhanced IoT systems.

11.4.2 Privacy-Preserving behavioral analysis

Behavioral analysis is a cornerstone of many IoT applications, enabling functionalities like anomaly detection, user personalization, and predictive maintenance [8]. However, the analysis of behavioral patterns often exposes users to privacy risks. GAI offers innovative solutions for anonymizing behavioral data while retaining its utility [9–11].

- **Anonymizing Behavioral Patterns:** GAI can learn and replicate behavioral patterns observed in IoT data, such as activity logs or sensor readings, while obfuscating identifiable details. For instance, a GAN can produce anonymized user activity data for analysis.
- **Preventing Profiling and Inference Attacks:** Behavioral data is susceptible to profiling and inference attacks. GAI can dynamically mask sensitive features within the data, preventing unauthorized entities from deriving personal information or behavioral trends.
- **Behavioral Synthesis for Model Testing:** GAI-generated synthetic behavioral data can be used to test machine learning models without exposing real user patterns, ensuring both security and usability.

11.4.3 Dynamic access control

Access control mechanisms in IoT environments must balance security and usability while adapting to dynamic conditions. GAI enables the creation of adaptive, privacy-centric access rules that respond to changing contexts and threats [12–14].

- **Adaptive Access Policies:** GAI models can generate context-aware access policies by analyzing patterns of device usage, user behavior, and environmental factors. For example, access to a smart lock could be dynamically granted based on real-time behavior and location data synthesized by GAI.
- **Minimizing Overexposure of Data:** By generating granular access control rules, GAI ensures that IoT devices and data are only accessible to authorized entities with the minimal necessary permissions.
- **Securing IoT Identity Management:** GAI can enhance identity management systems by creating anonymized identities or secure authentication tokens. This reduces the risk of identity theft or unauthorized impersonation within IoT ecosystems.

GAI's applications in FL, behavioral analysis, and dynamic access control demonstrate its potential to enhance privacy in IoT systems. By leveraging these capabilities, IoT environments can achieve robust privacy protections while maintaining functionality and user trust. In the upcoming section, we give case studies of the application of GAI in enhancing privacy within IoT ecosystems. These case studies are depicted in Figure 11.2, which gives a comprehensive view.

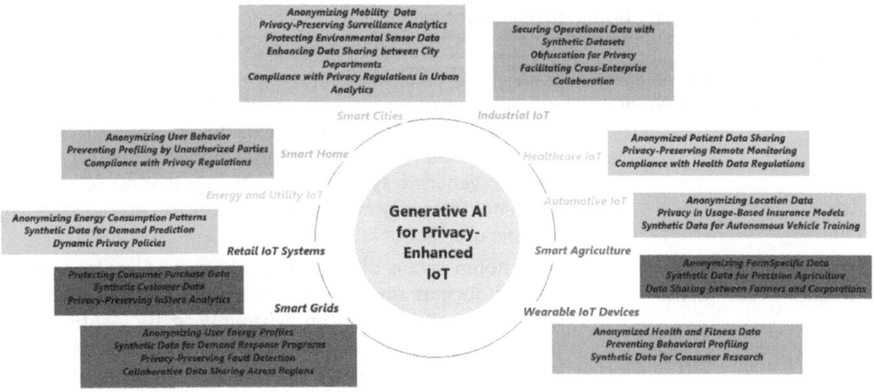

Figure 11.2 Case studies of generative AI in privacy-enhanced IoT systems.

11.5 CASE STUDIES AND EXAMPLES

GAI demonstrates practical efficacy in addressing privacy challenges in diverse IoT settings. This section presents ten illustrative examples to showcase the application of GAI in enhancing privacy within IoT ecosystems: smart home environments, smart cities, industrial IoT, healthcare, automotive IoT, smart agriculture, wearable IoT devices, energy, retail IoT systems, and smart grids.

11.5.1 GAI in smart home environments

Smart homes leverage IoT devices like voice assistants, smart thermostats, and security cameras to improve convenience and automation. However, these devices generate detailed behavioral data that can expose users to privacy risks, such as profiling and unauthorized tracking. GAI offers innovative solutions to safeguard user privacy in these scenarios [15, 16]. Table 11.1 summarizes some enhanced scenarios using GAI in a smart home environment.

11.5.2 GAI in smart cities

Smart cities rely on IoT networks to improve urban infrastructure, public safety, and resource management. These systems collect vast amounts of data from devices such as traffic cameras, environmental sensors, and public transportation trackers. While this data is crucial for efficient city operations, it also poses significant privacy risks for residents. GAI can play a critical role in safeguarding individual privacy while enabling the functionality of smart city applications [17, 18]. Table 11.2 gives several improved examples using GAI in smart cities networks.

Table 11.1 GAI in smart home environment scenarios

Scenario	*Description*
Anonymizing User Behavior	GAI can anonymize the behavioral data captured by smart home devices while preserving its utility for analytics. For example, a Generative Adversarial Network (GAN) can learn to generate synthetic activity logs that represent a household's energy consumption patterns without revealing specific user actions.
Preventing Profiling by Unauthorized Parties	Smart home data is often susceptible to profiling by external entities, such as advertisers or malicious actors. GAI-driven obfuscation techniques can dynamically mask identifiable patterns in data streams, such as sleep schedules or daily routines, ensuring that unauthorized entities cannot infer sensitive information.
Compliance with Privacy Regulations	By anonymizing data before sharing it with external service providers, GAI enables smart home systems to comply with privacy regulations like GDPR while maintaining service quality.

Table 11.2 GAI in smart cities

Scenario	*Description*
Anonymizing Mobility Data	Smart city systems frequently track mobility patterns, such as vehicle routes or pedestrian movements, to optimize traffic flow and public transit. GAI can anonymize mobility data by generating synthetic trajectories that mimic real-world patterns without exposing individual travel details. For example, GANs can produce synthetic transportation data that supports urban planning without risking resident privacy.
Privacy-Preserving Surveillance Analytics	Public safety systems in smart cities often employ surveillance cameras with facial recognition and activity monitoring capabilities. GAI can blur or replace identifiable features in video feeds with synthetic representations while retaining actionable insights for law enforcement or city management.
Protecting Environmental Sensor Data	Smart cities utilize environmental sensors to monitor air quality, noise levels, and water usage. GAI can anonymize location-specific sensor data, ensuring that the aggregated results do not reveal the behavior or habits of individuals or specific households contributing to the data.
Enhancing Data Sharing between City Departments	GAI can facilitate secure data sharing between city departments and external partners by synthesizing anonymized datasets. For instance, synthetic energy usage data generated by GAI can be shared with utility companies for load balancing without compromising household privacy.
Compliance with Privacy Regulations in Urban Analytics	As cities adopt IoT-driven solutions, they must adhere to strict privacy regulations to protect citizens. GAI-driven anonymization and synthetic data generation ensure that smart city systems remain compliant while continuing to deliver public services effectively.

11.5.3 Industrial IoT privacy solutions

Industrial IoT (IIoT) systems integrate connected sensors, machinery, and analytics platforms to optimize operations across manufacturing, logistics, and energy sectors. These systems often handle sensitive operational data, including proprietary processes, and performance metrics, which require robust privacy safeguards [19–23]. Table 11.3 describes particular upgraded cases in IIoT privacy solutions.

11.5.4 GAI in healthcare IoT systems

Healthcare IoT devices, such as wearable fitness trackers, smart insulin pumps, and remote patient monitoring systems, collect highly sensitive personal and medical data. GAI can help protect patient privacy while ensuring data usability for healthcare providers and researchers [24–28]. Table 11.4 enumerates particular revised contexts applying GAI in healthcare IoT systems.

11.5.5 GAI in automotive IoT (connected cars)

Connected cars generate a wealth of data related to driving behavior, location, and vehicle diagnostics. Protecting this data is critical to prevent misuse and ensure user privacy [29–34]. Table 11.5 lists specific optimized situations exploiting GAI in automotive IoT ecosystems.

11.5.6 GAI in smart agriculture

Smart agriculture employs IoT devices like soil sensors, weather trackers, and drone imaging to optimize farming practices. These devices collect sensitive

Table 11.3 GENAI in industrial IoT privacy solutions

Scenario	*Description*
Securing Operational Data with Synthetic Datasets	GAI can create synthetic versions of operational datasets that retain key statistical properties while concealing sensitive information. For instance, synthetic sensor data generated by a VAE can enable third-party analysis without exposing proprietary details about production processes.
GAI-Driven Obfuscation for Privacy	GAI models can obfuscate real-time IIoT data streams, ensuring that operational insights can be extracted without compromising privacy. For example, data on equipment failures or maintenance schedules can be anonymized before being transmitted to cloud platforms for predictive analytics.
Facilitating Cross-Enterprise Collaboration	Synthetic data generated by GAI allows enterprises to collaborate securely by sharing anonymized performance metrics or usage patterns. This promotes innovation and joint problem-solving without risking the exposure of competitive or sensitive information.

Table 11.4 GAI in healthcare IoT systems scenarios

Scenario	*Description*
Anonymized Patient Data Sharing	GAI can generate synthetic medical records or health data that maintain the statistical properties of real patient data. This allows healthcare providers and researchers to share anonymized datasets for analysis and medical innovation without compromising patient confidentiality.
Privacy-Preserving Remote Monitoring	In remote patient monitoring systems, GAI can obfuscate sensitive health metrics before transmitting them to cloud-based platforms, reducing the risk of interception or unauthorized access.
Compliance with Health Data Regulations	GAI can help healthcare IoT systems comply with regulations like HIPAA and GDPR by anonymizing identifiable patient information before storage or analysis.

Table 11.5 GAI in automotive IoT scenarios

Scenario	*Description*
Anonymizing Location Data	GAI can anonymize real-time GPS data to prevent tracking or profiling of drivers while still providing aggregated insights for traffic management systems.
Privacy in Usage-Based Insurance Models	Usage-based car insurance often relies on sensitive driving behavior data. GAI can generate anonymized driving profiles that preserve the accuracy of risk assessments without exposing individual driving habits.
Synthetic Data for Autonomous Vehicle Training	GAI can create synthetic datasets for training autonomous driving algorithms, reducing reliance on real-world data that may contain identifiable or sensitive information.

data about land usage and crop production, which could be exploited if not adequately protected [35–37]. Table 11.6 specifies certain refined circumstances regarding GAI in a smart agriculture environment.

11.5.7 GAI in wearable IoT devices

Wearable IoT devices, such as smartwatches, fitness bands, and health trackers, collect personal metrics like heart rate, activity levels, and sleep patterns [38, 39]. Table 11.7 presents a few enhanced conditions using GAI in wearable IoT devices.

11.5.8 GAI in energy and utility IoT systems

Smart meters and IoT-based energy monitoring systems collect detailed data on household energy consumption, which can reveal personal habits [40–44]. Table 11.8 gathers several advanced experiences regarding GAI in energy and utility IoT systems.

Table 11.6 GAI in smart agriculture scenarios

Scenario	*Description*
Anonymizing Farm-Specific Data	GAI can anonymize agricultural data, such as soil composition or yield predictions, to prevent competitive exploitation while allowing data sharing for research or policy-making.
Synthetic Data for Precision Agriculture	By generating synthetic datasets, GAI can support precision agriculture algorithms, enabling better crop management without exposing real farm data.
Data Sharing between Farmers and Corporations	GAI facilitates secure data sharing by creating anonymized versions of operational data, fostering collaboration without risking privacy breaches.

Table 11.7 GAI in wearable IoT device scenarios

Scenario	*Description*
Anonymized Health and Fitness Data	GAI can anonymize data collected by wearables, enabling users to share aggregated health metrics with fitness apps or researchers without revealing individual patterns.
Preventing Behavioral Profiling	GAI can obfuscate activity data, ensuring that wearable devices do not expose habits or routines to unauthorized entities.
Synthetic Data for Consumer Research	GAI-generated synthetic datasets can be used for product development and consumer behavior analysis without compromising the privacy of real users.

Table 11.8 GAI in energy and utility IoT systems scenarios

Scenario	*Description*
Anonymizing Energy Consumption Patterns	GAI can anonymize energy usage data, ensuring that utilities can optimize grid management without accessing identifiable household behaviors.
Synthetic Data for Demand Prediction	Synthetic datasets generated by GAI can help utilities predict energy demand patterns for grid optimization while maintaining consumer privacy.
Dynamic Privacy Policies	GAI can create adaptive privacy policies for smart energy systems, allowing households to control how their energy data is shared with third parties.

11.5.9 GAI in retail IoT systems

Retail IoT systems, such as smart shelves, customer tracking, and personalized recommendation engines, generate data about consumer preferences and shopping behavior [45–47]. Table 11.9 summarizes necessary upgraded situations regarding GAI in retail IoT systems.

Table 11.9 GAI in retail IoT systems scenarios

Scenario	*Description*
Protecting Consumer Purchase Data	GAI can anonymize purchase histories and shopping patterns, ensuring that retailers can analyze trends without exposing individual preferences.
Synthetic Customer Data	GAI can create synthetic customer profiles for training recommendation systems, reducing the risk of privacy breaches while maintaining system accuracy.
Privacy-Preserving In-Store Analytics	By obfuscating shopper movement data captured by in-store IoT systems, GAI ensures compliance with privacy regulations and prevents misuse.

11.5.10 GAI in smart grids

Smart grids leverage IoT technologies to monitor and manage energy production, distribution, and consumption in real time. These systems collect extensive data from consumers, producers, and grid operators, which can raise privacy concerns if improperly handled [48, 49]. Table 11.10 shows certain advanced scenarios concerning GAI in smart grids ecosystems.

11.6 CHALLENGES AND ETHICAL CONSIDERATIONS

While GAI holds immense potential for enhancing privacy in IoT environments, its application is not without challenges and ethical concerns. This

Table 11.10 GAI in smart grid scenarios

Scenario	*Description*
Anonymizing User Energy Profiles	Smart grid systems collect detailed household energy usage data to optimize distribution and detect anomalies. GAI can anonymize these profiles, ensuring that patterns of appliance usage or daily routines remain private while still allowing utility companies to analyze trends.
Synthetic Data for Demand Response Programs	GAI can create synthetic datasets to simulate user participation in demand response programs. This enables energy providers to test and improve systems without exposing actual customer data.
Privacy-Preserving Fault Detection	GAI can obfuscate sensitive data in fault reports generated by smart grid sensors, ensuring that privacy is maintained while enabling quick responses to infrastructure issues.
Collaborative Data Sharing Across Regions	Regional energy providers often collaborate by sharing grid performance data. GAI can generate anonymized or synthetic datasets that allow such collaborations without compromising local consumer privacy.

section discusses the risks and responsibilities associated with the use of GAI in privacy preservation.

11.6.1 Risks of adversarial attacks on GAI models

One of the primary challenges in leveraging GAI for privacy is the risk of adversarial attacks targeting the models or the data they generate.

- **Exploitation of Vulnerabilities:** Adversaries may exploit weaknesses in GAI models to reverse-engineer anonymized data or inject malicious inputs. For instance, attackers might manipulate GAI outputs to extract sensitive information from synthetic datasets, undermining privacy protections.
- **Integrity of Generated Data:** GAI models could unintentionally generate misleading or incomplete data, leading to inaccuracies in decision-making processes. This is especially critical in IoT environments, where real-time and high-precision data are essential.

To mitigate the risks of adversarial attacks on GAN models, various defensive strategies must be employed, including robust testing, monitoring, adversarial system detection, and enhanced anomaly detection techniques to ensure the security and reliability of GAI-generated outputs. Recently in [50], researchers explored GANs for enhancing IoT security by generating system call frequencies to detect zero-day malware. Their findings emphasized GANs potential in identifying malicious patterns and evading traditional detection methods, contributing to more resilient IDS mechanisms for IoT environments.

11.6.2 Ethical use of synthetic data

The ethical implications of synthetic data generation warrant careful consideration to ensure the responsible use of GAI technologies.

- **Avoiding Bias Propagation:** Synthetic data generated by GAI models must not perpetuate or amplify biases present in the training data. For example, biased training data could result in discriminatory outputs that affect underrepresented groups in IoT systems.
- **Ensuring Data Accuracy:** While synthetic data aims to anonymize sensitive information, inaccuracies in generated datasets can lead to flawed analytics or erroneous conclusions. Striking a balance between privacy and data fidelity is critical for ethical applications.
- **Transparency in Usage:** Stakeholders must be transparent about the use of synthetic data, particularly in scenarios involving decision-making or policy formulation. Clearly distinguishing between real and synthetic data helps maintain trust and accountability.

11.6.3 Balancing utility and privacy

One of the fundamental challenges in privacy-preserving IoT systems is maintaining the utility of data while protecting sensitive information.

- **Trade-offs between Privacy and Usability:** Overly aggressive anonymization or obfuscation techniques may reduce the utility of data for legitimate analytics and decision-making. GAI must be designed to balance these trade-offs, ensuring that privacy does not come at the expense of functionality.
- **Context-Specific Privacy Strategies:** IoT environments vary significantly in their data requirements and privacy concerns. GAI solutions must be tailored to the specific needs of each context, whether it is healthcare, IIoT, or smart cities.
- **Scalability of Privacy Mechanisms:** As IoT systems grow in scale and complexity, GAI models must remain efficient and scalable to handle increasing volumes of data without compromising privacy standards.

Addressing these challenges requires a multifaceted approach, combining technical innovation with ethical oversight. By recognizing and mitigating the risks associated with adversarial attacks, ensuring the ethical use of synthetic data, and balancing utility with privacy, GAI can fulfill its potential as a cornerstone technology for privacy preservation in IoT ecosystems.

11.7 CONCLUSION

GAI has emerged as a transformative technology for addressing privacy challenges in IoT environments. By enabling data anonymization, synthetic data generation, and secure sharing mechanisms, GAI empowers IoT systems to handle sensitive data responsibly while maintaining functionality and compliance with privacy regulations. The case studies and examples provided illustrate GAI's versatility in various IoT domains, such as smart homes, smart cities, IIoT, and healthcare, showcasing its potential to safeguard privacy while supporting innovation.

However, the adoption of GAI also brings challenges and ethical considerations. Risks such as adversarial attacks, the propagation of biases in synthetic data, and the trade-off between data utility and privacy must be carefully addressed.

REFERENCES

1. I. Goodfellow, J. Pouget-Abadie, M. Mirza, B. Xu, D. Warde-Farley, S. Ozair, A. Courville and Y. Bengio, "Generative adversarial nets." Z. Ghahramani, M. Welling, C. Cortes, N.D. Lawrence, K.Q. Weinberger, eds. Advances in Neural Information Processing Systems 27, Curran Associates, Inc., Boston, 2014, 2672–2680.
2. P. K. Diederik and M. Welling, "Auto-encoding variational bayes", arXiv, 2013, 1312.6114 [stat.ML], https://doi.org/10.48550/arXiv.1312.6114.

3. H. Kandil and H. Benaboud, "Using machine learning to Deal with privacy and confidentiality in internet of things: An overview," in Innovations in Smart Cities Applications, Volume 8. SCA 2024. Lecture Notes in Networks and Systems, vol 1310. Springer, Cham, 2025, https://link.springer.com/book/9783031886522https://link.springer.com/book/9783031886522
4. M. Goyal and Q. H. Mahmoud, "A systematic review of synthetic data generation techniques using generative AI," Electronics, vol. 13, no. 17, p. 3509, 2024, https://doi.org/10.3390/electronics13173509.
5. X. Cao, G. Sun, H. Yu and M. Guizani, "PerFED-GAN: Personalized federated learning via generative adversarial networks," IEEE Internet of Things Journal, vol. 10, no. 5, pp. 3749–3762, 1 March1, 2023, https://ieeexplore.ieee.org/document/9766407, https://doi.org/10.1109/JIOT.2022.3172114.
6. A. Triastcyn and B. Faltings, "Federated generative privacy," IEEE Intelligent Systems, vol. 35, no. 4, pp. 50–57, 1 July-Aug. 2020, https://ieeexplore.ieee.org/document/9091604, https://doi.org/10.1109/MIS.2020.2993966.
7. H. Wang, Y. Han, S. Yang, A. Song and T. Zhang, "Privacy-Preserving Federated Generative Adversarial Network for IoT," 2021 International Conference on Networking and Network Applications (NaNA), Lijiang City, China, 2021, pp. 75–80, https://ieeexplore.ieee.org/abstract/document/9634942, https://doi.org/10.1109/NaNA53684.2021.00021.
8. H. Yzzogh, H. Kandil and H. Benaboud, "A comprehensive overview of AI-driven behavioral analysis for security in internet of things." Youssef Baddi, Mohammed Amin Almaiah, Omar Almomani, Yassine Maleh, eds. The Art of Cyber Defense from Risk Assessment to Threat Intelligence, 2024, 40–51.
9. Z. Zaman, W. Xue, P. Gauravaram, W. Hu, J. Jiang and S. K. Jha, "Privacy-preserving probabilistic data encoding for IoT data analysis," IEEE Transactions on Information Forensics and Security, vol. 19, pp. 9173–9187, 2024, https://ieeexplore.ieee.org/document/10693594, https://doi.org/10.1109/TIFS.2024.3468150.
10. J. Yu, H. Xue, B. Liu, Y. Wang, S. Zhu and M. Ding, "GAN-based differential private image privacy protection framework for the internet of multimedia things," Sensors, vol. 21, no. 1, p. 58, 2021, https://doi.org/10.3390/s21010058.
11. G. Feretzakis, K. Papaspyridis, A. Gkoulalas-Divanis and V. S. Verykios, "Privacy-preserving techniques in generative AI and large language models: A narrative review," Information, vol. 15, no. 11, p. 697, 2024, https://doi.org/10.3390/info15110697.
12. S. Thummala, S. Thammishetti, S. Varkol, A. Thirunahari and V. L. Kanthey, "Event Management System Using Generative AI," in 2024 7th International Conference on Circuit Power and Computing Technologies (ICCPCT), Aug. 2024, pp. 624–628, https://doi.org/10.1109/ICCPCT61902.2024.10673057.
13. C. Shah, "Generative AI and the Future of Information Access," in Proceedings of the 32nd ACM International Conference on Information and Knowledge Management, in CIKM '23. New York, NY, USA: Association for Computing Machinery, Oct. 2023, p. 3, https://doi.org/10.1145/3583780.3615317.
14. C. Zhao et al., "Generative AI for secure physical layer communications: A survey," ArXiv, vol. abs/2402, p. 13553, 2024, https://doi.org/10.48550/arXiv.2402.13553.
15. M. Razghandi, H. Zhou, M. Erol-Kantarci and D. Turgut, "Variational Autoencoder Generative Adversarial Network for Synthetic Data Generation in Smart Home," ICC 2022 – IEEE International Conference on Communications, Seoul, Korea, Republic of, 2022, pp. 4781–4786, https://ieeexplore.ieee.org/document/9839249, https://doi.org/10.1109/ICC45855.2022.9839249.
16. M. Razghandi, H. Zhou, M. Erol-Kantarci and D. Turgut, "Smart home energy management: VAE-GAN synthetic dataset generator and q-learning,"

IEEE Transactions on Smart Grid, vol. 15, no. 2, pp. 1562–1573, March 2024, https://ieeexplore.ieee.org/document/10171153, https://doi.org/10.1109/TSG.2023.3288824.
17. A. Kapp, J. Hansmeyer and H. Mihaljević. "Generative models for synthetic urban mobility data: A systematic literature review," ACM Comput. Surv, vol. 56, no. 4, 2023, Article 93 (April 2024), 37 pages, https://doi.org/10.1145/3610224.
18. M. A. Sai, O. Balamurali, M. Karthikeya and S. Anand, "A Web-Based Chatbot for Indian Cities: A Comparison of CNN, ANN, and LSTM Models," in 2023 14th International Conference on Computing Communication and Networking Technologies (ICCCNT), Jul. 2023, pp. 1–6, https://doi.org/10.1109/ICCCNT56998.2023.10307912.
19. S. Lalos, E. Vlachos, K. Berberidis, A. P. Fournaris and C. Koulamas, "Privacy preservation in industrial IoT via fast adaptive correlation matrix completion," IEEE Transactions on Industrial Informatics, vol. 16, no. 12, pp. 7765–7773, Dec. 2020, https://doi.org/10.1109/TII.2019.2960275.
20. Y. Huo, C. Meng, R. Li and T. Jing, "An overview of privacy preserving schemes for industrial internet of things," China Communications, vol. 17, no. 10, pp. 1–18, Oct. 2020, https://doi.org/10.23919/JCC.2020.10.001.
21. S. Lalos, E. Vlachos, K. Berberidis, A. Fournaris and C. Koulamas, "Robust and Efficient Privacy Preservation in Industrial IoT via correlation completion and tracking," in 2019 IEEE 17th International Conference on Industrial Informatics (INDIN), Jul. 2019, pp. 1225–1228, https://doi.org/10.1109/INDIN41052.2019.8972154.
22. C. Huang, S. Chen, Y. Zhang, W. Zhou, J. P. C. Rodrigues and V. H. C. de Albuquerque, "A robust approach for privacy data protection: IoT security assurance using generative adversarial imitation learning," IEEE Internet of Things Journal, vol. 9, no. 18, pp. 17089–17097, 15 Sept.15, 2022, https://ieeexplore.ieee.org/document/9615364, https://doi.org/10.1109/JIOT.2021.3128531.
23. Y. S. Hindistan and E. F. Yetkin, "A hybrid approach with GAN and DP for privacy preservation of IIoT data," IEEE Access, vol. 11, pp. 5837–5849, 2023, https://ieeexplore.ieee.org/document/10013656, https://doi.org/10.1109/ACCESS.2023.3235969.
24. Y. Ning et al., "Generative artificial intelligence in healthcare: Ethical considerations and assessment checklist," arXiv, Feb. 23, 2024, arXiv:2311.02107, https://doi.org/10.48550/arXiv.2311.02107.
25. P. Zhang and M. N. Kamel Boulos, "Generative AI in medicine and healthcare: Promises, opportunities and challenges," Future Internet, vol. 15, no. 9, Art. no. 9, Sep. 2023, https://doi.org/10.3390/fi15090286.
26. Y. Shokrollahi, S. Yarmohammadtoosky, M. M. Nikahd, P. Dong, X. Li and L. Gu, "A comprehensive review of generative AI in healthcare," arXiv, Oct. 01, 2023, arXiv:2310.00795, https://doi.org/10.48550/arXiv.2310.00795.
27. A. Jadon and S. Kumar, "Leveraging Generative AI Models for Synthetic Data Generation in Healthcare: Balancing Research and Privacy," 2023 International Conference on Smart Applications, Communications and Networking (SmartNets), Istanbul, Turkiye, 2023, pp. 1–4, https://ieeexplore.ieee.org/document/10215825, https://doi.org/10.1109/SmartNets58706.2023.10215825.
28. S. Imtiaz, M. Arsalan, V. Vlassov and R. Sadre, "Synthetic and Private Smart Health Care Data Generation using GANs," 2021 International Conference on Computer Communications and Networks (ICCCN), Athens, Greece, 2021, pp. 1–7, https://ieeexplore.ieee.org/document/9522203, https://doi.org/10.1109/ICCCN52240.2021.9522203.
29. C. Anastasiou, S. H. Kim and C. Shahabi, "Generation of Synthetic Urban Vehicle Trajectories," 2022 IEEE International Conference on Big Data (Big Data), Osaka, Japan, 2022, pp. 359–366, https://ieeexplore.ieee.org/document/10020237, https://doi.org/10.1109/BigData55660.2022.10020237.

30. R. Zhang et al., "Generative AI-enabled vehicular networks: Fundamentals, framework, and case study," IEEE Network, vol. 38, no. 4, pp. 259–267, Jul. 2024, https://doi.org/10.1109/MNET.2024.3391767.
31. L. Stappen, J. Dillmann, S. Striegel, H.-J. Vögel, N. Flores-Herr and B. W. Schuller, "Integrating Generative Artificial Intelligence in Intelligent Vehicle Systems," in 2023 IEEE 26th International Conference on Intelligent Transportation Systems (ITSC), Sep. 2023, pp. 5790–5797, https://doi.org/10.1109/ITSC57777.2023.10422003.
32. M. Xu et al., "Generative AI-empowered simulation for autonomous driving in vehicular mixed reality metaverses," IEEE Journal of Selected Topics in Signal Processing, vol. 17, no. 5, pp. 1064–1079, Sep. 2023, https://doi.org/10.1109/JSTSP.2023.3293650.
33. Z. Xiong, W. Li, Q. Han and Z. Cai, "Privacy-Preserving Auto-Driving: A GAN-Based Approach to Protect Vehicular Camera Data," 2019 IEEE International Conference on Data Mining (ICDM), Beijing, China, 2019, pp. 668–677, https://ieeexplore.ieee.org/document/8970962, https://doi.org/10.1109/ICDM.2019.00077.
34. Z. Xiong, Z. Cai, Q. Han, A. Alrawais and W. Li, "ADGAN: Protect your location privacy in camera data of auto-driving vehicles," IEEE Transactions on Industrial Informatics, vol. 17, no. 9, pp. 6200–6210, Sept. 2021, https://ieeexplore.ieee.org/document/9234081, https://doi.org/10.1109/TII.2020.3032352.
35. H. Al Naqbi, Z. Bahroun and V. Ahmed, "Enhancing work productivity through generative artificial intelligence: A comprehensive literature review," Sustainability, vol. 16, no. 3, Jan. 2024, https://doi.org/10.3390/su16031166.
36. J. Liu et al., "Exploring the Integration of Digital Twin and Generative AI in Agriculture," in 2023 15th International Conference on Intelligent Human-Machine Systems and Cybernetics (IHMSC), Aug. 2023, pp. 223–228, https://doi.org/10.1109/IHMSC58761.2023.00059.
37. Y. Lu, D. Chen, E. Olaniyi and Y. Huang, "Generative adversarial networks (GANs) for image augmentation in agriculture: A systematic review," Computers and Electronics in Agriculture, vol. 200, p. 107208, Sep. 2022, https://doi.org/10.1016/j.compag.2022.107208.
38. A. Khan, N. Jhanjhi, G. A. A. Abdulhabeb, S. K. Ray, M. A. Ghazanfar and M. Humayun, "Securing IoT devices using generative AI techniques," in Reshaping CyberSecurity with Generative AI Techniques, IGI Global Scientific Publishing, 2025, 219–264, https://doi.org/10.4018/979-8-3693-5415-5.ch007.
39. M. A. Ferrag, M. Debbah and M. Al-Hawawreh, "Generative AI for Cyber Threat-Hunting in 6G-enabled IoT Networks," in 2023 IEEE/ACM 23rd International Symposium on Cluster, Cloud and Internet Computing Workshops (CCGridW), May 2023, pp. 16–25, https://doi.org/10.1109/CCGridW59191.2023.00018.
40. J. D. Weisz, M. Muller, J. He and S. Houde, "Toward general design principles for generative AI applications," arXiv, Jan. 13, 2023, arXiv:2301.05578, https://doi.org/10.48550/arXiv.2301.05578.
41. E. Avcı, "Generative ai in electricity distribution: A qualitative exploration," PAP, vol. 17, no. 1, pp. 208–211, Jul. 2023, https://doi.org/10.17261/Pressacademia.2023.1788.
42. P. A. DeCotis, "The generative artificial intelligence utility," Climate and Energy, vol. 40, no. 5, pp. 21–26, 2023, https://doi.org/10.1002/gas.22378.
43. X. Feng, J. Lan, Z. Peng, Z. Huang and Q. Guo, "A Novel Privacy Protection Framework for Power Generation Data based on Generative Adversarial Networks," 2019 IEEE PES Asia-Pacific Power and Energy Engineering Conference (APPEEC), Macao, China, 2019, pp. 1–5, https://ieeexplore.ieee.org/document/8994702, https://doi.org/10.1109/APPEEC45492.2019.8994702.
44. Z. Wang, Z. Liu, C. Fu, A. Wen, M. Zhang and W. Zhang "Privacy-preserving multiparty power data sharing based on generative adversarial network",

Proc. SPIE 13159, Eighth International Conference on Energy System, Electricity, and Power (ESEP 2023), 13159A9 (13 May 2024), https://doi.org/10.1117/12.3024222.
45. B. Chen, Z. Wu and R. Zhao, "From fiction to fact: The growing role of generative AI in business and finance," Journal of Chinese Economic and Business Studies, vol. 21, no. 4, pp. 471–496, Oct. 2023, https://doi.org/10.1080/14765284.2023.2245279.
46. A. Korinek, "Generative AI for economic research: Use cases and implications for economists," Journal of Economic Literature, vol. 61, no. 4, pp. 1281–1317, Jan. 2023, https://doi.org/10.1257/jel.20231736.
47. I. Anica-Popa et al, "The integration of artificial intelligence in retail: Benefits, challenges and a dedicated conceptual framework," Amfiteatru Economic Journal, vol. 23, no. 56, pp. 120–136, 2021, https://doi.org/10.24818/EA/2021/56/120.
48. S. Desai, N. R. Sabar, R. Alhadad, A. Mahmood and N. Chilamkurti, "Mitigating consumer privacy breach in smart grid using obfuscation-based generative adversarial network", Mathematical Biosciences and Engineering, vol. 19, no. 4, pp. 3350–3368, 2022, https://www.aimspress.com/article/10.3934/mbe.2022155.
49. S. M. Sajjadi Mohammadabadi, M. Entezami, A. Karimi Moghaddam, M. Orangian and S. Nejadshamsi, "Generative artificial intelligence for distributed learning to enhance smart grid communication," International Journal of Intelligent Networks, vol. 5, pp. 267–274, Jan. 2024, https://doi.org/10.1016/j.ijin.2024.05.007.
50. A. Chhaybi and S. Lazaar, "System call frequency analysis-based generative adversarial network model for zero-day malware detection in IoT," International Journal of Electrical and Computer Engineering (IJECE), vol. 14, no. 2, pp. 1969–1978, 2024, http://doi.org/10.11591/ijece.v14i2.pp1969-1978.

Chapter 12

Navigating dualities

Generative AI's role in cybersecurity for defense and attacks

Garrett Crumrine, Michael J. O'Brien, Izzat Alsmadi, and Yuvaraj Munian

12.1 INTRODUCTION

Generative artificial intelligence (GenAI), particularly in the form of deep-learning models, has ushered in transformative capabilities for creating synthetic content such as images, videos, medical imaging, and text. Unlike traditional AI models, which are designed primarily for pattern recognition and decision-making, GenAI can produce novel data, including text, images, and even music. Techniques such as generative adversarial networks (GANs), variational auto-encoders (VAEs), and transformer-based models such as OpenAI's GPT-4 have demonstrated remarkable capabilities in generating realistic and coherent outputs.

On the one hand, GenAI offers incredible potential for advances in any number of fields (Gruetzemacher & Whittlestone, 2022; Mollick & Euchner, 2023; Taddeo & Floridi, 2018), especially in medicine (Bekbolatova *et al.*, 2024; Chino, 2023; Dossantos *et al.*, 2023; Park *et al.*, 2023), biomedical research (Baumgartner *et al.*, 2023), education (Ahmad, 2023; Bezzina & Dingli, 2024; George, 2023), and the social sciences (Bail, 2024; Böhm *et al.*, 2023; Capraro *et al.*, 2024; Grossman *et al.*, 2023; Mannuru *et al.*, 2023). On the other hand, it offers profound risks across the board when exploited for nefarious purposes by adversaries (Bostrom, 2017; Wach *et al.*, 2023). We are reminded of what historian of technology Melvin Kranzberg (1985) said in his presidential address before the Society for the History of Technology in 1985: "Technology is neither good nor bad; nor is it neutral." In other words, we walk a fine line when using GenAI, and addressing the challenges requires a multifaceted approach encompassing technical innovation, ethical guidelines, and robust regulatory frameworks.

Walking that fine line also requires an understanding of the ways in which GenAI can be misused and how stakeholders can proactively develop strategies to safeguard individuals, organizations, and society at large. Our objective here is to provide a brief overview of applications of GenAI in cybersecurity, using the following outline:

- Identifying cybersecurity threats posed by GenAI;
- Evaluating the effectiveness of GenAI to both predict and thwart cybersecurity threats;

DOI: 10.1201/9781003597476-16

- Highlighting the challenges and ethical considerations associated with the use of GenAI in cybersecurity; and
- Proposing future research directions.

12.2 CYBERSECURITY THREATS

What follows below represents just the tip of the iceberg in terms of the threats posed by GenAI when malicious intent is involved. We identified six families of threats that are the most commonly recognized, each with subcategories. We note that the subcategories are not necessarily exclusive to one family.

12.2.1 Deepfakes: Weaponizing synthetic media

One of the most prominent and concerning uses of GenAI is in the creation of deepfakes, which convincingly depict individuals saying or doing things they neither said nor did (de Ruiter, 2021; Mirsky & Lee, 2021; Reardon, 2024). This technology has been leveraged for various malicious purposes, most if not all of which we place in the category "social engineering," although other categorizations are sometimes used. Social-information methods are implicated in a staggering 50 percent to 90 percent of all cybersecurity incidents, highlighting their predominant role in the landscape of digital threats (Teal, 2024).

- ***Political Manipulation:*** Adversaries can create deepfake videos of political figures making controversial statements or engaging in unethical behavior, aiming to sway public opinion or destabilize governance (Dobber *et al.*, 2021; Liao *et al.*, 2019; Rubin, 2020; Schwartz, 2020). Further, elections can be swayed, public trust in institutions can be diminished, and social unrest can erupt (Brody, 2024; Li & Callegari, 2024). This has never been truer than it is today, with unrest spreading across the globe at a seemingly increasing rate. In the United States, the run-up to the 2024 presidential election has been a laboratory in which both political adversaries and outside activists have honed their skills.
- ***Impersonation:*** Generate fake audio or video clips to impersonate individuals in positions of power, influencing public opinion or policy decisions (Galston, 2019; Salman *et al.*, 2023).
- ***Financial Fraud:*** Deepfake technology has been used to impersonate business executives in video calls, deceiving employees into transferring funds or disclosing sensitive information (O'Donnell, 2020).
- ***Phishing:*** Mimic the writing style and content of trusted entities to deceive recipients into disclosing sensitive information or downloading malware (Alkhalil *et al.*, 2021; Moustafa *et al.*, 2021).
- ***Baiting:*** Whereas phishing attacks exploit trust and often fear, baiting exploits curiosity. Baiting attacks use a false promise to lure users into a trap that steals their personal information or inflicts their systems with

malware (Eisner, 2023). For example, attackers leave the bait—typically malware-infected flash drives—in conspicuous areas where potential victims are certain to see them, such as in parking lots and bathrooms of a targeted company. Victims pick up the bait, which appears authentic, and, out of curiosity, insert it into a work or home computer, resulting in automatic malware installation on the system.

- ***Fake Profiles:*** Create realistic social media profiles to establish rapport with targets for further manipulation or access (Bhosale & Mane, 2024; Moore, 2023).
- ***Fraudulent Content:*** Generate fake invoices, receipts, or login pages that appear legitimate to deceive users into providing credentials or financial details. Technically, the "fake" invoices are not fake at all. Rather, they are real invoices created to mimic an invoice from a real entity such as PayPal or GoDaddy. And it is not only small customers who get hit. In 2019, for example, a Lithuanian pleaded guilty to bilking Facebook and Google out of $123 million over a three-year period (Fazzini, 2019).
- ***Phony Videos:*** Malicious actors use deepfake videos to impersonate trusted individuals (e.g., friends and family members) in order to extract personal information or manipulate social relationships (Rossler *et al.*, 2019).

12.2.2 Disinformation campaigns and fake news

GenAI enables the rapid generation of convincing textual content that is used in disinformation campaigns (Galston, 2019; Stirland, 2020). Here we need to make an important distinction based on the kind of incorrect information being transmitted and, more importantly, on the motives of the actors behind it (O'Brien & Alsmadi, 2021). Is the incorrect information innocent or superfluous, or is it insidious? *Misinformation* is misleading information created or shared without the intent to manipulate people. An example would be sharing a rumor that a celebrity died before finding out that it is false. *Disinformation*, by contrast, refers to deliberate attempts to confuse or manipulate people with dishonest information. These campaigns, at times orchestrated by groups outside the United States, such as the Internet Research Agency, a well-known Russian troll factory (or farm) in St. Petersburg (Motyl, 2023), can be coordinated across multiple social media accounts and might also use automated systems—bots—to post and share information online. Two examples are

- ***Automated Fake-News Generation:*** Adversaries use AI-generated text to fabricate news articles, social media posts, and reviews that appear authentic, aiming to spread false information and manipulate public opinion (Zellers *et al.*, 2019).
- ***Political and Social Instability:*** AI-driven text generation can fuel societal divisions by spreading divisive narratives, inciting unrest, and undermining trust in institutions (Koplin, 2023; Rakowski & Kowaliková, 2024).

12.2.3 Cybersecurity threats and malware

GenAI techniques are also employed in cybersecurity threats and malware:

- *Malware Evasion:* Exploiting vulnerabilities in AI-based security solutions (Yuan *et al.*, 2019) through the development of polymorphic malware that constantly evolves its code in order to bypass traditional signature-based detection systems.
- *Zero-Day Exploitation:* Predicting and exploiting vulnerabilities faster than traditional methods by analyzing code patterns and system behaviors (Ahmad *et al.*, 2023).
- *Targeted Attacks:* Customizing malware payloads and attack vectors based on detailed reconnaissance data in order to maximize effectiveness against specific targets (Ferdous *et al.*, 2023).

12.2.4 Identity theft and fraud

GenAI facilitates sophisticated identity-theft techniques:

- *Synthetic Identities:* AI-generated personas are used to create fake social media profiles, open fraudulent accounts, and conduct financial transactions under false identities (Angwin *et al.*, 2020).
- *Biometric Spoofing:* GenAI can create synthetic biometric data (e.g., fingerprints and facial features) to bypass biometric authentication systems, thus enabling unauthorized access to devices and facilities (Ratha *et al.*, 2021).

12.2.5 Automated cyberattacks and defense evasion

GenAI enables cyber adversaries to automate and optimize various aspects of cyberattacks:

- *Automated Vulnerability Discovery:* Development of AI algorithms that can autonomously identify and exploit vulnerabilities in software or network configurations.
- *Dynamic Attack Adaptation:* Adjustment of attack strategies in real-time based on defensive responses or changing network conditions.
- *Adversarial Machine Learning:* Development of AI models that learn to bypass detection mechanisms or manipulate datasets to degrade the performance of defensive AI systems.

12.2.6 Blockchain and cryptocurrency exploitation

In the realm of blockchain and cryptocurrencies, GenAI can be used for

- *Cryptojacking:* Using AI-powered malware to hijack computational resources for cryptocurrency mining without the user's consent (Hwang, 2021).

- ***Blockchain Manipulation:*** Predicting cryptographic keys or manipulating consensus algorithms to execute fraudulent transactions or compromise decentralized applications (Zheng *et al.*, 2019).
- ***Scams:*** Creating convincing fake cryptocurrency wallets or exchanges in order to steal credentials or deceive users into transferring funds.

12.3 GENERATIVE AI AND RISK MITIGATION

Detecting and countering malicious uses of GenAI require innovative approaches and advanced technologies that can differentiate between genuine and fabricated content, identify anomalies, and anticipate adversarial tactics. Not coincidentally, GenAI has shown significant promise in automating threat detection and response mechanisms. Traditional methods often rely on predefined rules and signature-based detection, which can be limited in identifying new and sophisticated threats. GenAI, however, because it learns from historical data, can detect anomalies that might indicate malicious activities. Below we outline five key strategies for identifying cases where GenAI is being used by cyber adversaries. Our goal is to highlight the practical benefits of different strategies, explore potential limitations, and suggest future research directions that can further integrate GenAI into cybersecurity strategies.

12.3.1 Pattern recognition and anomaly detection

Pattern-recognition and anomaly-detection techniques are fundamental for identifying deviations from expected behaviors or patterns in data generated by GenAI models. Generative models can identify unusual patterns or behaviors that deviate from the norm, flagging potential threats that might be missed by conventional systems. For example, GANs can create simulations of cyberattacks, helping to train detection systems to recognize these anomalies more effectively.

- ***Statistical Analysis:*** Using statistical methods to establish baseline behaviors and detect deviations. For example, anomaly-detection algorithms such as isolation forests or one-class small vector machines can identify unusual patterns in data distributions (Kagumire, 2021)
- ***Machine Learning Models:*** Training supervised and unsupervised machine-learning models on datasets that include examples of both benign and malicious GenAI outputs. Models such as recurrent neural networks (RNNs) and convolutional neural networks (CNNs) can learn to classify generated content based on learned features (Tealab, 2018). Similarly, GenAI can also play a crucial role in malware detection and analysis. Traditional signature-based detection methods struggle with the sheer volume and variety of malware, but generative models, such as VAEs, can learn the characteristics of benign software and identify deviations that might indicate the presence of malware.

- *Behavioral Analysis:* Monitoring user behavior, network traffic, and/or system interactions to detect unusual patterns that might indicate the presence of generative AI-driven attacks. Behavioral biometrics and anomaly-based intrusion detection systems (IDS) play crucial roles.

12.3.1.1 Implementation challenges

- *Adversarial Techniques:* Adversaries might adapt GenAI outputs to mimic benign behavior or evade detection algorithms. Continual model retraining and updating detection strategies are essential to staying ahead (Dilmegani, 2024). An example would be training detection systems to recognize phishing emails by having them learn about fake emails.
- *Data Quality and Diversity:* Ensure training datasets are diverse and representative of potential attack scenarios to improve detection accuracy and minimize false positives (Gupta, 2023).

12.3.2 Multimodal detection systems

Multimodal detection systems combine different kinds of data sources and analytical techniques to enhance the accuracy and robustness of detecting GenAI-driven attacks. By integrating data from various modalities such as audio, video, text, and metadata, these systems can provide a comprehensive view for identifying anomalies and confirming malicious activities.

- *Fusion of Data Streams:* Integrating outputs from different sensors or data streams (e.g., video frames, audio spectrograms, and metadata from digital communications) to detect inconsistencies or discrepancies that suggest manipulation by GenAI.
- *Cross-Modal Analysis:* Using techniques such as cross-modal retrieval or cross-modal fusion to correlate information across different modalities and validate the authenticity of generated content against known patterns or ground-truth data (Wang *et al.*, 2022).
- *Feature Extraction:* Employing advanced feature-extraction methods tailored to each modality (e.g., image-feature extraction using CNNs and audio-feature extraction using Mel Frequency Cepstral Coefficients) to capture unique characteristics indicative of GenAI manipulation (Lark Editorial Team, 2023).

12.3.2.1 Implementation challenges

- *Scalability and Integration:* Ensuring interoperability and scalability of multimodal detection systems across diverse platforms and environments to support real-time monitoring and response capabilities.

- *Computational Complexity:* Addressing the computational demands associated with processing and analyzing multimodal data streams in real-time or near-real-time.

12.3.3 Adversarial AI detection techniques

Adversarial AI detection focuses on developing countermeasures specifically designed to identify and mitigate threats posed by GenAI-driven attacks. These techniques involve leveraging adversarial training, game theory, and model introspection to detect and respond to malicious activities effectively.

- *Adversarial Training:* Training defensive AI models using adversarial examples generated by GenAI to improve robustness and resilience against manipulation attempts (Siva Kumar *et al.*, 2020). The adaptability of GenAI allows for the development of dynamic security measures that can evolve with the threat landscape. For example, adaptable security protocols can be created using generative models to adjust security protocols based on real-time threat intelligence, thus reducing the time required to counteract threats. GenAI can also aggregate and analyze threat intelligence from diverse sources to create a comprehensive threat profile.
- *Game-Theoretic Approaches:* Applying principles of game theory to model interactions between defenders and adversaries and optimizing strategies for detecting and mitigating GenAI attacks (Ho *et al.*, 2022; Shan & Zhuang, 2020).
- *Model Introspection:* Implementing techniques for inspecting internal model states, gradients, or activations to detect anomalies introduced by GenAI-generated inputs (Carrasco Ramírez, 2024).

12.3.3.1 Implementation challenges

- *Dynamic Adversarial Tactics:* Adversaries continually evolve their tactics and techniques to evade detection systems. Adaptive defenses that can rapidly adjust and learn from new adversarial behaviors are critical. AI models can analyze software and system configurations to predict potential vulnerabilities, and GenAI can simulate attack scenarios to identify weak points that might be exploited.
- *Patch Management:* Creating patches, especially when there is an immediate need, is a vulnerability, but by generating potential patches and evaluating their effectiveness in simulated environments, AI systems can expedite the patching process and reduce the window of exposure.
- *Overhead and Performance Impact:* Minimizing the computational overhead and performance impact associated with deploying adversarial AI detection techniques in operational environments (Ren *et al.*, 2019).

12.3.4 Enhancing security operations

Security operations centers face the challenge of managing and analyzing large volumes of security data. GenAI assists in this area by

- ***Automating Routine Tasks:*** GenAI can automate repetitive tasks such as log analysis, incident categorization, and alert prioritization. This automation reduces the burden on security analysts and allows them to focus on more complex tasks.
- ***Generating Incident Reports:*** It can also produce detailed incident reports by synthesizing data from multiple sources. The reports can provide insights into attack vectors, impact analysis, and response actions, which facilitates better decision-making and post-incident analysis.
- ***Simulating Attack Scenarios:*** Finally, GenAI can simulate various attack scenarios to test the effectiveness of existing security measures. These simulations help in identifying gaps in the defense infrastructure and refining security protocols.

12.3.5 Blockchain and decentralized approaches

Blockchain and decentralized technologies offer novel approaches for enhancing the trustworthiness and transparency of data generated and transmitted using generative AI. These approaches leverage distributed consensus mechanisms and cryptographic techniques to verify authenticity and detect tampering or manipulation.

- ***Blockchain Timestamping:*** Using blockchain to timestamp and securely store metadata associated with GenAI-generated content, thus enabling traceability and verification of authenticity (Meng & Chen, 2022).
- ***Smart Contracts:*** Implementing smart contracts to enforce predefined rules or agreements regarding the usage and validation of GenAI outputs within decentralized applications or ecosystems (Ouyang *et al.*, 2022).
- ***Decentralized Oracles:*** Using decentralized oracles to retrieve and validate external data sources that corroborate the authenticity or integrity of GenAI-generated content (Caldarelli, 2022).

12.3.5.1 Implementation challenges

- ***Scalability and Throughput:*** Addressing scalability limitations inherent in current blockchain architectures to support high-volume transactions and data processing required for real-time GenAI detection (Haefner *et al.*, 2023).
- ***Regulatory Compliance:*** Navigating regulatory challenges related to data privacy, intellectual property rights, and legal implications associated with blockchain-based solutions for detecting GenAI misuse. China apparently was the first country to crack down on deepfakes in any

serious manner, trying to change its negative reputation for producing fake information. Rules put in place in January 2023 mandated, among other things, that GenAI content that goes against existing laws is prohibited, as is content that endangers national security and interests, damages the national image, or disrupts the economy (Kharpal, 2022).

12.3.6 Collaborative and cross-domain approaches

Effective detection of GenAI misuse requires collaboration and information sharing among multiple stakeholders, including researchers, industry partners, and governmental agencies (Li & Callegari, 2024). Cross-domain approaches integrate expertise from diverse fields to develop holistic solutions that address the multifaceted nature of GenAI-driven threats.

- *Information-Sharing Platforms:* Establishing collaborative platforms and frameworks for sharing threat intelligence, best practices, and detection methods related to GenAI misuse. The Coalition for Content Provenance and Authenticity (C2PA), for example, addresses the prevalence of misleading information online through the development of technical standards for certifying the source and history of media content. C2PA is a Joint Development Foundation project (Olin, 2018), formed through an alliance among companies such as Adobe, Intel, and Microsoft.
- *Interdisciplinary Research:* Fostering interdisciplinary research initiatives that combine expertise in AI, cybersecurity, psychology, law enforcement, and policy-making to develop comprehensive strategies for detecting and mitigating GenAI-driven attacks.
- *Public–Private Partnerships:* Promoting partnerships among academia, industry, and government agencies to leverage resources, expertise, and capabilities for detecting and combating GenAI misuse effectively.

12.3.6.1 Implementation challenges

- *Data Privacy and Security:* Safeguarding sensitive information shared across collaborative platforms while ensuring compliance with data protection regulations and confidentiality agreements.
- *Resource Allocation:* Allocating resources and funding to support collaborative research efforts, infrastructure development, and capacity-building initiatives aimed at combating GenAI-driven threats.

12.4 ETHICAL CONSIDERATIONS

In an effort to relentlessly pursue technological advancement, GenAI has emerged as a formidable force, reshaping the cybersecurity threat landscape with both promise and peril. The duality of this technology, as explored in the previous sections, underscores the complexity of its rapid integration into the digital age (Alwahedi *et al.*, 2024; Huang et al., 2023; Saddi *et al.*, 2024; Zhang *et al.*, 2018). The benefits of GenAI in enhancing cybersecurity defenses are undeniable, but as we detailed in the previous sections, those same benefits can—and are—being used against us (Das, 2024; Ferrag *et al.*, 2023; Gupta, 2023; Schmitt & Flechais, 2023). Mixed in with this duality are ethical considerations that need to be brought to the forefront.

12.4.1 News media

The ethical quandaries faced by the news media are multifaceted, and here we're not even including social media. On the one hand, GenAI can streamline content production and enhance journalistic throughput, but on the other hand, it opens the door to a new era of digital deception where the lines are blurred between truth and reconciliation (Dobber *et al.*, 2021; Güera & Delp, 2018). The societal implications of this are profound, as the erosion of trust in media could lead to widespread skepticism and the destabilization of political process (Brody, 2024). The ethical responsibility is paramount, yet the challenges are immense, particularly in an environment where, yet again, the speed of AI-generated content far outpaces the ability to fact-check and verify.

12.4.2 Financial and legal sectors

The finance and legal sectors are not immune to the ethical challenges posed by GenAI. In finance, the automation of trading, report generation, and even financial advisement through GenAI has the potential to revolutionize the industry, but this automation comes with the inherent risk of unintended consequences, such as the amplification of market volatility or the execution of unethical trading strategies that exploit AI-generated insights. How do we ethically balance the benefits of automation with the risks of empowering adversaries with advanced tools? This question is not easily answered, yet doing so is essential to the responsible development and deployment of GenAI in cybersecurity (Brundage *et al.*, 2018).

12.4.3 The black-box conundrum

One of the more pressing ethical issues associated with GenAI is its "black-box" nature—its inherent opacity that leaves users in the dark about how decisions are made. This lack of transparency is particularly problematic in cybersecurity, where the ethical implications of deploying black-box AI models challenge the principles of accountability and trust that underpin effective cybersecurity practices.

12.4.4 Environmental impact

Compounding these concerns is the environmental impact of GenAI. The computational power required to train and run these models is immense, leading to significant energy consumption and corresponding carbon footprint

(Haefner *et al.*, 2023). As data centers continue to expand to accommodate the growing demands of AI, the environmental cost of these technologies becomes increasingly difficult to ignore. The ethical dilemma here lies in balancing the benefits of AI with its environmental impact—a challenge that requires careful consideration and a commitment to sustainability. Taking a step back in order to better understand the basics could provide a better foundation for the future.

12.4.5 Academia

The rapid adoption of GenAI into technical writing and academia presents a profound ethical dilemma. At its core, academia is built on the pillars of originality, integrity, and the thirst for knowledge. On the positive side, GenAI can enable clear and effective communication, but on the negative side, using it to generate scholarly content threatens to destroy the foundations of research and education. The potential for harm comes in many forms, one of which is plagiarism, which goes against the very nature of academic integrity (George, 2023; O'Brien *et al.*, 2024). Moreover, the reliance on AI to increase productivity in technical writing and academia inadvertently encourages a culture of complacency, where the rigor of critical thinking and human creativity in expression is diminished in favor of automated efficiency (Ahmad, 2023; Bezzina & Dingli, 2024).

With the financial wellness of individuals and families being tied, to one degree or another, to the number of publications and citations produced, the ethical implications for academia are profound. As research increasingly incorporates AI-generated content, the risk of perpetuating bias in the data used for training large language models is especially concerning (Baumgartner *et al.*, 2023). This could ultimately lead to a reinforcement of existing disparities rather than to the advancement of knowledge (Bail, 2024; Capraro *et al.*, 2024; Grossmann *et al.*, 2023; Mannuru *et al.*, 2023). Cybersecurity adversaries already have an advantage in that they need to find only a single loophole or mistake for a successful attack, whereas developers have often spent their careers developing one product and trying to make it as secure as possible. Perpetuating bias in cutting-edge research further enables hacking.

12.4.5.1 An unintentional road map

Perhaps one of the most unsettling ethical considerations is the role of academia in inadvertently providing a road map for adversaries to use. As scholars and researchers publish their findings and develop new means of navigating the cyber landscape, they also unintentionally leave breadcrumbs that can lead to potential vulnerabilities and methods of exploitation. The paradox here is striking: The pursuit of knowledge and technological advancement, which is intended to benefit society, is equipping those who seek to do harm with the same tools needed for success.

This reality forces us to confront a difficult truth: In our quest to push the boundaries of what is possible with AI, we also need to acknowledge the unintended consequences of what we do. The challenge lies in finding a balance among open academic inquiry, transparency, and the need to protect sensitive information that could be used to undermine cybersecurity advances. This reminds us of a quote from French fabulist Jean de la Fontaine's "The Horoscope": "A person often meets his destiny on the road he took to avoid it." It is our ethical responsibility to ensure that GenAI serves the greater good rather than enabling harm.

12.5 FOR THE FUTURE

The challenges and opportunities outlined in this chapter point to the need for continual discussion of GenAI methods to defend against cyberattacks. GenAI improves threat detection because it can identify anomalies and patterns that are often missed by traditional methods. Most importantly, advances in AI in general have allowed for the *early* detection of threats, and GenAI adds significantly to the momentum. To identify and neutralize attacks, especially large-scale attacks, machine learning, deep learning, natural-language models, and large-language models are essential for security. By streamlining security protocols, GenAI allows for more time being allocated to more complex challenges. To approach cybersecurity challenges more effectively, real-time AI must be enabled to analyze a large amount of data, automate security threat detection, and create an attack defense system. Scalability is a definite concern because of the massive amount of data being generated by online activities (Dunsin *et al.*, 2024).

Biometrics is one of the biggest challenges in cybercrime; fingerprint and facial authentication are the two types of biometric authentication considered for high-level security (Kaur *et al.*, 2023). In addition to these techniques, the standard traditional methods, such as the use of passwords, decrease crime by increasing the authentication of multiple gateways. These combinations increase the challenge in network model design. For dealing with these kinds of systems, a highly complex network model is needed, which can be found in GenAI.

By using the advanced technology easily available today, creating fake information about a person, counterfeit news in general, and eliminating jobs are manipulated malicious tasks that overlook the capability of the highly complex growing technology, such as OpenAI's ChatGPT. Fake-generated sound effects also cause security issues, and voice recognition must consider the GenAI network models. Nowadays, technology is generating naturistic fake voices for theft and security violations.

12.5.1 Future directions

The pivotal gaps identified in the previous sections are categorized into advancement in AI technique, data collection and representation, cyberinfrastructure, digital crime attack analysis, and multiverse applications. In the current forensic investigation, the complexity of malware artifacts is high. To reduce the high risk of malware detection, combining deep learning with machine-learning techniques and combining AI methods with traditional identification techniques is required (Dunsin *et al.*, 2024).

Recognizing the limitations of the technology and data representation, pattern recognition, and scalability within an allotted framework will further strengthen strategies aimed at solving cyber challenges. By considering all these parameters, a GenAI system must be designed for all sorts of cybersecurity applications, such as key-risk indicators, attack detection, malware identification, predictive automated intelligent systems, cyber defense and resilience, data-breach preclusion, context crime, fake documentation, fake checks in banking, and real-time scenarios.

The advancement in AI for future researchers takes us first to data-source analysis, the use of data sources from multiple databases, and the identification of the correlation among those datasets, all of which need improvement. For multi-data-source analysis, promising approaches such as multitask algorithms, matching algorithms, and deep-learning algorithms must be considered (Kaur *et al.*, 2023). Instead of using the AI technique alone for this cybersecurity attack identification and defense technique, human-based AI must be considered. The human will be the decision-maker, and the AI will handle the prediction and detection section. Combining humans and AI techniques paves the path to improving tomorrow's methods.

GenAI will increase a system's transparency by explaining how and why a particular algorithm was chosen for different datasets. Multimodal analysis must be considered for video- and text-based classification approaches and for calculating a correlation matrix for analyzing data relationships. There is, however, a lack of vast datasets with preferred information—a gap that must be filled for future cyberattack and cyber-environment analysis. The cyber-infrastructure data's features, patterns, contexts, and characteristics are significant for the analysis.

12.6 CONCLUSION

This chapter explores the dual nature of GenAI in the cybersecurity landscape, where it serves both as a powerful tool for defense and as a weapon for attackers. On the defensive side, GenAI enhances threat detection, anomaly identification, and response automation, significantly improving the ability to protect systems from emerging threats. It can generate realistic threat scenarios for training, simulate attacks for vulnerability assessment, and even create advanced encryption algorithms.

However, the same capabilities that make GenAI a robust tool for defense can be exploited by attackers. Malicious actors can use it to develop sophisticated phishing attacks, generate deepfake content for social engineering, and create malware that adapts and evolves to evade detection. We emphasize the importance of understanding this duality and the need for robust ethical frameworks and regulations to mitigate the risks associated with the misuse of GenAI.

Traditional detection systems often struggle to identify sophisticated threats, but GenAI's ability to learn from historical data and detect anomalies has proven promising. Key strategies for leveraging GenAI in cybersecurity include pattern recognition, anomaly detection, and behavioral analysis. Deep-learning models such as RNNs and VAEs are particularly effective for identifying unusual patterns and detecting malware. However, implementing these systems faces challenges such as adversarial techniques and data quality. Multimodal detection systems and adversarial AI detection techniques offer comprehensive solutions by integrating data from various sources and using game theory or adversarial training to enhance detection. Further, GenAI can automate tasks in security operations, generate incident reports, and simulate attack scenarios, easing the burden on analysts. Blockchain and decentralized technologies also play a role in ensuring the trustworthiness of GenAI-generated content. Ethical considerations, as well as issues related to transparency, data privacy, and environmental impact, require careful attention as GenAI continues to transform cybersecurity.

REFERENCES

Ahmad, J. (2023). AI and beyond: The transformative role of interdisciplinary learning in education. *Journal Environmental Sciences and Technology* 2, 191–197.

Ahmad, R., Alsmadi, I., Alhamdani, W., and Tawalbeh, L. (2023). Zero-day attack detection: A systematic literature review. *Artificial Intelligence Review* 56, 10733–10811.

Alkhalil, Z., Hewage, C., Nawaf, L., & Khan, I. (2021). Phishing attacks: A recent comprehensive study and a new anatomy. *Frontiers in Computer Science* 3, 536060.

Alwahedi, F., Aldhaheri, A., Ferrag, M. A., Battah, A., & Tihanyi, N. (2024). Machine learning techniques for IoT security: Current research and future vision with generative AI and large language models. *Internet of Things and Cyber-Physical Systems*, 4, 167–185.

Angwin, J., Larson, J., Mattu, S., & Kirchner, L. (2020). *The Age of Surveillance Capitalism: The Fight for a Human Future at the New Frontier of Power.* Profile Books, London.

Bail, C. (2024). Can generative AI improve social science? *Proceedings of the National Academy of Sciences* 121, e2314021121.

Baumgartner, R., Arora, P., & Bath, C. (2023). Fair and equitable AI in biomedical research and healthcare: Social science perspectives. *Artificial Intelligence in Medicine* 144, 102658.

Bekbolatova, M., Mayer, J., Ong, C. W., & Toma, M. (2024). Transformative potential of AI in healthcare: Definitions, applications, and navigating the ethical landscape and public perspectives. *Healthcare* 12(2), 125.

Bezzina, S., & Dingli, A. (2024). The transformative potential of artificial intelligence for education. *Networked Learning Conference* 14(1). doi.org/10.54337/nlc.v14i1.8077.

Bhosale, R., & Mane, V. (2024). Enhancing user trust: A novel hybrid model to detect fake profiles in online social networks. *International Journal of Intelligent Systems and Applications in Engineering* 12, 542–551.

Böhm, R., Jörling, M., Reiter, L., & Fuchs, C. (2023). People devalue generative AI's competence but not its advice in addressing societal and personal challenges. *Communications Psychology* 1, 32. doi.org/10.1038/s44271-023-00032-x.

Bostrom, N. (2017). *Superintelligence*. Dunod, Paris.

Brody, G. C. (2024). Generative AI model shows fake news has a greater influence on elections when released at a steady pace without interruption. *The Conversation*, https://theconversation.com/generative-ai-model-shows-fake-news-has-a-greater-influence-on-elections-when-released-at-a-steady-pace-without-interruption-227332, accessed July 25, 2025.

Brundage, M., Avin, S., Clark, J., *et al.* (2018). The malicious use of artificial intelligence: Forecasting, prevention, and mitigation. *arXiv*,1802.07228. https://doi.org/10.48550/arXiv.1802.07228

Caldarelli, G. (2022). Overview of blockchain research. *Future Internet* 14(6), 175.

Capraro, V., Lentsch, A., Acemoglu, D., *et al.* (2024). The impact of generative artificial intelligence on socioeconomic inequalities and policy making. *Proceedings of the National Academy of Sciences Nexus* 3(6), 191.

Carrasco Ramírez, J. G. (2024). Crafting explainable artificial intelligence through active inference: A model for transparent introspection and decision-making. *Journal of Artificial Intelligence General* 4, 13–26.

Chino, Y. (2023). AI in medicine: Creating a safe and equitable future. *Lancet* 402, 503.

Das, R. (2024). *Generative AI: Phishing and cybersecurity metrics*. CRC Press. https://doi.org/10.1201/9781003503781

de Ruiter, A. (2021). The distinct wrong of deepfakes. *Philosophy & Technology* 34, 1311–1332.

Dilmegani, C. (2024). Model retraining in 2025: Why & how to retrain ML models? *AIMultiple Research*, January 11. research.aimultiple.com/model-retraining.

Dobber, T., Metoui, N., Trilling, D., Helberger, N., & De Vreese, C. (2021). Do (microtargeted) deepfakes have real effects on political attitudes? *International Journal of Press/Politics* 26, 69–91.

Dossantos J., An, J., & Javan, R. (2023). Eyes on AI: ChatGPT's transformative potential impact on ophthalmology. *Cureus* 15(6), e40765.

Dunsin, D., Ghanem, M. C., Ouazzane, K., & Vassilev, V. (2024). A comprehensive analysis of the role of artificial intelligence and machine learning in modern digital forensics and incident response. *Forensic Science International: Digital Investigation* 48, 301675.

Eisner, D. (2023). Phishing bait: The AI-fueled social engineering tactics plaguing SMEs. *Forbes*, August 23. www.forbes.com/sites/forbestechcouncil/2023/08/23/phishing-bait-the-ai-fueled-social-engineering-tactics-plaguing-smes.

Fazzini, K. (2019). Google and Facebook got tricked out of $123 million by a scam that costs small businesses billions every year—here's how to avoid it. *CNBC*, March 28. www.cnbc.com/2019/03/28/how-to-avoid-invoice-theft-scam-that-cost-google-facebook-123m.html.

Ferdous, J., Islam, R., Mahboubi, A., & Islam, M. A. (2023). A review of state-of-the-art malware attack trends and defense mechanisms. *IEEE Access*, 11, 121118–121141.

Ferrag, M. A., Debbah, M., & Al-Hawawreh, M. (2023, May). Generative ai for cyber threat-hunting in 6g-enabled iot networks. In *2023 IEEE/ACM 23rd International Symposium on Cluster, Cloud and Internet Computing Workshops (CCGridW)* (pp. 16–25). IEEE.

Galston, W. A. (2019). *Is Seeing Still Believing? The Deepfake Challenge to Truth in Politics*. Brookings Institution, Washington, D.C.

George, A. S. (2023). The potential of generative AI to reform graduate education. *Partners Universal International Research Journal* 2(4), 36–50.

Grossmann, I., Feinberg, M., Parker, D. C., *et al.* (2023). AI and the transformation of social science research. *Science* 380, 1108–1109.

Gruetzemacher, R., & Whittlestone, J. (2022). The transformative potential of artificial intelligence. *Futures* 135, 102884.

Güera, D., & Delp, E. J. (2018) Deepfake video detection using recurrent neural networks. In *15th IEEE International Conference on Advanced Video and Signal Based Surveillance*. doi.org/10.1109/AVSS.2018.8639163

Gupta, T. (2023). Data-driven AI: Understanding the risks and mitigations. *Cloud Security Alliance*, August 15. cloudsecurityalliance.org/blog/2023/08/15/data-driven-ai-understanding-the-risks-and-mitigations

Haefner, N., Parida, V., Gassmann, O., & Wincent, J. (2023). Implementing and scaling artificial intelligence: A review, framework, and research agenda. *Technological Forecasting and Social Change* 197, 122878.

Ho, E., Rajagopalan, A., Skvortsov, A., *et al.* (2022). Game theory in defence applications: A review. *Sensors* 22, 1032.

Huang, C., Zhang, Z., Mao, B., & Yao, X. (2023). An overview of artificial intelligence ethics. *IEEE Transactions on Artificial Intelligence* 4, 799–819.

Hwang, I. (2021). What is cryptojacking? How to detect mining malware. *Mediafeed*, May 7. mediafeed.org/what-is-cryptojacking-how-to-detect-mining-malware.

Kagumire, S. (2021). Anomaly detection with machine learning. *Medium*, May 12. sulaimank.medium.com/anomaly-detection-with-machine-learning-8fa942fb5adc.

Kaur, R., Gabrijelčič, D., & Klobučar, T. (2023). Artificial intelligence for cybersecurity: Literature review and future research directions. *Information Fusion* 97, 101804.

Kharpal, A. (2022). China is about to get tougher on deepfakes in an unprecedented way. Here's what the rules mean. *CNBC*, December 22.

Koplin, J. J. (2023). Dual-use implications of AI text generation. *Ethics and Information Technology* 25, 32.

Kranzberg, M. (1985). Technology and history: "Kranzberg's Laws." *Technology and Culture* 27, 544–560.

Lark Editorial Team. (2023). Some common methods for feature extraction in AI, December 28. www.larksuite.com/en_us/topics/ai-glossary/some-common-methods-for-feature-extraction-in-ai#.

Li, C., & Callegari, A. (2024). Stopping AI disinformation: Protecting truth in the digital world. *World Economic Forum*, June 14.

Liao, Q. V., Ma, Y., Jin, Z., Zhang, S., & Hoi, S. C. (2019). Deepfake video detection using recurrent neural networks. *IEEE Transactions on Circuits and Systems for Video Technology* 30, 3832–3846.

Mannuru, N. R., Shahriar, S., Teel, Z. A., Wang, T., Lund, B. D., Tijani, S., Vaidya, P. (2023). Artificial intelligence in developing countries: The impact of generative artificial intelligence (AI) technologies for development. *Information Development*. Advance online publication, vol39, issue 5, 710–728. https://doi.org/10.1177/02666669231200628

Meng, L., & Chen, L. (2022). A blockchain-based long-term time-stamping scheme. eprint.iacr.org/2022/319.pdf.

Mirsky, Y., & Lee, W. (2021). The creation and detection of deepfakes: A survey. *ACM Computing Surveys* 54, 1–41.

Mollick, E., & Euchner, J. (2023). The transformative potential of generative AI: A conversation with Ethan Mollick. *Research-Technology Management* 66(4), 11–16.

Moore, M. (2023). Fake accounts on social media, epistemic uncertainty and the need for an independent auditing of accounts. *Internet Policy Review* 12, doi.org/10.14763/2023.1.1680.

Motyl, A. J. (2023). What a peek inside a 'troll factory' reveals about Putin's Russia. *The Hill*, July 17.

Moustafa, N., Sitnikova, E., Jager, J., & Slay, J. (2021). Using deep learning to create and detect fake news for internet of things applications. *IEEE Access* 9, 46054–46071.

O'Brien, M. J., & Alsmadi, I. (2021). Misinformation, disinformation, and hoaxes: What's the difference? *The Conversation*, April 21.

O'Brien, M. J., Alsmadi, I., Bentley, R. A., & Tuba, M. (2024). OpenAI ChatGPT and biased information in higher education. In Lahby, M. (ed.), *Empowering Digital Education with ChatGPT: From Theoretical to Practical Applications*, pp. 223–234. Routledge, New York.

O'Donnell, R. (2020). Deepfakes and synthetic media in the financial industry: Fraud and other issues. *Journal of Financial Transformation* 52, 63–70.

Olin, E. (2018). The Joint Development Foundation joins the Linux Foundation family to drive adoption of open source and standards. Linux Foundation, December 11.

Ouyang, L., Zhang, W., & Wang, F.-Y. (2022). Intelligent contracts: Making smart contracts smart for blockchain intelligence. *Computers and Electrical Engineering* 104 (Part B), 108421.

Park, I., Joshi, A. S., & Javan, R. (2023). Potential role of ChatGPT in clinical otolaryngology explained by ChatGPT. *American Journal of Otolaryngology* 44, 103873.

Rakowski, R., Kowaliková, P. (2024). The political and social contradictions of the human and online environment in the context of artificial intelligence applications. *Humanities and Social Sciences Communications* 11, 289. doi.org/10.1057/s41599-024-02725-y.

Ratha, N. K., Chikkerur, S., & Connell, J. (2021). Can generative adversarial networks create adversarial examples for biometric systems? *IEEE International Conference on Identity, Security and Behavior Analysis*, 1–8.

Reardon, S. (2024). How to spot a deepfake—and prevent it from causing political chaos. *ScienceInsider*, January 29. doi.org/10.1126/science.zw0xbf6.

Ren, K., Zheng, T. Qin, Z., & Liu, X. (2019). Adversarial attacks and defenses in deep learning. *Engineering* 6, 346–360.

Rossler, A., Cozzolino, D., Verdoliva, L., Riess, C., & Thies, J. (2019). FaceForensics++: Learning to detect manipulated facial images. *IEEE Transactions on Information Forensics and Security*, 15, 2984–2998.

Rubin, A. J. (2020). *Deepfakes and the New Disinformation War.* HarperCollins, New York City.

Saddi, V. R., Gopal, S. K., Mohammed, A. S., Dhanasekaran, S., & Naruka, M. S. (2024, March). Examine the role of generative AI in enhancing threat intelligence and cyber security measures. In *2024 2nd International Conference on Disruptive Technologies (ICDT)* (pp. 537–542). IEEE.

Salman, H., Khadda, A., Leclerc, G., & Ilyas, A. (2023). Raising the cost of malicious AI-powered image editing. *arXiv:2302.06588v.*

Schmitt, M., & Flechais, I. (2023). Digital deception: Generative artificial intelligence in social engineering and phishing. *arXiv preprint arXiv:2310.13715.*

Schwartz, L. (2020). *Deep Fakes and the National Security State.* Brookings Institution, Washington, D.C.

Shan, X. G., & Zhuang, J. (2020). A game-theoretic approach to modeling attacks and defenses of smart grids at three levels. *Reliability Engineering & System Safety* 195, 106683.

Siva Kumar, S. R. *et al.* (2020). Adversarial Machine Learning—Industry Perspectives. *IEEE Security and Privacy Workshops*, (pp. 69–75), doi.org/10.1109/SPW50608.2020.00028.

Stirland, S. (2020). Can AI be trusted to tackle misinformation? *Nature* 585, S60–S62.

Taddeo, M., & Floridi, L. (2018). How AI can be a force for good. *Science* 361, 751–752.

Teal (Corporation). (2024). What are baiting attacks and how can you prevent them? May 15. tealtech.com/blog/how-to-prevent-baiting-attacks.

Tealab, A. (2018). Time series forecasting using artificial neural networks methodologies: A systematic review. *Future Computing and Informatics Journal* 3, 334–340.

Wach, K., Duong, C. D., Ejdys, J., *et al.* (2023). The dark side of generative artificial intelligence: A critical analysis of controversies and risks of ChatGPT. *Entrepreneurial Business and Economics Review* 11(2), 7–30.

Wang, S., Liu, J., Lan, X. *et al.* (2022). Cross-modal association analysis and matching model construction of perceptual attributes of multiple colors and combined tones. *Frontiers in Psychology* 13, 970219.

Yuan, X., He, P., Zhu, Q., & Li, X. (2019). Adversarial examples: Attacks and defenses for deep learning. *IEEE Transactions on Neural Networks and Learning Systems* 30, 2805–2824.

Zellers, R., Holtzman, A., Rashkin, H., *et al.* (2019). Defending against neural fake news. *Advances in Neural Information Processing Systems* 32, 9057–9068.

Zhang, C., Kuppannagari, S. R., Kannan, R., & Prasanna, V. K. (2018, October). Generative adversarial network for synthetic time series data generation in smart grids. In *2018 IEEE International Conference on Communications, Control, and Computing Technologies for Smart Grids (SmartGridComm)* (pp. 1–6). IEEE.

Zheng, X., Zhu, Y., & Si, X. (2019). A survey on challenges and progresses in blockchain technologies: A performance and security perspective. *Applied Sciences* 9, 22.

Chapter 13

Generative AI-driven penetration testing

Frameworks, methodologies, and ethical considerations

Yassine Maleh

13.1 INTRODUCTION

In this modern time when the digital ecosystem drives most functions of contemporary living, the idea of trustworthiness is significantly determined by cybersecurity. As cyber threats multiply in diverse forms and complexities, it requires organizations to respond proactively to those threats that jeopardize their digital assets. Among such proactive measures, penetration testing (PT) emerges as one of the foremost practices to calibrate and promote the defensive strategy of an organization. PT applies real-world experience in cyberattack simulations, which combine vulnerability identification with resilience assessments of networks, applications, and systems (Maleh, 2024).

This chapter examines the foundational methodologies, frameworks, and the interplay of artificial intelligence (AI) in modern practices of PT. In contrast to vulnerability assessments or security audits, PT relies on an offensive technique that seeks to look inside a computer in order to find weaknesses that could be exploited by malicious actors. Equally important to PT are its ethical and legal aspects; to ensure accountability and clarity with regard to testing activities, sufficient RoE and NDAs must be set up. This chapter presents an overview of core methodologies and frameworks, including OWASP, MITRE ATT&CK, PTES, and the Cyber Kill Chain. These frameworks represent structured methodologies of PT that standardize the individual approaches in managing cybersecurity problems, and their interconnectedness creates a foundation for responding to increasingly sophisticated cyber threats. The chapter further analyzes how integrating AI tools into PT will transform it into a field where performance, precision, and scalability will witness exponential growth.

Evolving traditional PT techniques and emerging AI capabilities are at the forefront of this chapter's focus. The rise of sophisticated AI-driven tools suggests unprecedented opportunities for the automation of reconnaissance, vulnerability identification, and adversarial attack simulation (Zaydi & Maleh, 2024). With such advantages come manifold ethical challenges that stem from AI applications and will require additional industry regulations. Critical to this chapter is the mandate for a counterbalancing of innovations against

DOI: 10.1201/9781003597476-17

their responsibilities, ensuring that AI-driven PT practices align with ethical guidelines and carry no danger of becoming operational weapons in the hands of ill-intentioned parties.

Apart from the technical points of interest, this chapter emphasizes how PT serves strategic goals for the organization. By aiding the identification of vulnerabilities and determining the effectiveness of security measures, PT enables organizations to safeguard their critical assets, minimize risks, and comply with regulatory frameworks. Moreover, embedding AI into PT workflows enhances these benefits, such as employing predictive analytics, real-time threat detection, and continuous monitoring.

PT will continue to be something that organizations do desperately in order to stave off potential threats and attacks. This chapter amalgamates an exhaustive survey of methodologies, frameworks, and innovations driven by AI in modern PT. In helping readers utilize the strengths of AI and appreciate the implications therein, this chapter empowers cybersecurity professionals to externalize the challenges posed by the contemporary threat landscape and hence build a more resilient future-ready defense.

13.2 WHAT IS A PT?

In security evaluation, PT is more critical than vulnerability assessments. Vulnerability scanning examines individual devices, applications, or computers inside a network, whereas PT provides a comprehensive overview of the network's security framework (Bishop, 2007). Through PT, executives, managers, and administrators of computer networks may observe the potential consequences of a legitimate hacker getting into their accounts. Additionally, they can illuminate security vulnerabilities that standard evaluations overlook (Zaoui et al., 2024).

If the PT has expertise in social engineering, they can ascertain whether employees frequently provide strangers access to the office and utilize the network. The PT can also assess processes such as the patch management cycle. If security updates are not implemented within three days of their release, attackers would have a three-day window to exploit known server vulnerabilities; a penetration test can reveal this procedural deficiency.

The PT is a security assessment that measures a company's effectiveness in safeguarding its network, applications, systems, and personnel from internal and external threats.

Conducting a "penetration test," or "Pentest," is a method to assess the security of a computer network. It is a proactive method to assess the efficacy of an organization's infrastructure protection by simulating real attacks.

A penetration test systematically evaluates security protocols for weaknesses, design flaws, and technology deficiencies.

Test outcomes are recorded and conveyed in a detailed report for management and technicians.

13.3 BENEFITS OF PRODUCING A PT

- It assesses the probability of information assets being targeted and implement appropriate safeguards.
- It ensures the organization adheres to permitted limits for information security risk.
- This tool may provide a more accurate evaluation of the commercial impact of an assault and the feasibility of various attack paths.
- It provides a comprehensive framework for preemptive measures that may be undertaken to prevent future exploitation.
- It optimizes the advantages of investments in information technology security by ensuring the effective implementation of security protocols.
- It compliances with all relevant industry regulations and standards (e.g., ISO/IEC 27001:2022, PCI DSS, HIPAA, FISMA) (Maleh et al., 2021).
- It focuses on significant vulnerabilities and emphasizes security issues at the application level for management and development teams.
- It evaluates the effectiveness of web servers, firewalls, and routers as security mechanisms for a network.

Revealing vulnerabilities: A pentest identifies vulnerabilities in a company's systems and applications while also assessing the potential for employee-induced data breaches. The tester produces a report that encompasses current security vulnerabilities along with recommendations and guidelines to improve overall security.

Show the real risks: The tester emulates the behavior of a genuine attacker by leveraging identified vulnerabilities.

Ensuring business continuity: A little disturbance might significantly impact a firm. The enterprise may incur losses amounting to hundreds, if not thousands, of dollars. Consequently, it is imperative for the company's operations that the network is perpetually accessible, resources are readily available, and communications are consistently operational. A penetration test identifies potential vulnerabilities and recommends solutions to safeguard the business's operations from unforeseen disruptions or loss of access.

Reduce client-side attacks: An attacker can exploit client-side vulnerabilities in online forms and web services to gain access to a company's systems. Enterprises must be prepared to safeguard their systems against such attacks. If a firm recognizes the common threats it may encounter, it may proactively enhance its application to address identified weaknesses.

Establish the company's safety status: One method to ascertain the security of a company is to employ the PT. The tester provides an overview of the company's infrastructure protection, evaluates the effectiveness of existing security measures, and identifies the overall security system along with areas requiring enhancement.

Preserving the company's reputation: Companies must strive to maintain their esteemed reputations among clients and business allies. Following a data breach or attack, even the most loyal partners may hesitate to support the business anew. Safeguarding sensitive information and preserving reputation with clients and business partners requires regular PT.

13.4 COMPARISON OF SECURITY AUDIT, VULNERABILITY ASSESSMENT, AND PT

These approaches encompass security audits, vulnerability assessments, and PT, employed to evaluate the security of a computer system in compliance with stringent laws. Nonetheless, each possesses distinct qualities and objectives.

According to Sabillon et al. (2017), a security audit is a systematic process for analyzing and assessing the security of an IT system. It is typically done using various recognized standards and best practices, for instance, ISO 27001 (Malatji, 2023). The security audit scrutinizes the security policies, procedures, and controls to understand the weaknesses, risks, gaps, and more. The security audit gives an overall assessment of an IT system's security but does not give details regarding the specific vulnerabilities.

It is a way to scan a computer system to find identified and other potential vulnerabilities. In short, this technique deploys automated tools to scan open ports, running services, and known vulnerabilities (Samtani et al., 2016). The vulnerability assessment is usually conducted using vulnerability scanning software, which compares the information obtained against a database of known vulnerabilities. The assessment prioritizes the results of the vulnerability assessment such that the most threatening vulnerabilities are mitigated or patched first.

PT is a sophisticated method that simulates a genuine assault on a computer system to identify further vulnerabilities in its security. PT may be conducted either manually or with various automated methods. Pentest employs attack tactics akin to those of hackers; however, operates within a regulated and ethical framework. The penetration test findings enumerate identified vulnerabilities and security shortcomings, along with advice for remediation.

Consequently, the security audit provides a comprehensive evaluation of an IT system's security state, the vulnerability assessment identifies possible vulnerabilities inside the system, and PT replicates an actual assault to ascertain security weaknesses. These approaches are frequently employed in conjunction to deliver a comprehensive security evaluation of a computer system. Figure 13.1 delineates the distinctions among a security audit, vulnerability assessment, and PT.

Pentesting vs Ethical hacking

- PT is an authorized, methodical procedure that uses known vulnerabilities to try to access to a system, network, or application resources.

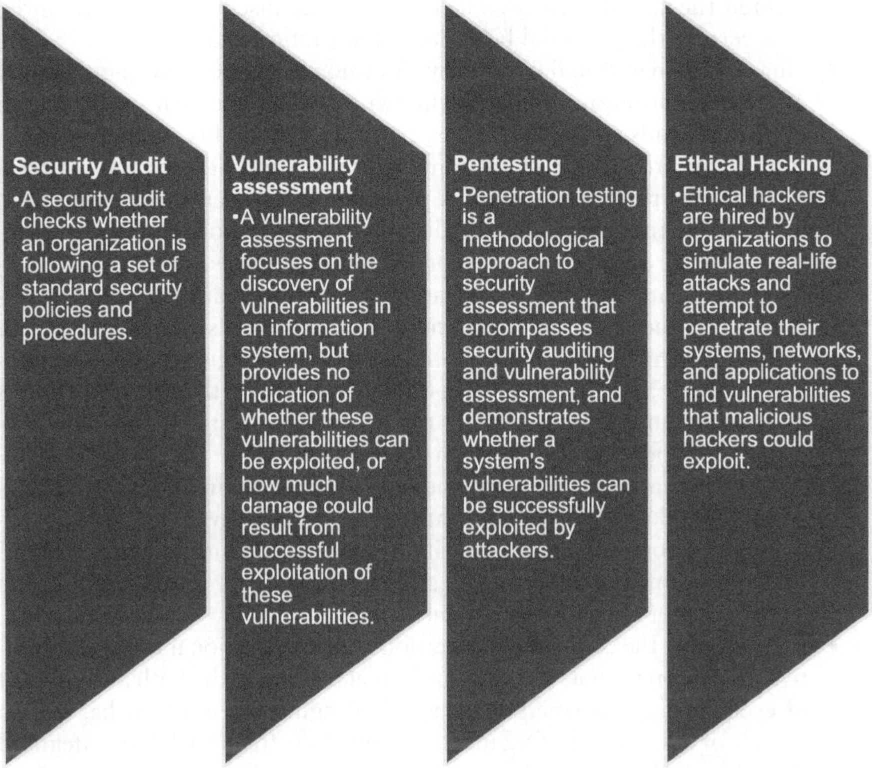

Figure 13.1 Difference between security audit, vulnerability assessment, and PT.

- PT seeks to uncover system vulnerabilities and recommend remedial actions prior to their detection and exploitation by hackers or cybercriminals.
- PT may be conducted internally (with partial access to the organization's information system) or externally (without access to the organization's information system). This often entails employing automated or manual instruments to evaluate the organization's assets.
- It is essential to recognize that PT is distinct from both hacking and ethical hacking.

Pentesting benefits

- Identifying vulnerabilities: A penetration test not only uncovers current deficiencies in system or application setups but also evaluates the activities and behaviors of an organization's workers that may result in a data leak. The tester delivers a report including updates on security vulnerabilities along with recommendations and rules designed to enhance overall security.

- Exhibit the actual hazards: The tester utilizes discovered vulnerabilities to ascertain the potential behaviors of a genuine attacker.
- Guarantee operational continuity: A minor disruption may significantly affect a corporation. It may incur expenses for the firm up to tens or even thousands of dollars. Thus, network availability, resource accessibility, and round-the-clock communication are vital for the seamless operation of the organization. A penetration test identifies possible vulnerabilities and proposes remedies to safeguard corporate operations against unforeseen disruptions or accessibility losses.
- Mitigate client-side attacks: An assailant can infiltrate a company's systems from the client side, especially through web services and online forms. Organizations must be equipped to safeguard their systems against such assaults. If a corporation is aware of the types of threats it may encounter, it can identify the warning indications and should be capable of updating the program accordingly.
- Assess the company's security status: PT can ascertain a company's security level and overall security status. The tester delivers a report on the company's comprehensive security system and identifies opportunities for enhancement, detailing the safeguarding of its infrastructure and the efficacy of current security measures.
- Safeguarding the company's reputation: An organization must keep a positive reputation with its partners and clients. Gaining the faith and support of even steadfast partners becomes challenging when a firm has a data breach or cyberattack. Organizations must do frequent PT to safeguard their data and maintain the confidence of their partners and consumers.

13.5 PT STRATEGIES

Intrusion testing can be carried out using three approaches:

- Black box PT is conducted under circumstances that closely resemble an external assault by an unidentified remote attacker. This indicates that the penetration testers receive minimal or no knowledge prior to commencing the assessment (Maleh, 2025).
- White box PT is conducted with comprehensive information provided to the pentesters prior to the assessment. The information necessary for the penetration test is supplied with total transparency. The action of the target is then disclosed and rendered apparent, thus the white box.
- Grey box PT is conducted with minimal information provided to the testers prior to the assessment. This may entail supplying information on the functionality of the target, granting user accounts on a platform with limited access, and providing access to a target that is not publicly available, among other actions. This facilitates more comprehensive testing and an enhanced comprehension of the situation.

13.6 BLACK-BOX PT

- The penetration tester doing the black-box assessment has no prior knowledge of the target infrastructure.
- The tester possesses limited knowledge of the target firm. Following comprehensive research and data acquisition, the penetration test may be executed.
- This test collects publicly available information, including domain and IP addresses, and then simulates the hacking process.
- Assessing the infrastructure's attributes and interrelations occupies a substantial segment of the project timetable.
- It is neither inexpensive nor time-efficient.

13.7 WHITE-BOX PT

- The tester receives extensive information on the infrastructure to be evaluated.
- This examination is structured to replicate the operational methods of a company's workforce.
- It swiftly uncovers security deficiencies and vulnerabilities.
- The tester will evaluate all necessary components since he is acutely aware of what to examine.

13.8 GRAY-BOX PT

- Gray-box employs both white-box and black-box PT approaches.
- In gray-box testing, the tester often possesses limited information.
- All requisite safety testing and assessments are performed internally.
- They seek vulnerabilities that an assailant may use to undermine a program.
- During a black-box test of secure systems, it is standard procedure to employ this approach if the tester identifies that specific background information is essential for the test's accuracy.

13.8.1 Pentesting vs red teaming

Red teaming and PT are two methodologies in information technology security designed to evaluate the security of a system or network. Despite their similarities, significant differences exist between the two.

Pentesting, or PT, is the evaluation of a system or network's security through simulated attacks. The objective is to identify vulnerabilities and security deficiencies that could be exploited by an adversary. PT frequently employs automated tools, including vulnerability scanners, alongside manual testing to uncover vulnerabilities that automated methods may overlook. The outcomes of these assessments enable organizations to enhance their security stance by addressing identified vulnerabilities. Red teaming, conversely, constitutes a more extensive methodology that entails the simulation of a genuine attack. Red Teams consist of IT security specialists who attempt to infiltrate a system or network employing authentic attack methodologies, including social engineering, email deception, network reconnaissance, and vulnerability exploitation, among others. Red Teams collaborate with organizations to evaluate their resilience against complex and realistic assaults. The objective is to evaluate the organization's capacity to detect, prevent, and respond to an actual attack, as well as to identify areas for enhancement.

The decision between red teaming and PT is contingent upon the organization's IT security maturity and objectives. For a company that is relatively inexperienced in IT security and seeks to routinely evaluate its security posture, PT may serve as an effective initial measure. PT can identify superficial vulnerabilities and prevalent misconfigurations while also offering actionable recommendations to enhance enterprise security. Nonetheless, if the organization possesses a well-established security strategy and seeks to evaluate the robustness of its defenses, red teaming may be a more suitable alternative. Red teaming can effectively simulate realistic scenarios of advanced attacks that incorporate sophisticated tactics, techniques, and procedures (TTPs). Moreover, red teaming can assist in identifying deficiencies in organizational security, including security policies, incident management protocols, and employee training programs.

13.9 COMMON AREAS OF PT

1. **PT network:**
   - Assists in identifying security vulnerabilities in network architecture and execution
   - Prevalent network security issues
   - Utilization of insecure protocols
   - Unutilized open ports and services
   - Unpatched operating system and applications
   - Improper configuration of firewalls, intrusion detection systems (IDS), servers, workstations, network services, etc.
2. **PT Web applications:**
   - Facilitates the identification of security vulnerabilities in web applications resulting from inadequate design and development methodologies
   - Prevalent vulnerabilities in web application security

    - Injection vulnerabilities
    - Failures in authentication and authorization
    - Inadequate session management
    - Inadequate cryptography
    - Inadequate error management
3. **PT by social engineering:**
    - Assists in identifying personnel who do not authenticate, adhere to, validate, and manage procedures and technology appropriately
    - Prevalent employee behavioral issues might provide significant security threats to the firm
    - Dissemination of deceptive electronic correspondence
    - Fall prey to phishing emails and telephone calls
    - Disclosing confidential information to unfamiliar individuals
    - Permitting unlawful access to non-nationals
    - Establishing a connection between a USB device and a workstation
4. **PT wireless networks:**
    - Assists in identifying settings inside wireless network systems
    - Prevalent security vulnerabilities in a wireless network framework
    - Insecure wireless encryption protocols
    - Unauthorized drug access points
    - Inadequate encryption passphrase
    - Wireless technology is unsupported
5. **PT mobile devices:**
    - Facilitates the identification of security issues related to mobile devices and their utilization. Prevalent security issues associated with mobile devices:
        - Lack or inadequate execution of BYOD (Bring Your Own Device) policy
        - Utilization of rooted or compromised mobile devices
        - Inadequate security implementation on mobile devices
6. **PT in cloud**

Assists in identifying security vulnerabilities inside cloud infrastructure (Maleh, 2023). Alongside traditional security concerns, cloud services introduce distinct security challenges related to the cloud environment:

- Inadequate data security during storage
- Network connection and bandwidth issues in relation to minimal criteria
- Inadequate user access management
- Unsecured interfaces and access points
- Inadequate secrecy of user activities in the cloud
- Insider security risks

13.10 PT PROCESS

The PT method is often segmented into many phases to guarantee thorough and effective evaluation. The stages may differ based on the employed technique; nevertheless, below is a standard five-step process:

Strategic planning and reconnaissance: The preliminary stage entails comprehending the PT's goals and objectives. In the information-gathering phase, the tester aims to obtain data on the target's architecture, operating systems, applications, communication protocols, and possible entry points. This can be achieved via the use of automated technologies or human techniques, including public information searches, log analysis, and others.

Vulnerability scanning: This step entails identifying the target's vulnerabilities and weaknesses using automated tools and human methods. The tester may employ vulnerability scanners, file explorers, fuzzing tools, and network traffic analysis tools to identify potential entry points and vulnerabilities.

Exploitation and post-exploitation: At this phase, the tester leverages vulnerabilities to determine possible access to sensitive systems or information. The exploitation strategy may differ depending on the vulnerability and circumstances, perhaps utilizing automated tools, bespoke scripts, or manual approaches.

Reporting: This phase entails the documentation of PT outcomes and their presentation in report format. Reports must be lucid, concise, and systematically organized to facilitate the comprehension of findings and suggestions. Reports must encompass facts regarding techniques, used tools, detected vulnerabilities, and security suggestions.

Cleanup and follow-up: Documenting the results from the PT requires presenting them in a reporting manner. The reports must be lucid, succinct, and systematically organized to effectively communicate findings and suggestions. They should also provide details about the used approach, utilized tools, detected vulnerabilities, and security suggestions.

13.11 CODE OF GOOD PRACTICE

PT is permitted exclusively on approved systems and requires the explicit approval of the system owner. Unapproved physical training results in considerable legal and ethical consequences.

Unethical and irresponsible action in ethical hacking and PT might result in adverse outcomes. This chapter will examine ethical hacking protocols, highlighting the significance of ethics, transparency, and accountability.

The ethics of ethical hacking are grounded on moral principles to guarantee that the procedure is conducted with the highest degree of responsibility and legality. The ethical hacker must adhere to a code of behavior designed to ensure that this discipline delivers an ethical service. The following norms of behavior encompass:

- Refraining from employing any nefarious techniques to gain access to a computer system or its information
- Adhering to relevant laws and regulations
- Securing prior authorization from the proprietor of the computer system
- Preserving the integrity of a computer system
- Honor user confidentiality
- Transparency: The ethical hacking movement is frequently defined by aspects of enigma and confidentiality. For ethical hacking to attain societal acceptability.
- Communication: Ethical hackers must transparently disclose their operations and engage with pertinent stakeholders, including IT system proprietors, security administrators, and users. They must go from first authorization to results reporting in a completely communicative way with all stakeholders involved in the process.

13.12 LEGAL FRAMEWORK: RULES OF ENGAGEMENT

Rules of Engagement (RoE) is a document that outlines the procedures for conducting the penetration test. Certain parameters must be explicitly articulated in a RoE document prior to commencing the penetration test.

Test type and framework: delineates the kind of penetration test (black box, white box, or grey box) according to the information supplied by the client.

Client contact information: Contact details and escalation procedures in the event of an issue or emergency. The customer-side technical staff must be accessible 24/7 during the penetration test.

Notification from the customer's IT team: penetration tests are utilized to assess the overall preparedness of the IT team and specifically the cyber defense team in responding to events and intrusion attempts. It is essential to clarify if a penetration test is scheduled or unscheduled. For an advertised test, it is necessary to mention the day and time of the testing, along with the source IP addresses from which the test (attack) would be conducted. In the event of an unannounced test, outline the procedure to be adhered to if identified or obstructed by a detection/prevention system.

Management of sensitive data: throughout the preparation and execution of tests, the penetration testers may encounter or get sensitive information pertaining to the firm, its systems, and/or its users. Managing sensitive data necessitates meticulous consideration in the engagement agreement, with the implementation of suitable storage and communication protocols (e.g., complete disk encryption on the pentesters' devices, encryption of reports transmitted via email, etc.). It is important to verify the alignment of the necessary tests and the designated framework with the applicable regulatory statutes to which the client is bound (GDPR, HDS, PCI ...).

Progress meetings and reporting: delineates the frequency of progress meetings with the client and the reports to be produced during and/or upon the conclusion of the penetration test.

13.13 LEGAL FRAMEWORK: NON-DISCLOSURE AGREEMENT

A non-disclosure agreement (NDA) is a legal contract between two parties that stipulates the obligation not to reveal secret information to third parties. An NDA is frequently employed to safeguard the client's data and systems during testing in the realm of ethical hacking and PT.

The NDA safeguards confidential information, including customer data, payment details, trade secrets, and intellectual property. Ethical hackers and corporate customers must establish consensus on the information to be safeguarded and the measures to be implemented in the event of a violation of the agreement.

The NDA must be formulated prior to the commencement of testing and executed by all parties concerned. It may be incorporated into the comprehensive security services agreement or established as an independent contract.

Noncompliance with an NDA may result in significant legal repercussions, including litigation for damages. Corporate clients must guarantee that ethical hackers adhere to all NDA stipulations to safeguard their information and systems. Figure 13.2 shows an example of a confidentiality agreement NDA.

13.13.1 Understanding the restrictions

Upon defining the primary objectives, the team should analyze several elements related to the testing process. Despite the assets and environment being delineated within the scope, the team must be cognizant of the constraints that may impact testing, including:

> The team must ascertain what is being tested and what is not to refine the scope further. It is essential to ascertain the parameters of acceptable conduct during physical and social engineering assessments.

The governing documents will delineate which locations, systems, applications, or other potential targets are to be included or excluded based on the defined scope. A team member may want to test an alternative subnetwork during the testing procedure. The team member must specify that, for legal reasons, they cannot perform the test unless it is expressly incorporated within the scope.

NON-DISCLOSURE AGREEMENT

PARTIES

- This Non-Disclosure Agreement (hereinafter referred to as the **"Agreement"**) is entered into on ________________ (the **"Effective Date"**), by and between __________________________, with an address of ________________, (hereinafter referred to as the **"Disclosing Party"**) and ________________, with an address of ________________, (hereinafter referred to as the **"Receiving Party"**) (collectively referred to as the **"Parties"**).

CONFIDENTIAL INFORMATION

- The Receiving Party agrees not to disclose, copy, clone, or modify any confidential information related to the Disclosing Party and agrees not to use any such information without obtaining consent.
- "Confidential information" refers to any data and/or information that is related to the Disclosing Party, in any form, including, but not limited to, oral or written. Such confidential information includes, but is not limited to, any information related to the business or industry of the Disclosing Party, such as discoveries, processes, techniques, programs, knowledge bases, customer lists, potential customers, business partners, affiliated partners, leads, know-how, or any other services related to the Disclosing Party.

RETURN OF CONFIDENTIAL INFORMATION

- The Receiving Party agrees to return all the confidential information to the Disclosing Party upon the termination of this Agreement.

OWNERSHIP

- This Agreement is not transferable and may only be transferred by written consent provided by both Parties.

GOVERNING LAW

- This Agreement shall be governed by and construed in accordance with the laws of ________________.

SIGNATURE AND DATE

- The Parties hereby agree to the terms and conditions set forth in this Agreement and such is demonstrated by their signatures below:

Figure 13.2 Example of a non-disclosure agreement (NDA).

The particulars of the Pentest may further include other constraints, such as potential geographical or technical limitations, to address these restrictions. A legacy system may have a history of issues with automated scanning.

Minimize intrusiveness based on the defined scope—what is specifically under inquiry and what is not? Activities such as physical security tasks and social engineering should be classified as acceptable. Furthermore, request the stakeholder to delineate any constraints that may impact susceptible systems in the event of a planned invasive assault, such as a Denial of Service (DoS) attack, during the testing phase.

Limit tool utilization to a singular engagement—In some instances, a regulatory body mandates the tools that the team must employ during the assessment. In that scenario, the group will receive a comprehensive overview of all available resources pertinent to that particular activity.

To ensure precise testing outcomes, the team must account for all pertinent elements. Is it feasible to reach the distant location utilizing existing technology if an installation in a foreign country must be included in the test? The parties must concur on the extent of travel required to conduct the Pentest at the remote site, should an on-site visit be deemed essential.

13.14 CHARACTERISTICS OF A GOOD PT

- Define physical therapy parameters, including aims, constraints, and rationale for operations.
- Engage proficient, seasoned experts to conduct the assessment.
- Choose an appropriate array of assessments, weighing expenses against advantages.
- Adhere to a technique that incorporates suitable planning and documentation.
- Meticulously record the outcomes and ensure they are understandable to the client.

13.15 WHEN SHOULD A PT?

To maintain a record of all existing and newly identified vulnerabilities that have been addressed prior to exploitation by cybercriminals, PT must be conducted often. Hackers seem to be exploring novel methodologies and strategies, as seen by several recent reports of new assaults. Any novel kind of aggression necessitates that a corporation be prepared with treatments. Regrettably, the majority of firms neglect to consider the probability of such occurrences and defer doing PT until it becomes obligatory, either due to legal requirements or, more critically, following an assault.

13.16 PENTESTER ETHICS

- Execute PT solely upon obtaining the customer's written authorization.
- Adhere to the stipulations of the contract, encompassing all responsibility and non-disclosure clauses.
- Prior to conducting the PT test, evaluate the equipment in a different laboratory setting.

- Ensure the customer is informed of any potential risks associated with the testing.
- Immediately inform the customer upon the discovery of a highly vulnerable vulnerability.
- Kindly provide just the statistically summarized outcomes of the social engineering assessment.
- The security guard and the cybercriminal should maintain a considerable distance from one another.

13.17 PT METHODOLOGIES

During the PT, specific systematic and reproducible procedures are utilized to guarantee the process's efficacy. A multitude of techniques has been developed throughout the years, each with distinct advantages and limitations. This chapter concisely analyzes the primary PT approaches, emphasizing their merits and drawbacks, and provides a comparative table to aid in the selection of the most appropriate method for particular situations.

13.18 OSSTMM METHODOLOGY

Open Source Security Testing Methodology Manual (OSSTMM) is an open-source methodology for PT that employs a holistic approach to information collecting, vulnerability assessment, PT, system takeover, information leaking, and test coverage (Giuseppi et al., 2019). OSSTMM is generally employed in intricate PT scenarios and is organized into many phases that function inside certain channels. Every channel has unique methods and phases, with a broad structure that may vary in implementation details according to domain, technological, and legal limitations. The OSSTMM delineates four modules necessitating further specification:

Phase I: Regulatory

- Evaluate posture: examine the relevant standards and regulatory frameworks.
- Logistics: document every process constraint inside the channel, encompassing both technical and physical limitations.
- Validation of active detection: Examining the identification and response to interactions.

Phase II: Definitions

- Conduct a visibility audit to evaluate the accessibility of information, systems, and procedures pertinent to the goal.
- Access verification: assess target access points.
- Evaluating trust: analyzing the trust connection between systems or individuals.

- Controls audit: assess controls to preserve confidentiality, integrity, and non-repudiation inside systems.

Phase III: Information phase

- Conduct a process audit to evaluate the company's safety protocols.
- Verification of configuration: testing protocols with differing levels of protection.
- Asset evaluation: examine the organization's tangible and intangible properties.
- Analyzing segregation: assessing the degree to which sensitive data has been compromised.
- Exposure assessment: analyzing potential interaction with personal information.
- Competitive intelligence: identify data breaches that may confer an edge to competitors.

Phase IV: Interactive control test phase

- Quarantine assessment: evaluate the effects of quarantine protocols on the designated recipient.
- Privilege audit: assess the effectiveness of permission and the potential ramifications of unauthorized privilege escalation.
- Survivability validation: assessing the resilience and recovery of the system.
- Examine alarms and logs: assess audit protocols to ensure precise event documentation.

OSSTMM encompasses all facets of a security assessment, including preparation, execution, and data analysis. The chapter in OSSTMM addressing international standards, laws, rules, and best practices is quite beneficial.

Advantages:

- Comprehensive strategy to ensure thorough test coverage.
- Ability to adjust to intricate physical therapy settings.
- Comprehensive documentation to guarantee a thorough comprehension of the procedure.

Limits:

- It may be overly complicated for basic PT.
- Demands extensive skill for efficient utilization.
- Absence of established criteria for physical therapy.

13.19 PTES METHODOLOGY

The Penetration Testing Execution Standard (PTES) is a standardized PT technique including five phases: pre-engagement, information collecting, discovery, operation, and reporting. PTES is frequently employed in less intricate

PT contexts (Dinis & Serrão, 2014). The PTES technique consists of seven (7) main components. The process encompasses the initial discussion regarding the necessity for a penetration test, followed by the stages of intelligence gathering and threat modeling, wherein testers acquire background information about the target organization. This is succeeded by the scanning, exploitation, and post-exploitation of vulnerabilities, where the testers' technical security expertise and business insight converge. Finally, the reporting phase encapsulates the entire procedure in a manner comprehensible and advantageous to the client.

13.20 THE STAGES OF THE PTES METHODOLOGY

13.20.1 Pre-commitment interactions

Pre-engagement meetings with the client facilitate discussions on the extent of coverage for the forthcoming penetration test. All obligations established with the client are delineated at this phase.

13.20.2 Information gathering

The information-gathering step involves collecting all relevant data on the firm being evaluated. To accomplish this, the tester employs social networks, Google hacking (to obtain sensitive data through specialized search queries), or footprinting (to gather publicly accessible information on target computer systems using techniques such as network enumeration, operating system identification, and Whois queries, among others). Network enumeration, operating system identification, Whois inquiries, SNMP requests, port scanning, etc. The acquired information on the target offers significant insights into the security protocols.

13.20.3 Threat modeling

Threat modeling utilizes the information acquired during intelligence collection. The data are examined to identify the most efficient strategy for assaulting the target system. The primary objective is to ascertain the vulnerabilities of the target and formulate an assault strategy.

13.20.4 Vulnerability analysis

Upon identifying the most successful assault on the target, the subsequent stage is to ascertain the method of access. At this step, the information collected in prior rounds is analyzed to assess the feasibility of the selected assault. Specifically, data obtained from port scans, vulnerability assessments, or intelligence collection is taken into account.

13.20.5 Operation

The exploitation phase predominantly employs brute force methods. This step is initiated only if a certain sort of exploit is guaranteed to accomplish the intended objective. It is possible that enhanced security measures might restrict access to the target system.

13.20.6 Post-op

The post-exploitation phase is an essential component of PT. The process begins upon the breach of the targeted system and assesses which data within the system holds the most value. The objective is to demonstrate the financial repercussions that a leak or loss of this information might impose on the firm.

13.20.7 Reports

The reporting step is unequivocally the most critical aspect of an intrusion test since it must substantiate its need. The report delineates the outcomes of the penetration test and the methodology employed. Primarily, it should emphasize the vulnerabilities that require rectification and the methods to safeguard the target system from such assaults. Engaging a professional services firm to conduct an information systems vulnerability audit is strongly advised in an increasingly complex IT landscape, which is therefore expanding its attack surface. Regularly scheduling penetration tests is recommended, as information systems develop concurrently with infrastructure changes, leading to the emergence of vulnerabilities. Figure 13.3 illustrates the several phases of the PTES technique.

Benefits:

- Systematic methodology to ensure test repeatability.
- Appropriate for less intricate physical therapy settings.
- Comprehensive documentation to guarantee a thorough comprehension of the procedure.

Limits:

- May exhibit insufficient adaptability to intricate physical therapy situations.
- The testing steps may be restrictive and fail to encompass all facets of PT.
- Certain elements of PT are up to the examiner's discretion.

13.21 NIST METHODOLOGY SP 800-115

NIST SP 800-115 is a PT methodology developed by the US National Institute of Standards and Technology (NIST) (Pascoe, 2023). The process consists of four phases: planning, information collecting, PT, and reporting. NIST SP 800-115 is frequently utilized in governmental and regulated settings.

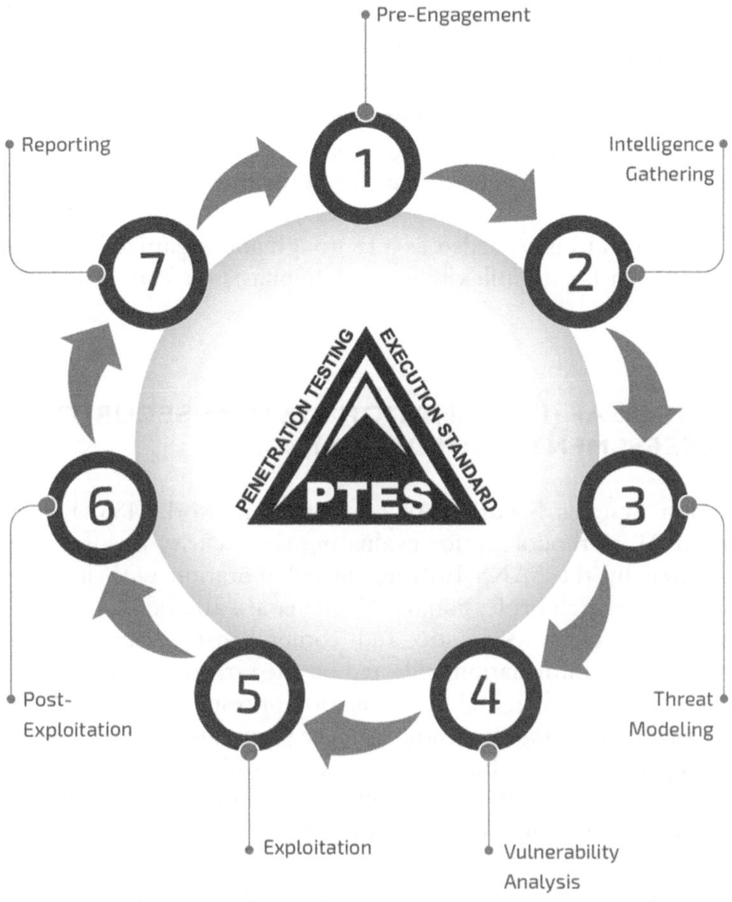

Figure 13.3 The stages in the PTES methodology.

The NIST SP 800-115 approach comprises six primary phases:

- The planning and preparation phase entails establishing the PT objectives, securing requisite authorizations, and formulating a roadmap for subsequent operations.
- Information acquisition: This phase seeks to collect data about the PT target, including IP addresses, domain names, and contact details.
- Vulnerability detection: This phase entails scanning the target to ascertain known and prospective vulnerabilities. Vulnerability scanning software can automate this process.
- Exploitation: In this phase, you will gain unauthorized access to the targeted systems by leveraging the identified vulnerabilities. There exist two categories of attacks: manual and automated.

- Preserve access: Should the attacker get illegal entry, this phase involves sustaining that access to further investigate and compromise the target systems.
- Results Analysis: This step involves examining the PT results and composing a comprehensive report on the found vulnerabilities, attack methodologies, and suggestions for mitigating the vulnerabilities.

NIST SP 800-115 is regarded as a thorough and organized technique; yet, it faces criticism for its inflexibility and emphasis on known vulnerabilities over new ones.

13.22 THE ISSAF (INFORMATION SYSTEMS SECURITY ASSESSMENT FRAMEWORK)

Information Systems Security Assessment Framework (ISSAF) is a well-recognized PT methodology for evaluating the security of information systems, created by the SANS Institute in collaboration with its IT security teaching and research professionals (Nabila et al., 2023).

ISSAF conducts a systematic and comprehensive security assessment encompassing the information collected on the target, the vulnerability finding phase, exploit testing, and the evaluation of results. The ISSAF outlines a seven-phase methodology for doing PT. The preparatory phase: This involves strategizing the PT by delineating objectives and expectations, identifying stakeholders, establishing test parameters, defining RoE, selecting tools, forming work teams, and outlining processes to be adhered to.

- The data collecting step include understanding the target system and its environment. At this juncture, reconnaissance methods may be utilized to ascertain hosts, open ports, active services, operating systems, web applications, and analogous components.
- The threat modeling step involves risk assessments utilizing risk analysis methods to identify essential assets and weaknesses that may be exploited by attackers. This phase also formulates a framework for prospective assault scenarios and their corresponding repercussions.
- The vulnerability finding process entails doing automated vulnerability assessments to detect security flaws inside the system. This phase may also involve doing manual testing to verify the discovered results.
- In the exploitation phase, vulnerabilities are utilized to obtain unauthorized access to the system or data. This phase may also involve the application of social engineering strategies to mislead consumers into revealing confidential information.
- The post-exploitation phase must concentrate on maintaining illicit access to the system or data. It may include creating additional accounts, modifying permissions, and deleting files and/or activity records.

- The reporting step entails articulating the outcomes of the PT and communicating them to the stakeholders. This must include the repair of detected vulnerabilities and suggestions to assess the overall security posture.

The benefits of ISSAF are numerous:

- Systematic approach: ISSAF employs a methodical and organized methodology that ensures comprehensive coverage of all security facets of the target system.
- Flexibility: ISSAF is engineered to be adaptive to many circumstances and physical training conditions, rendering it exceptionally versatile.
- ISSAF offers a comprehensive analysis of the target system's security by finding vulnerabilities and evaluating their possible consequences.
- ISSAF advocates for comprehensive recording of each phase in the PT process, hence enhancing the analysis and presentation of outcomes.
- Nonetheless, ISSAF possesses several limitations:
- Complexity: Owing to its systematic characteristics, ISSAF may be intricate, necessitating comprehensive training and experience for its utilization.
- Time and expense: ISSAF may be labor-intensive and expensive, necessitating meticulous preparation, and the participation of several specialists.
- Insufficient updates: While ISSAF is extensively utilized, its most recent version is from 2005, potentially overlooking contemporary technology and vulnerabilities.
- ISSAF is a comprehensive and adaptable technique that provides a profound insight into the security of target systems. Nonetheless, its intricacy and possible expense may not be appropriate for many physical therapy situations. Furthermore, its absence of recent upgrades may restrict its applicability in some instances.

13.23 OWASP METHODOLOGY

Open Worldwide Application Security Project (OWASP) is a nonprofit organization dedicated to enhancing online application security by providing information, tools, and standards. The OWASP PT methodology addresses web application vulnerabilities and is among the most prevalent methods for web application security testing (Bach-Nutman, 2020). Therefore, let us examine the OWASP approach in greater detail: stages, advantages and disadvantages, and so forth.

13.23.1 OWASP phases

- Planning and reconnaissance: This step entails collecting information on the web application to be evaluated, encompassing its objectives, users, foundational technologies, and architecture. It also delineates the application's access points and danger zones.

- Application mapping: This step entails delineating the architecture and content of the web application, encompassing URLs, forms, cookies, parameters, and dynamic components. It facilitates a deeper comprehension of the application and enhances the planning of the following examinations.
- Vulnerability identification: This phase employs automated techniques to identify known vulnerabilities in the online application, including SQL injections, cross-site scripting (XSS), and authentication weaknesses, among others. It also recognizes application-specific vulnerabilities that may only be identified by manual testing.
- Manual assessment: This step involves manual testing to identify application-specific vulnerabilities, including business logic flaws, session management issues, and data validation mistakes. It facilitates a deeper comprehension of the vulnerabilities identified in the prior phase and allows for the identification of vulnerabilities that can only be uncovered through manual testing.
- Exploitation: This phase entails leveraging identified vulnerabilities to illustrate their possible effects on the application and data. It also validates the vulnerabilities identified in the earlier rounds.
- Documentation and reporting: This phase involves cataloging the identified vulnerabilities, assessing their possible effect, detailing the reproduction steps, and providing suggestions for remediation. It facilitates the clear and succinct presentation of test results.

13.23.2 Benefits of OWASP

- OWASP offers free, open-source PT tools and materials to enhance online application security.
- The OWASP approach emphasizes online application vulnerabilities and offers precise rules for their detection and remediation.
- OWASP advocates for a comprehensive strategy for web application security, incorporating security testing at every stage of the software development lifecycle.
- The OWASP methodology is continuously revised to address emerging threats and technology.

13.23.3 Limits of OWASP

While the OWASP approach has several benefits, it also possesses specific limitations:

- Complexity: OWASP is an intricate approach necessitating a profound comprehension of IT security and PT methodologies. Employing this approach for security testing may be exceedingly time-intensive and frequently necessitates substantial technological and human resources.

- Inconsistency: The intricate nature of the OWASP approach results in significant variability in testing outcomes across different testers. This complicates the comparison of outcomes and the formulation of security judgments.
- Update: As information technology security advances swiftly, tools, methodologies, and vulnerabilities are in a state of perpetual flux. The OWASP approach requires continuous updates to maintain its efficacy. Maintaining an intricate current process might prove to be difficult.
- Technical orientation: OWASP is a framework centered on the technical dimensions of information technology security. It neglects the organizational, human, and procedural dimensions of security, which are equally vital in security management.
- Tool dependency: While the OWASP methodology does not mandate certain PT tools, it does depend on several tools to enhance security testing. This may render the process reliant on specific tools, perhaps leading to complications if these tools become outdated or unsupported.

13.24 CYBER KILL CHAIN METHODOLOGY

The cyber kill chain methodology is a component of intelligence-driven protection aimed at identifying and thwarting malicious infiltration efforts. Security professionals may employ this strategy to understand how assailants achieve their objectives (Yadav & Rao, 2015).

Cyber death chains extend the concept of military kill chains, offering a framework for safeguarding cyberspace. This method aims to improve the capacity for proactive detection and response to intrusions. The Cyber Elimination Chain comprises a seven-step security protocol designed to mitigate the effects of cyber threats.

Lockheed Martin asserts that cyberattacks can progress through seven separate phases, commencing with identification and concluding with the effective execution of the operation. Familiarity with the cyberattack kill chain enables security professionals to more effectively implement security measures at different stages of the attack lifecycle to prevent assaults. It also aids in comprehending the phases of an assault, which is advantageous for predicting the strategies employed by an adversary. Figure 13.4 shows the several steps that make up the Cyber Kill Chain methodology:

- Reconnaissance: Acquiring information about the target to identify vulnerabilities.
- Weaponization: Develop a deployable hostile payload utilizing an exploit and a backdoor.
- Delivery: Transmit the armed package to the recipient by email, USB, etc.

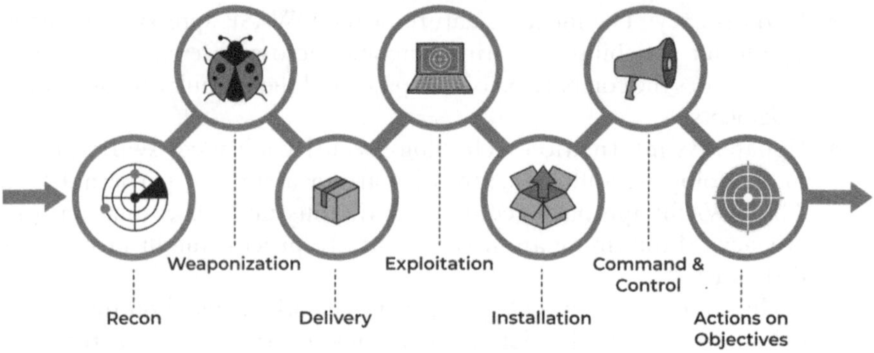

Figure 13.4 Cyber kill chain methodology.

- Utilization Exploiting a vulnerability through the execution of code on the victim's machine.
- Installation: Execute malware on a designated system.
- Command & Control: Establish a command and control channel for bidirectional communication and data transmission.
- Actions on objectives: Executing steps to attain objectives/goals.

Figure 13.5 shows an example of each Cyber Kill Chain Methodology step.

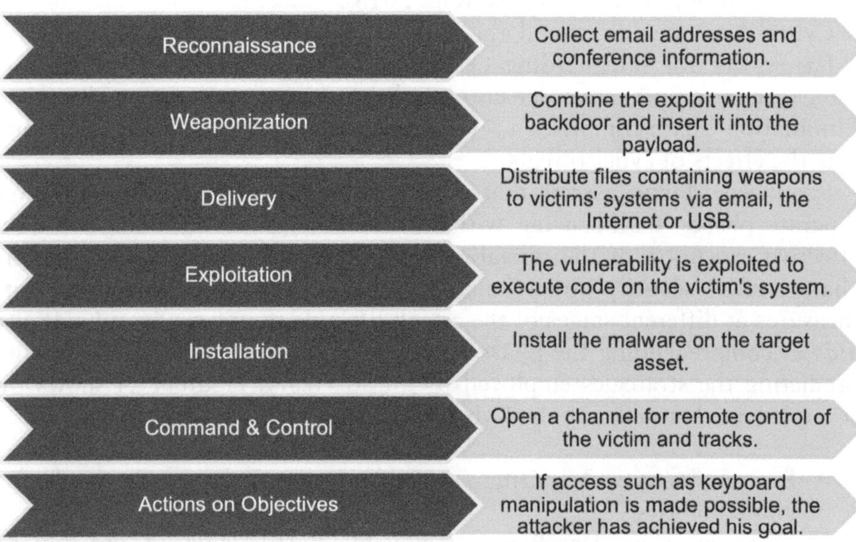

Figure 13.5 Cyber Kill Chain illustration.

13.25 MITRE ATT&CK

MITRE ATT&CK (Adversarial Tactics, Techniques, and Common Knowledge) is a framework and knowledge repository that delineates an adversary's actions during the execution of cyberattacks (Pennington et al., 2019). It came from the MITRE Corporation, a nonprofit entity that oversees federally financed research and development institutions. It provides a comprehensive database of methods and strategies utilized by adversaries during assaults, including initial access, execution, persistence, and exfiltration. It outlines supplementary techniques and methodologies, including reconnaissance, credential acquisition, lateral movement, and data exfiltration. ATT&CK is widely employed by cybersecurity experts, threat intelligence analysts, and researchers to understand certain cyber risks and formulate effective protection tactics against attacks by threat actors (Chamkar et al., 2024; Hubbard, 2020). MITRE ATT&CK provides a standardized lexicon and architecture for defining and categorizing adversary actions to improve cybersecurity across various enterprises. The framework is regularly updated to incorporate new knowledge on strategies, approaches, and processes based on actual cases (Chamkar et al., 2022). Thus, it is relevant, valid, and advantageous in aiding firms in their struggle against escalating cyber dangers.

The fundamental principle of MITRE ATT&CK is straightforward: although attackers may vary, their modus operandi, specifically TTPs, remains consistent. MITRE ATT&CK, or Adversarial Tactics, Techniques, and Common Knowledge, is a prominent framework within the MITRE FMX project, functioning as a knowledge repository that systematically catalogs the common TTPs employed by Advanced Persistent Threats (APTs). This framework serves as a fundamental reference for security professionals to begin understanding, analyzing, and safeguarding against advanced cyber threats. The framework's additional objective is to unify risk identification and mitigation strategies across diverse environments by modeling adversaries' behavior instead of their identity.

The MITRE ATT&CK framework is based on a matrix that describes the typical stages of a computer attack, from preparation to post-exploitation. Here are the steps of MITRE ATT&CK:

1. Reconnaissance: In this initial phase, attackers gather information about their targets to identify potential vulnerabilities and weaknesses in their defenses. This can include activities such as social engineering, Open Source Intelligence (OSINT) collection, and port analysis.
2. Initial access: Once attackers have identified potential weaknesses, they use a variety of methods to gain initial access to their target environment. This can include exploiting vulnerabilities, phishing, or using stolen credentials.
3. Execution: Once attackers gain initial access, they typically execute code or tools to achieve their goals. This can include running malware,

performing command and control (C2) communications, or exploiting vulnerabilities to elevate privileges.

4. Persistence: To maintain access to the target environment, attackers often use a variety of persistence techniques to ensure that their tools and malware remain active even after the initial attack vector has been removed.
5. Elevation of privilege: To gain deeper access to the target environment, attackers often seek to elevate their privileges, allowing them to perform actions that are typically reserved for administrators or other high-level users.
6. Defense evasion: To avoid detection, attackers use various techniques to evade detection and remain undetected for as long as possible. This can include activities such as evading antivirus, obfuscation, and using encryption.
7. Credential access: Once in the target environment, attackers often seek to obtain legitimate user credentials, which can provide them with additional access and privileges.
8. Discovery: At this point, attackers perform reconnaissance on the target environment to gather information about the network topology, user accounts, and installed software.
9. Lateral movement: Once attackers have gained credentials or other access, they often move laterally into the target environment to gain access to additional systems or data.
10. Collection: Once attackers gain access to target systems, they typically begin collecting information or stealing data from those systems.
11. Exfiltration: Attackers will often seek to exfiltrate data or other assets they have collected from the target environment, using a variety of techniques to avoid detection.
12. Command and Control (C2): Refers to an attack technique used by attackers to establish communication with a compromised system and give instructions remotely from a command and control (C&C) server. Attackers use this technique to gain access to confidential information, to download or execute malicious files on the compromised system, to exfiltrate sensitive data, or to extend their grip on the organization's network.

These steps are not necessarily linear or sequential, and different attackers may use different combinations of tactics and techniques depending on their goals and the target environment.

The fundamental principle of MITRE ATT&CK is straightforward: although attackers may vary, their modus operandi, specifically TTPs, remains consistent (Al-Sada et al., 2024; Copeland & Copeland, 2021). MITRE ATT&CK, or Adversarial Tactics, Techniques, and Common Knowledge, is a prominent framework within the MITRE FMX project, functioning as a knowledge repository that systematically catalogs the common TTPs employed by

APTs (Kinnunen, 2022). This framework serves as a fundamental reference for security professionals to begin understanding, analyzing, and safeguarding against advanced cyber threats. The framework's additional objective is to unify risk identification and mitigation strategies across diverse environments by modeling adversaries' behavior instead of their identity (Figure 13.6).

13.25.1 Adversary profile

Creating an opponent profile is an efficient approach to build a strategy plan for the red team's performance in evaluations. It may be as simple as the table seen above. The aim is to produce a succinct statement detailing the acts the red team will emulate. The profile above is based on the extraction of TTPs from a threat intelligence report on APT19. Alternatively, one may discover APT19 on the MITRE ATT&CK website to obtain a similar description and associated procedures, as seen in Table 13.1.

13.25.2 Contribution of MITRE

The MITRE ATT&CK architecture constitutes a universally accessible repository of adversary strategies and methods derived from empirical observations. It serves as a basis for formulating certain threat models and approaches within the business sector, government, and cybersecurity community. MITRE ATT&CK offers a detailed matrix of tactics and strategies employed by threat actors, facilitating the comprehension of attack behaviors and improving the detection, protection, and analysis of cybersecurity threats. Its contribution enhances security posture by fostering educated decision-making, establishing a shared lexicon for cybersecurity risks, and strategically orchestrating defenses against advanced cyber threats. The ATT&CK architecture, bolstered by ongoing updates and contributions from global cybersecurity experts, is an essential tool for effectively countering and mitigating cyberattacks. Figure 13.7 shows the contribution of MITRE ATT&CK.

13.25.3 Tools for pentesting according to MITRE ATT&CK

For each stage of the MITRE ATT&CK framework, there are a variety of tools and techniques that attackers can use to carry out their attack. Here is a non-exhaustive list of tools commonly used for each step:

1. Reconnaissance:
    - Amass: A tool for gathering information about targets, using various techniques such as crawling, scraping, and brute force DNS.
    - Sn1per: An automated vulnerability scanning and network reconnaissance tool, which performs port, service, and vulnerability scans.

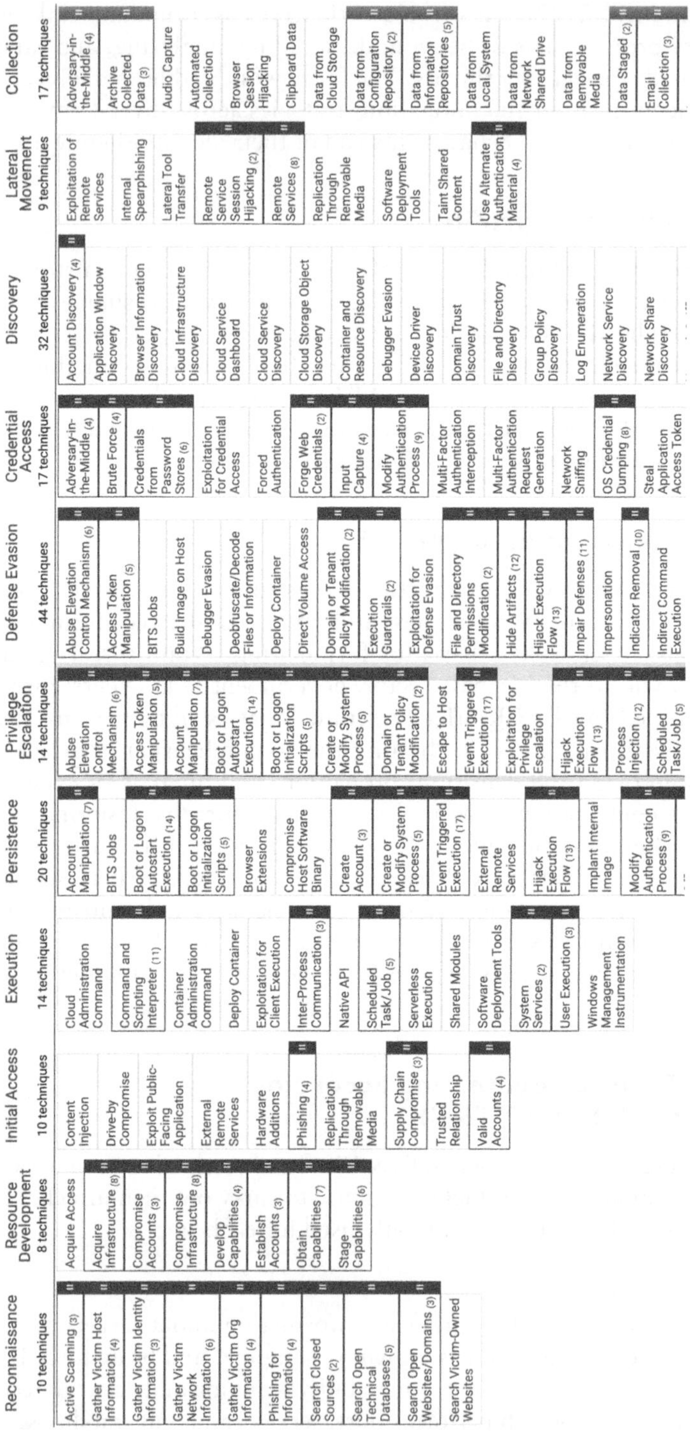

Figure 13.6 MITRE ATT&CK matrix.

Table 13.1 TTPs of APT19

Category	*Description*
Description	APT19 is a China-based threat group that has targeted various industries, including defense, finance, energy, pharmaceuticals, telecommunications, high-tech, education, manufacturing, and legal services.
But et intention	Exist in the network to enumerate systems and information to maintain command and control to support future attacks.
Initial Access	Phishing emails with malicious RTF and XLSM attachments to deliver the initial exploits.
Execution/Evasion	PowerShell; Regsvr32; Rundll32; Scripting
C2 Overview	HTTP via common port—TCP port 80 for C2
Persistence	Modify existing service—Port 22 malware is registered as a service

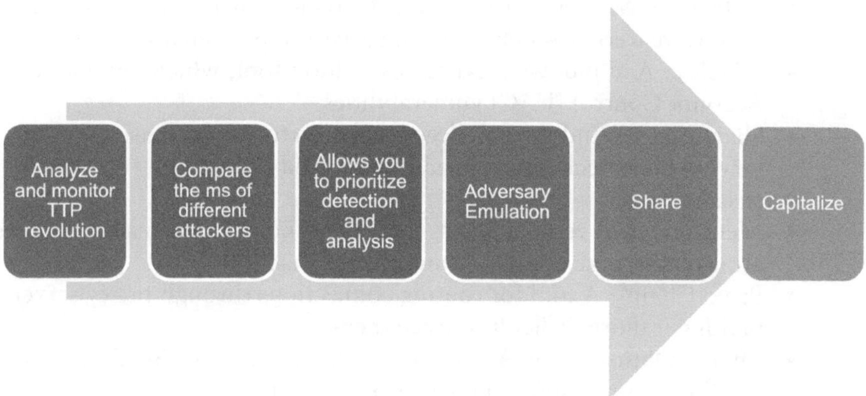

Figure 13.7 MITRE ATT&CK contribution.

- theHarvester: A tool for gathering information about targets by retrieving email addresses, domain names, and subdomains.
- Recon-ng: An automated web reconnaissance tool, which collects information about targets from public and private sources.
- Maltego: A tool for information gathering and network mapping, which uses graphs to visualize the relationships between the different elements of a target.

2. Initial Access:
   - Aircrack-ng: A WiFi password cracking tool, used to recover WiFi encryption keys.
   - Gophish: An automated phishing tool, which allows you to create and launch phishing campaigns targeting an organization's employees.
   - Bash Bunny: A hardware hacking tool, which can be inserted into a computer to execute malicious commands or steal data.

3. Execution:
    - macro_pack: A tool for creating malicious Office macros, which can be used to execute code remotely.
    - Donut: A stealth tool to run malicious PE files without being detected by antivirus software.
4. Persistence:
    - Empire: A post-exploitation tool, which allows attackers to maintain access to a target over the long term.
    - Impacket: A Python script library for communication with network protocols, which can be used to gain persistent access to a target system.
    - pwncat: A post-exploitation tool that allows communication with a compromised system via a network connection.
5. Privilege Escalation:
    - Rubeus: A Windows privilege escalation tool, which allows attackers to retrieve Kerberos tickets to gain access to protected systems.
    - UACMe: A Windows privilege escalation tool, which exploits User Account Control (UAC) vulnerabilities.
    - SharpUp: A Windows privilege escalation tool, which uses Windows service abuse techniques to gain privileged access.
6. Defense Evasion:
    - Meterpreter: A remote access tool for Windows systems that allows attackers to take control of an infected machine.
    - ProxyChains: A tool for routing connections through proxy servers, making it more difficult to trace them.
    - Invoke-Obfuscation: A tool for obfuscating PowerShell code and evading security software detection mechanisms.
    - Veil: A shellcode generator for creating custom payloads for social engineering attacks and PT.
7. Credentials Access:
    - Mimikatz: A password recovery tool for Windows systems that can extract passwords stored in memory.
    - Hashcat: A password cracking tool used to recover passwords from hashes.
    - Responder: A tool that can be used to capture credentials in response to network service requests.
    - Cain and Abel: A password recovery tool for Windows systems that can recover passwords stored locally or on the network.
    - John the Ripper: An open-source password cracking tool that supports many hashing algorithms.
    - THC Hydra: A command-line password cracking tool that supports many protocols.
    - LaZagne: An open-source password recovery tool that can recover passwords stored on the system.

8. Discovery:
    - BloodHound: An Active Directory topology visualization tool for mapping potential attacks.
    - Seatbelt: A tool for collecting system information about Windows machines.
    - Kismet: A tool for detecting and analyzing wireless networks.
    - ADRecon: A tool for collecting Active Directory information.
9. Lateral movement:
    - Mimikatz: A password recovery tool for Windows systems that can be used to compromise user accounts and move laterally across the network.
    - PsExec: A tool for executing commands remotely on Windows machines.
    - WMIOps: A tool for running WMI commands remotely on Windows machines.
    - CrackMapExec: A tool that can be used to run remote commands on Windows and Linux machines.
    - Infection Monkey: A tool to test the security of a network by simulating real attacks.
10. Collection:
    - PowerSploit: A suite of PowerShell tools for vulnerability scanning and data extraction on Windows systems.
    - PowerUpSQL: A tool for detecting and exploiting security vulnerabilities in SQL Server database servers.
11. Exfiltration:
    - DnsCat2: It is a data tunneling tool that allows data to be sent through the DNS protocol. It is often used to exfiltrate data by bypassing firewalls or IDS.
    - CloakifyFactory: It is a tool that allows you to clothes data by transforming it into harmless formats, such as images or audio files, in order to exfiltrate it without being detected.
    - PowerShell-RAT: It is a remote control tool that allows attackers to access a compromised system and take control remotely. It uses PowerShell to execute commands and retrieve data remotely and can be used to exfiltrate sensitive data.
12. Command and Control:
    - Metasploit: This is a project related to the security of computer systems. Its purpose is to provide information on vulnerabilities in computer systems and to assist in penetration and the development of signatures for IDS.
    - Covenant: Covenant is a. NET command and control framework that aims to highlight the. NET attack surface, facilitate the use of. NET offensive crafting, and serve as a collaborative command and control platform for red teams.

- Empire: This is a post-exploitation and adversary emulation framework that is used to help red teams and penetration testers. The Empire server is written in Python 3 and is modular to allow for operator flexibility. Empire comes with a built-in client that can be used remotely to access the server. There is also a graphical interface available to remotely access the Empire server, Starkiller.

13.25.4 Challenges in PT

PT is essential for assessing the security of systems and networks by mimicking actual attacks to identify vulnerabilities. Nevertheless, as technology advances swiftly, PT encounters numerous substantial hurdles, rendering it a vital domain for continuous research. This literature analysis examines the primary challenges in PT and identifies deficiencies in current approaches.

A principal problem is the rapid advancement of foundational technologies, like Wi-Fi, 5G, and IoT, which generate progressively intricate testing settings (Dalalana Bertoglio & Zorzo, 2017). Although research has thoroughly examined PT in multilayered networks, a deficiency persists in evaluating security within highly protected systems where a singular important hardware component is linked via Ethernet, especially in white-box testing contexts (insider threats). Moreover, current PT frameworks frequently prioritize automated testing, which, although efficient, may generate false positives and overlook subtle attack routes (Hilario et al., 2024). Moreover, most frameworks adopt a black-box methodology, presuming the attacker had no prior knowledge of the system, hence diminishing their efficacy in situations where an insider has access to system specifications. The extensive nature of these frameworks may result in inefficiencies by assessing unnecessary vulnerabilities, hence depleting critical time and resources.

Automation poses an additional challenge in PT. Although automated technologies aid in detecting vulnerabilities, they cannot fully replace manual testing. Automated scans frequently fail to identify complex vulnerabilities and may produce false positives and false negatives, resulting in inaccurate security evaluations (Gupta et al., 2023). Furthermore, in settings characterized by intricate configurations or outdated systems, automation may be unfeasible or inefficient.

The deficiency of proficient penetration testers exacerbates the process. Successful PT necessitates a comprehensive comprehension of system architectures, network security, and adversarial techniques. Many businesses, especially those with constrained resources, encounter challenges in finding and developing competent security experts. Accessibility is a challenge, as PT necessitates authorized access to systems, networks, and applications. This can be especially challenging in large organizations with rigorous access constraints.

A significant problem is the potential for false positives produced by PT technologies. These technologies may identify fictitious or non-exploitable vulnerabilities, causing security teams to waste time and resources on issues that present no genuine threat. Moreover, PT may interfere with business operations, requiring meticulous preparation to reduce downtime and operational disturbances. Legal and ethical considerations must be addressed, as PT entails simulating attacks on organizational systems. Adhering to legislation and securing clear authorization from stakeholders is crucial for conducting testing responsibly (Fatima et al., 2023).

In summary, PT encounters various problems, such as the swift advancement of technology, the inadequacies of existing testing procedures, the restrictions of automation, and the necessity for proficient individuals. These problems underscore the necessity for additional study to improve PT methodologies. To effectively address these difficulties, companies must set clear testing objectives, utilize suitable tools and processes, perform comprehensive risk assessments, and engage key stakeholders throughout the testing process. Engaging with seasoned penetration testers is essential for mitigating security threats and maintaining adherence to legal and ethical norms.

13.25.5 AI-driven PT

Generative AI (GenAI) and Large Language Models (LLMs), including OpenAI's ChatGPT, are transforming the PT (pentesting) sector by automating tasks, enhancing creativity, and enabling real-time adaptability. The integration of AI-driven tools in PT enhances efficiency, accuracy, and proactive threat management. GenAI has advanced PT (pentesting) by offering innovative insights to improve cybersecurity evaluations. Organizations can utilize advanced AI model capabilities to simulate real-world attacks for automated reconnaissance and to defend against complex cyber threats. GenAI facilitates automated data collection from public sources, customization of phishing emails, and the development of persuasive social engineering scenarios, encompassing deepfakes and personalized impersonations. These tools enable ethical hackers to replicate attack techniques with compelling realism, focusing on credential harvesting, phishing campaigns, and malware deployment targeting specific vulnerabilities and behavioral patterns. GenAI facilitates the creation of comprehensive pentesting reports, examines attack patterns, and suggests security strategies relevant to the proactive defense. Although scalable, efficient, and adaptable, GenAI presents new challenges, including ethical dilemmas, data privacy issues, instances of false positives, and the potential for undue reliance on systems. The conduct of an unethical individual with access to GenAI technology underscores the necessity of ethical guidelines, prior consent-based testing, and robust data protection strategies. The risks associated with GenAI are mitigated by its ability to simulate and capture evolving threat tactics in response to contemporary cybersecurity challenges. In the future, GenAI may facilitate advancements in proactive threat hunting, IoT and cloud security testing, and real-time defense. Organizations integrating GenAI into their PT workflows will establish security infrastructures that are resilient to contemporary cyber threats while adhering to ethical AI practices.

13.25.6 Key features of AI-driven PT

1. **Automation of Repetitive Tasks:** AI tools can automate mundane but critical tasks such as scanning for vulnerabilities, generating reports, and monitoring network traffic. This allows penetration testers to focus on more complex, high-level analysis.
2. **Advanced Threat Detection:** AI-driven systems excel at detecting sophisticated and zero-day vulnerabilities that may go unnoticed using traditional methods. Machine learning models are trained to identify patterns and anomalies indicative of potential breaches.
3. **Predictive Analytics:** Leveraging past attack data, AI tools predict potential vulnerabilities and attack vectors. This enables penetration testers to anticipate and mitigate risks before they are exploited.
4. **Real-Time Analysis:** AI enhances the speed of PT by providing real-time analysis of systems, applications, and networks. This significantly reduces the time required to uncover critical vulnerabilities.
5. **Enhanced Reporting and Insights:** AI tools can generate comprehensive and detailed reports on identified vulnerabilities and their potential impact. This helps organizations prioritize and address issues more effectively.

13.25.7 Benefits of AI-driven PT

- **Efficiency:** AI processes large datasets and performs reconnaissance tasks rapidly, saving significant time.
- **Scalability:** AI-driven solutions can handle testing across extensive and complex systems, making them ideal for enterprise-level environments.
- **Accuracy:** Machine learning algorithms reduce human error, ensuring precise identification of vulnerabilities.
- **Cost-Effectiveness:** By automating processes, AI reduces the need for extensive human resources, cutting operational costs.
- **Continuous Testing:** AI tools enable ongoing assessments, providing organizations with real-time insights into their security posture.

13.25.8 Tools for AI-driven PT

AI-powered PT tools have become indispensable for ethical hackers and security professionals. Below is a curated list of tools along with their features and sources:

1. **HackerGPT**

   A versatile tool designed to assist in identifying vulnerabilities and automating tasks.

   Source: HackerGPT

2. **BurpGPT**
   Integrates with Burp Suite to enhance vulnerability scanning using AI-powered insights.
   Source: BurpGPT
3. **PentestGPT**
   Automates reconnaissance, scanning, and reporting to support penetration testers.
   Source: PentestGPT
4. **BugBountyGPT**
   Tailored for bug bounty professionals to identify and report vulnerabilities.
   Source: BugBountyGPT
5. **CybGPT**
   A comprehensive tool offering AI-powered security assessments and threat intelligence integration.
   Source: CybGPT
6. **h4ckGPT**
   Real-time assistance and insights for vulnerability identification.
   Source: h4ckGPT
7. **Hacking APIs GPT**
   Automates API vulnerability scanning and reporting.
   Source: Hacking APIs GPT
8. **BugHunterGPT**
   Designed to detect and report security vulnerabilities efficiently.
   Source: BugHunterGPT
9. **Ethical Hacker GPT**
   Provides AI-driven vulnerability assessments and real-time hacking insights.
   Source: Ethical Hacker GPT
10. **GPT White Hack**
    Real-time recommendations for mitigating identified vulnerabilities during PT.
    Source: GPT White Hack
11. **DeepExploit**
    An AI-powered PT tool designed to automate and optimize the process of identifying and exploiting vulnerabilities in target systems.
    Source: DeepExploit

13.25.9 Applications of AI in pentesting

1. **Reconnaissance:** AI tools automate information gathering, providing comprehensive target profiles quickly. This phase includes identifying subdomains, analyzing exposed credentials, and mapping network topologies.

2. **Vulnerability Scanning**: AI enhances vulnerability scanners by identifying misconfigurations, outdated software, and potential entry points more accurately.
3. **Phishing Simulations**: AI-driven tools can craft realistic phishing emails to test organizational security awareness and employee susceptibility to social engineering.
4. **Web Application Testing**: AI tools focus on application-specific vulnerabilities, such as SQL injections, cross-site scripting (XSS), and broken authentication.
5. **Network Security Analysis**: AI monitors traffic patterns to detect unusual behavior that may signify breaches or attack attempts.
6. **Continuous Monitoring**: AI-driven systems offer real-time insights into security vulnerabilities, enabling immediate mitigation.

13.25.10 Challenges and ethical considerations

- **Overreliance on AI**: Although GenAI offers substantial benefits, excessive dependence on its outputs may result in critical oversights. AI models like ChatGPT frequently generate responses based on environmental patterns and lack the contextual understanding of a human expert. A false positive, which refers to the erroneous identification of a non-existent vulnerability, or a false negative, which involves the failure to detect existing vulnerabilities, can lead to penetration tests, data exfiltration, or even remote-access cyberattacks. The outputs of AI may lack accuracy; it can hallucinate or misinterpret a query, potentially causing confusion among testers. Human intervention is essential to validate AI insights and guarantee an equitable and impartial evaluation of security vulnerabilities.
- **Ethical and Legal Concerns**: The function of AI in PT raises significant ethical dilemmas. There exists a risk that, if exploited due to imprudent maximization, ChatGPT may become vulnerable to jailbreaking or manipulation, thereby providing tangible opportunities for malicious entities to automate the development of exploits, phishing schemes, or malware. Additional ethical considerations may arise when AI begins to simulate attacks that could potentially expose sensitive information. Moreover, there exists a potential violation of human privacy when sensitive information is unintentionally extracted for training AI models utilizing publicly accessible data. The misapplication by unauthorized individuals poses a risk, thereby exposing AI providers for PT organizations to potential legal complications.
- **Inherent Bias in AI Models**: GenAI systems are beneficial or detrimental based on the quality of their training data. Biases or omissions in training data may result in distorted or unreliable outcomes. If an AI model is predominantly trained on contemporary attack techniques, it may fail to identify vulnerabilities in legacy systems or nonstandard environments. Likewise, unrepresentative data may cause the AI to overlook vulnerabilities pertinent solely to niche industries or specific

organizational configurations. Addressing this necessitates a meticulous selection of training datasets, followed by periodic updates to adapt to emerging cyber threats.

- **Skill Gap in Using AI Tools**: The integration of AI into PT workflows may pose a daunting learning curve for many security professionals. Numerous individuals may lack the technical expertise to effectively utilize GenAI tools and interpret their results, leading to inefficiency or misapplication. Moreover, the lack of seamless integration with other PT tools, such as Nmap, Nessus, or Burp Suite, may hinder their overall utility without the necessary technical expertise.

13.25.11 Risks associated with generative AI in PT

- **Escalation of Cyber Threats**: While GenAI can enhance the capabilities of security professionals, it may also be leveraged to benefit attackers. An assailant could employ AI to create advanced phishing emails, produce polymorphic malware, or automate the reconnaissance and exploitation stages. The proficient application of AI for social engineering exemplifies this capability by nefarious individuals. Europol highlighted the utilization of LLMs in creating deepfakes or impersonating individuals, undermining trust, and amplifying the effects of social engineering attacks. The accessibility of these AI tools facilitates even the most ordinary hacker's ability to exploit and manipulate them for intricate, evolving attack strategies.
- **Advanced Persistent Threats (APTs)**: Hackers can exploit GenAI tools to create highly targeted and covert APTs. Malefactors may employ AI to assess vulnerabilities and develop customized exploits, thereby securing extended access to a network while evading detection. Utilizing APTs enabled by polymorphic malware, which allows for dynamic code alteration to circumvent conventional detection systems, hackers are poised to cause significantly greater harm to an organization.
- **Autonomous and Self-Propagating Attacks**: Due to the rapid advancement of AI technologies, the risks of autonomous cyberattacks may further evolve to adapt to new environments. Rapid self-propagating attacks can extensively infect networks from various perspectives, exploiting vulnerabilities autonomously. The researchers demonstrated that AI-generated malware can evade traditional security systems and can replicate itself with minor modifications, thereby increasing its difficulty to detect and contain.
- **Uncontrolled AI Development**: The swift progression of AI technologies may lead to the evolution of autonomous cyberattack risks, enabling adaptation to new environments. Rapid self-propagating attacks can extensively compromise networks from multiple angles, autonomously exploiting vulnerabilities. The researchers illustrated that AI-generated malware can circumvent conventional security systems and can self-replicate with minimal alterations, thus enhancing its detectability and containment challenges.

13.26 CONCLUSION

PT is essential in contemporary cyber defense, enabling organizations to proactively identify vulnerabilities and assess security measures. In addition to the technical advantages of PT, there are numerous actionable insights that align with the organization's business objectives, enhancing the protection of critical assets, mitigating risk, and ensuring compliance. This chapter discusses methodologies, ranging from structural approaches like OSSTMM and NIST SP 800-115 to dynamic frameworks such as MITRE ATT&CK and the Cyber Kill Chain, emphasizing the necessity and significance of standardized and repeatable processes to attain reliable outcomes. The integration of AI tools signifies a significant transformation in the efficiency, accuracy, and scalability of PT operations. As cyber threats continue to evolve, PT emerges as a fundamental component of an organization's defensive strategy, allowing it to stay ahead of potential attackers while fostering trust and resilience in the dynamic realm of cyberspace.

The future of AI in PT is promising, featuring enhanced convergence, predictive analytics, advanced natural language processing, and adaptive learning. Organizations that embrace AI-driven PT solutions will enhance the efficiency of their security assessments and improve their preparedness for mitigating risks associated with an evolving array of cyber threats.

REFERENCES

Al-Sada, B., Sadighian, A., & Oligeri, G. (2024). MITRE ATT&CK: State of the art and way forward. *ACM Computing Surveys*, *57*(1), 1–37.

Bach-Nutman, M. (2020). Understanding the top 10 OWASP vulnerabilities. *ArXiv Preprint ArXiv:2012.09960*.

Bishop, M. (2007). About penetration testing. *IEEE Security & Privacy*, *5*(6), 84–87. https://doi.org/10.1109/MSP.2007.159

Chamkar, S. A., Maleh, Y., & Gherabi, N. (2022). The human factor capabilities in Security Operation Center (SOC). *EDPACS*, *66*(1), 1–14. https://doi.org/10.1080/07366981.2021.1977026

Chamkar, S. A., Maleh, Y., & Gherabi, N. (2024). Security operations centers: Use case best practices, coverage, and gap analysis based on MITRE adversarial tactics, techniques, and common knowledge. *Journal of Cybersecurity and Privacy*, 4(4), 777–793.

Copeland, M., & Copeland, M. (2021). Introduction to the MITRE Matrix. *Cloud Defense Strategies with Azure Sentinel: Hands-on Threat Hunting in Cloud Logs and Services*, 213–254.

Dinis, B., & Serrão, C. (2014). Using PTES and open-source tools as a way to conduct external footprinting security assessments for intelligence gathering. *Journal of Internet Technology and Secured Transactions (JITST)*, *3/4*, 271–279.

Fatima, A., Khan, T. A., Abdellatif, T. M., Zulfiqar, S., Asif, M., Safi, W., Al Hamadi, H., & Al-Kassem, A. H. (2023). Impact and research challenges of penetrating testing and vulnerability assessment on network threat. *2023 International Conference on Business Analytics for Technology and Security (ICBATS)*, 1–8.

Giuseppi, A., Tortorelli, A., Germanà, R., Liberati, F., & Fiaschetti, A. (2019). Securing cyber-physical systems: An optimization framework based on OSSTMM and genetic algorithms. *2019 27th Mediterranean Conference on Control and Automation (MED)*, 50–56.

Gupta, M., Akiri, C., Aryal, K., Parker, E., & Praharaj, L. (2023). From ChatGPT to ThreatGPT: Impact of generative AI in cybersecurity and privacy. *IEEE Access*, *11*, 80218–80245.

Hilario, E., Azam, S., Sundaram, J., Imran Mohammed, K., & Shanmugam, B. (2024). Generative AI for pentesting: The good, the bad, the ugly. *International Journal of Information Security*, *23*(3), 2075–2097.

Hubbard, J. (2020). Measuring and improving cyber defense using the MITRE ATT&CK framework. *SANS Whitepaper*.

Kinnunen, J. (2022). *Threat Detection Gap Analysis Using MITRE ATT&CK Framework*.

Malatji, M. (2023). Management of enterprise cyber security: A review of ISO/IEC 27001: 2022. *2023 International Conference on Cyber Management and Engineering (CyMaEn)*, 117–122.

Maleh, Y. (2023). Enhancing e-learning security in cloud environments: Risk assessment and penetration testing. In *Cybersecurity Management in Education Technologies: Risks and Countermeasures for Advancements in E-Learning* (pp. 171–210). https://doi.org/10.1201/9781003369042-9

Maleh, Y. (2024). *Web Application PenTesting: A Comprehensive Guide for Professionals*. CRC Press.

Maleh, Y., Sahid, A., Alazab, M., & Belaissaoui, M. (2021). *IT Governance and Information Security: Guides, Standards, and Frameworks*. CRC Press. https://doi.org/10.1201/9781003161998

Maleh, Y. (2025). *Traditional vs Generative AI Pentesting: A Hands-On Approach to Hacking*. CRC Press.

Nabila, M. A., Mas' udia, P. E., & Saptono, R. (2023). Analysis and implementation of the ISSAF framework on OSSTMM on website security vulnerabilities testing in polinema. *Journal of Telecommunication Network (Jurnal Jaringan Telekomunikasi)*, *13*(1), 87–94.

Pascoe, C. E. (2023). *Public Draft: The NIST Cybersecurity Framework 2.0*.

Pennington, A., Applebaum, A., Nickels, K., Schulz, T., Strom, B., & Wunder, J. (2019). Getting started with ATT&CK. *MITRE Corporation*.

Sabillon, R., Serra-Ruiz, J., Cavaller, V., & Cano, J. (2017). A comprehensive cybersecurity audit model to improve cybersecurity assurance: The CyberSecurity Audit Model (CSAM). *2017 International Conference on Information Systems and Computer Science (INCISCOS)*, 253–259. https://doi.org/10.1109/INCISCOS.2017.20

Samtani, S., Yu, S., Zhu, H., Patton, M., & Chen, H. (2016). Identifying SCADA vulnerabilities using passive and active vulnerability assessment techniques. *2016 IEEE Conference on Intelligence and Security Informatics (ISI)*, 25–30. https://doi.org/10.1109/ISI.2016.7745438

Yadav, T., & Rao, A. M. (2015). Technical aspects of cyber kill chain. *Security in Computing and Communications: Third International Symposium, SSCC 2015, Kochi, India, August 10–13, 2015. Proceedings 3*, 438–452.

Zaoui, M., Yousra, B., Yassine, S., Yassine, M., & Karim, O. (2024). A comprehensive taxonomy of social engineering attacks and defense mechanisms: Toward effective mitigation strategies. *IEEE Access*, 12, 72224–72241.

Zaydi, M., & Maleh, Y. (2024). Empowering red teams with generative AI: Transforming penetration testing through adaptive intelligence. *EDPACS*, 1–26. https://doi.org/10.1080/07366981.2024.2439628

Index

D

E

F

G

H

I

For Product Safety Concerns and Information please contact our
EU representative GPSR@taylorandfrancis.com Taylor & Francis
Verlag GmbH, Kaufingerstraße 24, 80331 München, Germany